RECONSIDERED

Afterword by RICHARD RORTY

RECONSIDERED

Edited by MATTHEW J. COTTER

 Prometheus Books

59 John Glenn Drive
Amherst, New York 14228-2197

Published 2004 by Prometheus Books

Inquiries should be addressed to
Prometheus Books
59 John Glenn Drive
Amherst, New York 14228–2197
VOICE: 716–691–0133, ext. 207
FAX: 716–564–2711
WWW.PROMETHEUSBOOKS.COM

08 07 06 05 04   5 4 3 2 1

Library of Congress Cataloging-in-Publication Data

Sidney Hook reconsidered / edited by Matthew J. Cotter.
     p. cm.
   Includes bibliographical references.
   ISBN 1–59102–193–6 (alk. paper)
   1. Hook, Sidney, 1902–1989. I. Cotter, Matthew J.

B945.H684.S57 2004
191—dc22

2004004499

Printed in the United States of America on acid-free paper

Contents

Preface   9
    Matthew J. Cotter

Acknowledgments   15

Introduction. Charting the Intellectual Career
         of Sidney Hook: Five Major Steps   19
    David Sidorsky

**Part 1. Sidney Hook's Place in the American Philosophical
      Tradition**

   1. A Defense of Naturalism as a Defense of Secularism   69
    Barbara Forrest

Contents

2. Politics without Dogmas: Hook's Basic Ideals   117
   Robert B. Talisse

3. Dewey's Bulldog and the Eclipse of Pragmatism   129
   Michael Eldridge

4. Sidney Hook's Secular Humanism
   Appraised Retrospectively   147
   Paul Kurtz

5. Right to Life and the Use of Violence   161
   Marvin Kohl

**Part 2. Sidney Hook's Place in the American
   Intellectual Tradition**

6. Sidney Hook and Education   171
   Steven M. Cahn

7. Flexibility and Revolution   175
   Christopher Phelps

8. Sidney Hook, Higher Education,
   and the New Failure of Nerve   183
   Edward Shapiro

9. From Dewey to Hook: World War II
   and the Crisis of Democracy   203
   Gary Bullert

10. Polemics, Open Discussion, and Tolerance   225
    Neil Jumonville

Part 3. Reminiscence

11. Concerning Sidney Hook   247
    Nathan Glazer

12. Sidney Hook's Prescience   257
    Tibor R. Machan

13. Sidney Hook: Teacher and Public Philosopher   271
    Bruce Wilshire

Afterword   281
    Richard Rorty

A Complete Bibliography of Sidney Hook's
Published Work   287
    *Jo-Ann Boydston, Kathleen Poulos, and
    Matthew J. Cotter*

Contributors   387

7

Preface

Matthew J. Cotter

t was altogether fitting that the celebration of the centenary of Sidney Hook's birth took place on October 25 and 26, 2002, at the Graduate Center of the City University of New York (CUNY). For, prior to his legendary affiliation with the Hoover Institution, his nearly forty-year tenure in the philosophy department at New York University, and his years at Columbia under John Dewey's tutelage, Sidney Hook began his unquiet life as a student in the CUNY system at City College.[1]

The essays in this book were originally presented at that conference, which, like much of Hook's career, was not without controversy. Although this is not the place for reminiscing about the difficulties associated with planning, organizing, and eventually carrying out such an event, the conference, especially the possibility that there might not have been one, brought the career of Sidney Hook once more to the forefront of American intellectual affairs, briefly garnering him national attention.[2] Moreover, given the current scholarly interest in McCarthyism and the cold war, the increasing influence of neoconservatism in shaping US public policy, the involvement of the US military in what appears to be an interminable conflict, and the perennial problems facing many of the United States' educational institutions, the work of Sidney Hook is more relevant than ever. The times are ripe for revisiting and appraising his entire corpus responsibly in lieu of simply dismissing him wholesale because of some of the controversial stands he took.

Although some of the essays that follow have been revised to varying degrees, most of them stand largely as they were originally presented at the conference.[3] The reader will soon discover that the contributors represent all points on the ideological compass—Hook would not have had it any other way. What is of particular interest is that many of them were either Hook's students, colleagues, or adversaries. More importantly, also included for the first time are several fresh insights by a younger generation of scholars, many of whom are far removed from the turbulent times that repeatedly shaped and transformed Hook's thought.

I have divided the essays that follow into an introduction and three parts. This does not mean that they are to be taken as isolated evaluations distinct from all the rest. When taken as a whole, they represent the collective attempt to bring the work of one of the United States' most complex and misunderstood intellectuals to bear on our current circumstances. The first part of this volume brings attention to the significance of Hook's chosen profession—that of a philosopher committed to *advancing*, and not merely *espousing*, as some have charged, John Dewey's pragmatism. The essays in part 2 address the degree to which Hook was engaged with the larger cultural issues of his day. Whereas discussions of the latter tend to be dismissed as more polemical than substantive, the essays included actually show an organic connection in Hook's own thinking between his philosophical commitments and his political, cultural, and educational proposals. As proposals (and not mere blueprints), Hook maintained that they functioned more like suggestions whose soundness was contingent upon the degree to which they could withstand the scrutiny of honest, open, and independent inquiry. Finally, the group of essays collected in part 3 combines analysis of Hook's life and work with personal reminiscence.

One aim of this volume is to stimulate further inquiry into Hook's philosophy, influence, and intellectual development. These essays will hopefully encourage future scholars to carefully examine the complex intersections between his philosophical commitment to pragmatism—or "experimentalism," as he preferred— and the manifold and often controversial positions he took on a wide variety of cultural and political issues, of which only a few are addressed in this volume. Another, more important aim of this book is to illustrate the dangers associated with discussing Hook's significance exclusively in terms of his anti-Communism. Retrospective historical analyses have focused strictly on whether Hook was "right" or "wrong" (or Left or Right) about the severity of the Communist threat throughout the cold war are not sufficient for an evaluation of his life's work in its full complexity. Furthermore, such analyses occlude other themes central to Hook's philosophy: his naturalism, moral philosophy, philosophy of education, secular humanism, and democratic theory. It is only against the backdrop of these broader themes that Hook's unflagging commitment to democracy as a way of life in the face of totalitarianism can be fully understood; any other approach falls short when defining Hook as a thinker and public inquirer.

The value of Sidney Hook's life and work can best be estimated

by the degree to which they speak to our own experiences, especially in a time when our own democratic institutions and principles
appear to be in retreat and when in the face of innumerable human
tragedies we are again reminded of the precariousness of human life
in a dangerous world. In light of his philosophical vigor, vigilance,
and resoluteness, Hook may thus be thought of as *the* philosopher of
modern US democracy and education in the most meaningful sense
of the terms. For, throughout his unquiet life, Hook never wavered
in his commitment to John Dewey's philosophical ideals. But unlike
those of his mentor Dewey, Hook's own ideas have not become "so
much a part of the cultural climate of our time" as one might think.[4]
Paradoxically, until recently they lay dormant. But if the recent
expanded edition of Hook's landmark *Towards the Understanding
of Karl Marx* (Prometheus Books, 2002), as well as an anthology
titled *Sidney Hook on Pragmatism, Democracy, and Freedom: The
Essential Essays* (Prometheus Books, 2002) is any indication of the
revival of interest in Hook's philosophical relevance, then perhaps
this volume joins them in the ambitious attempt to resurrect, make
explicit, and advance his work.

NOTES

1. The CUNY conference was preceded by centennial celebrations at
the Hoover Institution on October 4, 2002, and was followed by one at
New York University on December 2, 2002.

2. The reader will find discussions of the various controversies in the
following publications, all of which appeared in the summer of 2002:
Chronicle of Higher Education (June 20, July 5); *Boston Globe* (June 23);
New York Times (June 29); *Washington Post* (July 7, August 11); *New
Yorker* (July 8); and *Nation* (July 15), to name a few. These articles
spurred on the efforts of several noteworthy Internet news and discussion
sites as well. For an overview of the conference, see Matthew J. Cotter,

Robert Talisse, and Robert Tempio, "The Relevance of Sidney Hook Today," *Free Inquiry* 23 (Winter 2002–2003): 51–53.

3. A videotape of the conference has been added to the Sidney Hook Collection at the Hoover Institution.

4. Sidney Hook, *John Dewey: An Intellectual Portrait* (1939; reprint, Amherst, NY: Prometheus Books, 1995), p. 27.

Acknowledgments

In preparation for this volume, my thanks go to those who made its predecessor possible. The generous contributions of the John M. Olin Foundation, David Nasaw at the Center for the Humanities, and Paul Kurtz at the Council on Secular Humanism were the chief sources of financial support for it.

I take great pleasure in thanking the surviving members of Sidney Hook's immediate and extended family. Many of them traveled, at their own expense and at a considerable distance, to attend the conference in its entirety. I am particularly indebted to Sidney Hook's son Ben, whose concerns for a good conference equaled if not surpassed my own.

Despite the fact that the conference occupied the better part of two years of my life, it was by no means an isolated experience.

Planning, organizing, and executing required, literally, a community of scholars and nonscholars alike, all of whom were committed to "get Sidney's name out there" despite innumerable obstacles. Although there was considerable disagreement over what his name signified, at least everyone agreed that getting Hook's name out there—to this degree—was long overdue. In addition to the conference participants for their individual capacities and comments, I would like to thank Stephen Motika and Aoibheann Sweeney of the Center for the Humanities for their advice, guidance, and assistance throughout the organizing process.

It is a pleasure to state my gratitude to my friends Robert B. Talisse and Robert Tempio, who approached me with the idea for a centennial celebration nearly two years before it occurred. In addition to placing the conference squarely in my lap, they were the first to introduce me to Hook's relevance as an independent thinker.

At the Graduate Center, I owe special thanks to professors Carol Berkin and James Oakes, whose patience permitted me to renege on many commitments to deliver already late papers and to skip a few classes in order to attend to matters of planning and organizing. My friends and colleagues there, especially Tevah Platt, Ryan Swihart, and Ted Wiesniewski each found themselves on several occasions privy to the details of both Hook's and my travails during frequent sojourns to the local tavern. Tevah and her husband Daniel Thiel were invaluable sources of inspiration, advice, and camaraderie throughout the editing process for this volume. I would also like to single out Prof. Martin Burke for his expert advice and Lucas Waltzer for his instrumental computer expertise.

Even though my wife, Laura, met me prior to my long affair with Sidney Hook, she soon forgave me for my constant transgressions in our own relationship with unyielding support.

Finally, I would like to acknowledge my father, James Cotter, who despite the slings and arrows associated with severe illness found the strength to attend some of the conference's sessions. In addition to a lifetime of support, criticism, and encouragement, my father (and mother, of course) survived with me the controversies and frustrations associated with celebrating Sidney Hook's life and work. My only regret is that my father did not survive long enough to see this volume published. Although it is somewhat unorthodox to commemorate an anthology to a loved one, since he was so worried about me throughout and so intimately involved in the conference from its inception by simply asking me "so what's new with Sidney?" each time I saw him, I lovingly dedicate this book to him.

Charting the Intellectual Career of Sidney Hook

Five Major Steps

David Sidorsky

*T*he centennial of Sidney Hook's birth provides a unique vantage point for surveying of the main intellectual movements current throughout the twentieth century. These movements can be observed from the perspective afforded by each of the five major steps of Hook's intellectual career. He was, probably to a degree unparalleled by any other philosopher of his generation, actively involved in the cultural and political conflicts of his time.

Sidney Hook's engagement with pragmatism was the first major step in his intellectual maturity, and it represented a commitment to which he remained constant throughout his life. Pragmatism is generally considered to be the first indigenously US philosophical movement, and its birth and coming of age took place shortly after the turn of the century. The founding fathers of US pragmatism are generally identified as Charles Peirce and William James, with John Dewey emerging as its major thinker immediately after the founding generation. Sidney Hook became a partisan of pragmatic philosophy during his graduate studies at Columbia with John Dewey in the early 1920s. Pragmatism was to dominate the US philosophical scene for the first five decades of the century. During much of this period of pragmatism's heyday in the United States, Sidney Hook became a central figure in the justification and defense of pragmatic views. His support for John Dewey's version of pragmatism earned for him, among both the proponents and critics of the movement, the title of Dewey's "bulldog."

Sidney Hook's involvement with pragmatism did not erase his continuing interest in Marxist theory. After his doctoral dissertation at Columbia on *The Metaphysics of Pragmatism*, his succeeding work in the history of ideas was not directed toward the search for the origins of Deweyan thought in the transformation of Hegelianism, which was a major topic of investigation among pragmatists, including Ralph Barton Perry and Morton G. White. Rather, Hook wrote an account of the genesis of Marxism through a series of neo-Hegelian thinkers in a work titled *From Hegel to Marx*. Hook was a scholarly analyst of Marxist theories and an advocate of a very special interpretation of Marxism. He sought to unite his interpretation of Marxism with Deweyan pragmatism in the late 1920s and early 1930s in a way that would allow him to be faithful to both the pragmatic spirit of critical intelligence and Marxism as a scientific program for social change. Thus Hook's particular interpretation of Marxism can be identified as the second major step in charting his intellectual career.

Hook's position as a major interpreter of Marxism led to a deep involvement with the political and cultural movements of the Left. These movements came to be riven by the issue of opposition to or support for the Soviet Union and the official line of the Communist

Party, particularly after Joseph Stalin's consolidation of power in the Soviet Union in the 1930s. The result of this rift was that the passion that was to become dominant in the middle span of Hook's intellectual career was his concern for the truth about the nature of Communism, whether in the Soviet Union, in the international arena, or on the US scene. Thus Hook's anti-Communism, as the third step of his intellectual career, became the defining factor of his position within US culture and was responsible for the passions that swirled around him from the 1930s onward, perhaps even to this very time.

Hook had originally sought, as noted above, to unite his pragmatic philosophy with the Marxist perspective, and similarly, for many decades, he remained loyal to a belief in socialism alongside his strong anti-Communism. In the 1960s, however, there was a significant change in the agenda of the Left that had been brought about by its displacement by the New Left. The New Left initiated a forceful attack upon many US traditional institutions, including a number of proposals for the transformation of the university. Hook's response to these challenges brought him to a reevaluation of the important social and political values of US society, particularly on aspects of contemporary culture and the university. The result of this reevaluation can be understood as a new emphasis in his political philosophy on what might appropriately be termed *value pluralism*. This new emphasis was to lead to the general identification of Hook as sympathetic to neoconservatism in US politics, particularly in what have been termed the "culture wars." Thus Hook's writings on social, cultural, and educational issues that were grounded by his value pluralism or neoconservatism mark the fourth major step of his intellectual career.

Hook's continual commitment to pragmatism was also expressed in the more general, and personal, idiom of Enlightenment naturalism, a motif that represents a fifth major step of his intellectual career. (This fifth step, unlike the others, is not chronologically sequential but represents a continuing aspect of his thought from beginning to end.) As a naturalist, Hook did not believe that there could be any guarantee for human redemption from history or for spiritual transcendence and liberation from the forces of nature. As a partisan of the Enlightenment, he believed that human intelligence might succeed in progressing toward the perfectibility of the human condition and the scientific transformation of natural processes for human ends. Thus Hook's Enlightenment naturalism holds that neither the ultimate triumph nor the ultimate defeat of mankind is religiously ordained or inevitable.

Accordingly, the course of Sidney Hook's intellectual career can be charted by a survey of these five major steps. Some of these steps remained constant commitments throughout while others shifted, changed, and developed during a life continually engaged in theoretical social inquiry as well as in public forums for the exchange of ideas.

The advent of the pragmatic movement in US philosophy, which gained Hook's lifetime loyalty, was heralded in a remarkable letter from William James, the author of *Pragmatism*, to his younger brother, novelist Henry James, dated May 4, 1907. This letter begins with William's praise for *The American Scene*, the work that resulted from Henry's rediscovery and reexploration of the United States. Since William had continually urged Henry to write about the United States and appreciate its culture rather than to become an expatriate critic of US values in favor of "European" culture, it is appropriate that William recognizes this work to be "supremely great," although he cannot refrain from the characteristic remonstration that it is "supremely great . . . in its peculiar way."

It is relevant in the context of Hook's birth in 1902 to an immigrant family in New York to note Henry's comments in *The American Scene* on his visit to the Lower East Side of New York at about that time. He visited the Yiddish-language theater and dropped in to observe the activity at that public meeting place for actors, musicians, intellectuals, journalists, writers, and hangers-on: the Café Royale. Henry's response to this visit included the speculative comment that the new energy and vitality of this strange society of immigrants would soon make its way into the mainstream of English-speaking theater, thought, and letters. He could not refrain from expressing his concern about the future sounds and accent of the English language, once this happy event had taken place.

After a number of "elder brother" counsels urging the abandonment of his excessively mannered style, despite the acknowledged "paradoxical success" of Henry's later novels, William moved on to the communicative point of the letter about his own forthcoming work, *Pragmatism*:

> I have just finished the proofs of a little book called "Pragmatism," which even you *may* enjoy reading. It is a very "sincere" and, from the point of view of ordinary philosophy-professorial manners, a very unconventional utterance, not particularly original at any one point, yet, in the midst of the literature of the way of thinking which it represents, with just that amount of squeak or shrillness of the voice that enables one book to *tell*, when others don't, to supersede its brethren, and be treated later as "representative." I shouldn't be surprised if ten years hence it should be rated as "epoch-making," for of the definitive triumph of that general way of thinking I can entertain no doubt whatever—I believe it to be something quite like the protestant reformation.

If we change the European reference to a reformation to the more American idiom that Dewey introduced of a "reconstruction" in philosophy, then James's prophecy may be considered to have been vindicated. This reconstruction in philosophy was hailed as marking a new philosophical beginning after the dead end of the main fin-de-siècle philosophical tendencies of materialism and idealism.

Pragmatism was to provide a thoroughgoing reconstruction in major areas of philosophical thought that was to gain Sidney Hook's loyalty, for he, like William James, was confident of the "definitive triumph of that general way of thinking." More specifically, Hook supported pragmatism in four significant areas: an interpretation of metaphysics; a methodology that placed great value on scientific method; an epistemology that stressed the instrumental role of knowledge in reshaping the human environment; and a moral theory that required the application of critical intelligence to "problematic situations."

Sidney Hook's doctoral dissertation was written on the metaphysics of pragmatism. The details of this analysis did not become relevant for his later intellectual career, but like William James or John Dewey, Hook shared the pragmatic approach to metaphysics, according to which the exploration of the question of the nature of ultimate reality is philosophically significant, unlike the contemporaneous positivistic position or the nascent analysis of logical positivism.

James had argued that the traditional method of metaphysics represented a way of turning to the *past* for the truth about reality. This turn to the past was evident in both the "tough minded" materialist views and the "tender minded" idealism that, according to James, had arrived at their climactic dead end by the end of the nineteenth century. James's reference to the past was his characterization of materialism as appealing to the *presuppositions* of current phenomena. For materialism, the necessary existence of matter is presupposed or required in order to explain the phenomena and happenings of the present situation. Similarly, the metaphysical idealists, in the grand tradition of Hegel, formulated at the end of the century by such powerful exponents as Bradley in England, Croce in Italy, and James's friend Josiah Royce in the United States, had argued that the *presupposition* of the phenomena of experience was the necessary existence of a mind in which the objects of experience were articulated, perceived, and cohered. For James, these two tendencies shared the perspective of looking backward to what was considered as having necessarily existed in order to explain the data of contemporaneous experience.

At the same time, early positivists like Ernst Mach, in the great tradition of David Hume, were restricted by their own interpretation of what could be known from direct experience to what was *given* in the *present*. Their metaphysics could not extend beyond the "impressions" or *sense data* perceived by observers in the here and now. Such a metaphysics might well succeed in constraining speculation through its requirement of correspondence between what was perceived as real and any true statement about the world, but the price to be paid for such an impressionistic interpretation of reality was the denial of the way in which knowledge sometimes permits human beings to predict and control the future.

For James, as for Dewey, these metaphysical emphases upon the past (i.e., the presuppositions of experience) and upon the present (i.e., the given sense data) were remediable. The remedy was a metaphysical account that involves necessary reference to future experience. Both James and Dewey followed Peirce in his interpretation of what was real as what a community of inquiry would ultimately, in the *future*, discover to exist at the asymptotic conclusion of scientific inquiry.

An oversimplified illustration may serve to clarify this perspective. For many decades, the standard textbooks of chemistry affirmed that the world was composed of ninety-two chemical elements. Current textbooks of chemistry assert the thesis that the real fact of the matter is that the universe is composed of about 130 elements. The answer to the question "How many elements are there really?" is the number of elements that will be said to exist when the process of inquiry in chemistry has approached its (unattainable) final end or limit. Perhaps there will never be a final answer to any specific scientific question, but the correct form of the answer to the perennial metaphysical question—namely, "What is there?" or "What is real?"—is what is asserted to exist in the scientific theories about the world as they approach their asymptotic limit. Neopragmatist philosopher Willard Van Ormond Quine has described this view as an interpretation of reality in terms of the values of the variables asserted to exist in the languages of the empirical sciences.

This connection between metaphysics and the future progress of scientific discovery and confirmation, rather than the inquiry into the presuppositions of experience or to the structures of sensation and sense data, can be identified as James's partisanship for "futurism." Interestingly, if somewhat digressively, Giovanni Papini took James's references to futurism to be the central thesis of pragmatism. He interpreted the idea in both a religious and artistic context and became its advocate in journals in both prewar Italy and Russia. In a very short time, pragmatism had receded into the background of the futurist movement, which emerged as a distinctive artistic response in twentieth-century painting and sculpture to the presumed future evolution of the technological age.

The relevant thesis for the pragmatic tradition, as exemplified by Sidney Hook, is that the truths of metaphysics, according to this reconstruction of philosophy, even though it may provide an examination of the most general and pervasive features of experience and existence, cannot transcend the boundaries of the empirical truths of science. Consequently, in the pragmatic reconstruction of philosophy, metaphysical truth is connected to the application and use of scientific method.

Accordingly, in the second area—that is, methodology—pragmatism considered the methods of science to be paradigmatic for all reliable knowledge. Charles Peirce had stressed that scientific method was characterized by the development of hypotheses, which were fallible but which could be tested and confirmed or refuted by future experiments. Hence, scientific hypotheses, though fallible, were corrigible and represented a way of progressively arriving at hypotheses with greater degrees of confirmation. This model, or paradigm, of scientific method as requiring testable or verifiable hypotheses that were accepted or rejected as their degree of confirmation was increased or decreased represented a generalized methodology that could be applied to all areas of inquiry.

John Dewey pursued the preceding model and extended it such that he arrived at confidence in the hypotheses of the social sciences as a way for realizing truths that should be applied in the area of public policy. Dewey also believed that scientific method could be applied in education, allowing for sweeping reform of traditional education. Dewey's support for democracy involved the thesis that the democratic method could parallel the scientific method in arriving progressively at truth about social hypotheses, in light of the evidence.

Sidney Hook shared the pragmatic view that scientific method provided a paradigm for rational inquiry, and he also shared the Deweyan hope and desire for the application of methods analogous to scientific inquiry in areas of public policy. But he recognized the significant distance between experimental research in the natural sciences and research on educational issues, or between the progress of knowledge in the natural sciences and the limits to progress in historical studies and social thought. Hook's methodological claim was therefore restricted to the narrower but still optimistic view that "critical intelligence" could be carried out so as to arrive at more probable or more "warrantedly assertable" beliefs, which would guide human choice and human action.

As the third aspect of Hook's pragmatism, his emphasis on the application of critical intelligence to social practice, or what Dewey had referred to as the "problems of men," was given an extended theoretical basis in the area of epistemology. The pragmatic theory of knowledge or truth was formulated by means of the drawing of a sharp distinction between it and its two dominant predecessor theories. On the one hand, the materialists and positivists had argued for a correspondence theory of truth. Thus, according to the traditional correspondence theory of truth, a statement was true if it *mirrored* the real state of affairs, that is, if it reported, in Wittgenstein's phrase, the facts of "the world . . . which is the case," or in the Shakespearean idiom, "held the mirror up to nature." On the other hand, the idealists maintained a coherence theory of truth: any individual proposition could be validated (i.e., accepted) based upon its coherence or consistency with the set of antecedently accepted propositions. For idealism, this epistemology was crucial for understanding how the phenomena of experience were the partial appearances of an absolute mind that structured and cohered the totality of human experience. If there were a contradiction or negation of the prior structure of experience, it would represent an incoherence within the entire system similar to the way in which a single contradiction invalidates an entire mathematical structure. Accordingly, the way in which mind structures the world of experience resembles a holistic or organic system in which coherence designates truth and incoherence is a mark of falsity.

For the pragmatist, both the theory of correspondence as well as the theory of coherence failed to explain why knowledge was useful; that is, they failed to account for the evident fact of human history that knowledge about the world had allowed human beings to predict and control some aspects of the environment in which they lived. Thus pragmatism rejected an account of knowledge as a passive spectator process in which individuals mirror or cohere the objects of the real world. Rather, knowledge was an active process that necessarily involved prediction and verification by future experience.

The pragmatic epistemology, or theory of knowledge, accordingly sought to connect the truth of any hypotheses in an inquiry with its ability to predict or control future experience. Consequently, truth was considered an instrument both for the adaptation of human beings to the world in which they were situated and for greater control of the environment, which was potentially capable of transformation. This instrumental theory of truth placed great stress upon prediction or verification as the criterion for the adequacy of the acceptance of hypotheses. Significantly, it provides an understanding of the possibility of knowledge to change the antecedently "given" realities of the world. The pragmatic connection between truth and utility was derided from the outset by philosophers such as Moore and Russell, who considered that such connection violated the requirement that the objective truth be completely independent of its psychological and sociological consequences. James Joyce, for example, had argued against the connection between truth and utility by pointing out an apparent contradiction. Joyce noted that he had always preferred the Italian encyclopedia to the *Britannica*, since it provided him with more "useless truths." Throughout his long teaching career, however, Hook continually defended pragmatic epistemology against such criticism on the ground that it alone made sense of the recognized relationship between knowledge and the possibility of improving the human condition.

As the philosophical context shifted with the rise of logical positivism and existentialism after the 1930s, Hook taught pragmatic epistemology as a golden mean between these two philosophical extremes. At one pole, the correspondence theory of truth had been replaced by the more sophisticated "semantic theory of truth" versions advanced by the logical positivists and Polish logician Alfred Tarski. The relationship of mirroring the facts of the world by correspondence was developed in a formal linguistic structure according to which "truth" was identified as the semantic property of propositions, disconnected from the process of inquiry. At the other pole, with the demise of idealist metaphysics, there were the more subjectivist accounts of truth that had been developed in existentialist thought, in which the truth of a phenomenological experience could be identified with its authenticity as self-expression, including, in Heideggerian terms, the "unconcealment" of being. In Hook's view, pragmatism alone provided an account of true statements that both met the standards of objectivity and connected the realization of truth with the activities of human beings in conducting inquiries about their environment. In this account, statements could be asserted to be true based on their public or intersubjective confirmation by a critical community of inquiry.

Hook's analysis antedated later challenges to the pragmatic theory of truth, but it is not difficult to extrapolate from his position what the general nature of his response would be to major lines of criticism. Thus Kuhn's historical investigation of "scientific revolutions" would negate the Peircean thesis of the convergence of the process of inquiry to a single limit. Hook's view is closer to the criticism of Kuhn that has been developed by Israel Scheffler in *Science and Subjectivity*. In that view, "paradigm shifts" are not analogous to subjective conversions; rather, they reflect the ways in which the framework or categories of discourse are changed and revised under the impact of experience so as to yield a higher degree of confirmation and afford a greater degree of control of the environment. Similarly, the "neopragmatic" interpretation of truth that has been advanced by Quine in *Pursuit of Truth* is compatible with Hook's pragmatism. For while Hook stressed, like Peirce and Dewey, the essential incompleteness of inquiry such that inquiry was always fallible and open to revision, there would be no objection within this process to an attempt to define truth conditions or the ultimate limit of a progression of verified statements in semantic terms or by use of Quine's criteria "disquotation." For Hook, the significant point remained that a theory of truth must explain why truth matters in the sense that knowledge will be able, in principle, to ameliorate the human condition.

Fourth and finally, the most thoroughgoing area for the reconstruction of philosophy concerned the nature of moral judgments. These judgments were not accorded the status of absolutes supported by moral intuitions or by religious commandment exemplified by the assertion that "killing is wrong"; yet for the pragmatists, moral judgments could not be reduced to expressions of emotive attitude or to mere cultural conventions. Hook wrote an early paper on Tolstoyan pacifism. The question obviously arises, in the Tolstoyan context, as to whether killing in self-defense or even committing oneself to a war of national self-defense, which inevitably involves the killing of some persons, is justified. The absolute intuition or command that forbids killing does not respond to the requirement of the problematic situation to develop a policy or hypothesis that will best meet the needs of the human beings involved in that situation. More generally, moral decisions can be understood as hypotheses about what would effectively and optimally resolve a concrete situation in ways that satisfy the needs of human beings, applied in general terms and over the long run. Thus the absolute intuition that killing was wrong was itself a hypothesis that could be refuted in cases where killing was justified as a necessary means of self-defense or as a justified act of restoration of a violated moral order. This interpretation of morals as empirical hypotheses about optimal policies required great confidence in the ability of human beings to exercise critical intelligence in evaluating moral conflict and in developing social norms. Sidney Hook's career found its greatest fulfillment in the attempt to use critical intelligence on the most important moral issues that confronted the society in which he lived.

Hook remained faithful to these four aspects of pragmatism throughout his entire intellectual career. It is this commitment to pragmatism that was to shape his subsequent interpretation of Marxist theory.

Morton G. White, a philosopher who has written on the origins of pragmatism and is a historian of US social thought, has narrated, in his memoir of G. E. Moore's influence at Columbia, a recurrent phenomenon in the careers of numerous philosophy students of the City College of New York. They developed their self-identification as New York intellectuals and radicals, often Marxist, during their undergraduate years in the 1920s and '30s and were subsequently to succumb to the power of John Dewey's teaching and thought during their graduate studies at Columbia. Hook's career appears to have followed this trajectory, paralleling his closest friend and colleague at the City College of New York, Ernest Nagel. Nagel's relationship to their teacher Morris Raphael Cohen was closer than Hook's, since Cohen worked in his special area of the theory of logic. Nagel's support of Deweyan thought was joined by his effort to build a bridge between US pragmatism and European analytical philosophy, including logical positivism. In the case of Sidney Hook, even after his embrace of pragmatic philosophy he became a leading interpreter of Marx's thought and an advocate of a special interpretation of Marxism compatible with the pragmatic stress on scientific method. Thus, in charting the intellectual career of Sidney Hook, an account of his views on Marxism, both supportive and critical, marks a second major step.

After completing his doctoral dissertation on the metaphysics of pragmatism, Hook turned to the project of tracing the origins of Marxist thought to their Hegelian roots in a previously mentioned classic of the history of ideas: *From Hegel to Marx*. Hook outlined the restructuring of Hegelian philosophy in a series of thinkers who had been precursors of Marxism. Subsequently, in *Towards the*

Understanding of Karl Marx, Hook examined the grounds for reconciliation between Marxism and pragmatism.

Hook emphasized two elements of affinity. First, Marx had been the philosopher of scientific socialism as opposed to utopian socialism. This identification of Marxist theory as "scientific" provided a basis for the view that Marxist theory could be developed in the form of a scientific hypothesis about future social structures. More specifically, Marx's theory was interpreted in the form of a scientific hypothesis that involved a prediction—subject to confirmation or refutation by future historical experience—that socializing the means of production would resolve the current "problematic situation," that is, would lead to a great advance of the technology and productivity of a cyclically depressed capitalist economy.

The empirical assessment of this problematic situation was that it was caused by the ways in which class ownership of the means of production had fettered the technological forces of production, as evidenced by the intensity of cyclical depression in free-market economies. The Marxist prediction, allegedly derived from these empirical phenomena, was that the cyclical depressions would worsen in what was referred to as the "contradictions" of capitalism, the "crisis" of "late capitalism." The experimental hypothesis that was to be tested was that the socialization of the means of production would function to free or unfetter the technological forces and to generate an economy that would have "production for use" with the corollary result of full employment, increased total wealth, and the greater equality of a classless society. During the period of the early thirties, many Deweyan pragmatists, including at times John Dewey himself, considered socialization of the means of production as an experimental hypothesis that could be introduced in order to improve the established economic order. Thus Hook's interpretation, which rested upon a close identification of pragmatism and Marxism, had a basis in the rhetorical similarity of the commitment to scientific method as the instrument for resolution of social problems. If the rhetorical slogan that Marxism is "scientific socialism" represents the acceptance of the scientific method for socioeconomic transformation and excludes the dogmatic thesis that all of history is governed by dialectically materialist laws of inevitable revolutionary progress toward socialism, then the bridge between pragmatism and Marxism can be established. (It is perhaps appropriate to note, in light of current philosophical discussion, how great the distance is between the Marxist prescription for social justice through the increase in the productive forces in the society that would result from the socialization of the means of production and more recent theories of distributive justice that propose in some way to justify a more equal distribution of goods that have been realized through growth in a free-market economy. It may also be relevant to note the distance between both of these models of an egalitarian society and the limited possibilities for the application of scientific method to the prediction and control of economic change.)

A second basis for Hook's proposed reconciliation between Marxism and pragmatism was the similarity of the two movements' views on the relationship between knowledge and action. Hook cited the famous thesis of Marx on the philosophy of Feuerbach, namely, that previous philosophies had sought to understand the world, whereas his sought to change it. For Hook, this indicated more than a mere rhetorical connection between the Marxist and the pragmatic epistemology, in that the verification of the truth of the theoretical proposition was its ability to transform experience. This indicated that Marxism, like pragmatism, rejected a theory of knowledge in which men were "passive spectators" of the "given" world. For Marxism, as in the pragmatic epistemology, knowledge is an instrument that enables the control or prediction of future experience; although pragmatism diverges from the Marxist hypothesis that the uniquely dynamic agent for historical change is the self-consciousness of the proletariat. Despite the differences between Marxism and pragmatism, Hook supported the view that these affinities could serve as a basis for an appropriate synthesis of these two philosophical perspectives.

Such an interpretation of Marxist theory has the additional advantage of not ascribing to Marxism itself the responsibility for the ways in which it was subsequently used as a dogma that brooked no heresy in the Leninist, Trotskyist, Stalinist, or Maoist interpretation. Even in his early steps as a Marxist, Hook did not embrace the Marxist view of history as a kind of monist science that could explain the relevant data of diverse human cultures and ages as necessarily implying a prediction about the inevitable future course of history. Thus in explicit confrontation with Marxism, Hook was soon to write *The Hero in History*. In this work, he refuted the claims of historical determinism, in which the actions of great individuals are irrelevant because they merely reflect the working out of the underlying dialectical laws that govern historical structures. Hook recognized that in some cases individual agents had been event-makers in the historical process. He also published a series of analytical criticisms of the concept of the "dialectic," refuting the thesis that had been advanced in Soviet ideology that the method of dialectical materialism could be considered an alternative or an enhancement to the methodology that had governed the achievements of natural sciences in modern times. Hook's studies in Marxist thought led him to a period of residence both in the Weimar Republic and, for a short period, in the Soviet Union. His experience in those two countries had a lasting impact on his political philosophy.

In Germany, Hook observed firsthand the dilemma of a liberal democracy that offered the protection of civil liberties and electoral participation to antidemocratic movements like the National Workers' Socialist Party. The challenge for a democracy was to adopt procedures that, without undermining its own constitutional institutions, would appropriately constrain and resist subversion by antidemocratic movements that exploited the opportunities afforded by a free society in order to achieve political power and to end future democratic processes. Thus the Nazi party was able to achieve a plurality in a free and fair election in Germany and use its political power to abolish future elections. This challenge has become even more evident since Hook's early perception of the dilemma for democracy. The notion that there should be "one person, one vote" for only one election has been exemplified in a number of fledgling democracies. Similarly, the possibility of electoral victory for an Islamist party that is dedicated to any possible transfer of power to secular authority derived from the outcome of future elections provides other current exemplifications of this dilemma. For Hook, the possibility that Communist political parties dedicated to totalitarian transformation of the society would achieve electoral victories was central for his conception of the need to strengthen the defense of democracy in periods of crisis.

In the Soviet Union, his writings on Marxism brought him in contact with the scholarly work of the Marx-Engels Institute in Moscow. The institute's director, David Riazanov, was a very early victim of Stalin's purges. Thus Hook's political radar received an early warning signal of the nature of emerging totalitarianism in the Soviet Union.

Whatever be the final verdict on Hook's interpretation of Marxist theory or his own retrospective assessment of that phase of his intellectual career, his involvement with Marxism brought him into a close engagement with the political movements of the Left during the late 1920s and the early '30s. Moreover, Hook's role was not limited to theoretical analysis in Marxism but led to a series of activist projects in support of socialism and of the agenda of the Left in the United States during that period.

One turning point can be identified as Hook's essay in 1934, titled "The Democratic and Dictatorial Aspects of Communism," which referred to the Russian Revolution in terms of its great transformational potential for human history. It is significant that Hook's terminology at that time identified the Soviet Union as the product of a historic revolution, for the concept of revolution had an "approbative" force as the fulfillment of historic aspirations; this stands in contrast to the subsequent identification of the Soviet Union that was to become standard in anti-Communist circles. From that perspective, the USSR was the result of a successful coup or putsch carried out by Lenin and a small cadre of followers against the reformist and democratically oriented government of Alexander Kerensky. It was also recognized in this alternative historical account that Lenin and many of his closest followers had arrived in St. Petersburg through an arrangement with the German government. The German regime, knowing of Lenin's intention to overthrow a government that was in a wartime alliance against Germany, had provided a sealed train for the transport of this group of potential revolutionaries from Switzerland to Russia. Yet this essay of 1934, which still held out hope for revolutionary socialism, concluded with Hook's reference to what he termed a series of "horrendous excrescences," which provided an alarm regarding the significance, values, and direction of the developing society of the Soviet Union under the rule of Joseph Stalin. Sidney Hook's sensitivity to these horrendous excrescences, which involved the murder or the purging of many persons who were loyal to the Communist ideology as well as hundreds of thousands of liberals, journalists, writers, and intellectuals and millions of peasants and workers, grew very rapidly after 1934. This led him to take sides in the single most important moral conflict of his intellectual career: the commitment to the cause of anti-Communism. As previously stated, this third step of his career was to become the defining phase of his intellectual life.

It is probably this step in Hook's intellectual career that, more than any other, provides the basis for the self-characterization present in the title of his own autobiography: *Out of Step*. For when Marxism or Communism were unpopular beliefs held only by a minority of the intellectual community, Sidney Hook was at the vanguard of its interpreters. He taught the first course on Marxism to be offered in a college curriculum in the United States. When, in the 1930s, support for the Soviet Union and for socialism became widespread and was a major force in the intellectual, literary, and artistic communities in the West, including the United States, Sidney Hook was to be numbered among the very small group of dedicated anti-Communists.

This circle of anti-Communists occupied a fringe position within US political culture in the 1930s. It was a minority view, even compared to the intellectual influence of the Communist Party after the Party had adopted the tactical expansion of its message through the use of such vehicles as the Popular Front or the National Front coalitions in Europe and its merging into the diverse ranks that could be unified under the slogan of "antifascism." This expansion of Communist influence took place in the United States through its support for the politics of the New Deal and its prominence in the development of a liberal-Left "progressive" culture. The sense of being a counterminority whose experience had given them an important truth reinforced the morale of the anti-Communist group.

In the mid-1930s, Stalin's purge trials of the original Kremlin leadership constituted the single most dramatic development and generated the greatest passion between pro-Soviet supporters and anti-Communist critics. A well-known incident indicates Hook's sense of the injustice of these show trials. Hook had hosted a party in his apartment in Greenwich Village at which the most identifiable literary celebrity was Bertolt Brecht. Brecht, an exile from

Hitler's Germany, had become a prominent figure in the "antifascist" movement and in theatrical circles in New York. He brought off a characteristically sardonic quip about the purge trials, saying that if the prominent defendants were not guilty, then they were all the more guilty, meaning that if they were not legally guilty at the bar of judicial justice, then they were guilty at the more important bar of historical justice. The dialectical basis for Brecht's quip is the view that these former leaders of a historically progressive revolution had now been cast in the role of opponents to the next phase of the development of the forces of historical progress, so they were being judged by the appropriate standard by which they had lived. Hook recognized that Brecht was saying that even if they had been framed by Stalin, they should be considered guilty—which rationalized the abuse of legal justice by ceding the right to tender the "verdict of history" to the Soviet state and to its dictatorial leader.

Hook had placed the coats of the guests as they arrived in an adjoining room. Now he went there, collected Brecht's coat, and handed it to him. Brecht took his coat and left without comment, either chagrined by the rebuke to the moral flippancy of his own remark, or, more probably, conceding the right of a host to decide upon his own guest list.

Hook's participation in the argument about the nature of the Communist revolution was joined, both intellectually and in practice, with his support for Deweyan views on the nature of democracy and freedom. Thus Hook sought to persuade John Dewey to become the chairman of a Commission of Inquiry that would investigate the charges against Leon Trotsky and would render a verdict regarding the truth of these charges. Despite the opposition of some of Dewey's closest family members, Dewey undertook this task at the request of Hook and, particularly, the urgings of US novelist and sympathizer with the Trotskyist movement James T. Farrell. Dewey went to Mexico for the public hearings of the Com-

39

mission of Inquiry. The result was a definitive assessment of the evidence with the verdict that Trotsky was not guilty of the various charges of treason and conspiracy that had been used to force him into exile.

Yet the conclusion of the Trotsky commission did mark another turning point in the development of Hook's anti-Communism. After the trial, Trotsky sought to further the bond between him and Dewey by developing the arguments in support of his general Marxist position. Dewey published a long essay, reflecting conversations and editorial consultations with Hook, that argued that the intellectual dogmatism and undemocratic approach that had characterized Soviet governmental policy toward Leon Trotsky were also present in the Leninist-Trotskyist conception of the state and of the Communist Party. In this view, the Soviet state could achieve legitimacy as a "dictatorship of the proletariat," and the Communist Party could be recognized as the vanguard instrument for directing political and social change within the society. The Trotskyist position, like the Stalinist position, did not consider itself a fallibilist hypothesis that sought scientific confirmation but was, in Dewey's phrase, "locked in absolutes." Thus Hook's anti-Communism evolved beyond the opposition to Stalin to the rejection of Trotskyism and onto the criticism of Marxist theory as bearing within itself the seeds of an antidemocratic approach to the question of political authority.

Hook's anti-Communism was supported by his Deweyan faith in political democracy and the possibilities a democratic society offered for societal change, including economic reform. This implies the refutation of the Marxist thesis that the political leadership within a capitalist democracy is only the executive committee of the bourgeois class.

In the anti-Communist community with which Sidney Hook was identified, the debate over Trotskyism was carried out primarily in the pages of *Partisan Review*. That journal, whose partisanship was originally Communist and subsequently partial to Trotsky, had continually sought to articulate a union of Marxism in political thought with modernism in literature and art criticism. It had become the leading intellectual forum for the critical discussion of the nature of the Stalinist regime in the Soviet Union. As the "dismal decade" of the thirties neared its end, one of the central issues of the debate about the role of the United States in world affairs was the legitimacy of US political action against Nazi Germany at the risk of entry into a second world war. In terms of the Trotskyist analysis of that period, the struggle between such democratic polities as the United Kingdom or the United States and Nazi Germany was viewed as a struggle between one oppressive domain of imperialist corporate capitalism and another, more oppressive domain, identified as the decadent last phase of capitalism in Nazi Germany. In this view, there was little to choose between these two forms or phases of the repressive capitalist society. It may be difficult to reconstruct this analysis in light of the later moral atrocities of Nazism that had their great impact on public consciousness only after the end of World War II.

The debate is reflected, however, in the leftist intellectual journalism of the period. The argument that there was no essential moral difference between the US capitalist state, despite its formal institutionalization of democratic freedom, and the German capitalist regime, despite its restructuring as the instrument of the National Workers' Socialist Party, was formulated in a last pro-Trotskyist editorial in *Partisan Review*. This argument continued to receive support from young Trotskyist literary critic Irving Howe as well as in the pages of *Politics*, a breakaway from *Partisan Review* that had been founded by Dwight McDonald.

For Sidney Hook, as for the changing views of *Partisan Review*, the struggle of World War II was essentially between the

41

imperfect societies of democratic freedom, which merited protection, and the evil polities of totalitarian expansionism, which ought to be ended. The political-philosophical principle that gained support for the future was that the distinction in the political structure between a free, democratic society and its totalitarian negation is far more morally significant than the distinction in economic structure between capitalist and socialist ownership of the means of production. This also marked another element in Hook's departure from Marxist theory, for it represented a rejection, as noted above, of the general Marxist thesis that political institutions are simply epiphenomenal to the economic substructure.

The issue of anti-Communism came to the fore even more strongly within a few years after World War II. The dispute over the nature of the Soviet Union in both its domestic and foreign policy emerged from the place it had occupied in the 1930s on the fringes of US political culture to become a central feature of the intellectual, media, and policy issues of the 1950s. Again, Hook defined the struggle that historians now identify as the cold war in moral terms, as one between democracy and totalitarianism. Accordingly, the enlistment of Hook for the cause of democracy led to his characterization as a "cold war warrior."

The current acceptance of the historical reality of the cold war between the Soviet bloc and the West between 1947 and 1989 has gone far toward erasing the historical memory of the actual usage of that term in the late 1940s and '50s. The contemporaneous use of the phrase *cold war warrior* was a pejorative term for a person who sought to foment an unnecessary war with a nonexistent enemy because of his paranoiac belief that the socialist countries, as supporters of alternative, noncapitalist societies, represented a hostile threat to the West. Thus Sidney Hook's anti-Communism was portrayed as an ideological vision whose moral absolutism overrode the arguments for prudent policies in pursuit of peace with the Soviet bloc in an age of nuclear arms. A portrait that moved further than the criticism of anti-Communism as a species of ideological zealotry was its dramatic representation, as in Arthur Miller's play *The Crucible*, as a form of moral puritanism that sought to repress the Communist movement, paralleling the paranoiac Puritanical suppression of the practice of witchcraft in an earlier age. (Although the terms used in this debate over the status of a "cold war warrior" like Sidney Hook may now appear alien or remote, they were objects of intense emotion during the culture wars of that period. Thus Elia Kazan's well-known film *On the Waterfront* represents in its hero's decision to testify before a congressional committee a direct response to Arthur Miller's praise for the silence of the martyred couple charged with practicing witchcraft in *The Crucible*. A dramatic footnote to this choosing of sides was the last word that Molly Kazan, the wife of Elia Kazan, directed toward Arthur Miller on their parting. As Miller left the Kazan home to proceed to the writing of *The Crucible*, she admonished him that their political concern in this early phase of the cold war was not focused upon "witches.")

Hook, who had observed the triumph of totalitarian forces in Germany, recognized that democratic societies could in principle and, in appropriate circumstances, must restrict the activities of antidemocratic political groups. He formulated this view in *Heresy, Yes—Conspiracy, No*. To the extent that Communist Party activities in democratic countries represented the expression or even the advocacy of heretical ideas and competing points of view, their rights ought not to be abridged on pain of violation of democratic principles. Yet, to the extent that these activities represented a conspiratorial organization against the procedures and methods of democracy, it would be legitimate for a democracy to pass legislation that would restrain the freedom of action of the conspiracy. Hook's distinction does not, of course, govern the application of this theoretical principle to particular cases and their adjudication in specific circumstances.

Sidney Hook was a member of the editorial board of *Partisan Review* in those years along with his colleague in the Philosophy Department, James Burnham, and his friend Lionel Trilling of Columbia, who had authored *The Middle of the Journey*, a novel whose hero is modeled upon the career of the most significant anti-Communist figure of the 1950s, Whittaker Chambers. The central focus of *Partisan Review* during Hook's tenure on the editorial board was the issue of anti-Communism, but, as noted above, it combined this interest with other tendencies of modern thought. Thus William Barrett, whom Hook had hired as a professor of philosophy at New York University, was an associate editor of *Partisan Review* and had pioneered in that magazine the introduction and interpretation of existentialist philosophical thought in the United States. In this context, it is relevant to note that Hook, who had earlier been a student of German philosophical thought, authored a critical study directed against Martin Heidegger's concept of being. This work, *The Quest for Being*, follows in part the line of Dewey's criticism of modern metaphysical tendencies in his *The Quest for Certainty*. Hook's criticism of Heidegger's metaphysics and epistemology was carried out independently of any assessment of his political views.

The response to Communism remained the dominant philosophical and political issue for Hook in the postwar period. In this context, the phenomenon of the mercurial rise of Senator Joseph McCarthy, who had emerged as a leading protagonist of an alternative type of anti-Communism, had to be confronted by the longtime supporters of the anti-Communist movement. Senator McCarthy's tactics led to a split among the members of the editorial board of *Partisan Review*: there was a division between Hook, Lionel Trilling, and William Phillips, on the one hand, and James Burnham on the other, who argued that it was a fallacy of moral equivalence or of false moral symmetry to equate the millions of murders that the Communists had carried out with the handful of errors of Senator McCarthy's anti-Communism. For Burnham, this would be analogous in today's terms to an equation between deaths caused by terrorism and deaths that result from collateral damage caused by counterterrorism.

The contrary position apparently held by Hook, Trilling, and Phillips was that the anti-Communist cause must dissociate itself completely from the activities of Senator McCarthy for both prudential and moral reasons. In prudential terms, the failure to dissociate would facilitate the agenda of the Left to use the epithet of "McCarthyism" to condemn any kind of anti-Communist activity. Burnham's rejoinder was that the Left would condemn anti-Communists as "McCarthyites" no matter how strongly they criticized McCarthy's tactics.

Furthermore, "McCarthyism," as a cherished intellectual construct of the Left, was being advanced to indicate a portent of an incipient nativist US fascism. This construct would be exploited by the Left to develop a politically useful, broad front of anti-McCarthyism or antifascism, in which hardcore Communists would be mixed with anti–cold war neutralists, anti-anti-Communists of various political kinds, advocates of peace, and true believers in civil liberties, who objected to actions against Communists that were carried out in the name of or for the sake of national security.

A forceful response, however, was advanced on moral grounds. Since the anti-Communist movement had its roots in a protest against the injustice of Stalin's methods, it was untenable that this movement should fail to reject any action that involved an abuse of individuals' legal and civil rights. The requirement was that no innocent person should be charged with a fault for reasons of poli-

45

tics or propaganda in the absence of the highest standard of evidence. Thus procedural fairness ought to be maintained regardless of the ways in which the political Left would exploit the anti-Communist movement's criticism of McCarthy. This position was accepted by the *Partisan Review* board and led to James Burnham's resignation from it.

The split between Sidney Hook and James Burnham provides an illuminating perspective on the positions that Sidney Hook supported at that time. Burnham had decided to resign his post of professor of philosophy at New York University in order to pursue his political interests more actively. These involved, primarily, a criticism of the US foreign policy of containment of the Soviet bloc in favor of active measures to intervene in areas of Soviet control and to "roll back" the expansion of Soviet power. In contrast, Hook supported the more constrained policy of containment practiced by the Eisenhower administration, even during the anti-Communist insurrection in Hungary, on the grounds of its greater prudence. Burnham became a regular writer for the conservative magazine *The National Review*, founded by William Buckley, whereas Hook's advocacy of secularism brought him in sharp disagreement with Buckley's formulation of conservative ideology during that period. Burnham described liberalism in terms of a suicidal ideology for the West that essentially represented a death wish for the institutions of traditional liberal, democratic culture. Hook, though critical of that segment of the liberal political movement that constituted the "fellow travelers" of the Communist movement, was prepared to join forces in anti-Communist coalitions with leading liberal figures on the US political scene.

The disagreement between Hook and Burnham also points to an interesting problem in the interpretation of pragmatic moral theory. It would appear that, for pragmatic moral theory, the moral justification for any policy involves its confirmation as a predictive hypothesis about a particular "problematic situation." Accordingly, it could be argued that Burnham's position has been justified on the pragmatic ground that the subsequent factual record has confirmed the charges advanced by Senator McCarthy. The opening of the documented files of the KGB has confirmed that McCarthy, far from exaggerating the degree of Communist penetration in the United States, had significantly underestimated its dimensions, both in the sphere of culture through "agents of influence" and in the sphere of politics, particularly through the placing of espionage agents in important government positions. Yet the rejoinder of the pragmatic moralist such as Hook is that the issue remains whether the falseness of the charges made by McCarthy against some or many individuals has been confirmed or refuted in light of the ensuing evidence. The principle that persons ought to accept responsibility for the accuracy and complete truth of charges made against other persons holds for pragmatic moralists, although its status may not be an a priori categorical imperative or absolute moral intuition but is more like a policy guideline that has been vindicated and "verified" in practice, by human experience, in many cultures over great periods of time.

In any event, the significance of McCarthyism has remained a historical issue for both the Left and the Right, even though the fall of McCarthyism was as rapid and spectacular as its meteoric rise had been. At the apparent peak of his power, Senator McCarthy had adopted the self-destructive strategy of attacking the Eisenhower presidency for being "soft" on Communism. This attack soon brought about his political demise.

At the opposite ideological pole, even after McCarthy's mortal political wounds, McCarthyism continued to be portrayed as the growing threat of US fascism. In Paris in late 1954, for example, I heard Jean-Paul Sartre develop this analysis of US politics and galvanize his audience with the rhetorical refrain of "*À bas le McCarthyisme! À bas le fascisme!*"

47

This seemed to me at that time an extraordinary response by a French intellectual who had himself lived through the German occupation and had witnessed General Eisenhower's liberation of France and Paris, including the magnanimous and politically astute ascription of that liberation to the forces of the Resistance and of Free France. Sartre's expressed tilt toward Soviet Communist policies in the 1950s in opposition to Eisenhower and US "proto-fascism" also suggests an impulse to self-destructiveness. This tendency to self-destructiveness makes McCarthy's pale in comparison, for the stakes were not the rise or fall of an individual political career but whether the freedom of French cultural and political life would suffer the fate of Warsaw, Prague, or East Berlin.

Hook's characterization of the conflict between the West and the Soviet Union as a struggle between democracy and totalitarianism resulted in his role as an ideological and intellectual leader in the 1950s, not only in the United States but throughout what was referred to as the "free world." He organized the American Committee for Cultural Freedom, which sponsored a series of symposia and conferences in the United States, and the Congress for Cultural Freedom in Western Europe. The Congress for Cultural Freedom sponsored a number of publications, including *Encounter* in the United Kingdom, edited by Irving Kristol and Stephen Spender; *Der Monat* in Berlin, edited by Melvin Lasky; and *Les Preuves* in Paris, which published several anti-Communist essays of François Mitterrand, who was later to become the longtime socialist president of France. Although each of these three journals had its own distinctive style and approach, each had, as its dominant moral theme, the opposition between democracy and totalitarianism. In a sense, *Partisan Review* was the model for each of them in its successful combination of aspects of cultural modernism, artistic avant-garde criticism, and the recognition of the significance of anti-Communism for the politics of the period.

48

Despite this international expansion of Hook's influence in the anti-Communist movement, he remained constant to both pragmatism and socialism. Hook reasserted the justification of pragmatism, which Dewey had formulated against metaphysical antiempirical views in *The Quest for Certainty*, with a parallel criticism of Heideggerian existentialism in *The Quest for Being*.

Hook continued to declare himself to be a socialist and was generally identified with the politics of the Left, rather than the Right, in Europe and the United States. One confirmation of his position is that the money supplied by the US government to help fund the work for the Congress for Cultural Freedom was administered under the acronym of "NCL," that is, support for the non-Communist Left.

Hook's support for socialism did not imply any view about the relationship of free market economics and political democracy. In a front-page essay on Friedrich August von Hayek's *Road to Serfdom* for the *New York Times Book Review*, he criticized von Hayek's thesis that free-market pluralism leads to democracy and that socialism's concentration of economic and political power leads to the denial of freedom. For Hook, who had rejected Marxist economic determinism, there was no necessary connection between the economic order and the political order. Consequently, he believed in the possibility of democratic socialist governments, just as he recognized the reality of socialist regimes that were dictatorial. He also believed that there could be democratic capitalist governments, contrary to the standard Marxist view, and that capitalist societies might not be democratic, but authoritarian or even dictatorial. (The development of the free-market economy in China will presumably provide a crucial test case for the Hayek hypothesis that Hook criticized. The issue is whether the Communist Party leadership's monopoly of political power can be sustained after the introduction of rule of law in the domestic commercial sphere and international economic relations, as well as with the rise of an entrepreneurial and managerial class whose role and wealth provide a degree of protection from political coercion.)

Hook's subsequent turn toward neoconservatism did not originate from a new belief in the importance of free-market economies for political freedom; nor did it derive from any fundamental change in his secular and naturalist opposition to religious views. Thus, Hook did not become, at the outset of his neoconservatism, in contemporaneous political terms, either an economic or a religious conservative. The change in his views was primarily a response to the new political and cultural situation that developed in the 1960s. In light of that response, Hook came to represent and strongly express the voice of cultural conservatism, particularly on the nature of the US university.

The rise of the New Left in the 1960s, with its attack on academic freedom and academic integrity in major universities, provided the impetus for the fourth major step in Hook's intellectual career—in which his views were to be linked with the neoconservative movement in US political thought. Hook remained "out of step." For as the New Left gained powerful faculty support within the academy and university administrations shifted to compromise with and absorb the onslaught of the New Left faculty and student groups through a series of changes in their standards and curricula, Hook stressed his loyalty to the essential aspects of the traditional, free university.

By this time, Hook had abandoned his self-identification with Marxism, partly because it had become evident to him that the Marxist corpus had been interpreted in ways that differed significantly from his own preferred interpretation of Marxism as an empirical hypothesis about "scientific" socialism. In contrast to this interpretation, Marxism included a theory of existentialist Marxism, derived from a reading of Marx's youthful 1848 manuscripts, as well as the construction of a Nietzschean Marxism, derived from the rejection of the primacy of economic theory combined with the Romantic attractiveness of revolutionary transformation of social institutions. In a 1975 essay signaling this abandonment, Hook recognized that Marx's texts and legacy had permitted these diverse interpretations of Marxism, as well as those of Lenin, Trotsky, Stalin, and Mao, which had been used to legitimate totalitarian power.

In theory, it would have been possible for Hook to continue his advocacy of socialism even as he shifted away from Marxism to a conservative position on current cultural issues. Yet he appears to have changed his position on socialism.

At an interview for Hook's oral biography at Teacher's College, Columbia, Prof. Diane Ravitch began by asking Hook whether he had always been a socialist. He replied that in his boyhood, the family had voted for William Howard Taft and he had shared the family's political loyalty. This surprised Professor Ravitch, and Hook explained that his father had been a worker in the garment industry and at that time there had been two seasons: "employment" and "slack." Taft was perceived as supporting tariffs on imported textiles, thereby helping employment and reducing "slack." Accordingly, the family supported his candidacy.

After this reminiscence, Hook pointed out that he prided himself on his ability to apply logic and critical intelligence to political and social issues. Yet he declared that embarrassing as the confession might be in respect to this ability, he had concluded that he had been guilty of a fallacy in the logic of practical reasoning. That fallacy was embedded in his comparison of the realities of the capitalist system as he had himself experienced them in the Williamsburg neighborhood of his youth and in the poverty of the Depression, with the ideal portrait of the socialist system as it was envisaged in Marxism or in other theoretical projections of the socialist economy. He had never corrected this bias by comparing the realities of capitalism with the economic realities of socialism as they had emerged in country after country where socialist governments had come to power. Alternatively, he had not adopted a perspective in which the ideal theory of socialism, with its vision of unfettered production for use, would be compared with its ideal counterpart in the theory of a capitalist free-market society, in which the invisible hand works to bring forth optimal prices, wages, and rates of economic growth and never allows equilibrium to be permanently established at depressed levels of economic performance.

Hook's cultural conservatism was expressed in his criticism of those radical perspectives that absolutized some values like civil liberty and neglected the importance of correlative values like civic order or national security. Hook founded the newsletter *Measure*, whose title reflected his effort to stress the importance of balance among competing, plural values.

In the 1970s, an important confrontation was taking place in the university over the value of equality. Egalitarians were seeking to achieve virtual universality of access without considering the price to be paid in the loss of standards in US education. Thus, the open enrollment that was introduced—in order not to increase student frustration and failure—necessarily implied that a large proportion of the work carried out in postsecondary school institutions would not take place at historical levels of college achievement. Generally, it is a truism that social institutions require the recognition or reward of hierarchical duties and of differences in performance among persons engaged in the work of the institution. Hook's focus upon "measure" sharpened the realization that the attempt to obliterate all relevant distinctions for the sake of the maximization of equality could violate a value like excellence and deny fairness in the standards of admission, employment, grading, or promotion in any human enterprise, including the university.

Consequently, Hook's criticism of a lack of balance among maximalist advocates of egalitarianism led him to become an opponent of those interpretations of "affirmative action" policies that involve group quotas. Hook did not oppose affirmative action as the positive search for able persons among minority groups, just as he did not oppose the development of educational and training programs for minorities and disadvantaged groups. But Hook opposed any interpretation of affirmative action or of the extension of equality that would undermine or ignore standards of talent, merit, or achievement in the workplace and particularly in the academy.

One focus of Hook's concern in the educational confrontation that formed part of the "culture wars" that were the legacy of "sixtyism" was on the issue of "multiculturalism." Hook had always supported the Deweyan emphasis upon free inquiry that is critical of inherited traditions in any domain of experience, including some of Dewey's innovations in progressive education. Yet he recognized that a valid conception of liberal education must also transmit the major cultural monuments of the tradition from one generation to the next.

In many of the areas of cultural studies that have developed since the 1960s, the class becomes a shared community of faith organized around a search for group identity in which there is little room for skeptical intelligence or critical inquiry, particularly about the assumptions of the common faith. This is especially true where the cultural studies are those of a group assumed to have shared the fate of victimhood, such that the academic study of its condition is often fused with an advocacy for an activist agenda. Hook's criticism of this kind of multicultural education was to assert the standards of critical discussion and research in all areas of university teaching, rejecting any politicized instruction, even in such academically sacrosanct fields as black studies, women's studies, or gay and lesbian studies. Hook's criticism of these ideological multicultural tendencies was conjoined with his opposition to efforts to delegitimate the teaching of Western classics. He welcomed the introduction of nonpoliticized courses that would increase knowledge of non-Western cultures; yet the university curriculum required balance between the introduction of new areas of study in non-Western cultures and the appreciation and critical interpretation of the Western and US cultural heritage. On the whole, Hook's views as a cultural conservative were compatible with the approach he had adopted in support of Dewey's liberal pragmatism. He continued to stress the importance of freedom of inquiry, the use of critical intelligence, and the need for measured evaluation among plural values, along lines that were consistent with the systematic formulation he had published in 1946 in *Education for Modern Man*. In that work, Hook had been critical of the "great books" curriculum advanced by Saint John's College in Annapolis, particularly in its use of classical historical texts for the teaching of the natural sciences. Yet Hook had always supported an important place in the curriculum for the great works of the Western cultural tradition, whether in literary humanities, the history of philosophy, or political theory. His final essays on the philosophy of the curriculum placed more explicit emphasis, as noted below, on the teaching of the Western tradition, particularly in political thought.

Hook's confrontation with totalitarian ideologies, combined with his pragmatic philosophical approach, involved him in an advocacy of the strategic priority of the value of cultural freedom and of free inquiry over other important social values. Yet Hook's neoconservatism complemented this view, even as it recognized the need for balance or measure, rather than for the absolute maximization of liberty. Hook would have found it incoherent to suggest that a free society could survive and flourish if it did not find a balance among freedom and a range of plural values, including the constraints that may be required for the realization of excellence in cultural standards and civic order and security in domestic practices.

Hook's continuous defense of the pragmatic philosophical perspective was expressed, in terms of his personal beliefs, as a position that can be characterized as "Enlightenment naturalism." This position represents a fifth step, or aspect, of his intellectual career.

There is an interesting item of biographical evidence that underscores the continuity of Hook's commitment to the Enlightenment. When Aleksandr Solzhenitsyn had burst upon the consciousness of the West, particularly in his early autobiographical novel, *The First Circle*, there was little awareness of the nature of his views. The president of the American PEN Society, apparently seeking to defend Solzhenitsyn from arrest by the Soviet authorities, wrote an op-ed essay in the *New York Times* arguing that Solzhenitsyn was only a critic of Stalin's crimes, a criticism that did not merit his imprisonment. According to this essay, Solzhenitsyn had never criticized Communism, Leninism, socialism, or Marxism. The *Times* published a response that argued that this interpretation was incorrect. The evidence for Solzhenitsyn's actual views included the harsh castigation he directed against the French fellow-traveler journalist of the publication *Liberation*, which marks the closing words of his novel. The journalist had observed the many vans that moved around Moscow bearing the label of food delivery and, not knowing the interior of these vans, which actually contained political prisoners, noted for his newspaper that the city was well provisioned.

Subsequently, Solzhenitsyn emerged as a severe critic not only of Stalin's oppressive rule but of Communism, Leninism, socialism, and Marxism. Hook's admiration for Solzhenitsyn virtually knew no bounds, both because of his great suffering and courage in the gulag and his determination to bear witness to the events of that "Archipelago." Hook recognized that Solzhenitsyn was a severe critic of Communism, Leninism, socialism, and Marxism, and did not express disagreement with his views. Yet Solzhenitsyn had moved beyond these criticisms to a counter Enlightenment thesis that located the flaw of Communist or National Socialist totalitarianism in the Enlightenment's negation of a religious sensibility with the subsequent abandonment of transcendental constraints upon the expansion and concentration of power in the secular sphere of human affairs. From Solzhenitsyn's perspective of modern history, the secularism and the "scientism" of the Enlightenment had weakened the religious tradition and through this weakening bore responsibility for the phenomena of Marxism and Leninism, with their consequences in the Stalinist state or, by a different route, for the post-Christian National Socialist state. Hook recognized and could identify the true range of Solzhenitsyn's anti-Communist criticism; he drew the line, however, at Solzhenitsyn's negative interpretation of the Enlightenment. Hook continued to sustain his belief in the potential triumph of the values associated with this Western philosophical movement.

This belief implied Hook's continuing faith in historical perfectibility through the application of critical intelligence to institutional change and to the reformation of human nature. The pragmatic focus upon scientific method as a paradigm for truth-seeking was part of both a rejection of antinaturalist or religious perspectives of reality as well as a continuation of the rational worldview that had become central to Western thought during the Enlightenment.

Hook's naturalism assumed that nature was neutral with respect to human endeavor. Nature was not malicious or hostile with an ultimate sentence of doom for human aspiration; nor was it beneficent, even though natural events had given rise to human life and intelligence. Thus Hook rejected any place for the supernatural in an account of human experience. Unlike James or Dewey, who had explored positively the possibilities of a naturalistic theism in which God may be considered, in Matthew Arnold's phrase, as a name for "the power not ourselves that makes for good in the Universe," Hook excluded any reinterpretation of theism within the confines of naturalism.

Similarly, Hook rejected as "antinaturalistic" any interpretation of human nature that considered mankind to be irremediably evil, as in the Christian doctrine of original sin, or even in the Kantian dictum, canonized by Isaiah Berlin, that "out of the crooked timber of humanity, nothing straight can be made." For Hook, the neutralism of nature left open the question of the possibilities of human perfectibility through the melioration of the human environment or the scientific mastery of psychological motivation.

Hook's naturalism included a belief in the possibilities of the transformation of nature and of human nature. This Enlightenment faith in the possibility of progress through science was reinforced by the pragmatic methodology that stressed the systematic application of scientific method to human affairs. Consequently, if Hook's naturalism viewed any divine guarantee of human triumph to be wishful, it also led to his optimistic belief that any interpretation of human history as tragically fated to destruction went beyond the empirical record of a neutralist naturalism.

He was sensitive to the counterclaim that this version of naturalism could be characterized as projecting an excessively optimistic vision of the future of the human condition. Thus, Hook's justification of naturalism sought to confront the criticism that George Santayana had directed specifically against pragmatic naturalism. Santayana had argued that the pragmatists looked at the foreground of the vast scene of nature, in which human beings were capable of transforming some natural processes, and overlooked the "background" dimensions of the scale of natural forces that could place in perspective the smallness of the theater of human possibilities. Hook's Enlightenment naturalism rejected any ultimate pessimism that was derived either from the view that the immensity of nature, with its potentialities for catastrophe, was bound to overwhelm the transformative capacities of human intelligence or from the view that the perverse and self-destructive tendencies of human nature were irremediable and imperfectible.

The optimistic naturalism of US pragmatism had as part of its tacit framework an emphasis on the possibility of realizing human ideals rather than an emphasis upon suffering, resisting, or enduring inevitable suffering and evil. Such a framework is presupposed in Dewey's formulation of a pragmatic, naturalist moral philosophy as aiming to realize a world in which "frail goods are secured, secure goods are extended, and the precarious promise of good that haunts experienced things be more liberally fulfilled."

Hook was acutely aware that his optimistic projection was required to confront the twentieth-century phenomena that moved beyond the "horrendous excrescences" of the nascent Soviet state to the subsequent development of the "Gulag archipelago" and to the unimagined concentration camp universe with its death camps. Moreover, recent scientific and technological development indicated, in Winston Churchill's memorable phrase about the bombing of London by unmanned rockets, that "the Dark Ages return on the winged tips of Science."

Hook confronted this challenge in several essays on evil in history and in his presidential address to the American Philosophical Association, when he chose to question whether pragmatism had an adequate "tragic sense of life." Hook's pragmatic view of tragedy allows for innumerable sites for human failure and defeat. He also stressed that history is not simply a drama of good against evil but involves a tragic conflict between one good and another good, between the good and the right, as well as between one form of the right and another form of the right.

Yet Hook remained adamant in his denial of the inevitability of the defeat of human ideals in history. With a characteristic Enlightenment optimism whose roots can be traced to Condorcet or even to Descartes, he speculated whether science, which seemed to be on the brink of the realization of technological achievements that would mean "the poor" would not "always be with us," would also be able to realize progress in biology that eradicated sickness.

Hook ended his address by stating, "Pragmatism, as I interpret it, is the theory and practice of enlarging human freedom in a precarious and tragic world by the arts of intelligent social control." And he went on to conclude that this practice may not be a lost cause "if we can summon the courage and intelligence to support our faith in freedom—and enjoy the blessings of a little luck."

This naturalistic profession of faith in the possibility of the remediation of human nature and the transformation of human history, which Hook found to be compatible with the pragmatic sense of the tragic, stands in sharp contrast to Hellenic naturalism, with its sense of tragic necessity that insists that any lasting human triumph is unattainable. This pragmatic faith also stands in ironic contrast to those texts of "Biblical naturalism" such as the books of Job and Ecclesiastes, which assert limits to the human condition: Job recognizes the ways in which the immensities of nature overwhelm any human aspiration for just rewards in this life; similarly, Ecclesiastes can only counsel resignation to the tragic circumstance that human endeavor is ultimately futile and vain in a world "under the sun" (1:3) where "Time and Chance happen to all of mankind" (9:11). Hook's Enlightenment naturalism was the complement of his own personal optimism and feistiness. These formed the ground for his faith that whatever be the numerous setbacks to human progress, the realistic acceptance of these facts does not logically permit an inference about the ultimate defeat of human ideals in history.

This sequential survey of the five major steps of Hook's intel-

59

lectual career calls for an epilogue that considers his career as a whole. Throughout most of the five phases of his intellectual career, Hook persisted in his willingness to be "out of step." He had been, as previously noted, a Marxist before the thirties and an anti-Communist during the heyday of progressivism. He was a secularist supporter of Enlightenment naturalism during the public revival of religious conformism in the Eisenhower fifties. In his last decades, he was activist advocate of neoconservative policies for the university during the period when the academic community of which he was a member grew increasingly radicalized by the culture of sixtyism.

In his own field of political philosophy, the Deweyan approach that Hook had championed, which required the empirical evaluation of competing pragmatic hypotheses about possible social change, had been replaced by an aprioristic Kantian theory for the rational support of distributive justice. Hook did not shift his support to this type of Rawlsian theory, which was so enthusiastically embraced by postpragmatic philosophers, in search of a post-Marxist formulation of egalitarianism. Hook maintained an approach to political philosophy that stressed the evaluation of competing hypotheses on the grounds of empirical historical experience rather than a methodology of rational ideal construction. This pragmatic methodology, which had resulted in Hook's radical assessment of the need for social change in the prewar period, remained a continuing aspect of Hook's philosophy, although his empirical judgment of postwar developments tended to confirm his neoconservative views about the need to defend liberal and democratic traditions against the onslaught of the new ideological forces that challenged them.

This awareness of being out of step was sustained by Hook's willingness to be a member of a minority. It is the courage to maintain a minority position that Sigmund Freud (a thinker whose psychoanalytic theories Hook had criticized for half a century as lacking scientific verifiability) had identified as a crucial aspect of his own ethnic identity. Freud had argued that even when a person abandons the traditional doctrine and practice of a minority religious group, the psychological residue in personal identity and character formation provides a source of the courage to function as a member of a minority.

In evaluating Hook's intellectual career, two contrary perspectives can be sketched. There are those who would characterize his career as a kind of "autumnal" work, stressing his disillusionment with the transformative vision and radical zeal of his early views that led him to retreat to activities in defense and conservation of imperfect, traditional institutions. From this perspective, the narrative, in its entirety, constitutes a tragic fall from the promise, ardor, and idealism of his youth.

Others would represent Hook's career within the genre of the works of "spring." In these works, like *Twelfth Night* or *As You Like It*, the quixotic lover is initially infatuated with an impossible or absolutely inappropriate object for his yearning. The happy outcome takes place only when a disillusioning discovery is made and the lover is rematched to an appropriate, true, and lasting object for his affection.

The decision in favor of the latter perspective seems straightforward. It rests upon the unavoidable facts about the illusory character of those idealistically visionary yet catastrophically regressive political constructions that Hook came to oppose. It also rests upon the recognition of the paramount importance and resilient endurance into the twenty-first century of the institutions of democracy, cultural freedom, and scientific inquiry that gained Hook's loyalty and support through most of the past century.

In the last decade of his life, Hook organized a number of conferences on the role of the university in education for democracy, for the enhancement of cultural freedom, and for the development of scientific inquiry. In Hook's lectures at these conferences, he placed great emphasis upon the teaching of the classics in the curriculum.

After one such conference, in which I had participated, I followed up with a letter to Hook on the limits of the classic texts in protecting the curriculum from politicization. That letter had two parts. In the first part, which was written during the period of Gorbachev's *glasnost*, I referred to recent news items about the fate of a Soviet dissenter whose case Hook had championed five decades earlier. This relatively minor official in the Soviet foreign ministry of foreign affairs had criticized Stalin openly while in France and was subsequently found dead in that country. This case had recently been reopened in the Soviet Union. Surviving relatives had been allowed to speak publicly about the circumstances of his murder and had petitioned the Kremlin for redress. It appeared that the false historical record was being corrected by the Soviet authorities. Since Hook had long pursued this case without a veil, I suggested to him that the day might not be far off when Hook's contested criticisms of the Soviet Union would be vindicated by the Soviet governmental leadership itself. This would amount to a declaration of victory in the long moral struggle that Hook had waged so vigorously throughout his life about the truth of the crimes of the Soviet Union.

In the second part of the letter, there was advanced a critical view of Hook's faith in the power of a curriculum containing the great classics of political philosophy to sustain a culture of political freedom. The argument was that in the current university, these classics could be interpreted and read to reinforce an opposing ideological agenda. Thus, Aristotle's texts in politics could be redirected away from his own special theories of democracy and justice toward a caricature of his views as a supporter of slavery, anti-feminism, and political exclusion. Similarly, the reading of John

62

Locke's classic text that pioneered human rights to life, liberty, and property in the West could be readily subverted. Locke's doctrine of natural rights could be interpreted as a rhetorical device for legitimizing the power of the propertied class and excluding the participation of many groups from the institutions of democratic government. The presence of such great books in the curriculum would not itself serve as a barrier to the corruption of the process of free inquiry or to the erosion of the standards of scholarship. If the method of classroom teaching were to represent a form of advocacy, then access to the text itself would not be sufficient to provide the great majority of students with immunity from politicization.

I received in response a note from the hospital that Professor Hook had read the letter and was too ill to answer it immediately but that he would do so shortly. A few days later, I received a follow-up communication that Hook had not yet been able to answer the letter because of illness but would do so in the near future.

After a few more days had passed, I received a brief reply. Hook did not respond to the first part of the letter, with its reference to the significance of recent events for the eventual vindication of his own political position. I believe that this characterized his general attitude, which tended to pass over any expression of praise and also tended not to be interested in battles that had previously been waged and won. Instead, he replied only to the second part, indicating his agreement with the criticism of his own essay on the curriculum. To my surprise, Hook urged me to immediately submit this comment to *Partisan Review.* He expressed the thought that an article that would criticize his own views in a magazine with which he had been associated for so long would merit publication.

A day or so later, I received the news of Hook's death. Despite Hook's suggestion, the comment in my letter was far too brief for publication. Yet I was able to follow his advice, and an expanded version on that comment did appear subsequently on "Multicultural

Education and the University" in the *Partisan Review* volume *Our Country, Our Culture*. Hook's last brief note can only be understood as belonging to a form or genre of pedagogical expression, which is characterized by its recurrent motif of the paramount value that is placed upon the development of the student's capacity for self-expression and for the pursuit of his own line of thought whether it disagrees with, or even because it disagrees with and challenged, the opinion of his teacher.

For any account of Hook's intellectual career would be incomplete without the realization that Hook's thought and writings were constantly accompanied by his teaching and self-identification as a teacher of philosophy. He was continuously energized by his activity as a teacher, whether in the undergraduate classroom, the graduate seminar, the public lecture, or the forum of controversial and polemical debate.

As a teacher of introductory philosophy, one of his favorite books was a work with which he disagreed greatly: Plato's *Republic*. Hook enjoyed drawing out the "contradiction" between Plato's detailed construction of the imperatives for the ways of life of the citizens of his Republic and his concluding theme in the Myth of Er that each person must and should be free to make his own choices for the next stage of his life or reincarnation. One class assignment required the students to examine their own choices for a future life.

The range of personal projections for an alternative life surprised Hook, and he discontinued this assignment as risking an invasion of privacy. For it is a private question whether Sidney Hook himself would have chosen to be born again in a career that pursued the steps of pragmatism, Marxism, anti-Communism, cultural conservatism, and Enlightenment naturalism. In Er's account, for example, of the choice made by Ulysses, as Plato envisaged it and Joyce later renarrated it, that great adventurer who was "never at a loss" chose to be reincarnated as an Everyman who set forth for no venture beyond his native city and sought to enjoy the home-grown pleasures of the quiet life.

The related public question, however, is whether the kind of intellectual career that Hook pursued provides a form of life that can serve as a model for later generations as they make their own choices in the new century. It would appear that the model of Hook's life, as a philosopher and public intellectual, does provide a guide for making the right choices about greatly contested issues so that, in the final words of the *Republic*, "Both for this life and for the journey of a thousand years that may follow, we shall fare well."

The last two words of the *Republic*, commonly translated into English as "fare well," contain an ambiguity that combines the idea of "acting well" with the connotation of an ending. Yet I am informed (by my colleague Prof. Katja Vogt) that the original words thus translated do not contain any reference to an ending, even though they retain an ambiguity. That ambiguity is found in the fact that the Greek phrase *eu prattomen*—that is, literally "acting well"—combines both the idea of being well or happy and the idea of doing good. The intellectual career of Sidney Hook represents a life in which his well-being was related to the moral causes and purposes to which each of the five steps of his career were dedicated.

PART 1

SIDNEY HOOK'S PLACE IN THE AMERICAN PHILOSOPHICAL TRADITION

A Defense of Naturalism as a Defense of Secularism

Barbara Forrest

I.

$\mathcal{S}$idney Hook believed that "philosophy is legitimately concerned with large problems of human affairs, that philosophers should have something to say to their fellow citizens."[1] And indeed, Hook had much to say to his fellow citizens about two very important areas of human affairs: education and public policy. First a teacher, then a philosopher, and always a citizen who celebrated democracy as the necessary foundation of both education and philosophy, he saw education, philosophy, and public policy as organically related. Hook also knew the lessons of history, from which he learned that not only *his* intellectual interests as a pragmatic naturalist but those of his theistically committed opponents, with whom

69

he so loved to argue, were best served by a secular democracy. Arguing that the only reliable way to substantively advance knowledge was through the naturalistic methodology exemplified in science (referred to nowadays as *methodological naturalism*) and rooted in an empiricist epistemology reflecting our natural cognitive capabilities, Hook correspondingly held that a secular democracy was the best political safeguard of the freedom this methodology requires.[2] I maintain also that the converse is true, specifically, that a naturalistic methodology provides a defense of secularism in public policy. I specifically include here *educational* policy, in which sound cognitive procedures and principles are of paramount importance.

Secularism provides a framework for peaceful coexistence in a religiously pluralistic society. Although religious pluralism can exist, as in England, in a society with a state church, justice and equality demand that the church's political influence be so circumscribed either by law or custom (or both) that the government is functionally secular, that is, neutral with respect to religion. Any attempt to govern by overtly religious (or antireligious) principle leads to political inequities and social unrest, as attested by centuries of European history (and much recent history elsewhere). Robert Audi, in *Religious Commitment and Secular Reason*, outlines the problem for public policy when the state violates its religious neutrality: "Religion . . . can be a divisive force in democratic politics. . . . A holy cause can sanctify extreme measures. . . . Once the state favors the religious over the non-religious, . . . religious disagreements are likely to polarize government, especially regarding law and policy concerning religion."[3] Given the compelling historical reasons for secularism, I see it as less in need of strenuous defense and will devote more time to the discussion of naturalism.

Although, in defending separation of church and state, Audi rightly notes the polarizing effect of religion in politics, the naturalist points to a deeper rationale for separation: the conflicts engendered by religion are, at their deepest level, intractable epistemological conflicts. Humans have no known, common, cognitive faculties for knowing the supernatural. Moreover, of the ways in which people claim to acquire the knowledge of nature and society needed to navigate the problems of practical, social, and moral life, a naturalistic methodology is our only *common, public* way of acquiring this knowledge.[4] Consequently, the knowledge of nature and society gained through the use of a naturalistic methodology, relying upon our common cognitive capabilities, is the only reliable basis for public policy in a secular democracy. And in no area of public policy is the epistemological aspect of the issue more important than in education.

Furthermore, naturalistic methodology is not intrinsically *anti*-supernaturalist. It actually preserves a metaphysical "neutral zone" while being necessary in a practical sense because of the lack of a methodology for testing supernatural claims. Indeed, we have no choice but to proceed naturalistically if any practical tasks are to be accomplished successfully. (I include making policy as a practical task; I am not speaking merely about solving technological problems.) For exactly the same reason, secularism is not properly understood as *anti*religious but as providing a religious neutral zone in *civic* life. It is necessary to civic life in a practical sense for the same reason that naturalistic methodology is necessary in science and other cognitive tasks: the methodological and epistemological deficiencies of supernaturalism. Since there is neither a methodology for testing supernatural claims nor an epistemology for knowing the supernatural, public policy should not be grounded at any level in theistic belief. The epistemological and methodological constraints within which we must work in order to understand nature and society are the same constraints within which we must construct public policy, especially educational policy.

71

In making this argument, I am actually resurrecting arguments Hook made over half a century ago.

II.

Hook pointed out that "The history of naturalism . . . has been marked by two main tendencies. The first has interpreted God in the same way as the great historical religions; *viz.*, as an omnipotent personal power who guides the destinies of the world He has created. . . . The second has reinterpreted the conception of God . . . to signify a principle of order in the universe, the totality of all things, the possibility of good in the world, or the object of human allegiance."[5] Since the first is the conception governing the religious lives of most theists, in arguing for the superiority of naturalism over theism as a basis for public policy, I use the terms *theism* and *religion* in the first sense, that is, as designating belief in a transcendent, supernatural deity. Audi lists the features of religion as most Westerners understand it:

1. Belief in one or more supernatural beings.
2. A distinction between sacred and profane objects.
3. Ritual acts focused on those objects.
4. A moral code believed to be sanctioned by the god(s).
5. Religious feelings (awe, mystery, etc.) that tend to be aroused by the sacred objects during rituals.
6. Prayer and other communicative forms of conduct concerning the god(s).
7. A worldview according adherents a significant place in the universe.
8. A more or less comprehensive organization of one's life based on the worldview.
9. A social organization bound together by (1)–(8).[6]

72

(For my purposes, 1, 4, 8, and 9 are especially important.) In addition, Audi lists the sources of religious obligation, which I include because of the role they may play in efforts by theists to shape public policy in light of them: "(1) scripture; (2) non-scriptural religious authority, especially that of the clergy, but including the relevant community, such as the . . . theological community . . . ; (3) tradition . . . ; (4) religious experience; and (5) natural theology," the latter exemplified by Aquinas's five arguments for the existence of God.[7]

Next, three descriptive terms must be kept distinct: (1) *religious*, which describes traditional belief in a supernatural deity and behavior consonant with such belief; (2) *secular*, which describes a neutral, or simply nonreligious, position with respect to religious belief; and (3) *antireligious*," which describes an overtly hostile or antagonistic attitude toward religious belief and behavior consonant with such hostility. Those differences can be highlighted by looking at the respective ways in which they can be and have been manifested in public policy. Overtly religious public policy is openly and unambiguously founded on supernaturalism, that is, the acceptance of a transcendent deity who is the source of values and rules governing human conduct. (Such policy is the goal of many Religious Right political activists in the United States; their views are often unambiguously theocratic. Islamic theocracies provide a current example of overtly theistic public policy.) To the extent that public policy reflects theistic belief, public institutions will almost surely incorporate some body of doctrine considered exclusively true and will require conduct consistent with this doctrine. Such theistic government policy may also manifest itself in the persecution not only of nontheists, but of other *theistic* groups whose doctrinal commitments are unacceptable. Educational policy will reflect government-sanctioned orthodoxies.

On the other hand, *anti*religious public policy actively discourages or prohibits the free exercise of religious belief, even in areas of life that do *not* affect people outside the religious group. Antireligious policy is openly and unambiguously atheistic, as in the former Soviet Union and, currently, in the People's Republic of China. It is grounded in the outright *rejection* of supernaturalism and, correspondingly, in the rejection of supernatural rules governing human values and conduct. To the extent that public policy reflects state atheism, it, too, will almost certainly include some body of doctrine (e.g., Marxist-Leninist) considered authoritative over public institutions and private life. Institutions will reflect the government's hostility to religion, which can be manifested in the closing of churches, the harassment of believers, the imprisonment of clergy, and so on. In a hypothetical twist based on the current—and perennial—issue of American creationism (about which I shall speak shortly), antireligious public policy might prohibit the teaching of creationism in *religious* institutions, requiring instead that churches and sectarian schools teach evolution, or that they teach evolution along with creationism, or that they teach the controversies surrounding creationism.[8]

Secular democracies, however, refrain from enacting policies dictating the content of religious instruction in churches and sectarian schools. Such coercion would constitute the totalitarianism Hook abominated, though he himself was not religious. Contrary to the increasing tendency of the Religious Right to (mis)construe *secular* as *antireligious*, secular public policy is merely *not religious*, that is, neither justified by nor incorporating theistic belief.[9] Nothing in the concept of secularism requires the rejection of theism. Properly understood, secularism connotes neutrality toward the content of religious belief and religious practice, though secular policy may properly proscribe certain instances of the latter. (Law and public policy may, for example, restrict religious *practices* that interfere with the rights of other citizens without thereby taking any

74

position on the beliefs sanctioning those practices.) Neutrality implies the freedom to adopt any religious, nonreligious, or even antireligious view that does not adversely affect one's fellow citizens. Secular public policy maximizes each person's freedom to embrace any preferred view, limited by the right of others not to support it either financially or behaviorally and the right not to live under policies constrained either by theism or atheism. Moreover, the government's disallowance of certain religious *practices* and of the incorporation of religious ideas in public institutions does not constitute *anti*religious policy. Not only are there practical and constitutional reasons for such disallowals, but, as I try to show, methodological and epistemological reasons as well.

The writers of the US Constitution designed such a secular democracy, although in practice it has at various times been *more or less* secular. (I would argue that we are presently experiencing one of the pendular swings away from secularism and that the religious neutrality of the US government is being compromised by the political influence of the Religious Right.[10]) In such a system, public policy should be determined by common needs, interests, and values; it should incorporate neither theism nor atheism but should protect an individual's (or a private organization's) right to embrace either. Secular democracy is not a doctrine but a political *methodology* for constructing policy according to constitutional procedures and principles. And insofar as the policy-making process is carried out within the constraints of our shared cognitive capabilities (as opposed to being based on appeals to intuition or religious revelation), it is a distinctly naturalistic process. The secular democratic process is the political analog of the naturalistic methodology employed in understanding the natural and social world and in successfully meeting the practical demands of life in that world.

The next clarification concerns what I mean by "naturalistic methodology." A methodology is a systematic procedure or set of procedures for answering a question and/or accomplishing a task, such procedure(s) reflecting a basic pattern of inquiry that is a unified response both to the objective features of a problematic situation and to the cognitive faculties and technical capabilities we bring to its resolution. By *naturalistic* methodology, I mean what is done generally, *but not exclusively*, in science: the search for natural explanations of what we experience in the world, using the common cognitive faculties that we know humans to have and that therefore make experience intersubjective. Most simply stated, these faculties are the ability to detect phenomena accessible to sense experience and the ability to reflect critically upon that experience, drawing conclusions using the well-established rules of logic and evidence. There are no known, common faculties for detecting anything that may lie beyond the reach of experience and of inferences grounded in experience.

Naturalistic methodology, in short, is *any* way of doing things that does not call upon or require the invocation of supernaturalist beliefs in order to get them done. Such methodology is employed in everyone's daily tasks, and it was in use long before the advent of modern science. Law enforcement officers, for example, whether theist or nontheist, if they are to do their jobs effectively, must conduct investigations by considering the features of the crime scene. Any hypotheses they construct regarding the identity of the perpetrator(s) must be consistent with these features and must adhere to accepted standards of evidence and reasoning. They do not rely upon their capacities for religious experience to find criminals, nor do lawyers in the prosecution and defense of those accused. Many such examples could be added to this one, but all would reveal a common (because successful) approach to carrying out such tasks: people assess the problems they face, draw from the information they have or gather more as they need it, construct explanations of their situations and potential solutions to their problems, and then test their explanations and proposed solutions—that is, they try them out to see if they work. If they do, then these explanations and solutions are used to anticipate and forestall future problems. In short, naturalistic methodology is nothing other than what *both theists and nontheists already commonly do* in the course of daily life. Hook points out several features of naturalism that are relevant here:

> [D]espite all the basic conflicts over the first principles of thinking or evidence, there are working truths on the level of practical living which are everywhere recognized and which everywhere determine the pattern of reasonable conduct in secular affairs, viz., the effective use of means to achieve ends. Rationality on this level is . . . so using the means and materials of the situation in which final causes are pursued as to achieve a maximum of functional adaptation between means and ends. . . . [S]cientific method is the *refinement* of the canons of rationality and intelligibility exhibited by the techniques of behavior and habits of inference involved in the arts and crafts of men; its pattern is everywhere discernible even when overlaid with myth and ritual.[11]

Hook adds "that there is only one reliable method of reaching the truth about the nature of things anywhere and at any time, that this reliable method comes to full fruition in the methods of science, and that a man's normal behavior in adapting means to ends belies his words whenever he denies it."[12]

So is naturalistic methodology the application of *laboratory-like* procedures to vexing, complicated social and moral problems, devoid of any consideration of the uniqueness and complexity of human experience? Is it scientism? To answer affirmatively would be to misunderstand Hook, who would say that this is too rigid an understanding even of science (since science also comprises more than just laboratory procedures). Naturalistic methodology assumes a more conscious, systematic, and stepwise form in science than in nonscientific contexts, but it is simply the *extension into* science, with appropriate adaptations, of ways of solving problems and constructing explanations already proven successful *outside* science. The rules of logic and evidence are the same in either context.

Naturalism has proven its mettle by making possible extraordinary advances in human knowledge. Secularism has made possible an extraordinary degree of civic harmony in the midst of great religious variety. But one hundred years after Hook's birth, both are under strenuous attack by people who, despite being their beneficiaries, are trying to derail them.

III.

When Hook wrote his essay "The New Failure of Nerve" in 1943, during World War II, he was apprehensive about the future of secular democracy. He feared for "liberalism as an intellectual temper, as faith in intelligence."[13] He was worried not only about the war itself but about the response to it by some US intellectuals—a response he called the "new failure of nerve," that is, the failure of confidence in intelligence and the power of reason to resolve problems that lead to wars and the consequent turn to religion as the only sure salvation of society. As diagnosed by Hook, this failure manifested itself in many intellectuals' "abandoning the hard-won critical positions of the last few centuries."[14] Hook saw the implications of the view that public policy must be buttressed by divine sanction and moral absolutes, namely, "that our children cannot be properly educated unless they are inoculated with 'proper' religious beliefs; that theology and metaphysics must be given a dominant place in the curriculum of our universities; that churchmen should cultivate sacred theology before applying the social gospel; that business needs an inspired church that speaks authoritatively about absolutes . . . [and] that what is basically at stake in this war is Christian civilization."[15]

If Hook were here now, he would no doubt be providing a similar analysis of the current "culture war" that has become the mantra of the Religious Right. Noting the latter's rising influence on public policy, he would recall the prescient statement he made almost sixty years ago: "Fundamentalism is no longer beyond the pale; it has donned a top hat and gone high church."[16] He would point now to signs of what he saw in 1943 as "intellectual panic, heralded as portents of spiritual revival," manifested in "the recrudescence of beliefs in the original depravity of human nature; prophecies of doom for western culture, . . . the frenzied search for a center of value that transcends human interests; . . . posturing about the cultivation of spiritual purity; . . . and a veritable campaign to 'prove' that without a belief in God and immortality, democracy—or even plain moral decency—cannot be reasonably justified."[17] Hook would today be sharpening his formidable polemical skills in response.

In 1943, Hook located most of such intellectual panic in the Protestant response to "Catholic agitation," leading these panicked Protestants to "call for a society organized on [Protestant] Christian foundations."[18] According to Hook, if history and the internal characteristics of this response were reliable indications of the nature of a society thus organized, the state's neutrality toward religion would be destroyed, and "Education would have to be purged of all freethinkers to prevent them from examining the 'truths' of religion as critically as the truths of other branches of knowledge. . . . The new orthodoxy . . . would require the contraction, if not the proscription, of the scientific temper in order to diminish the hazards of belief. The social usefulness of ideas to those who possessed power, and their comfort and consolation to those who did not, would become the criteria of accepted truth."[19]

The "new currents of Protestantism" that Hook then saw washing over the intellectual landscape were strikingly similar to conservative Christians' call today for the United States' return to its putatively Christian foundations: "These new currents of Protestantism which profess sincere acceptance of present day democracy employ arguments . . . [assuming] that modern democracy has been derived from, and can only be justified by, the theological dogmas of Hebraic-Christianity according to which all men are created by God and equal before Him."[20] Hook saw then, as he would see now, that some "religious groups are seeking, as they always have, to make of God an instrument of national policy."[21]

In 1949, when Hook wrote "Nature and the Human Spirit," his earlier concern was still active, but he observed that the "anti-naturalist movement" that in 1943 he had called "the new failure of nerve" had since "taken on the proportions of a tidal wave in philosophy, theology, literature and the philosophy of history":

Characteristic of . . . [the] views [of this antinaturalistic movement] are two beliefs: (1) that our time of troubles is primarily an historical and logical consequence of the abandonment of the religious and metaphysical foundations of Western civilization and of a shift to secular life; and (2) that what gives genuine happiness to man, and relief from the multiple alienations which fragmentize both personality and society, in the words of St. Augustine "is something which does not proceed from human nature but which is above human nature." And from these beliefs the criticism follows that naturalism in any form is incapable of doing justice to the actually experienced qualities of human life, particularly the nature of man's moral experience.[22]

In the aftermath of the war, antinaturalism had not subsided but, according to Hook, had worsened, accompanied by a correspondingly stronger antisecularism.

The intellectual panic Hook highlighted then is virtually identical to that now coming from similarly panicked people. Therefore, my defense of naturalism as a defense of secularism is rooted in a *new* new failure of nerve. It is today the failure of moderate and progressive, but also some conservative, intellectuals who, comfortable in the religious and political freedom of a secular, constitutional democracy, are paying insufficient attention to the panic of the Religious Right and its influence on public policy. The panic is coming from mostly, but not exclusively, Protestant evangelicals and fundamentalists (although there are examples from the Catholic right as well). It takes the form of an explicit rejection of both naturalism and secularism, typified but not exhausted by Religious Right leaders such as James Dobson, Pat Robertson, Jerry Falwell, and D. James Kennedy; by such organizations as the Family Research Council and the American Family Association; and by other cultural movements ideologically aligned with them.[23]

Among the latter is the Discovery Institute–sponsored intelligent design (ID) movement, the newest manifestation of creationism, which has joined the Religious Right's project of making naturalism and secularism the bogeymen of modern culture. Headquartered in the Center for Science and Culture, the Discovery Institute's creationist subsidiary, ID has two primary goals: (1) to create in the public mind the idea that science (and, by extension, science education) is better governed by the principle of theistic rather than naturalistic explanation; and (2) to have this view incorporated into policy governing public education. To this end, ID proponents are urging boards of education to permit teachers to "teach the controversy" surrounding the theory of evolution (a cultural controversy that is nonexistent within science itself). Moreover, the movement's antinaturalism reflects its antisecularism. One of its advisers, George Gilder, explicitly rejects secularism: "Secular culture is in general corrupt, degraded, and depraved. . . . I don't believe in secular culture."[24] (In rejecting secular culture, Gilder was specifically rejecting public education, sanctioning parochial schools as the only genuine educational system.) The movement's founder, Phillip E. Johnson, has written extensively about the spiritual dangers of sending American youth into secular universities doctrinally unequipped to deal with what he sees as the pervasive naturalism that threatens their religious faith.[25] Proponents of ID and the Religious Right in general are deeply distrustful of both science and secular culture. And it is this distrust that threatens ultimately to undermine not only the scientific underpinnings of American education but the secular underpinnings of democracy as well.[26]

Many current antinaturalists are seeking influence over public policy by cultivating political connections. But I speak with special reference to the ID movement because it targets two institutions about which Hook cared deeply—public education and science, both of which thrive most effectively in a secular democracy. Intelligent design is not a scientific program but a political and religious movement; it cultivates followers among conservative Christians, whom its tactical document, "The Wedge Strategy," specifies as its chief constituency.[27] Its political goal is made explicit by Johnson: "[I]t is nearly inevitable that 'teach the controversy' will become public policy."[28] Its religious essence is expressed by the movement's leading apologist, William Dembski: "Indeed, intelligent design is just the Logos of John's Gospel restated in the idiom of information theory."[29] But ID proponents are also advancing their cause through the use of the secular media. And like other soldiers in the "culture war" (as they see themselves), ID has sought to influence one of democracy's most important secular processes: the drafting of federal legislation concerning public education; and it urgently desires a chance to test its claims in a vital secular institution—the federal courts.[30]

IV.

The ID movement's charges against naturalism boil down to two: (1) that its methodology rules out the supernatural, that is, God, a priori and (2) that having ruled out God, naturalism dismisses the need for transcendent, absolute moral truths, leading to moral relativism. The antinaturalism of the ID movement, which it shares with segments of the evangelical community (though not all evangelicals support either its aims or its message), is exactly the kind of antinaturalism Hook recognized in 1956, when he published "Naturalism and First Principles," prompted by "recent criticisms of naturalism which charge that it arbitrarily imposes its own canons of rationality or intelligibility on human behavior and therefore denies certain important truths about the world and human experience on a priori grounds."[31] He specifies the truths that naturalism supposedly eliminates at the outset: "The most powerful opposition to naturalism comes . . . from those who fear that it arbitrarily excludes from the realm of existence and knowledge something which we actually have good reason to believe in, viz., God and man's immortal soul . . . because its first principles and categories of explanation are such as to make the very assertion of their existence meaningless. If true this charge would be serious indeed, for the naturalist professes to be open-minded about the possibilities of existence in a world in which his greatest efforts seem so modest in the cosmic scale."[32]

Almost fifty years after Hook wrote "Naturalism and First Principles," this charge is precisely the one that Phillip Johnson,

83

founder of the intelligent design movement, today makes against naturalism in his effort to equate evolutionary theory with atheism: "The neo-Darwinian theory was discovered by a science that was committed a priori to methodological naturalism."[33] Johnson sees the latter as pervasive in American academia:

> The domination of the intellectual world by naturalism has important consequences for the popular culture, where theism remains prevalent. The United States is formally a democracy, but on matters involving "religion" the Constitution is supreme, and the judges have the authority to say what the Constitution means. . . . The judges . . . get their education at the universities, and they normally interpret events in the light of what they have been taught. To the extent that they have learned to take a naturalistic understanding of reality for granted, they will tend to assume that persons who base their thinking on the premise that God is real are irrational and hence dangerous when they influence public policy.
>
> Suppose that parents in a particular public school district want their children to be exposed to the arguments against the theory of evolution. . . . Those parents are unlikely ever to get their way. . . . The educational bureaucracies, backed by the courts, will make sure that "rationality" prevails. . . .
> . . . Rational beliefs are . . . consonant . . . with reality, and in the intellectual world of today, reality means naturalism.[34]

Johnson considers the secular educational process to be the seedbed of naturalism and the judicial system to be its culmination, from whence naturalism pervades US culture. In his view, the exclusive teaching of evolutionary theory, the product of science's naturalistic methodology, discriminates against religious believers because it excludes intelligent design. The clear implication of his antinaturalism is that he favors allowing *supernaturalism*, that is, theistic religion, a voice in the determination of both educational

84

and judicial policy; there *is* no other alternative to naturalism. Johnson persistently refuses to recognize the distinction between *methodological* naturalism and *ontological* or *philosophical* naturalism, the latter being a comprehensive, nontheistic worldview that, as Hook says, "generalize[s] the cumulative evidence won by the results of this method."[35] For Johnson, however, the two are without any substantive distinction. He maintains that in teaching only the naturalistic *methodology* of science, without even mentioning *philosophical* naturalism, public schools in effect are promoting atheism. This charge is exactly the one Hook was concerned to address: "Are naturalists guilty of this kind of dogmatism?"[36]

How is this issue as raised by the intelligent design movement related to the question of public policy? It is related in that precisely the fear that Hook described, which Johnson so persistently enunciates, is now fueling the Religious Right's attempt to ground public policy in a "transcendent truth." But Hook's answer to the question he posed shows that when ID proponents charge that teaching only evolution is equivalent to government sanction of atheism, they make a significant mistake: they label a *secular* way of knowing as an *atheistic* way.

V.

Hook's response to the antinaturalists' charge that naturalism dogmatically excludes God reveals that a naturalistic *methodology*, which he pointed out was unavoidable even for theists, does not require the a priori assumption of *philosophical* naturalism, that is, naturalism as an ontology. The use of naturalistic methodology does not bind the philosophical naturalist a priori to any ontological category:

> Naturalism is not committed to any theory concerning which categorical *terms* are irreducible or basic in explanation. Naturalists

85

differ among themselves about this in the same way that scientists may differ among themselves as to what terms in the language of science should be taken as primary. What all naturalists agree on is "the irreducibility" of a certain method by which new knowledge is achieved and tested. . . . It is a complete non sequitur to assume that because one asserts that the fundamental categories of description are X and Y and Z, and that they hold universally, he is therefore asserting that the world cannot be significantly described *except* in terms of X, Y, and Z, or as so many critics assume, that the world consists of "nothing but" X and Y and Z.[37]

To the extent that naturalistic methodology is "irreducible," Hook means it is the only workable methodology we *currently possess* for addressing questions of existential fact; some other methodology could certainly supplant it if the new methodology were equally or more successful at what the naturalistic one does. This is hardly dogmatism.

Indeed, according to Hook, such dogmatism would "remove the sting" from philosophical naturalism, in which criticism of theistic belief rests on the "weight of scientific discovery," that is, the weight of evidence relevant to questions of existential fact. The metaphysical viability of theism (or any other ontological commitment) rests on its facticity; God's existence is as much a question of existential fact as the existence of any natural entity. Thus the a priori denial of the possibility of theism would require ignoring the very thing upon which philosophical naturalism depends—evidence. The naturalist treats God's existence as an important factual question rather than a question of mere semantics in which various definitions of God must compete for acceptance.[38] And since God's existence is as meaningful and serious as any other factual question, the philosophical naturalist maintains that it must pass the same test as any other existential fact: the empirical test.

Intelligent design proponents recognize the legitimacy of this requirement by claiming that "intelligent design theory" *can* pass this test, thereby earning it entry into the public school science class. Dembski claims that the handiwork of a transcendent intelligent designer can be detected empirically.[39] (Ironically, if this were true, it would make the designer a *natural* entity, not the transcendent entity Dembski claims it is.) To Dembski and his creationist fellows, Hook would say, "If you have a workable methodology for detecting the supernatural, please produce it. And we must all be able to use your *super*naturalistic methodology as successfully as we have used the naturalistic methodology in science." Any uncertainty about whether theism can function as a principle of scientific explanation, warranting its inclusion in science instruction, would be instantly dispelled by producing a workable methodology for it and an intersubjective epistemology that enables us to justify supernaturalist truth claims.

But supernaturalism/theism has never been able to pass this test. As I remarked in an earlier essay, "Supernatural claims are existential claims . . . and so are subject to the same evidentiary requirements as claims about the natural order. . . . Yet despite this, . . . supernatural claims are beyond the reach of these requirements. *Paradoxically, supernatural claims are the kind of propositions for which empirical evidence is required, but impossible to obtain.*"[40] No methodology for resolving questions of existential fact is available other than the naturalistic one, which even theists must—and do—employ without protest in areas where the questions are less momentous. Since a supernatural designer by its nature is beyond the reach of scientific, that is, naturalistic, methodology, there is no possibility of doing the "theistic science" of intelligent design. Proponents of ID must produce a genuinely *scientific* methodology (and a corresponding epistemology) that are adequate to the verification of the designer's existence. Until they do, neither intelligent design nor any other antinaturalist position has any claim upon public policy, especially educational policy, in which the methodology and epistemology of cognition are of fundamental importance.

And in any case, antinaturalists' wholesale rejection of naturalistic methodology is logically inconsistent: the supernaturalist who invokes a transcendent, nonmaterial entity as an agent in natural processes cannot explain how such an entity can either instigate or influence these processes—the familiar supernaturalist dilemma of dualism. This dilemma forces even supernaturalists to explain physical processes by appealing to other physical processes—if they are concerned to *verify* their explanations. Moreover, a total rejection of naturalistic methodology is *practically* inconsistent because those who claim to reject it have no choice but to use it, even when, as Hook says, they punctuate its use with religious ritual and understand it conceptually within a wider, supernaturalist framework. Such necessity effectively *mandates* at least tacit acknowledgment of naturalism. When the theist wishes to find out why his lights have gone dark, he must employ a naturalistic methodology. He might pray or light a candle instead, but he would only delay the necessity of finding the problem. However, if he wishes to read the Bible by electric light rather than candlelight, he must inspect the breaker box and flip the switch. So even a thoroughgoing supernaturalist is, in a methodological sense, a naturalist, at least where such routine practical problems are concerned. The only difference between the philosophical naturalist and the theist lies in the way their paths diverge once they move beyond methodology to ontology.

Although the philosophical naturalist does not do so, the theist can consistently view (and implement) a naturalistic methodology as a way of understanding what he views as a divinely created universe. The philosophical naturalist's reasons for *not* seeing the world this way do not stem merely from reliance upon a naturalistic methodology but from other considerations, such as the *absence* of any methodology for detecting the supernatural, the problem of evil, etc. Hook points out, "Naturalism, as a philosophy, is a systematic *reflection upon, and elaboration of,* the procedures man employs in the successful resolution of the problems and difficulties of human experience" (emphasis added).[41] So philosophical naturalism is a product not of the mere employment of naturalistic methodology but of inferences based on the knowledge it yields *in combination with* other considerations. Reflecting *philosophically* upon what naturalistic methodology yields, the believer may indeed conclude that the universe is the product of a creator, or an "intelligent designer." The philosophical naturalist will view this conclusion not as a logical inconsistency but as simply the acceptance of a superfluous, evidentially unsupported *ontological* category.

The naturalist realizes, however, that failure to pass the existential tests, that is, the methodological and epistemological ones, does not thereby eliminate the *logical* possibility of God, even if the naturalist also believes that the *existential* possibility is negligible (note: "negligible" does not mean null). And because it does not nullify the logical possibility of theism, according to Hook, naturalist methodology actually preserves for theism an ontological category unavailable to atheism—the supernatural—which may be embraced, albeit without the benefit of scientific evidence. And it is both an existentially and semantically meaningful category, even if the naturalist does not consider it an evidentially supportable one. Atheism, on the other hand, has no categories beyond nature to which to appeal. Atheists must find existential meaning in the natural realm (a task that atheists affirm they can and do meet).[42]

The point, however, is that naturalistic methodology leaves the theistic question on the table, and this point absolves the naturalist of the antinaturalist's charge that the supernatural is ruled out a priori. The naturalist is in no position to deny theistic claims, as I have pointed out elsewhere: "Methodological naturalism does not disallow the logical possibility that the supernatural exists. To assert categorically that there is no dimension that transcends the natural order is to assert that human cognitive capabilities are sufficient to survey the whole of what there is; such a claim would amount to epistemological arrogance."[43] So not only are theists within their *political* rights in choosing to situate their secular lives conceptually within the framework of theistic belief, but naturalistic methodology also preserves rather than destroys the logical space within which they include the sacred above the mundane.

Correspondingly, functioning as citizens in the secular sphere does not require people to suspend their theism, which Robert Audi properly points out: "The relevant kind of thinking in secular terms does not require suspending one's theism, at least for any kind of theism of major importance in the world today. Even if one thinks of everything as created by God or under God's sovereignty, one will have ways of referring to people and (non-religious) things without mentioning God, and one can appeal to moral principles— including the ethical imperatives among the Ten Commandments— without depending on religious descriptions. This is entirely compatible with taking those principles to depend on God as much as anything in the Creation."[44] Audi is referring specifically to theists' obligation as citizens to provide adequate secular reasons for public policies they propose even when they also have religious reasons. (This, in effect, is what ID proponents purport to be doing when they claim that their pedagogical proposals are based on science.) Fulfilling this obligation need not jeopardize religious belief, since it is possible for a policy to be simultaneously justifiable on *both* secular and religious grounds. For example, one might support an aid program for the poor for both secular and religious reasons. However, offering secular reasons has the advantage of making a proposal attractive to people outside one's religious group by

90

giving them reasons they can accept, whereas using religious reasons tends to alienate them. Audi affirms, "As the Commandments themselves illustrate, one can take a standard having secular content to be theologically grounded without its cogency as providing a secular reason being undermined in the least."[45] Naturalistic methodology, therefore, is not an *anti*religious or atheistic methodology but a *non*religious, that is, a *secular*, methodology. Indeed, far from spelling the a priori negation of religious belief, both naturalistic methodology and secular public policy function as preservatives of it by leaving a space for it to exist: naturalism leaves a logical space, and secularism a civic space.

Another advantage of determining secular public policy according to the operating principles of a naturalistic methodology is the latter's intrinsic fallibilism. Public policy thereby incorporates the same process of self-correction as science. Moreover, secularism requires as a *civic* virtue the kind of justification for public policy that naturalistic methodology requires in science as an *epistemic* virtue: publicly accessible, evidentially adequate reasons.[46] Audi, having argued for the obligation to present such reasons, believes that once "mature, rational, religious" people recognize the potential for conflict stemming from religious belief, they will surely become fallibilists, open to the need for possible revision in their religious views.[47] Although Audi is generally correct, fallibilism is not a notable feature of the Religious Right or, indeed, of theocratic movements in general. And it is this unwillingness to consider their own fallibility, along with their insistence on founding government on religious absolutes, that produces the intolerance so characteristic of such movements and the resulting need for secular methods of making public policy.[48]

Naturalistic methodology, with its emphasis on experience as the epistemological touchstone for framing judgments about the world, must therefore be the working methodology of secular democracy.

We have no way of adjudicating the claims of discordant religious voices when those claims emanate from purportedly transcendent sources. We cannot base public policy on a foundation that produces discord that, by its very nature, is beyond resolution. A naturalistic operational approach to making public policy therefore precludes relying, either openly or covertly, upon supernatural sanction. A secular democracy requires a naturalistic methodology as its procedural protocol in the construction of public, including educational, policy.

VI.

As we have seen, the reliance upon a naturalistic methodology does not logically entail the acceptance of philosophical naturalism; it therefore need not nullify or prohibit the theist's functioning as a citizen in secular society while remaining a theist. Correspondingly, living in a secular society does not entail living every aspect of one's life in a secular way (for example, it does not logically preclude church attendance, the observance of religious ritual, or prayer). The use of naturalistic methodology in the public, secular sphere leaves one free to pursue whatever putative alternative methodologies, values, and ultimate explanations one wishes (though Hook argued that there are only *penultimate* explanations)[49] provided the lives of one's fellow citizens are not thereby constrained. Just as theistic religion may complement naturalistic methodology by addressing areas of concern beyond the reach of that methodology, so theistic religion may complement secular life by offering guidance in areas that lie beyond the proper reach of public policy. It may also incorporate a code of moral conduct that the believer sees as integral to religious life. However, antinaturalists insist upon the much stronger view that morality *must* have a theistic foundation, that naturalism is incapable of providing a foundation for anything except moral relativism.

Hook's remarks point again to the parallelism between the criticism of naturalism a half-century ago and that coming from the Religious Right today: "The most common objection to naturalistic humanism is not that it has no place for moral experience but that it has no place for an *authoritative* moral experience except one which rests merely on arbitrary preference, habit or force. In consequence, it is accused of lapsing into the morass of relativism despite its desire to discover inclusive and enduring ends which will enable human beings to live harmoniously together."[50]

So after the epistemological and methodological issues surrounding naturalism have been dealt with, the question arises of how naturalists propose to ground the moral principles that they agree are as important as the epistemological and methodological ones. Indeed, Phillip Johnson sees naturalism in education as the *source* of moral relativism:

> The combination of [naturalism's] absolutism in evolutionary science and relativism . . . in morals perfectly reflects the established religious philosophy of late-twentieth-century America. [Johnson views naturalism as a government-sanctioned religion.] Naturalism in science provides the foundation for liberal rationalism in morals, by keeping the possibility of divine authority effectively out of the picture. Belief in naturalistic evolution is foundational to a great deal else, and so it can hardly be presented as open to doubt. The schools accordingly teach that humans discover the profound truth of evolution but they *invent* moral standards and can change them as human needs change.[51]

Hook's response to the charge of relativism is that the principles and values guiding human conduct are grounded in their consequences; they are not self-justifying. This does indeed make them relative rather than absolute, but to say that moral values are relative means neither that they are subjective nor that they are arbitrary.[52]

93

Rather, it means simply that they are "related to" or "dependent upon" relevant, significant features of a moral situation. As a pragmatist, Hook argues that the value of any idea, whether a hypothesis guiding scientific research or a moral principle guiding human conduct, must be measured against its consequences. And as a naturalistic humanist, he used human well-being as the criterion against which consequences must be weighed. This criterion requires that moral principles be judged by whether they are *humane* rather than whether they are *doctrinally* acceptable under a governing religious orthodoxy. If the goal of moral conduct is to enhance the quality of human interaction, then human welfare is a better standard than religious orthodoxy, which has a significantly worse historical track record. If the antinaturalists who insist that public policy be grounded in transcendent moral absolutes disagree, then, as a pragmatist, Hook would suggest that the strength of their disagreement be tested by their willingness to allow other theists who insist on the very same point, for example, the Taliban, to determine the moral values under which they themselves must live.

But may not moral values be founded upon religious belief? They may indeed, but they may not be the basis for public policy on the basis of an exclusively religious justification. Although they may have strong religious justification, they must coincide with humane values for which, as Robert Audi stipulates, one can offer adequate, secular reasons that recommend themselves just as strongly to people of deep religious conviction:

> As important as civic virtue is in motivating citizen participation of any kind, it is needed above all where one is advocating or otherwise supporting coercive laws or public policies. Much of human life does not involve such conduct; much that does can be guided by cooperating religious and secular motives, motives that, like secular compassion and religious benevolence, urge one to roughly the same conduct. It is often noted how powerful reli-

gious considerations were in motivating the civil rights movement. Their prominence should not lead to underplaying the force of moral convictions entirely compatible with them, nor to thinking that those whose motivation might have been entirely religious would have been incapable of seeing and being adequately motivated by a moral case for the same social changes.[53]

This is not to deny that religion has made valuable contributions to the moral advancements of human society. But when it has done so, it has been because the values it recommended were those of inclusion rather than exclusion, desirable regardless of the doctrinal loyalties of its adherents. Catholics made admirable contributions to the civil rights struggle, but so did Jews, and so did atheists. In addition to the fact that racial harmony is a value embraced by enlightened theists, it is also a humane *secular* value that has advanced the well-being of a significant number of Americans. But there was no intrinsic connection between these values and the supernatural commitments of the religious believers who advanced them. Indeed, many theists, for example, Southern Baptists, invoked the same God as the Catholics but on behalf of continued segregation.

Antinaturalists who charge that naturalism has generated the worst of the world's evils must confront the record of history, which reveals an unflattering frequency of religious atrocity. To those who argue that secular government cannot embody the moral principles constitutive of a just society, one can point out that there is no more reason to consider a secular government *prone* to injustice and evil than there is to consider a theocracy *immune* from injustice and evil. Both are *logical* possibilities, but while there actually occurred a glaring historical example of the former, one is hard-pressed to find a historical example of the latter. To the extent that a government—or even a church—incorporates principles of justice, there are perfectly sound reasons to do so that have nothing to do with theology. Hook cited the example of Reinhold Niebuhr.

95

Speaking in 1943 of the fact that various religious groups had reached opposite positions on the war on the basis of the *same* religious premises, Hook cited the theology of Reinhold Niebuhr as an example of the irrelevance of religious belief when used as a "universal coefficient" of other beliefs. Saying that Niebuhr combined a "scientific attitude and rare courage" on social issues with a "rather reactionary theology," Hook pointed out that "not a single one of the positions that Niebuhr takes on the momentous issues of social and political life is dependent on his theology."[54] He highlighted this irrelevance by observing that Niebuhr seemed to appeal to his theology only "in situations where values and partial interests are locked in mortal combat."[55] Hook offered instead the naturalistic methodology on which even theists must rely, both in the solution of practical problems and in the civic space outside their faith:

> [I]n the history of thought it has been the naturalists who have exposed the pretensions of final truths and who have uncovered the nerve of interest behind the absolute values of church, state, and conscience. Science has known its dogmatism, too. But the cure of bad science is better science, not theology. . . .
>
> . . . Against Niebuhr's myth of a private and mysterious absolute, we counterpose the public and self-critical absolute of reflective intelligence or *scientific method in its most comprehensive sense.* By evaluating claims in light of their causes and consequences, it makes clear the interests from which they spring, and the meaning of what they propose. By guiding us to the construction of a social order whose institutions provide for the negotiation and compromise of claims on the basis of the completest knowledge available, it promises not absolute security but greater security. It does not pretend to make men gods but to treat more intelligently the problem always at hand. . . . How to get men to accept this absolute method—and to test it by its fruits, not only in the realm of nature but of human affairs—is a specific problem of scientific politics and education concerning which theology can tell us nothing.[56] (emphasis added)

The central fact for which the antinaturalist must account is that millions of people who *reject* supernatural religion live in as moral and meaningful a fashion as most of those who embrace it. Conversely, countless people, despite declaring moral values to be rooted in transcendent absolutes, have been quite willing to violate those absolutes in the most inhumane ways. Religion alone has never been a sufficient condition of humane behavior.[57] And it has not been true historically, nor does it follow logically, that understanding values to have a nontheistic origin in itself leads to immoral behavior. The truth in such matters is far more complex. There is no logical, and therefore no epistemological, connection between the acceptance of any particular supernaturalist belief and any particular moral position.

The agnostic Hook also pointed out what the theistic Kant recognized: that "the position that the validity of moral judgments rests upon transcendental truths of a metaphysical or theological nature" destroys the autonomy, and therefore the moral responsibility, of human moral agency.[58] Moreover, this recognition comes in addition to the historical and logical obstacles faced by theists who contend that both history and logic support the superiority of an absolutist, theistic foundation for public policy. Hook correctly points out that there is no guarantee that transcendent, absolute moral principles will in any way address the temporal situations humans face: "Any attempt to find a basis to improve the human estate by resort to a principle 'above human nature' is doomed to failure. . . . Ideals and ends that are out of time and so lack a natural basis can never be brought into logical and causal continuity with the means recommended to achieve them, for all such means are temporal acts with temporal consequences."[59] This observation would still be true even if the epistemological problem of knowing what these transcendent absolutes are could be overcome.

Hook thus recommends naturalistic humanism as a foundation

97

for moral conduct for the same reason he recommends naturalistic methodology and secular democracy: there is a greater chance of reaching consensus when we rely on common ways of knowing and of shared values, whereas there is no chance of doing so when moral values are rooted in contrary absolutes for which people are prepared to die—or to kill. Reflecting upon the strident admonitions of the Religious Right that the United States must retrieve its lost moral moorings by restoring the Christian foundations of government, I think Hook would today compare the advances of the sciences, both natural and social, to those of the various supernatural religions, making the same point he made in 1942:

> The social principles of Christianity have had almost two thousand years in which to order the world on a moral basis. It is not likely that anything new can be discovered from its principles or that its social gospel will succeed better in eliminating war, social distress, and intense factional strife, than it did during the historical periods in which religious institutions enjoyed chief authority. And when we examine the behavior and doctrines of different religious groups as they meet the trials of our world today, the impression is reinforced that there is no more unity of purpose among them, no more agreement in program and direction of effort, than among their secular brethren. But whereas the latter may rely upon a method by which to limit, adjudicate and negotiate the differences among them, the former must absolutize their differences if they are consistent.[60]

One might wonder *why* the various religious factions are still in the same place they were when Hook thus described them sixty years ago, when other areas of human inquiry are so far beyond where they were sixty years ago. The answer lies precisely in the fact that science, and all other naturalistic areas of inquiry, rely upon a methodology and epistemology that have no rivals in enabling us to answer the questions and solve the problems of human experience. The fact that naturalistic methodology cannot answer supernatural religious questions does not thereby obviate the need for it in *secular* life and practice. It simply highlights further the continuing lack of any comparable methodology and epistemology to answer the questions inevitably generated by supernatural belief systems—whether Christianity, Judaism, Islam, or any others. The most radical sects and the most mainstream, to the extent that they both rely on supernatural sources of authority, are in exactly the same epistemological position. Western theists, for example, may argue that however strongly the Taliban asserted supernatural sanction for their brutality, their assertions cannot be true: God cannot be on the side of people who resort to cruel punishments for the most trivial of social violations. However, when Western theists try to ground morality in supernaturalist religion, they can only appeal to the same sources as the Taliban for justification: scripture, tradition, divine revelation, clerical authority, and religious experience.

This common feature leads only to stalemate—and sometimes to violence—when religion is incorporated into public policy, a predicament that is not difficult for policy makers to understand, although other considerations may lead them to ignore it. But we should not build public policy on any beliefs regarding which there can be no epistemological consensus. And if policy makers fail to be impressed by the epistemological arguments, we may point to more pragmatic concerns expressed by Thomas Clark in "Faith, Science, and the Soul: On the Pragmatic Virtues of Naturalism": "[F]or many there are fundamental 'facts' about what exists that have nothing to do with observation, and there is nothing I can say that would convince them otherwise. The prospect looms, therefore, of two distinct cultures fighting over the same bit of ontological turf—but without enough in common ever to decide the contest. Such a picture has its own sort of melancholy appeal, if one likes perpetual combat."[61]

It is at the epistemological level, at which supernaturalists must show *how they know* what they insist must ground public policy, that the insufficiency of supernatural religion as this grounding becomes quite clear. And Hook points us once more to the advantages of relying upon the epistemology and the methodology of naturalism: "What is common to all forms of empiricism is the belief that truth is an affair of observational consequences. Although the hypothesis may turn out to be false, it is not unreasonable to assume that where men are willing to test their beliefs not by their alleged presuppositions, but by their observable consequences, they will probably be more willing to compromise their demands, to negotiate differences, to take the standpoint of the other, to live together and help each other to live rather than to fight and die together."[62]

But although the naturalist advocates that we continue in the moral context to abide by the rules of reasoning and evidence that we use in nonmoral contexts, these provide only the methodological framework for moral agency. Its content must always come from the factors relevant to the situation from which a moral problem springs and from the needs and interests of the human beings who stand to be affected by whatever decisions are made. And if naturalists lack supernal absolutes to support their moral judgments, they have a rich fund of philosophical resources from which to construct a conceptual moral framework. The naturalist can point to many good and honorable traditions from which to draw guidance in ways that are entirely secular. There is the utilitarian tradition, which requires that we consider the effects of our actions on others. Naturalists may also call upon the Kantian tradition, which requires that we treat our fellow humans as ends rather than means and that we accord them the dignity rooted in their own moral agency as rational beings. They can invoke pre-

100

Christian moral traditions such as Plato's belief that moral value is integrally related to knowledge and Aristotle's instruction in how to live with moral equilibrium and equanimity. All are compatible with theism. And naturalists may certainly adopt the best ethical teachings of the great religions, for they are entirely consonant with the best secular teachings and require no divisive doctrinal commitments: the Christian exhortation to love one's neighbor as oneself; the Jewish emphasis on active goodness, the *mitzvah*; the Islamic pillar of concern for the needy; and the Buddhist way of speaking truthfully and compassionately.

VII.

So what does all this mean regarding the methodology appropriate to the construction of public policy? The fact that there is (so far) no epistemology that explains how one acquires knowledge of the supernatural and no known methodology for testing supernatural claims implies that theists cannot justifiably demand that others be constrained by policies grounded in their theism. It also means that the *philosophical* naturalist has every right to demand an epistemological accounting for the theist's beliefs when such demands are made. In a secular democracy, it may well be true that theists who desire that public policy reflect their beliefs are asked to exercise more restraint than others in the arguments they offer for their policy positions. But for all the reasons cited above, this is altogether proper. The respect that any religion demands is directly proportional to the humility with which it asserts the truth of its doctrines. Although theism is entitled to the political respect accorded by the Constitution, it is not entitled to automatic epistemological respect in the absence of any method for verifying its foundational commitments. Hook rightly asserted, "Religion can escape showing its credentials concerning the inspiration of its knowledge but not concerning its validity. For the reliability of any knowledge is tested in the necessities of intelligent action. That test, together with the varying counsel of the Churches on specific social policies, is sufficient to indicate that there is no unique religious knowledge or religious guidance."[63] The lack of epistemological grounding for the supernatural therefore explains why it would be both bad pedagogical policy and bad public policy to teach as science intelligent design proponents' view that biological complexity requires a transcendent designer—whose existence cannot be *scientifically* established.

To the extent that theists ground their reasoning on public policy in their theism, they bear the ontological burden of proof; this burden compounds their civic responsibilities with an epistemological responsibility that no theist has ever been able to discharge. But their inability heretofore to meet this burden is not a reason to make secular democracy *less* secular in order to accommodate their theistic preferences, but rather to maintain its secularity in order to protect the rights of those who are under no obligation to live under theistically grounded policies that ignore the theist's burden of proof.

Theists who have not reached what Audi calls a state of "reflective equilibrium" will undoubtedly find this too restrictive. But the feeling of excessive constraint is the product of the theist's own supernaturalist commitments, to which no one is under any obligation to give any consideration until the theistic burden of proof is met. (But even if the burden of proof *could* be met, this would not mean that theism should be institutionalized in public policy.) However, *theism* per se is not being singled out for such constraint; anyone else whose public-policy positions depend on unverifiable claims reaching beyond common experience should receive the same response. Hence, paranormal claims would be subject to the same constraints where public policy is concerned. We do not incorporate into school science curricula the assertions of psychics for the simple reason that their claims remain resistant to scientific scrutiny; theistic claims have exactly the same epistemological status, even though they are accorded more social respect than those of psychics. Grounding public policy in overt atheism is also off limits for exactly the same reason: atheism cannot meet its epistemological burden of proof, a predicament that helps to explain why government-sponsored atheism such as existed in the former Soviet Union had to be implemented through enforced curtailment of religious practice.

To the extent that one does *not* inject one's religious beliefs into public-policy debates, one is less likely to feel restricted and therefore less likely to complain about the secularity of public policy. Among religious believers, those who understand that naturalistic methodology is not intrinsically antireligious and who have consequently achieved some equilibrium between their religious beliefs and their public-policy positions are less likely to feel constrained by secular public policies than are believers who reject naturalistic methodology as inherently antireligious. Secular public policy does *not* mean that religious voices should be silenced in the "public square," but it *does* mean that theism should *not* be incorporated into public policy. If the methodological naturalist is in no position to deny theistic claims, the theist is in no position to insist on them, that is, to insist that they be privileged in matters of public policy. By the same token, because we must limit the use of naturalistic methodology to the world of common experience, thus preserving a logical space for theism, we must limit the breadth of secular policy, preserving a zone of religious belief and practice.

The *philosophical* naturalist should find this completely agreeable. The methodology and epistemology of naturalism establish both the limits and the necessity of its employment as the methodology of democratic policy-making in a religiously pluralistic society.

VIII.

I am not proposing a societal conversion to philosophical naturalism (although it is an honest and eminently respectable point of view, despite the charges of antinaturalists). Not only will that never happen, but American and international life would lose much of the interest and cultural richness that come from religious variety. However, some attempt must be made to rehabilitate in the public mind the reputation of the naturalistic methodology upon which humans—even naturalism's detractors—have *always* relied and still rely, despite the current campaign to make "naturalism" a term of reprobation. Contrary to the Religious Right's theocratic rhetoric, the Founding Fathers had compelling historical reasons— indeed, life or death reasons—for adopting a secular constitution. But as I have argued, there are also compelling epistemological and methodological reasons for maintaining the secular foundation of public policy. The methodology of naturalism has advanced human knowledge in a way that religion has not (it is useful here to compare the knowledge yielded by this methodology in the sixty years since Hook wrote "The New Failure of Nerve" to the knowledge yielded by supernaturalism). Everyone can use it, and it leaves theists the option to make whatever additional, logically coherent ontological commitments they choose (though they also have the *political* freedom to make even logically *incoherent* commitments). Likewise, secular life is something that can be shared by theist and nontheist alike, in which each may function with broad, but not absolute, freedom. But we must restore our nerve, with Hook's prescient admonitions to guide us: "The new failure of nerve in contemporary culture is compounded of unwarranted hopes and unfounded beliefs. It is a desperate quest for a quick and all-inclusive faith that will save us from the trouble of thinking about difficult problems. These hopes, beliefs and faiths pretend to a knowl-

104

edge which is not knowledge and to a superior insight not responsible to the checks of intelligence. The more fervently they are held the more complete will be their failure."[64]

NOTES

1. Sidney Hook, *Philosophy and Public Policy* (Carbondale, IL: Southern Illinois University Press, 1980), p. 5.

2. Instead of *methodological naturalism*, which has become associated with scientific procedure in the strict sense, I shall use the term *naturalistic methodology*, which captures the broad connotation of the term Hook intended.

3. Robert Audi, *Religious Commitment and Secular Reason* (Cambridge: Cambridge University Press, 2000), pp. 3–4, 39. Audi himself is a Christian; he is currently the president of the Society of Christian Philosophers. (See the list of officers at www.siu.edu/departments/cola/philos/SCP/officers-committees.htm; accessed on March 22, 2004.) He acknowledges that "secular disputes can also polarize" but says that "other things [being] equal they have less tendency to do this or at least to produce irreconcilable differences" (p. 39). A notable example of how divisive religion can be when it is entangled with government is the reaction by the Family Research Council, a prominent US Religious Right organization, when a Hindu priest was invited to give the prayer at a September 2000 session of Congress. The September 21, 2000, FRC newsletter *Culture Facts* conveyed this reaction to readers (and was quickly taken offline after it prompted criticism): "[W]hile it is true that the United States of America was founded on the sacred principle of religious freedom for all, that liberty was never intended to exalt other religions to the level that Christianity holds in our country's heritage. Our Founders expected that Christianity—and no other religion—would receive support from the government as long as that support did not violate peoples' consciences and their right to worship. They would have found utterly incredible the idea that all religions . . . be treated with equal

deference. . . . As for our Hindu priest friend, the United States is a nation that has historically honored the One True God. Woe be to us on that day when we relegate Him to being merely one among countless other deities in the pantheon of theologies." Quoted in Steve Benen, "Invocation Intolerance," *Church and State*, November 2000, available at the Internet Archive at http://web.archive.org/web/20030624181657/http://www.au.org/churchstate/cs11001.htm (accessed April 5, 2004). An example of intragovernmental divisiveness stemming from the government's sponsorship of the congressional chaplaincy itself occurred only the previous year, when a Protestant minister was selected over a Catholic priest to fill the vacant position. See Rep. J. Dennis Hastert and Rep. Dick Armey, "Joint Letter to Republican Members Regarding Selection of the House Chaplain," Speaker of the House Web page, http://speaker.house.gov/library/misc/991210chaplainltr.asp (accessed March 22, 2004). See Juliet Eilperin, "Appointment of Chaplain Splits House," *Washington Post*, December 3, 1999.

4. Moral questions, though necessarily requiring us to work also from evaluative premises that are not statements of existential fact, nonetheless are related in important ways to the factual information we have at a given time. An example is the status of homosexuality: is it a moral choice, or is it an unchosen identity that some people—often against their will and upbringing—find themselves to have? If science establishes a genetic basis for homosexuality, such findings will have profound implications for how we view it morally. It would be no more acceptable to condemn homosexuals for their sexual identity than it is to condemn people of color for their racial identity.

5. Sidney Hook, "Naturalism and First Principles," in *The Quest for Being* (Amherst, NY: Prometheus Books, 1991), p. 190.

6. Audi, *Religious Commitment and Secular Reason*, p. 35.

7. Ibid., p. 117. I am not immediately concerned with religions that fall outside these parameters. Audi says, "Non-theistic religions (if indeed there are such in any full-blooded sense of 'religion') pose—other things being equal—far less serious church-state problems. This is in good part because theistic religions tend to be in certain ways authoritarian" (p. 34).

8. This hypothetical example reflects in reverse the history of US

creationism, which evolved from attempts to outlaw the teaching of evolution in public schools to attempts to require the teaching of creationism
along with evolution to the current attempt by the "intelligent design"
movement to persuade school officials to allow teachers to "teach the
controversy" surrounding evolutionary theory. See Ronald L. Numbers,
The Creationists (New York: A. A. Knopf, 1992). For background on the
most recent form of creationism, "intelligent design theory," see Steve
Benen, "The Discovery Institute: Genesis of Intelligent Design," *Church
and State*, May 2002, http://www.au.org/site/PageServer?pagename
=cs_2002_05 (accessed April 5, 2002). See also Eugenie C. Scott, "Anti-
evolutionists Form, Fund Think Tank," *Reports of the National Center for
Science Education* 17, no. 1 (January–February 1997): 25–26, http://
www.ncseweb.org/resources/rncse_content/vol17/3209_antievolution-
ists_form_fund__12_30_1899.asp (accessed April 5, 2004). See also Barbara Forrest, "The Wedge at Work: How Intelligent Design Creationism
Is Wedging Its Way into the Cultural and Academic Mainstream," in
Robert T. Pennock, *Intelligent Design and Its Critics: Philosophical, Theological, and Scientific Perspectives* (Cambridge, MA: MIT Press, 2001),
and available at http://www.talkreason.org/articles/Wedge.cfm (accessed
April 6, 2004).

9. See "secular," in *Oxford English Dictionary Online*, http://dic-
tionary.oed.com. One interesting facet of the OED definition is the ecclesiastical meaning, i.e., "secular clergy," who lived "in the world and not in
monastic seclusion, as distinguished from 'regular' and 'religious'" clergy.

10. A current example is President George W. Bush's support of
"faith-based" programs, in which public funds are being used to support
overtly sectarian programs. The Religious Right's influence on Bush's
domestic policy is detailed in Jim Whittle, "All in the Family: Top Bush
Administration Leaders, Religious Right Lieutenants Plot Strategy in
Culture 'War,'" *Church and State*, May 2002, http://www.au.org/site/
PageServer?pagename=cs_2002_05 (accessed April 6, 2004). For an
example of how Bush's foreign policy is being influenced by the Religious Right, see Steve Benen, "Strange Bedfellows," *Church and State*,
September 2002, http://www.au.org/site/PageServer?pagename=cs_2002
_09 (accessed April 5, 2004).

11. Hook, "Naturalism and First Principles," p. 173; emphasis added.

12. Ibid., p. 185. Hook cited anthropological data about primitive people pointing to their de facto recognition of the difference between the mundane and the supernatural, e.g., the use of technology to sow and cultivate crops and the use of religious ritual to ensure a good harvest. He argued that such recognition, even if only implicit, shows that religion arose not in competition with technology (which is the practical employment of naturalistic methodology) but as a complement to it. Hook also recognized religion's role in easing the pain and uncertainty that are an inevitable part of life (ibid., pp. 179–80). If Hook is right that technology and religion have always existed as complements rather than competitors, the argument that naturalistic methodology is not inherently antireligious is strengthened.

13. Sidney Hook, "The New Failure of Nerve," in *The Quest for Being*, p. 74. Hook originally published this article in *Partisan Review* 10 (January–February 1943): 2–23. Stephen Weldon writes that the "failure of nerve" concept was first expressed by Gilbert Murray in 1910 and was introduced to Americans in Murray's Columbia University lectures on ancient Greek religion. Murray contended that Greek culture declined because of a loss of confidence in scientific thinking and a consequent turn toward mystery religions. Stephen Weldon, "In Defense of Science: Secular Intellectuals and the Failure of Nerve Thesis," *Religious Humanism* 30, nos. 1–2 (Winter–Spring 1996), http://www.americanhumanist.org/hsfamily/rh/weldon.html (accessed March 22, 2004), refers to Hook's making *Partisan Review* the setting of a 1943 symposium entitled "A New Failure of Nerve."

14. Ibid., p. 74. The constitutional separation of church and state is clearly one such position.

15. Ibid.

16. Ibid., p. 75.

17. Ibid., p. 74.

18. Ibid., p. 90.

19. Ibid.

20. Ibid., p. 91.

21. Ibid., p. 82. Frederick Clarkson, *Eternal Hostility: The Struggle*

Between Theocracy and Democracy (Monroe, ME: Common Courage Press, 1997), documents the effort by various factions of the Religious Right to shape public policy.

22. Sidney Hook, "Nature and the Human Spirit," in *The Quest for Being*, pp. 197–98. This article was originally published in *Proceedings: 10th International Congress of Philosophy* (Amsterdam: North Holland Publishing, 1949).

23. James Dobson's panic shows in his spring 1998 remarks to the Council for National Policy, a secretive, hard-right organization that makes policy recommendations to conservative politicians. After reciting a litany of societal evils such as "moral relativism," Dobson begged the group to exert their influence on the Republican Party: "I came here today to . . . beg you shamelessly, to use your influence on the party at this critical stage of our history. You have a lot of influence on the party. A lot of you are politicians." See "James Dobson's CNP Address," Building Equality Web site, http://www.ifas.org/cnp/dobson/html (accessed April 13, 2004). Peter Kreeft, "How to Win the Culture War," *Crisis* 16, no. 6 (June 1998): 12–15, http://www.catholiceducation.org/articles/civilization//cc0076.html (accessed March 22, 2004), provides an example from the Catholic side: "We are engaged in the most serious war that the world has ever known. . . . America is the center of the culture of death. . . . Who is our enemy? Not Protestants. . . . Not Jews. . . . Not Muslims, . . . not the 'liberals.' . . . Not anti-Catholic bigots . . . not even the media of the culture of death, . . . not heretics within the Church. . . . Our enemies are demons. Fallen angels. Evil spirits." Seeing Satan at the heart of the world's evil, Kreeft proposes that Catholics give "A blank check to God. Complete submission." Both Dobson and Kreeft see religion as the key to cultural renewal. Although it is not clear that Kreeft is advising the direct influence of public policy (Dobson *is* urging this), his remarks reflect the kind of intellectual panic to which Hook referred.

24. "Freedom from Welfare Dependency," interview with George Gilder, *Religion and Liberty* 4, no. 2 (March–April 1994), http://www.acton.org/publicat/randl/interview.php?id=109 (accessed March 22, 2004).

25. See "Philip Wentworth Goes to Harvard," in Phillip E. Johnson, *The Wedge of Truth* (Downers Grove, IL: InterVarsity Press, 2000), pp. 19–38. William Dembski and Jay Richards, fellows of the Center for Sci-

ence and Culture, also see secularism as an *anti*religious concept in their introduction to *Unapologetic Apologetics: Meeting the Challenges of Theological Studies* (Downers Grove, IL: InterVarsity Press, 2001): "Anything that hints at a Christian worldview is routinely discarded within our secular society. . . . The great fault of secularism—and there's plenty of secularism at our seminaries—is that it actively hinders us from coming to . . . a belief in the unqualified goodness, wisdom and trustworthiness of God" (pp. 19, 21).

26. Phillip Johnson, the founder of the intelligent design movement, shows his disdain for secularism in "What (If Anything) Hath God Wrought? Academic Freedom and the Religious Professor," *Academe* (September–October 1995), http://www.arn.org/docs/johnson/aaup.htm (accessed March 22, 2004). See also Phillip E. Johnson, "How the Universities Were Lost," chapter 12 in *Objections Sustained: Subversive Essays on Evolution, Law, and Culture* (Downers Grove, IL: InterVarsity Press, 1998). For an example of antisecularism in the broader Religious Right, see Greg A. King, "Though the Heavens Fall: Standing Tall in a World of Secularism, Relativism, and Moral Inconsistency," *College and University Dialogue*, http://education.gc .adventist.org/dialogue/essays/King.htm (accessed March 22, 2004). King cites Johnson, reiterating the latter's dual indictment of naturalism and secularism: "As Phillip Johnson and others have capably documented, philosophical naturalism, with its concomitant materialist ideology, dominates the leading institutions of modern society. . . . This philosophy precludes the supernatural and therefore denies the reality of a transcendent creator God. Naturalism is a fundamentalist religion in its own right, for it is a closed system, and its adherents have a tendency to denigrate and demean anyone who questions the established orthodoxy. The crown jewel plundered by those committed to this religion of secularism is the educational system."

27. "[W]e also seek to build up a popular base of support among our natural constituency, namely, Christians." See "The Wedge Strategy," Antievolution: The Critic's Resource Web site, http://www.antievolution.org/features/wedge.html (accessed March 22, 2004). See also my discussion of the authenticity of this document and the religious nature of the Wedge Strategy in "The Wedge at Work: How Intelligent Design Creationism Is Wedging Its Way into the Cultural and Academic Mainstream," pp. 13–14.

28. Phillip E. Johnson, "Wells Hits a Home Run at Harvard," *Weekly Wedge Update*, December 2, 2001, http://www.arn.org/docs/pjweekly/pj_weekly_011202.htm (accessed March 22, 2004).

29. William A. Dembski, "Signs of Intelligence: A Primer on the Discernment of Intelligent Design," *Touchstone: A Journal of Mere Christianity* 12, no. 4 (July–August 1999): p. 84.

30. See David Applegate, "Federal Challenges to the Teaching of Evolution (6-17-02)," American Geological Institute: Governmental Affairs Program, http://www.agiweb.org/gap/legis107/evolution_congress.html (accessed April 13, 2004). See also Dembski's assertion that "the challenge of Intelligent Design to the evolutionary naturalism of Darwin is not the latest flash in the pan of the culture war but in fact constitutes ground zero of the culture war," in his foreword to Benjamin Wiker, *Moral Darwinism: How We Became Hedonists* (Downers Grove, IL: InterVarsity Press, 2002), Design Inference Web site, http://www.designinference.com/documents/2002.06.foreword_ben_wiker.htm (accessed March 22, 2004). See the Wedge's legal strategy for defending intelligent design in an eventual court case in David K. DeWolf, Stephen C. Meyer, and Mark Edward DeForrest, "Teaching the Origins Controversy: Science, or Religion, or Speech?" *Utah Law Review* 39 (2000), http://www.arn.org/docs/dewolf/utah.pdf (accessed March 22, 2004).

31. Hook, "Naturalism and First Principles," p. 172.

32. Ibid., pp. 188–89.

33. Phillip E. Johnson, review of Robert Pennock, *Tower of Babel: The Evidence against the New Creationism* (Cambridge, MA: MIT Press, 1999), for "Books and Culture," in *Christianity Today* (September–October 1999), http://www.ctlibrary.com/bc/1999/septoct/9b5030a.html (accessed March 22, 2004).

34. Phillip E. Johnson, *Reason in the Balance: The Case against Naturalism in Science, Law, and Education* (Downers Grove, IL: InterVarsity Press, 1995), pp. 9–10. Johnson desires that public school science instruction include the use of the supernatural as an explanatory principle so that it will become part of the cognitive equipment of the young, equal in importance and validity to naturalism. This desire is evident in his objection in an interview to what he sees as the public educational

system's "indoctrination" of students in naturalism: "[My] . . . book, *Defeating Darwinism by Opening Minds*, is specifically addressed to . . . high-school students, beginning college students and their parents and teachers. It is . . . intended to prepare these students for the . . . indoctrination they will receive in college, not only in . . . science . . . but throughout the curriculum. They will be presented material that presupposes that nature is all there is, that there has never been any supernatural influence from the ultimate beginning to the present and that God belongs in the category of what they call religious belief, which is to say subjective fantasy." See Jerry Aust, "Creation and Evolution," interview with Phillip Johnson, *The Good News* Magazine (July–August 1998), http://www.gnmagazine.org/issues/gn17/interview.html (accessed March 22, 2004).

35. Hook, "Naturalism and First Principles," pp. 173–74. William Dembski, "Naturalism's Argument from Invincible Ignorance: A Response to Howard Van Till," Design Inference Web site, http://www.designinference.com/documents/2002.09.Van_Till_Response .htm (accessed March 22, 2004), likewise ignores this distinction: "Naturalism, whether of the metaphysical or merely methodological varieties, treats nature as complete in terms of the causal principles inherent in it."

36. Hook, "Naturalism and First Principles," p. 189.

37. Ibid., p. 191.

38. "[Naturalism's] criticisms of the belief in Deity have not been based on semantic considerations but on what it presumed to be the weight of scientific discovery." Ibid., p. 189.

39. Dembski makes this assertion in "Intelligent Design Coming Clean," Counterbalance Meta Library Web site, www.meta-library.net/id-wd/index-frame.html (accessed March 22, 2004): "I believe that nature points to a transcendent reality, and that that reality is simultaneously reflected in a different idiom by the Scriptures of the Old and New Testaments. . . . [I argue that] when science points to a transcendent reality, it can do so as science and not merely as religion. In particular, I argue that design in nature is empirically detectable and that the claim that natural systems exhibit design can have empirical content."

40. Barbara Forrest, "Methodological Naturalism and Philosophical

Naturalism: Clarifying the Connection," *Philo* 3, no. 2 (Fall–Winter 2000): 16.

41. Hook, "Naturalism and First Principles," p. 195.

42. "Such a view is more devastating to atheism than to theism." Ibid., p. 189.

43. Forrest, "Methodological Naturalism and Philosophical Naturalism," pp. 15–16.

44. Audi, *Religious Commitment and Secular Reason*, pp. 94–95.

45. Ibid., p. 95.

46. See Audi, "Religious Convictions and Secular Reasons," chapter 4 in *Religious Commitment and Secular Reason*.

47. Ibid., p. 122.

48. The earlier citation from the Family Research Council's September 21, 2000, newsletter is a prime example of this.

49. Sidney Hook, "Scientific Knowledge and Philosophical 'Knowledge,'" in *The Quest for Being*, p. 226.

50. Hook, "Nature and the Human Spirit," p. 206.

51. Johnson, *Reason in the Balance*, p. 166.

52. Hook, "Nature and the Human Spirit," p. 206. A number of problems beset the supernaturalist's moral absolutism: (1) From a practical standpoint, no one can truly abide by moral absolutes; the push and pull of material conditions and of pressing situational circumstances make this impossible. (2) Absolutism makes *rules* more important than the *people* who are expected to abide by them. Attempting to live by a system of moral absolutes can be done only at the risk of the most inhumane consequences. (3) It produces irresolvable conflicts between equally binding rules. (4) It makes what to reasoned judgment is a relatively trivial, because reversible, offense (e.g., stealing) as wrong as a much more serious, because irreversible, offense (e.g., killing). And (5) it makes morality robotic and reflexive, rather than thoughtful and deliberative, thus depriving the moral agent of the autonomy requisite to both commendation for goodness and condemnation for evil.

53. Audi, *Religious Commitment and Secular Reason*, pp. 167–68.

54. Hook, "The New Failure of Nerve," p. 84.

55. Ibid., p. 87.

56. Ibid., pp. 87–88. Asserting absolutes, such as "this absolute method," is not typical of Hook. His use of the term here should be interpreted charitably, as meaning a *provisional* absolute: until someone invents a different methodology that is successful at enabling us to achieve the same advances in human knowledge that naturalistic methodology has, then the latter is the only reliable methodology. As always, the naturalist is open to being persuaded otherwise by the introduction of an equally successful alternative methodology. The same would be true if someone were to produce a methodology that enabled us to successfully verify the existence of the supernatural.

57. The Catholic Church's recent, well-publicized troubles with pedophile priests and ecclesiastical cover-ups of their misdeeds is proof of this. But the Church's moral failings in this regard do not address the truth or falsity of its theology, e.g., the doctrine of the Immaculate Conception. Rather, they point all the more vividly to the irrelevance of theological doctrine to human conduct.

58. Hook, "Nature and the Human Spirit," p. 199.

59. Ibid., p. 200.

60. Hook, "The New Failure of Nerve," pp. 81–82.

61. Thomas Clark, "Faith, Science, and the Soul: On the Pragmatic Virtues of Naturalism," *The Humanist* 53 (May–June 1993): 10. The conflict between the naturalist and theist is essentially the conflict that arises between science and religion when religion is taken to be a way of *knowing* the world rather than a framework within which one chooses to *experience* the world. Clark provides the best assessment I have seen of the unlikelihood of resolving this standoff:

Given the disparity in goals and cognitive strategies, it is no wonder that science and religion, although they exist in and make claims about the same world, have difficulty finding common ground. Each must justify itself . . . by success in its particular projects; *for there is not, I think, a larger cognitive perspective which could demonstrate that one is the 'best' approach to every problem or show, as a matter of principle, where we should apply*

114

one and not the other. . . . . [P]hilosophy . . . is not an agreed-upon platform that provides ready-made criteria to judge such issues; . . . like science, it is a process of open-ended inquiry. . . . Since science cannot categorically *disprove* the existence of the soul but . . . only cite lack of evidence for it, those unimpressed by the demand for evidence will happily take advantage of this apparent failing and postulate whatever they please; after all, part of the culture of faith is the gut feeling that revelation and authority alone *are* sufficient grounds for belief, that we need *not* consider what science has to say. Thus, there is no obvious point within science (or philosophy) from which to justify, to the true believer, the epistemic austerity of naturalism. (emphasis added)

62. Sidney Hook, "Philosophy and Human Conduct," in *The Quest for Being*, p. 24.

63. Hook, "The New Failure of Nerve," p. 83. Hook's denial that there is anything that qualifies uniquely as religious knowledge is not mere partisanship. He also denies this of his own discipline when he asserts that philosophy is not privileged with special knowledge or insights. See "Scientific Knowledge and Philosophical 'Knowledge,'" in *The Quest for Being*.

64. Hook, "The New Failure of Nerve," pp. 93–94.

CHAPTER 2

Politics without Dogmas
Hook's Basic Ideals

Robert B. Talisse

$\mathcal{A}$ny systematic attempt to understand Sidney Hook's political thought will have to come to terms with his 1987 claim: "When I look back on my long life, I am not aware of having undergone any serious conversions from the days of my youth, or of having abandoned my basic ideals."[1] One way of dealing with this statement would be to charge Hook with dishonesty. This reading would be maximally uncharitable; for this reason it should be avoided. Another way would be to claim that Hook was simply mistaken about the character of his own political trajectory. However, given the intellectual acuity of all of Hook's writings, this seems an unlikely explanation, and we would be entitled to it only after the failure of a sincere attempt to detect a set of basic ideals to which Hook was committed throughout his career. In this brief essay, I shall identify what I take to be Hook's "basic ideals." That is to say, I intend to vindicate his 1987 remark.

The proper way to work toward a unified reading of Hook would be to examine carefully Hook's straightforwardly philosophical pieces (as opposed to his overtly polemical writings) and identify a set of fundamental principles and basic commitments. I cannot undertake this project here; instead, I shall have to begin from a few principal contentions. Although I shall appeal to Hook's writings in what follows, I offer a promissory note on the full textual support.

It is vacuous to claim that Hook's basic ideals may be captured by the term *pragmatism*; for *pragmatism* is, as Richard Rorty has suggested, a "vague, ambiguous, and overworked word."[2] The important thing to note is that, at least as regards vagueness and ambiguity, it has *always* been this way. One does not find in the writings of the classical pragmatists a *single* pragmatism; and perhaps it is not too much of an overstatement to say that the only thing that Peirce, James, and Dewey had in common is that each was dissatisfied with the work of the other two. There is hence no real point in appealing to "pragmatism" *simpliciter*, and it is a mistake to do so.

Furthermore, it is unhelpful to identify Hook's basic ideals with the tenets of *Deweyan* pragmatism. Although he was certainly "Dewey's bulldog," Hook was not Dewey's parrot. Rather, Hook drew upon the work of traditional pragmatism to formulate a distinctive stripe of pragmatist philosophy. Although Alan Ryan has recently characterized this stripe as a "street fighter's version of Dewey's pragmatism," my own sense is that Hook drew heavily from Charles Peirce.[3] As ironic as it may seem in light of the notoriously apolitical nature of Peirce's thought, Hook developed Peirce's functionalist view of belief and fallibilist theory of inquiry into a fully experimentalist and politically activist conception of democratic citizenship. It is my contention that this conception of the democratic citizen constitutes Hook's most basic ideal. I maintain also that Hook never abandoned this fundamental commitment.

My task now is to explain this ideal. Hook took very seriously the Peircean project of displacing the traditional task of epistemology. Whereas traditional epistemologists fix on the analysis of beliefs and their justification in the hope of refuting skepticism, Peirce proposed to dismiss wholly the skeptic and attend primarily to the *methods* employed in arriving at beliefs in order to render those methods more transparent; he hoped thereby to render believers more capable and responsible in forming their beliefs.

In Peirce's view, then, the real threat to knowledge comes not from skeptical challenges to justification but from the dogmatist, the fanatic, and the dilettante in the form of a rejection of inquiry. Although Peirce's famous essays—namely his 1877 "Fixation of Belief" and later "How to Make Our Ideas Clear"—are most often read as early examples of an especially naive positivism, they are better understood as outlining a theory of epistemic responsibility.[4] To be sure, Peirce saw scientific practice as the paradigm of such responsibility, but his aim was not to inspire deference to science; rather, Peirce sought to encourage a certain *attitude* toward our beliefs. Simply put, Peirce attempted to show that *having a belief* or *asserting a judgment* is intrinsically connected to *having reasons* and *being prepared to articulate them*.[5] Hence, to assert that *p* is to incur a set of epistemic obligations associated with *justifying p*. Justifying *p* involves taking seriously objections, countervailing evidence, and opposing considerations; furthermore, it involves recognizing that *p* may be false.

In Peirce's view, then, *believing* and *inquiring* are internally connected such that a proper believer must also be a proper inquirer. Perhaps Peirce's most important insight is that proper inquiry can be conducted only within a certain kind of community.

That is, Peirce saw the project of justification as irreducibly social; to assert that p is to incur the epistemic obligations of *responding* to the questions, challenges, and objections of others. Hence, proper believing entails seeing others as partners in inquiry, as epistemic agents in their own right.

In his 1940 essay, "Conflicts in Ways of Belief," Hook captures well these Peircean insights: "Everything becomes subordinate to the question: What *method* shall we follow in developing new beliefs and testing the old?"[6] Hook's answer incorporates familiar pragmatist themes: he promotes the "method of intelligence," or "experimentalism," and points to the self-correcting practice of scientific inquiry as the paradigm of proper method. Whereas natural scientists look to data and results with a view to confirmation, inquirers in the most general sense attend to *reasons* and to *consequences* with a view to *resolving conflicts* and *keeping open channels of further inquiry*. Hence, in Hook's view, all proper inquiry involves "a perpetual invitation to sit down in the face of differences and reason together, to consider the evidence, explore alternative proposals, and assess the consequences."[7]

Yet Hook saw something that Peirce did not see and that Dewey did not articulate well, namely that methods of fixing belief can be paired with political systems. In anticipation of an argument now widely associated with Hilary Putnam and Jürgen Habermas, Hook saw that epistemology and politics are *mutually edifying*. That is, a democratic political order secures the conditions under which proper inquiry can commence and is enriched by the participation of citizens in inquiry. To employ the kind of biological jargon of which Dewey was so fond, the relationship between democracy and inquiry is symbiotic: the breakdown of democratic institutions obstructs or renders meaningless public inquiry, and the inability or unwillingness of citizens to participate in inquiry cripples democratic politics. Of course, the relation is not peculiar to democracy

120

and experimental inquiry: epistemic authoritarianism generates the dogmatism and servility necessary to keep a tyrant in place, and this is why aspiring tyrants seek to disable inquiry by controlling information and the exchange of ideas.

We see, then, that Hook's commitment to an experimentalist epistemology is internally connected with his commitment to democratic politics. We also see that the character of Hook's commitment is not merely a matter of logic; the commitment to democracy is a commitment to a life of inquiry. Like Peirce, Hook held that inquiry is necessarily a *social* activity—there must be a *community of inquiry* if there is to be an individual inquirer. Therefore, Hook's experimentalism implies a general ideal of democratic citizenship according to which the essence of democracy lies within the participation of citizens in the continuing activity of exchanging reasons with the mutual understanding that one ought to follow where the best argument, reasons, and evidence leads. The process of social inquiry is moreover open-ended in that it treats all questions as ultimately open questions; whereas a given inquiry may come to an end, inquiry never terminates in a final answer, no product of inquiry is beyond further revision and refinement. No truth, no matter how well confirmed or cherished, is treated as immune to further investigation. Properly democratic citizens, then, participate fully in the community of social inquiry; their most basic commitment is to the process of inquiry itself rather than to any particular outcome or desired result of inquiry. As Hook wrote, "In a democracy, the process of intelligence . . . must be supreme," for it is only by the persistent application of this process that "the raging fevers of stupid and cruel intolerance can be diminished."[8] In this way, Hook anticipates current discursive views of democracy; these views hold that "agreements . . . are to be sought for not at the level of substantive beliefs, but at that of procedures, processes, and practices for attaining and revising beliefs."[9]

121

Hook was not merely a theorist of democracy; he was a courageous democratic citizen. We find throughout his work a persistent engagement in inquiry, a steady willingness to address objections, an eagerness to reopen a question, and a readiness to change position in the light of new considerations. In short, Hook was committed to the way of life associated with free inquiry and was opposed to anything that obstructed inquiry. Following Peirce, who maintained that the chief commandment of the intellectual life is, "Do not block the way of inquiry," Hook claimed that the "cardinal sin" against inquiry is "refusal to discuss, or action which blocks discussion."[10]

Of course, citizenship in a democratic community of inquiry is demanding and risky. It is demanding in that it requires individuals to engage actively in the project of political justification; they must challenge, criticize, and question others and themselves. It is risky because inquiry, even at its best, is no guarantee of success in public affairs. The most conscientious inquirer with access to the fullest set of relevant data and the time to consider matters to a sufficient degree may yet err. Given the urgency that often accompanies questions of public policy and political judgment, we cannot wait until all the relevant facts are surveyed before making a judgment; we must gather the evidence as best we can in the time we have and then act, knowing always that our understanding is at best partial and that our conclusions are at best hypotheses.

Did Hook himself live up to his own image of citizenship? Given the argument thus far, a proper evaluation of Hook's own democratic practice must focus not simply on the *conclusions* he reached but the *reasons* he offered in support of those conclusions. That is, any responsible estimation of Hook as a citizen must examine Hook's record *qua* public inquirer. By this measure, Hook's life stands as an inspiring image of success, for success consists precisely in *the activity of political engagement by means of public inquiry*. Despite what some would consider political mistakes, one will *not* find in Hook a refusal to argue, a reluctance to listen to an opposing view, or an unwillingness to reconsider his own position in light of opposing considerations.

There is an apparent counterexample to this democratic image of Hook in his position, articulated in his 1953 book *Heresy, Yes—Conspiracy, No*, concerning Communist Party (CP) members holding teaching posts in public colleges and other areas of the public trust. Hook argued that membership in the CP constitutes prima facie evidence of unfitness for holding a teaching position. He is consequently often charged with violating his own democratic prescriptions of open debate and freedom of inquiry. However, when we examine Hook's actual position, the subtleties block any such easy refutation. Given the frequency of this criticism of Hook, it is worth looking briefly at his argument.

Three points are worth emphasizing at the start. First, Hook's argument did not apply to Communists but only to members of the CP.[11] Hook had no problem with *Communist* teachers. Secondly, Hook did not object to CP members in all areas of society but only to those who held "sensitive" or "strategic" posts; Hollywood actors were of no concern to Hook. Finally, Hook did not argue that CP membership should be *outlawed* or that CP members should be imprisoned. Rather, Hook argued that the CP was not merely a political party but a conspiratorial organization under the direct control of a dictator that expressly sought to dismantle Western democracy. According to Hook, the CP explicitly cited educational indoctrination as among the means by which it sought to undermine the United States, and it *required* of its members full endorsement of its stated objectives and methods. Hence membership in the CP signaled an individual's allegiance to the objectives of the CP. Hook concluded that CP members were unfit to hold "sensitive" public positions such as that of teacher in a public college, advocating the removal of CP members from the relevant positions.[12]

It is important to note the nuance of Hook's position at the level of policy. He argued that CP members should be *suspended* from their positions in order that a proper inquiry into their activities could be conducted.[13] In no case did Hook advocate the *automatic* removal from a post of a CP member; there was always to be an inquiry into the nature and extent of one's involvement. He held that "Each case and each situation will be considered in the light of the rule, and sometimes it will be sufficient to know that an individual is a member of the Communist Party to dismiss him."[14]

Now, of course, Hook's premises regarding the nature of the CP can be challenged. Today, we have good reason to think that Hook had an exaggerated sense of the threat posed by the CP, and his view may consequently seem to us inappropriately alarmist. However, our question again should not be whether Hook's premises and his estimations of the threat were correct, but whether he *at the time he posed the argument* was *warranted* in adopting these premises. As much of *Heresy, Yes—Conspiracy, No* is devoted to a detailed defense of these premises, it is difficult to maintain that Hook had not sufficient reason for them.

Granting the premises for the sake of evaluating the argument, there is no democratic failing on Hook's part. That is, supposing it *true* that the CP was a powerful conspiratorial organization devoted to the undermining of democracy in part by means of educational indoctrination that required of its members full and continuing obedience to its dictates, it is hard to see any problem with Hook's argument. It seems to me as reasonable as calling for the immediate dismissal of any New York City police officer who has been proven to belong to the mafia or of any airport baggage inspector who has been shown to be a member of al Qaeda.

Hook's position is that this does not constitute a violation of democratic principles. Recall that in Hook's view, democracy is bound up with the values of proper inquiry and the open exchange of argument; to oppose a force that openly seeks to destroy these democratic values is not to sacrifice democracy but to defend it. Far from a departure from his conception of democratic citizenship, Hook's stance against the CP is exactly what responsible democratic practice required.

If this general analysis of Hook's democratic vision is correct, it follows that analyses of Hook in terms of Left versus Right, liberal versus conservative, or young versus old are philosophically impotent. They are symptomatic of a tendency to think of politics in terms of competing platforms or programs. Democracy is hence construed as an adversarial contest for domination among conflicting interests. As such, democracy is divorced entirely from the practice of intelligent inquiry; it is merely a bargaining game, not the rational pursuit of self-government. Hook's 1938 insistence that democracy is essentially a *way of life* constitutes a rejection of the agonistic vision of politics; this rejection further entails a rejection of all prefabricated political platforms and any a priori social agendas. As Hook observed in 1934, "Philosophy at its best is not a hand-maiden to politics or theology . . . but a *critical activity* which aims to clarify to ourselves what we know, what we live for and die for, what we do and what we say."[15] This critical activity is necessarily opposed to the rote thinking and party-line dogmatism that is engendered by the adversarial model of politics. It is no wonder, then, that throughout his career Hook occupied a wide variety of positions on the standard political spectrum. It is also no surprise that at no point did Hook adopt any particular party line wholesale: he died an anti-Communist supporter of the cold war who was also a prochoice, prounion secular humanist and democratic socialist. Any attempt to "claim" Hook, or some part of him, for the Left or the Right is therefore fundamentally misguided, as it betrays a deep-seated misunderstanding of Hook's political vision. Democratic politics without dogmas is a politics that eschews categories, platforms, and parties. As Hook wrote in 1983, "The contrast between 'conservatism' and 'liberalism' today is not very instructive because these terms have been labels for varied and ambiguous positions. It is more illuminating to discuss *issues*. . . . When a problem arises our quest should be not for *the* liberal or *the* conservative solution, but for one we consider the most intelligent under the circumstances evaluated in light of the consequences of alternative courses of action on the preservation of a free society."[16] The extent to which this advice confounds us is the extent to which we have failed to grasp Hook's most essential philosophical message.

NOTES

1. Cf. Hook, "Communism without Dogmas," in *Sidney Hook on Pragmatism, Democracy, and Freedom: The Essential Essays*, ed. Robert B. Talisse and Robert Tempio (Amherst, NY: Prometheus Books, 2002), p. 145: "Only Communism can save the world from its social evils" (1934); and Hook, "Convictions," in *Convictions* (Amherst, NY: Prometheus Books, 1990), p. 24: "I am still an unreconstructed Social Democrat who regards the Communist danger as the main threat to human freedom."

2. Richard Rorty, "Pragmatism, Relativism, Irrationalism," in *Consequences of Pragmatism: Essays, 1972–1980* (Minneapolis: University of Minnesota Press, 1982).

3. Alan Ryan, foreword to Talisse and Tempio (eds.), *Sidney Hook on Pragmatism*, p. 10.

4. For a fuller interpretation of this view, see Robert Talisse, "Towards a Peircean Politics of Inquiry," *Transactions of the C. S. Peirce Society* 40, no. 1 (2004): 21–38.

5. I am here and in the paragraph that follows echoing Cheryl Misak, *Truth, Politics, Morality: Pragmatism and Deliberation* (New York: Routledge, 2000), especially chap. 2. Cf. Misak, "Making Disagreement Matter," *Journal of Speculative Philosophy* 18, no. 1 (2004): 9–22.

6. Sidney Hook, "Conflicts in Ways of Belief," in Talisse and Tempio (eds.), *Sidney Hook on Pragmatism*, p. 5.

7. Sidney Hook, "The Philosophical Heritage of the Atlantic Democracies," in Talisse and Tempio (eds.), *Sidney Hook on Pragmatism*, p. 38.

8. Sidney Hook, "How Democratic Is America? A Response to Howard Zinn," in *Convictions*, p. 35; "Experimental Naturalism," in Talisse and Tempio (eds.), *Sidney Hook on Pragmatism*, p. 210.

9. Seyla Benbahib, "Toward a Deliberative Model of Democratic Legitimacy," in *Democracy and Difference*, ed. Seyla Benhabib (Princeton, NJ: Princeton University Press, 1996). See Robert Talisse, "Liberty, Community, and Democracy: Sidney Hook's Pragmatic Deliberativism," *Journal of Speculative Philosophy* 15, no. 4 (2001): 286–304, for a more detailed discussion of Hook and current views of deliberative democracy. For an examination of Dewey's views of inquiry and democracy, see Robert Talisse, "Can Democracy Be a Way of Life? Deweyan Democracy and the Problem of Pluralism," *Transactions of the C. S. Peirce Society* 39, no. 1 (2003): 1–22.

10. Sidney Hook, "The Ethics of Controversy," in Talisse and Tempio (eds.), *Sidney Hook on Pragmatism*, p. 295.

11. Hook himself was for a long time a self-declared Communist but never a member of the CP.

12. On these points, see Sidney Hook, *Out of Step: An Unquiet Life in the 20th Century* (New York: Harper and Row, 1987), p. 505; *Heresy, Yes—Conspiracy, No* (New York: John Day, 1953), pp. 72, 26, 21–34, 181–83.

13. Hook, *Out of Step*, p. 504.

14. Hook, *Heresy, Yes—Conspiracy, No*, p. 206. Cf. Hook, *Out of Step*, p. 504: "Even though I believed that membership in the [CP] rendered an individual unfit . . . to be a member of the teaching staff, I did *not* believe that the mere fact of membership should result in automatic dismissal."

15. Hook, "Experimental Naturalism," p. 45.

16. Hook, "A Critique of Conservatism," in Talisse and Tempio (eds.), *Sidney Hook on Pragmatism*, p. 385.

CHAPTER 3

Dewey's Bulldog and the Eclipse of Pragmatism

Michael Eldridge

*T*here is not much that is uncontroversial about Sidney Hook. He was an energetic, even fierce social critic who did not hesitate to tackle tough issues and forcefully engage his intellectual opponents. Often his efforts were in behalf of his teacher, political ally, and friend, John Dewey. Hence the nickname that was initially given by an adversary but was readily embraced by Hook— "Dewey's bulldog." But there was one issue on which they appeared to differ—academic freedom for Communist Party members. Hook argued for their exclusion from teaching. Dewey's support for this policy was less ferocious than Hook's, and he was more insistent that attention should be paid to the actual behavior and not just to the fact of Party membership. Recently, the nature of Hook's opposition to Communist Party members as teachers has become an issue once again. But this time it is an issue in relation to the perceived decline in pragmatism following World War II. John Capps has suggested that the way in which Hook argued for the exclusion of teachers who were members of the Communist Party contributed to the eclipse of pragmatism and the rise of analytic philosophy in the midtwentieth century.[1]

Here I consider Hook and Dewey's relationship, assess Capps's argument and offer my own suggestions about what may have happened to pragmatism in the postwar years.

I.

Hook and Dewey had a long association. Hook had written his dissertation under Dewey's direction, earning high praise from his teacher. In 1927 Dewey wrote George Herbert Mead regarding Hook: "We have a man who is finishing soon who promises to be a prize, Sidney Hook—maybe you saw his articles in the *Journal* [*of Philosophy*]. He has a Section in his dissertation on the metaphysics of the instrument which is a corker—I almost feel that I am ready to quit, as he has not only got the point but sees many implications which I hadn't seen. He also has a training in Symbolic logic & can meet that crowd on its own ground."[2] But, it is important to note, Hook's recollection of this letter is inaccurate. In his autobiography he says the letter was written to James H. Tufts and that Dewey said that "he was ready to resign his post and withdraw from the field of philosophy because he had found a successor"— and that successor was Hook.[3] But despite the inaccuracy and the exaggeration, Hook and Dewey were close, and Dewey did hold Hook in high regard.

Over the next several years Dewey would often consult with Hook, who by this time was teaching at New York University,

130

about Dewey's writing projects. Dewey had sufficient confidence in Hook that he would trust him to make revisions in a manuscript. For instance, in 1938 Dewey wrote Hook regarding some chapters that were to be published later that year as part of *Logic: The Theory of Inquiry*: "When you have looked them over if you think they are substantially OK, please turn them over to [typist] Alice Davis at the Chelsea Hotel. Make such changes as you think desirable, or if too extensive let me know. These are the chapters (after XV) which I am most shaky about in technicalities tho [*sic*] pretty sure of the groundwork."[4] Hook also was involved with Dewey in a variety of political and intellectual efforts. Although Hook often assumed the organizer role, Dewey was not a passive participant who merely lent his name and prestige.

The first person of whom I am aware that called Hook "Dewey's bulldog" was Victor Lowe, a philosopher at Johns Hopkins University. He did so in a 1951 interchange in the *Journal of Philosophy* that we will consider later.[5] Hook did not take notice of Lowe's remark in his reply, but a year later, following Dewey's death, Hook embraced the appellation. In the closing paragraph of his reminiscence of Dewey, he recalled that he had once asked him "what he really saw in my stuff, since I felt I was merely developing ideas I had learned from him"—so much so that, Hook continues, "an unfriendly critic had even referred to me as 'Dewey's bulldog.'"[6]

There are many instances of Hook both interpreting Dewey and coming to his defense. A fine introduction to Dewey's thought is Hook's book *John Dewey: An Intellectual Portrait*, which was published in the fall of 1939 shortly before Dewey's eightieth birthday. An awkward example of Hook's aggressive defense of Dewey is his blocking the publication of V. J. McGill's contribution to the volume edited by Paul Schilpp that was published in the same year.[7]

But the defense of Dewey that I find interesting for our present purpose is Hook's response to Corliss Lamont's attack on the Commission of Inquiry into the Charges Made against Leon Trotsky in the Moscow Trials. We do not need to get into the details of Lamont's attack and Hook's counterattack; it is sufficient to notice some of Hook's statements and then Dewey's reaction. But I do need to provide some background. Lamont and Hook were classmates at Columbia University, where Dewey taught.[8] Lamont and his family were benefactors of the Columbia philosophy department and its prominent publication, the *Journal of Philosophy*.[9] Now specifically for what I am about to quote, one needs to know that in 1934 Lamont had publicly criticized Dewey's employment of the word *God* in *A Common Faith*, whereas Hook had done so privately.[10] With this background in mind, we can look at the last two paragraphs of Hook's essay "Corliss Lamont: 'Friend of the G.P.U.'" (G.P.U. is a reference to one of the early incarnations of the Soviet secret police.) It is important to quote these paragraphs, despite their length, because they convey the aggressiveness, sarcasm, ridicule, and "gotcha" quality of Hook's invective:

> Mr. Lamont's fervent faith in the experimental method is apparently compatible with some strange practices. The truth is that his allegiance to the experimental method—not to speak of his understanding of it—was never more than skin deep. It was a temporary verbal holiday between two phases of religious belief. He has simply substituted for the God of religious supernaturalism, the God of Stalinist orthodoxy. Ten years ago he lost theological innocence, and then campaigned with great diligence proving that many contemporary philosophers use religious terms ambiguously. But his heart still hungered for an enduring object of worship, and he found it in the "beloved disciple and leader," Stalin, who administers a regime of indivisible achievements with the high priests of the G.P.U. No more need he wander in the valley of doubt. He has a touchstone for all problems and difficulties. Under certain conditions he is inclined to

smile even on the supernaturalism against which he had recently led such a furious crusade. He proclaims now in reviewing a book by an Anglo-Catholic who is "militantly in favor" of "both the Soviet Union and the God of Christian supernaturalism," that "I feel much more akin to a religious supernaturalist who believes in a radical social and economic program [Hook's euphemism for Stalinism] than in an anti-supernaturalism of any school who believes in Capitalism."[11]

Mr. Lamont has given hostages to his new religion of Stalinism. I predict that he will be compelled more and more to perform its rituals of frame-up, and prevarication. He will take as his own its working maxim, "the end justifies *any* means." He will, if necessary, even publicly renounce his religion and say: "I am not a Stalinist; I am not even a Socialist" in order to do its work more effectively in the dark. His confusion and very innocence will give him seal, and his faith will give him solace. Together they will hasten him along the devious path which is the fate of everyone who defends the G.P.U. For in politics, he is already morally dead. And the politics of Stalinism spreads its shadow on the whole of life.[12]

Hook clearly employs ferocious language in defense of Dewey. In accusing the secular humanist Lamont of unwitting religiosity and moral deadness, Hook certainly earned his bulldog status.

Now notice Dewey's response. In a letter to Hook Dewey thanks him for his "devastating comments of the activities of Corliss Lamont" and suggests that the material in Hook's article should be brought to others' attention. Clearly Dewey embraces Hook's ferocious defense.[13]

II.

It was remarkable then in 1949 for Dewey and Hook to find themselves in apparent disagreement on an issue. Dewey wrote a letter to the editor of the *New York Times* in which he argued that a distinction should be made between the correct abstract principle of not employing a Communist Party member as a teacher and attention to "concrete conditions and probable consequences." He thought that dismissal of a teacher should only be on "evidence of bias in [the] conduct of work."[14] A few days later, after some chagrined private correspondence with Dewey, Hook published his own letter in the *Times* in which he argued, on pragmatic grounds, that it would be better to dismiss teachers who were active members of the Communist Party. It was important, Hook thought, that educational institutions remove Communists from employment to prevent legislatures from intervening in educational matters.[15]

A couple of months later Hook published a statement in the *Saturday Evening Post*. The way in which he formulated his position in this article permitted Dewey to observe that "there is no real difference between us" for Hook, according to Dewey, recognized that there were possible exceptions to the general principle. This was "in line with the point that I tried to make in the *New York Times*," Dewey noted. Still, Dewey observed, "it is quite likely that the exceptions in my view would carry further than on yours."[16] So one should not regard the two friends as being adamantly opposed to one another on this issue. Rather, there was agreement and some disagreement. A charitable person would say that the disagreement was a matter of emphasis.

Nevertheless, the common perception was that Dewey and Hook disagreed about the matter. Two years later Victor Lowe, with Hook as his target, initiated a discussion in the *Journal of Philosophy* on this same issue. Lowe took Hook's position to be that "members of the Communist party ought as such to be barred from the academic profession."[17] He then, using a phrase from William James, accused him (and others who held similar views) of "vicious intellectualism." He succinctly articulates what he has in mind in an

August 3, 1951, letter to Dewey: "I start with James, whose definition of 'vicious intellectualism' I extend so as to have a critical
weapon against all category thinking; and I briefly bring in your
empiricism too. Then I argue that American philosophers, brought
up as empiricists, have in the present 'hot' situation taken on the
habit of arguing from definitions to necessary conclusions about
questions of fact. The philosophers I have in mind are those who
have argued that if a professor is discovered to be a Communist you
can be sure, from the very nature of Communism, that he's no
teacher, but a propagandist. . . . Sidney Hook is my chief
example."[18] To my knowledge Dewey did not reply to this letter.

Hook, in his reply to Lowe's article, displayed considerable
dialectical skill and was able to score some verbal points. But
despite some "vicious intellectualism" of a sort different from what
Lowe had in mind but similar to what we saw in Hook's devastating
remarks about Corliss Lamont above, Hook did not deflect the main
charge. He thought it was an appropriate policy for academic institutions to bar current members of the Communist Party from
teaching, whereas Lowe, Hook acknowledges, thought that the
institution must show "something more" than membership. Hook,
to be sure, thought that membership in the Communist Party was
fundamentally incompatible with the professional responsibilities
of an academic. Thus it was a violation of trust for a teacher to be
a member of such an organization. Hence membership was sufficient for dismissal.[19]

Yet in his autobiography, *Out of Step*, Hook maintained that he
"did *not* believe that the mere fact of membership should result in
automatic dismissal." Rather, there must be evidence of party
activity. Then the accused academic would be given an opportunity
to defend himself. Moreover, "the burden of proof would rest with
him."[20] Setting aside the troublesome matter of presumed guilt, I
want to notice an apparent shift in Hook's public position. His rec-

ollection, late in life, is that he thought it took more than current membership in the Communist Party. He was thus closer to Dewey and Lowe's position that one had to pay attention to the specific circumstances of the case.

In fact this appears at first to be Hook's position in the final chapter, "Some Positive Proposals," of *Heresy, Yes—Conspiracy, No*.[21] He proposes, as a third step in a four-step process that included clear, faculty-adopted rules and a professional ethics committee of the faculty, that "admitted Communist Party membership, although prima facie evidence of unfitness and disqualification, will not *automatically* lead to dismissal without further consideration of the case and of the consequences of acting on it. . . . Each case and each situation will be considered in the light of the rule." But Hook, a few lines later, adds, "and sometimes it will be sufficient to know that an individual is a member of the Communist Party to dismiss him."[22] So, in some circumstances, the mere fact of current membership would be sufficient for dismissal.

I readily accept Robert Talisse's claim, with regard to the first chapter of *Heresy, Yes—Conspiracy, No* that "Hook's actual position is much more subtle than his communist critics acknowledge."[23] Yet it is this very subtlety, or, some would say, lack of precision, in his fundamental proposal that was a problem. Most of the time the message seemed to be that present membership was sufficient for dismissal. At other times it seemed to be that there could be relevant factors that would not require dismissal.

Following the publication of an article in the *Saturday Evening Post*, which, according to Hook, "substantially expresses the same position taken in" the final chapter of *Heresy, Yes—Conspiracy, No*, Dewey, as I noted above, thought that the difference between them on this point was one of emphasis. But it is more than that. Dewey's position is rather straightforward—one is to be dismissed for one's actions and not on the basis of membership alone. Hook's view is

136

more nuanced and subject to being misread. Active party membership is sometimes sufficient for dismissal. But at times in the heat of public debate, as in the *Journal of Philosophy* interchange with Lowe, Hook defended the position that membership was sufficient. Moreover, his criticism of the American Association of University Professors' position that party membership was not sufficient for dismissal could lead one to infer that he supported the contrary policy.

III.

In "Pragmatism and the McCarthy Era," John Capps considers several possible reasons for the eclipse of pragmatism during the cold war, including one that involves Hook. Capps begins his essay with the sentence, "While it may be undeniable that pragmatism fell into eclipse after World War II, there is little consensus as to why, exactly, this took place."[24] He then proceeds to survey the possible causes of this decline, discussing several explanations, including that of Richard Bernstein, a philosopher, and those of several intellectual historians—Bruce Kuklick, David Hollinger, and James Kloppenberg, as well as others—Louis Menand and John McCumber. The explanations of Bernstein and the intellectual historians are classified by Capps as "internal" explanations; those of Menand and McCumber as "external." The external explanations have to do with the larger, political pressures of the cold war on the profession; the internal, with the changes in the profession itself—increasing professionalization and the linguistic turn. Capps effectively shows that none of the proposed explanations are adequate. Hence he considers Hook's role during the McCarthy era.

Citing the *Journal of Philosophy* interchange with Lowe, Capps characterizes Hook's argument as one that could be put in the form of a deductive argument: "from the fact that Professor X was a member of the Communist party, and that all Communist party members were unfit to hold positions of public trust, it followed logically that Professor X, too, was unfit to hold a position of public trust, namely that of a college professor."[25] Capps then notes the similarity in reasoning between this and the sort of arguments offered by analytic philosophers of the time—"an emphasis on definitions and their logical consequences." Thus "the difference between pragmatic and non-pragmatic approaches is blurred, leaving us with a version of pragmatism that fails the pragmatic test: it is no longer clear, in this context, what difference is made by approaching matters pragmatically."[26]

Capps's suggestion is an intriguing one. It is not seriously compromised by the fact that Hook did not always argue in this fashion. He sometimes, as I have pointed out, allowed for the consideration of factors beyond party membership. Thus he sometimes reasoned in the contextual way that Capps thinks is more characteristic of pragmatism. That this is not fatal to Capps's suggestion is because Hook's subtle or nuanced or less than consistent position does precisely what Capps is concerned to point out. Hook failed upon occasion to offer a clear alternative to the emerging analytic movement on this prominent issue.

Capps, from a pragmatist perspective, is right to raise the issue of context. His concern is that Hook, like the analysts, is not paying sufficient attention to the actual circumstances of one's alleged Communist affiliation, that one is able to deduce a behavior from the meaning of the terms of one's affiliations. But this is not quite correct. Hook is not simply making a deduction from a concept; he is forming a judgment about the nature of one's party affiliation. His judgment is that the affiliation is such that membership alone shows that one is unfit to teach. This is an explicitly empirical, as Capps acknowledges, and evaluative claim; it is not armchair philosophizing.

Of course Hook may have been incorrect about the facts. It may have been that Communist Party (CP) membership did not entail the strict discipline that he thought it did. It is certainly troublesome that Hook in 1951 cites a CP publication from 1938.[27] Better evidence of duplicitous behavior on the part of CP teachers would have been from the period following World War II. But also one would want evidence of near universal duplicitous behavior before formulating a policy to bar someone from the teaching profession on the basis of membership alone. Capps is correct to point out that Hook's premise that "all Communist Party members are unfit to hold positions of public trust . . . is a very difficult claim to support in its full generality."[28]

But, as I suggested earlier, even if Capps's judgment that Hook leaned too far in the analytic direction to offer a distinct alternative to the rising analytic movement is incorrect, there is still the matter of Hook's "subtle position." Hook, for reasons other than what Capps thinks, could have failed as the needed pragmatist bulldog at a time when pragmatism was vulnerable to displacement. It may have been that he was perceived as a slippery, pragmatic (in the vulgar, opportunistic sense) exponent of a philosophical pragmatism that could not offer a precise, rigorous alternative to the analytic approach. If so, then his pragmatism would have contributed to the understanding of pragmatism that Bernstein identifies.

IV.

Bernstein, in the article discussed by Capps, writes, "After the Second World War, during a period of rapid growth of American universities, academic philosophy in the United States was completely transformed (except for a few pockets of resistance). Virtually every major 'respectable' graduate department reshaped itself in the new spirit of 'tough-minded' analytic philosophy. The classic

American pragmatists were marginalized, relegated to the dustbin of history." A few paragraphs earlier he had noted that from the late 1930s pragmatism was viewed among "professional academic philosophers" as "tender-minded"—"diffuse, fuzzy, and soft at the center." These critics did not think that pragmatism met "the high standards of 'rigor' required for serious philosophic investigation."[29] Bernstein then makes a persuasive case that an attenuated form of classical pragmatism can be found in the work of W. V. O. Quine, Wilfrid Sellars, and Donald Davidson. But this is a rather thin pragmatism, as both Bernstein and Capps point out, one that has let go of the ethical and political concerns that were central to James and Dewey.[30]

Capps, as noted earlier, categorizes Bernstein's as an "internal" explanation for the eclipse of pragmatism. Classic pragmatism, with its concern for a range of questions, including social and political, did not address the needs of the tough-minded analytic philosophers who were coming on the scene. We have to look no farther than the profession itself for an explanation. And these logically minded, rigor-demanding philosophers, who were in an important sense heirs of the Vienna Circle, did not share the logical positivists' or the classic pragmatist's social and political concerns.

Hook, in his autobiography, expresses regret that he "had not done more to amplify and defend [Dewey's] technical doctrines, resolve their difficulties, and carry out his ambitious program of philosophical reconstruction and deconstruction." In the next paragraph he adds, "had I not returned from Europe [in 1929] convinced that Germany would soon erupt into a new threat to the world, I would not have thrown myself so wholeheartedly into the political movement of the thirties, and would instead have done more work in academic philosophy to justify Dewey's faith in me."[31]

Thus, for very different reasons, both Capps and Hook suggest that if Hook had argued differently (Capps) or pursued a different agenda (Hook), then Hook could have—to overstate the case—prevented pragmatism's eclipse. I think not. For one reason, *eclipse* is not quite the right term for what happened, and, two, something more extensive was needed than a different style of argument or a different focus.

Hook himself wrote in the late fifties, "American philosophers, with some notable exceptions, no longer practice philosophy in the grand *tradition*, essaying wholesale views about the nature of man, existence, and eternity. Inspired by the results won in the sciences, they do not even practice philosophy in the grand *manner* but concentrate on the patient analysis of specific problems aiming at results which although piecemeal are more likely to withstand criticism."[32] This is from the introduction to a book Hook edited that was intended to represent what US philosophers were doing by asking them to select something they had already written and, in most cases, published elsewhere to be included in this volume. Notice the appeal to science as a justification for doing "patient analysis of specific problems" that are "more likely to withstand criticism." Within the profession, vision and speculation had given way to careful consideration of well-defined problems, whose solution many thought required careful attention to language and the use of the relatively new tools of mathematical logic.

But this is only one of the concerns to which pragmatism needed to respond. There were also religious and atheistic versions of existentialism that were found in academic departments and the society at large. Richard Rorty has remarked, "It was as if pragmatism had been crushed between [existentialist theologian Paul] Tillich and [logical empiricist Rudolf] Carnap, the upper and the nether millstones."[33] I think this is more or less right. Pragmatism had difficulty sustaining itself as a coherent approach in the face of the competing demands of the postwar generation. As we now know, pragmatism fragmented. Hook continued to articulate force-

141

fully in the public arena his own rational, secular blend of Dewey and Marx, while others in the public sphere embraced approaches that Hook regarded as irrational. And in the profession of philosophy itself, pragmatism became submerged in the work of Quine.

Of the same generation as Hook, Quine, by his wit, considerable knowledge, and technical brilliance became the most prominent philosopher of the third quarter of the twentieth century. But his pragmatism, as has been noted, was a narrow one and, although present as early as "Two Dogmas of Empiricism" (1950), was not as apparent as his logical positivist heritage. For Quine, pragmatism was a solution to an intellectual problem. Whereas for Dewey and Hook pragmatism was an intellectual tool for solving human problems, Quine's nonpolitical, logic-oriented philosophy appealed to a large number of philosophers, including, ironically, the analytic philosophers that his "Two Dogmas" essay, with its attack on analyticity, had disenfranchised.

But neither Dewey's nor Hook's audience was limited to academic philosophers; they spoke to a broad spectrum of academics and other intellectuals. In fact, the audience of academic philosophers was a relatively small one until late in Hook's life. The real growth in philosophy departments did not occur until sometime after World War II. Bruce Kuklick provides these numbers: "In 1920 the membership of the American Philosophical Association was about 260; in 1960 it was 1,500; in the 1990s it was well over 8,000."[34] So we can add an additional explanation for the growth of analytic philosophy and the submergence of pragmatism, one that is both external and internal. Because of what was happening in US society, higher education experienced tremendous growth in the latter half of the twentieth century. This enabled the philosophical profession to expand dramatically, providing an audience of specialists for an intellectually demanding Quine. But this expansion in numbers led to a narrowing in the scope of philosophy in this

142

sense. With the absolute rise in the number of philosophers and an increasing percentage of them making the linguistic turn, those taking other approaches felt marginalized.

A full-fledged pragmatism, one that addressed a wide range of issues both professional and public, apparently did not grow in adherents among professional philosophers nor as a perspective among nonphilosophers. Perhaps, as some have suggested, it lacked coherence or its proposals seemed stale. Perhaps, judging by those movements that were successful, the strain of the pulls from the increasingly technically oriented philosophers and, from the opposite direction, the more dramatic neo-orthodox theological and existentialist intellectuals and literary figures, was just too great for any single approach to accommodate.

So I come to the reluctant conclusion that the pragmatism that Hook sought to defend was vulnerable to internal and external pressures and failed to accommodate itself to the changing situation; it failed, ironically, to reconstruct itself. Hook's ferocious defense, I am suggesting (but have not shown), may have been "out of step" with the times. It could have been out of step in two ways: one, the coming apart of the Deweyan synthesis can be traced to the 1930s and hence in some measure to Dewey himself. So Hook may have missed his opportunity in the 1930s in his self-acknowledged preoccupation with other problems. Two, the manner of his defense may have been "out of step" with the 1950s and '60s. To be able to make such a claim, however, one would have to investigate what philosophers were actually saying about pragmatism in the middle part of the twentieth century and how they were reacting to Hook as a person and philosopher. Clearly Hook was a socially engaged philosopher of drive and distinction, with many accomplishments, but perhaps not the one best suited to respond to the challenges that confronted pragmatism in the middle of the century.

NOTES

1. John Capps, "Pragmatism and the McCarthy Era," *Transactions of the C. S. Peirce Society* 39 (Winter 2003): 61–76.

2. John Dewey, letter to George Herbert Mead, April 22, 1927 (05436), in *The Correspondence of John Dewey, 1919–1939*, Vol. 2, ed. Larry A. Hickman, CD-ROM (InteLex, 2001). The accession number is a convenient way to locate the item. Note that quotations from Dewey's letters are printed as they appear in the edited correspondence, including misspellings. The editors' clarifications, however, are retained, such as the insertion of "*of Philosophy*" in the present citation.

3. Sidney Hook, *Out of Step: An Unquiet Life in the 20th Century* (New York: Harper and Row, 1987), p. 90.

4. John Dewey, letter to Sidney Hook, January 17, 1938 (06008), in *The Correspondence of John Dewey.*

5. Victor Lowe, "A Resurgence of 'Vicious Intellectualism,'" *Journal of Philosophy* 48 (July 5, 1951): 440.

6. Sidney Hook, "Some Memories of John Dewey," in *Pragmatism and the Tragic Sense of Life* (New York: Basic Books, 1974), p. 114. Dewey replied that when he read Hook he understood himself better.

7. See Robert Westbrook's lengthy footnote in *John Dewey and American Democracy* (Ithaca, NY: Cornell University Press, 1991), p. 500n.

8. Christopher Phelps, *Young Sidney Hook: Marxist and Pragmatist* (Ithaca, NY: Cornell University Press, 1997), pp. 66f, 204.

9. John Herman Randall Jr., "The Department of Philosophy," in *A History of the Faculty of Philosophy, Columbia University* (New York: Columbia University Press, 1957), pp. 141f.

10. Michael Eldridge, *Transforming Experience: John Dewey's Cultural Instrumentalism* (Nashville: Vanderbilt University Press, 1998), pp. 154–60.

11. The quotes from Lamont are from his article in the *Humanist Bulletin*, February 1938.

12. Sidney Hook, "Corliss Lamont: 'Friend of the G.P.U.,'" *Modern Monthly*, March 1938, p. 8.

13. John Dewey, letter to Sidney Hook, March 16, 1938 (06015), in *The Correspondence of John Dewey*.

14. John Dewey, letter to the editor, *New York Times*, June 21, 1949; reprinted in *The Later Works of John Dewey*, ed. Jo Ann Boydston (Carbondale, IL: Southern Illinois University Press), 17:136.

15. Sidney Hook, letter to John Dewey, June 23, 1949 (13181). Correspondence written after 1939 has not yet been published but is in preparation. These items are available at the Center for Dewey Studies, Southern Illinois University Press, Carbondale.

16. John Dewey, letter to Sidney Hook, September 18, 1949 (13189), Center for Dewey Studies.

17. Lowe, "A Resurgence of 'Vicious Intellectualism,'" p. 438.

18. Victor Lowe, letter to John Dewey, August 3, 1951 (12749), Center for Dewey Studies.

19. Sidney Hook, "Mindless Empiricism," *Journal of Philosophy* 49 (February 14, 1952): 91.

20. Hook, *Out of Step*, p. 504.

21. Sidney Hook, *Heresy, Yes—Conspiracy, No* (New York: John Day, 1953).

22. Ibid., pp. 266f.

23. Robert Talisse, "Sidney Hook Reconsidered," The Pragmatism Cybrary, http://www.pragmatism.org/genealogy/hook.htm, endnote 13 (accessed March 23, 2004).

24. Capps, "Pragmatism and the McCarthy Era," p. 61.

25. Ibid., p. 72.

26. Ibid., p. 73.

27. Sidney Hook, "Not Mindful Enough," *Journal of Philosophy* 49:115n3.

28. Capps, "Pragmatism and the McCarthy Era, p. 72.

29. Richard Bernstein, "The Resurgence of Pragmatism," *Social Research* 59 (Winter 1992): 815f.

30. Ibid., p. 817; Capps, "Pragmatism and the McCarthy Era," p. 62.

31. Hook, *Out of Step*, p. 91.

32. Sidney Hook, introduction to *American Philosophers at Work:*

The Philosophic Scene in the United States, ed. Sidney Hook (New York: Criterion Books, 1956), p. 12.

33. Richard Rorty, "Pragmatism without Method," in *Objectivity, Relativism, and Truth: Philosophical Papers* (Cambridge: Cambridge University Press, 1991), 1:64.

34. Bruce Kuklick, *A History of Philosophy in America, 1720–2000* (Oxford: Oxford University Press, 2001), p. 259.

CHAPTER 4

Sidney Hook's Secular Humanism Appraised Retrospectively

Paul Kurtz

I.

e can get a clearer perspective of the legacy of Sidney Hook now that more than a decade has passed since his death. A seminal philosopher's writings mean different things to different commentators; and friends and foes invariably choose to emphasize, approve, or disapprove of one or another aspect of his thought. Thus, there were left- and right-wing Hegelians, left- and right-wing Marxists. Many Marxists in Eastern Europe focused in the post–World War II period on the earlier *Philosophical and Economic Manuscripts* of Karl Marx, using it to defend freedom against repressive regimes; others minimized the youthful Marx. Similarly, today there are left- and right-wing Heideggerians.

Many neoconservatives emphasize one aspect of Hook's work—his criticisms of totalitarian Communism; and other neo-Marxists disparage this aspect of Hook but herald his earlier revolutionary work. Hook undoubtedly will be remembered by history because of his early break with Communism and his persistent attacks on Leninism-Stalinism-Maoism; and now that the Soviet Union has collapsed, many consider this to be his major contribution. But I submit that Hook should not be read primarily or solely for his historic role in unmasking totalitarian influences and marshaling the cultural forces of freedom.

Some neoconservatives refused to take part in Hook's centennial celebration because they deplore the liberals and left-wingers who participated; possibly some neoconservatives also objected to its cosponsorship by secular humanists. If there is any aspect of Sidney Hook's thought that distances him from neoconservatism, it is undoubtedly his defense of secular humanism—long considered by many of them to be a subversive threat to Judaic-Christian culture. I submit that Sidney Hook's identification with secular humanism clearly distinguishes him from his erstwhile political cronies who were allies in his battles against totalitarianism. I am here referring to the fact that US intellectual, political, and cultural life today has been virtually dominated by the emergence of new forms of religiosity and spirituality, which most neoconservatives (such as Irving Kristol, Norman Podhoretz, Gertrude Himmelfarb, and many other disciples of the *Commentary* mantra) have welcomed, but which Sidney Hook adamantly refused to do. A graphic illustration of this difference is that at a packed memorial ceremony at New York University on July 18, 1989, immediately after Hook's death, Norman Podhoretz donned a skull cap and intoned Kaddish, a brazen affront to the atheist convictions of Hook.

II.

In retrospect, Hook stands out as one of the leading philosophical defenders of secular humanism in the twentieth century against its neoconservative, orthodox, and fundamentalist critics. Ronald Reagan, who conferred the Medal of Freedom on Hook in 1985 for his defense of democracy, at the same time was allied with political and religious forces that castigated secular humanism unremittingly, and their legions still continue to do so.[1] Sidney Hook's colleague Irving Kristol thought that the dominance of secularism throughout most of the century was an "anomaly," and Roman Catholic philosopher-theologian Michael Novak mistakenly declared that the "butcher block" of twentieth-century tyranny may be attributed primarily to secular ideologies; tracing secular humanism back five hundred years to the Renaissance, he declared that the next turn would be a renewal of interest in religiosity. This prophecy, I hope, will not be fulfilled; but no one can predict the future with certainty.

The world today is mired in conflicts between contending religious ideologues, in its most extreme form the *jihad* versus the Holy Crusade; uncompromising dogmatic attitudes pit Hindus against Sikhs and Muslims, and devout Christians, Jews, and Muslims at times against each other—and most of them against secularism. Everywhere demands are being heard that secularism and humanism need to be limited and that religious piety should dominate the public square, and this finds strong support in Mumbai and Islamabad, Tehran and Washington. This is not true, fortunately, of two continents, Europe and Australia, which are increasingly postreligious, though it is unfortunately applicable to the United States. Can anyone think of a political leader in the United States today who has the courage to admit that he is an agnostic, let alone an atheist?

Sidney Hook was an implacable foe of totalitarianism and a defender of democracy; by this he meant not simply political but also economic and social democracy. He differed with those neo-conservatives who worshiped unregulated free-market libertarianism; he consistently maintained that he was a social democrat, interested in social justice. Neoconservatives sometimes allied with Hook when he defended academic freedom; when he opposed the politicization of the universities, violence on campus, or the degradation of cultural values by a banal libertine consumerism; or when he thought that affirmative action undermined the idea of merit.[2]

But Hook was a critic of neoconservativism in a more basic sense: for he rejected their defense of religion as necessary for the social order. He insisted that there should be a divorce between ethics and religion. And he forcefully defended secular humanism, naturalism, and freethought.

As a preeminent master of polemical argument—he was perhaps the United States' leading Socratic gadfly of the twentieth century—he constantly adapted his philosophical outlook to new challenges—Trotskyism, Stalinism, and fascism in the 1930s and '40s; neo-Thomistic criticisms of naturalism in the 1940s and '50s; the New Left's assault on the universities in the 1960s and '70s; and the postmodernist defense of multicultural relativity in the 1980s and its undermining of scientific objectivity.

Throughout his career, Hook considered himself a naturalistic humanist. He began to use the term "secular humanist" especially in the last decade of his life (he was a charter founder of *Free Inquiry* magazine and a signer of the *Secular Humanist Declaration* of 1980), no doubt in response to the many attacks that secular humanists had suffered at the hands of the Religious Right. Their criticisms of secular humanism were multifaceted: they opposed Darwinian evolution and defended creationism, they attempted to bridge the separation of church and state, they attacked the labor movement and the liberal social-welfare state, they were vociferous in rejecting Dewey's experimental methods in education, and they did not think that a person could be moral without professing a belief in God.

The terms "secular humanism" and "naturalistic humanism" overlap and share a common agenda. They differ only in regard to focus and emphasis. "Secular humanism" came into vogue to differentiate it from "religious humanism," a term bandied about by many dedicated humanists. In *A Common Faith*, John Dewey was willing to use the term *religious* to denote our commitment to ideal ends that move us.[3] Indeed, Dewey, who was a nontheist, even used the term *God* in a metaphorical sense to refer to the "unification of our values." Many US humanists, even though they were nontheists and naturalists, were eager to accept this liberal interpretation; one could be religious and not believe in God. Both Sidney Hook and his humanist political adversary Corliss Lamont were critical of John Dewey's use of *religious*, which they thought was ambiguous and confusing. Thus the term *secular* was applied to humanism to differentiate it from fuzzy-minded religious humanism. Paradoxically, the Religious Right went on to declare that secular humanism was itself a religion; and they undertook a campaign to extirpate it from US public life, the courts, the liberal media, the universities, and especially the public schools. Thus the term *secular* was a meaningful term to append to humanism. But it also differed with the Religious Right and their neoconservative friends in pointing out that the United States was a secular republic (basing this on the First Amendment) and that a naturalistic ethics could replace a supernaturalistic one.

The term *secularism* thus became popular but only because of the need within the US political scene to defend it. The term *naturalism* is, however, the basic philosophical concept that underlies contemporary humanism. Sidney Hook's work is especially relevant to a revival of interest today in John Dewey's naturalism. Hook was a naturalist in three important senses: he was a methodological, scientific, and ethical naturalist.

III.

The first principle of Hook's naturalism is *methodological*, for he considered the methods of science to be the most effective way of understanding nature and solving human problems. He interpreted the methods of science broadly as "the method of intelligence." This presupposes that science is continuous with common sense; and it endeavors to test ideas, hypotheses, and theories by their experimental consequences. Hook maintains in his essay "Naturalism and First Principles" that "there are working truths on the level of practical living . . . *viz.*, the effective use of means to achieve ends."[4] These are the methods used by carpenters, cobblers, and gardeners as they go about their business of coping with the world, and these are implicit in technological behavior. This conception of rationality is not confined to our culture but is used generally, according to Hook, by primitive human beings as well as moderns. These involve rules of inference and techniques of resolving problems that are deeply embedded in the way we behave in the everyday world. Thus, "scientific method is the refinement of the canons of rationality and intelligibility exhibited . . . in the arts and crafts of men."[5] How to solve the problem of justification? asks Hook. Not by proving first principles in some ultimate way but by showing that the methods of science and practical reasoning are more effective than other approaches in understanding and adapting to the world—and hence more reasonable. There is no insuperable problem, says Hook, in justifying these first principles; for both scientists and ordinary men and women know when something is truer than something else.

The kind of methodological naturalism that Hook and his fellow US naturalists proposed was radical; for it wished to extend the methods of science to all aspects of human inquiry, everyday life, ethics, politics, social behavior, and religion.

Hook defended a second form of naturalism, which may be called *scientific* naturalism. This is an endeavor to develop a generalized account of experience in nature as humans transact in the world; it draws its knowledge primarily from the various sciences, not from religion, tradition, or the arts. It also defends, at root, the primacy of "matter" rather than "spirit." But Hook's materialism was nonreductive. He defended a form of emergent evolution, because he held that each kind of phenomenon encountered should be described and accounted for on its own level and in its own terms. This was consonant with his earlier defense of Marxist dialectics, which dealt with social and cultural phenomena without attempting to reduce them to physics or chemistry.

In a paper coauthored by John Dewey, Sidney Hook, and Ernest Nagel, the three pragmatic naturalists of the Columbia school attempted to respond to criticisms that naturalism's focus on "physical nature" excluded from the universe everything but the "physical,"[6] thus depriving us of knowledge of the "mental." Responding to this charge, they make it clear that they are not asserting that psychological qualities and conscious experiences, such as "the feeling of pain," are nothing but a "concourse of physical particles." The relationship to physical nature is not logical or analytical but contingent and causal. Clearly, human bodies are able to think and act rationally. Nevertheless, all of these processes are natural.

What is crucial is that naturalists reject supernatural claims because they do not meet the test of public verifiability. Critics of naturalism complain that this criterion exiles by definition private, introspective, and/or mystical encounters with the divine. Naturalists do not deny that human beings may have "mystical experiences" of what they call the "divine." They do deny, however, that *having* such experiences constitutes "knowledge." The testimony of a mystic is *testimony* but not necessarily *evidence* for the proposition that the divine exists; for introspective reports are uncorroborated and highly subjective, and they presuppose a questionable mind-body dualism.

In any case, Hook did not think that there was sufficient evidence or reasons that would demonstrate the existence of God, let alone enable us to define it. There are many conceptions of God and the soul, Hook maintained, that are so unintelligible and vague that nothing significant can be said of them. Concepts such as God have no empirically discernible effects, and no publicly observable evidence that can be brought to support the claim that God exists. Hook questions the cognitive legitimacy of purely speculative metaphysics or ontology. The quest for Being as such, "as an all-inclusive category," is not meaningful "for it does not seem to possess an intelligible opposite."[7]

Hook was skeptical of classical Thomistic arguments for the existence of God. He likewise questioned the famous queries posed by Heidegger, "Why is there something; why is there not nothing?" And he claimed that these are devoid of sense except as a "sign of emotional anxiety." Similarly for Paul Tillich's "shock of non-being or being not," which refers to unfulfilled or disappointed expectations, a "purely psychological category."[8] Neither of the above have any ontological status. Hook's analysis is in accord with Kant's critique of rational theology, for in talking about "Being as such," we are not referring to a predicate, attribute, or property. "There is no absurdity," paraphrasing Morris R. Cohen, "to which a philosopher will not resort to defend another absurdity!"

Can the sciences provide us with empirical metaphysical knowledge about the cosmos? John Dewey thought that we could uncover "the generic traits of the natural world."[9] Hook is cautious about this program, for "the specific traits of the world are the subject matter of the sciences." The only form of ontology that makes sense, he says, refers to common-sense statements that are "cognitively valid" and that assert that "something is true or false" and "are not found in any particular science . . . but which are obviously taken for granted by them."[10] These, he said, "have especial relevance to the career of human life on earth," a reflection of certain traits of nature involved in "the cosmic theater of human destiny."[11] In any case, Hook's naturalistic universe does not leave room for God; though he is aware of the tragic dimensions of human experience and the need for courage and resolve to deal with adversities.

In an influential paper published after World War II in *Partisan Review*, he indicted "the new failure of nerve" in contemporary culture.[12] This is based on "unwarranted hopes and unfounded beliefs . . . a desperate quest for a quick and all-inclusive faith that will save us from the trouble of thinking about difficult problems." One wonders what Sidney Hook would say today of the flight from reason that has overtaken us and the abandonment of scientific naturalism for ancient supernatural and/or paranormal dogmas. Most assuredly he would indict our current intellectuals for lacking the courage to defend naturalism.

A third form of naturalism that Hook defended is some form of naturalistic *ethics*. It is here that Hook has made his major contribution, for unlike his fellow philosophers of the 1950s, '60s, and '70s, who withdrew into the sanctuary of metaethics, he descended to the world of concrete moral and social problems and attempted to apply pragmatic intelligence to their solution. In this area he displayed a unique virtuosity in his moral perceptions and deliberations.

Can the methods of science be applied to normative questions and help us to make wise decisions? Dewey thought that the great problem that world civilization faced is the disparity between advances on the frontiers of scientific knowledge and the cultural lag

155

besetting our moral values, which were based upon custom and habit—ancient theological, artistic, or mystical doctrines. Hook no doubt agreed with Dewey's general observation that we ought to develop a science of valuation. He did not think, however, that ethical principles could be deduced from factual premises, or that good, bad, right, or wrong could simply be inferred from the sciences. Rather, the methods of scientific intelligence can help us to make prudent ethical choices by relating them within the contexts of inquiry to empirical data, the causes and conditions of behavior, means/ends analyses, and testing them by their experimental consequences.

Hook held that the subject matter of ethics was autonomous, not deducible from prior metaphysical or theological premises, and that it is possible to use critical thinking to modify our values in the light of evidence. Hook identified himself as an ethical humanist: "I would say that an ethical humanist today is one who relies on the arts of intelligence to defend, enlarge, and enhance the areas of human freedom in the world."[13]

Hook was a strong critic of command ethics, based on theistic premises. Today we hear from all sides that "one cannot be moral unless one believes in God." Hook denied that. There is no necessary logical relationship between God and specific moral principles. Indeed, he argues that from the Fatherhood of God, contradictory moral judgments have been derived by contending religious moralities, on issues such as capital punishment, suicide, the rights of women, slavery, pacifism, and war and peace.

The question often is raised, Where does the ethical naturalist begin? Are there first principles that govern human moral behavior? Hook expresses some skepticism. We cannot find first principles from which we can deduce moral imperatives. Rather, we must begin in the midst of life, embroiled in problematic situations that need resolution, and we make moral choices by appealing to various principles and norms that we accept; but we may evaluate and

156

modify them if need be in the light of their factual and consequential effects. Hook applied the empirical method of pragmatic intelligence to a wide range of topics: euthanasia, academic freedom, affirmative action, the ethics of scientific research, the curriculum in the schools, US foreign policy, and so on.

IV.

It is Hook's defense of democracy that perhaps best illustrates the approach of his naturalistic ethics to political questions. I should confess that I enrolled in Hook's brilliant course at New York University on the "Philosophy of Democracy" more than a half century ago. Hook denied that the justification of democracy was based upon a doctrine of natural rights, metaphysical concepts of human nature, or theological premises; he thought that any justification would have to be made on empirical grounds. We should treat democracy as a hypothesis, appraising it in the light of its consequences. Contrasting democracy with fascism and Communism, Hook made the case for political, economic, and social democracy—a rather radical position at that time. Hook drew upon a wide range of ethical principles and values that we widely shared to demonstrate the reasonableness of the democratic outlook. He opposed totalitarian society because it was closed, restricting dissent, the free market of ideas, and the right of opposition.

I am tempted to ask, How would Hook react today to the increasing corporate dominance of the media, which limits the free exchange of ideas, impoverishes dissent, and undermines democracy, or to the perversion of the electoral process by campaign financing by big money and lobbies? We sorely need his insight and reflections today about what many of us consider to be a drastic erosion of US democracy.

157

Historically, many philosophers were secular humanists, agnostics, atheists, materialists, and naturalists; they sought to relate ethics to human interests, needs, and values, not to some theological framework. Unfortunately, on the current cultural scene, the drums of religious fervor virtually drown out the naturalistic viewpoint. Moreover, all too few intellectuals have been willing to step forth as religious dissenters. Hook was able to do that with courage and virtuosity. In appraising the role of Hook's secular humanism and naturalism retrospectively, I submit that it is important that we appreciate its value. We need to ask, Is it possible to develop an authentic naturalistic outlook that has relevance to human interests and needs and that can ameliorate the human condition and help us to solve human problems? Sidney Hook surely did not think that all problems had easy solutions, and indeed there are conflicts in life that represent the tragic dimension of human existence. Nonetheless, he did not lose confidence in the ability of human beings to solve problems and to use critical inquiry for the benefit of humankind. This distinctive aspect of Hook's philosophical outlook is relevant to our current cultural context and needs to be restated anew—in sharp contrast with the prevailing sacred bias of our increasingly postmodern religious culture.

NOTES

1. Incidentally, I spoke to Hook on the phone a few days before he received the medal. He wondered if the Reagan administration knew that he was a secular humanist and whether he should accept the award. I urged him to do so since he was a fighter for freedom.

2. I do not agree with David Sidorsky that Hook was a "cultural conservative." He was only partially so about some excesses of the left in regard to moral behavior. His emphasis upon the experimental application of the method of intelligence was a *radical* proposal to reform society, as was his rejection of absolutes.

3. John Dewey, *A Common Faith* (New Haven, CT: Yale University Press, 1934).

4. Sidney Hook, "Naturalism and First Principles," reprinted in *The Quest for Being* (New York: St. Martin's Press, 1961; Amherst, NY: Prometheus Books, 1991), p. 173.

5. Ibid.

6. John Dewey, Sidney Hook, and Ernest Nagel, "Are Naturalists Materialist?" *Journal of Philosophy* 42 (September 13, 1945): 515–30.

7. Sidney Hook, "Two Types of Existentialist Religion and Ethics," in *The Quest for Being*, p. 147.

8. Ibid., p. 148.

9. Ibid., p. 160.

10. Ibid., p. 168.

11. Ibid., pp. 170–71.

12. Sidney Hook, "The New Failure of Nerve," reprinted in *The Quest for Being*, pp. 93–94.

13. Sidney Hook, "The Snare of Definitions," in *The Humanist Alternative*, ed. Paul Kurtz (Amherst, NY: Prometheus Books, 1973), p. 34.

CHAPTER 5

Right to Life and the Use of Violence

Marvin Kohl

I.

f I were allowed to pay tribute to Sidney Hook as a teacher and secular humanist and to comment on an important aspect of his work, what should I say? It would be necessary to be brief and simple, and I think I should concentrate upon two points. The first is that he was an inspiring and loving teacher. He cherished intellectual challenge, and when students were bold enough to do so his replies, more often than not, mixed good humor with warm admiration. Like Socrates, he loved the question-and-answer method of doing philosophy and, I suspect, was delighted even more when his students engaged him in intellectual battle. In class, as well as in other endeavors, there was a bottom line: to provide a supportive environment for free inquiry, for the use of intelligence to help understand and solve problems, especially the problem of how to nurture and protect the good life.

A distinction is often drawn between the brothers Prometheus and Epimetheus. Prometheus is the inner flame of desire for a better world; the will to aspire to the stature of the gods, even if that means open defiance. Epimetheus is the adapter to the past and the worshiper of the power that is. He is the supporter of the will of the gods and the archconservative. Hook, I would suggest, was neither a pure Promethean nor a pure Epimethean. Instead, there was a layering: sometimes one side would emerge and dominate, sometimes the other. He went where he believed intelligence, if not wisdom, commanded. Often he did battle as a Promethean for Epimethean or conservative causes. But only those who find comfort in oversimplification would call him, even during the latter decades of his life, a compassionate conservative. Compassionate he was; but it was a kind of compassion driven by his pragmatic secular humanism, and vice versa.

It is in this spirit that I wish to pay tribute to his work. I have chosen to focus on the problem of the value of life, more specifically on his discussion of the right to life and the use of violence, because the great ancient schools of philosophy concentrated essentially on the problem of what constitutes the best of lives as opposed to, say, the value of life and the importance of notions akin to the broader notion of the right to life.

II.

Rational suicide and euthanasia aside, Hook understood not only that most people want to live but that this kind of want has a special weight, often an overriding moral priority. The reason why most people want to live, if I may inject my own language, is that having a meaningful life is the primary material good, being virtually a necessary condition for the achievement of other goals. These goals may range in diversity from the simpler pleasure (like peeling an apple or just being able to get out of bed each day) to more lofty goals that involve levels of capacity and aspiration fulfillment. The fundamental point is that, whatever you may want to do, being alive is an almost necessary condition.

This in itself has implications for any theory of rights that does not beg the question concerning the equality of rights or the primacy of the right to freedom. For it suggests that the right to life has a moral and practical primacy and often trumps other considerations.

At this level, the argument presents only the choice of protecting life as opposed to other fundamental rights. But ethical life is not this simple. Within the kind of ethical life we find ourselves in, there are diversities and other kinds of challenge. At another level we are often faced with a choice between protecting life and protecting the good life. Hook appears to have been extremely sensitive to the fragility of each of these goods, especially the vulnerability of the good life. Thus he writes that it is not life itself that is worth living, but *only* the good life. "We must," he writes in his 1927 paper "The Ethics of Suicide," "recognize no categorical imperative 'to live,' but to 'live well.' From the above, two corollaries may be drawn significant for a theory of moral instruction: No rational morality can compel us to perpetuate lives that are irretrievably blasted by accident or birth, or blighted by some horrible malady before which remedial measures are unavailing; and more important, . . . no social morality can be equally binding upon everyone unless a social reconstruction makes possible a more equable distribution of the necessities of life."[1]

In other words, what may be lost in understanding his defense of democracy against violent civil disobedience and revolution is that it rests, in large part, on his identification of the good life with the good or democratic society.[2] "The good life," he insists, "cannot be pursued independently of the good society because a bad society can make the good life impossible."[3]

III.

Hook's analysis of human rights is penetratingly honest and often brilliant, and it still remains fruitful reading for all those who claim to be responsible social reformers. He maintains that "force is necessary to sustain or enforce legal rights wherever they are threatened—and human rights, too, which have a moral authority of their own to justify them. Otherwise they are no more than aspirations or pious hopes." However, there is an important difference between force and violence. Violence is usually taken to mean the exertion of any physical force so as to injure or abuse another. In contrast, Hook argues that "violence is not physical force *simpliciter* but the 'illegal' or 'immoral' use of physical force." He then claims that it is only permissible when there is no means of remedying grievances by peaceful constitutional change. In other words, the democrat may not use violence against a democratic system, since "the faith of the democrat is that the evils of a democracy—and it has many evils—can be remedied by the patient efforts to achieve a better democracy."

In the last three essays of *Revolution, Reform, and Social Justice*, he more carefully details his views about the role of protest, the position of human rights, and the nature of social justice in a democracy. According to Hook, there are human rights that, among other things, serve as a criterion for what should or should not be the basic legal rights enforced by the state. Human rights, no matter how carefully specified, sometimes conflict with each other, and in

164

any given situation our choice of which way to go is ultimately justified by personal and social utility in furthering human happiness. "Where there exists sufficient affluence to distribute to those in want, justice as well as prudence requires that their basic needs be met, independently of merit or desert." But where there does not exist more than enough of everything in the way of desirable goods, services, and opportunities, there must be "an equality of concern for all persons with the community to develop themselves to the full reach of their powers." Once we have established this equality of concern—which is the cardinal ethical belief of democracy as a way of life—then "what is wrong is not inequality of treatment but unwarranted or unreasonable inequality."

Two standard objections follow: first, it is not self-evident that a commitment to political democracy, which on its face seems only to be a commitment to a kind of electoral process, entails or requires a substantive ethic; second, if in any given situation our choice is ultimately justified by an appeal to personal and social utility, then why not say that human rights are important rules of thumb or thresholds that are really grounded in an act-utilitarianism or a situationalism akin to that of Dewey's?

Let us, however, leave these difficulties aside. Let us also assume that the notion of equality of concern is an important one and that, other things being equal, a society that feels and practices equality of concern is better than one that does not. There still remains the question whether or not Hook has aimed too low. Why not aim higher? Why not say that a commitment to the politics *and* ethics of democracy ought to rest on the freely given consent of the governed, where the governed recognize the right to life, liberty, and happiness as moral thresholds, where there is an equality of concern for all persons within the community to achieve excellence or develop themselves to the full reach of their powers, where there is an active concern and commitment to establish

165

institutions and laws that protect against circumstances that exceed these thresholds or actual violations, where violence is viewed as an extreme form of rescue for those in immediate, actual peril, and where every individual with moral standing has a basic right, when unjustly assaulted or unjustly deprived of basic sustenance and health care, to use violence to protect these goods if other means should prove ineffective?

This proposal is based—but not solely—on the general recognition that to knowingly allow people to suffer or die from lack of proper diet, basic and vital health treatment, or the like, when this could have been reasonably avoided—and to say that this is fully consistent with even the prima facie right to life—is to make a hollow mockery of that right. Neither justice nor wisdom warrants our telling a person whose right to life is being unfairly and seriously violated that he ought to be patient; that he should, after exhausting all the relevant nonviolent means, bide his time in the hope that a better society ultimately will triumph. Nor, it seems to me, can we rightfully say this to a man trying to save the life of an innocent child or some other loved one.[4]

Hook's opposition to violence in a democracy leaves him open to the criticism that his position cannot do justice to the nagging moral intuition that, when it comes to serious violations of the right to life, the threat or use of violence is sometimes permissible. For if it is true that a serious violation of the right to life (unlike more easily reversible violations of liberty) is not correctable at a later date, and if it has a unique moral primacy, then it seems to follow that certain circumstances permit the use of violence even in a democracy.

Hook, if I correctly recall his debate with Russell on the question of nuclear disarmament, argued that a major advantage of the nonpacifist is that, once the enemy knows you will fight, you have a considerably better chance of not being abused. The willingness to fight is a matter of strategic utility, albeit neither of a simple kind nor without possible loss. Isn't this especially true concerning the right to life? More generally, isn't it true that you have a considerably better chance of not having fundamental rights violated if it is generally known that you are prepared to fight in their defense?

With all this said, it must not be forgotten that Hook has rendered an inestimable service in describing the liberal faith in democracy. In a period of history when there seems to have been a mania of destroying valuable institutions, Sidney Hook reminded us that a rational man ought to love democracy and that only a fool destroys something he loves because it is imperfect. Like Hook, I believe the democratic way of life is one of the greatest of political goods. But I also believe, first, that democracy is not as vulnerable as he thought it was; and second, that Hook needlessly leaves himself open to the charge that, "when push comes to shove," secular humanism is not sufficiently responsive to the needs of the unfortunate.

NOTES

1. Sidney Hook, "The Ethics of Suicide," *International Journal of Ethics* 37 (1927): 186–87.

2. In *Revolution, Reform, and Social Justice: Studies in the Theory of Marxism* (New York: New York University Press, 1975), p. 249, Hook writes that civil disobedience "must be truly nonviolent—peaceful not only in form but in actuality" and that the "resort to civil disobedience is never morally legitimate where other methods of remedying the evil complained of are available."

3. Sidney Hook, *The Paradoxes of Freedom* (Berkeley and Los Angeles: University of California Press, 1962), p. 128.

4. There are many examples; however, there is a recent movie that graphically illustrates this point. In the film *John Q* (2002), the father (played by Denzel Washington) learns that his beloved young son needs

a heart transplant or he'll die soon—and because John Q is cash strapped and his insurance company refuses to pay, he's not going to get it. The story has its problems, one of which is what would follow if, instead of resorting to mild violence with only the threat of deadly violence, he had to actually resort to the latter. But another important point is that his use of violence appears to be the only effective way of saving his son's life, and therefore the use of it strikes a less conservative moral audience as being permissible, if not mandatory.

PART 2

SIDNEY HOOK'S PLACE IN THE AMERICAN INTELLECTUAL TRADITION

CHAPTER 6

Sidney Hook and Education

Steven M. Cahn

$\mathcal{S}$idney Hook is connected to education in at least three ways. First, he was an eminent philosopher of education, whose writings not only dealt with the educational controversies of his time but also addressed overarching issues regarding the aims of education. I especially admire his insightful book *Education for Modern Man*, which first appeared in 1946 and was revised in 1963.

The entire book repays careful study, but I have a special attachment to two chapters in particular. The first is his critique of the curriculum of St. John's College, with its exclusive concentration on great books. Here is some of Hook's response to the extravagant claims of the college's founders:

> Great books by all means; but why not also great pictures and symphonies, great plays and cinemas, great social changes, and mass movements, as well as the great Armageddons of our own time? We can learn at least as much from the heroic tragedy of Warsaw as from the last stand at Thermopylae.... Those who fulminate against the degeneration of modern education because some schools pay attention to the bridges, waterways, and sanitation systems of our large cities, together with other great feats of engineering, regard it as perfectly proper to study and glow about the marvels of Roman aqueducts, plumbing, and roads.... In education as in life we must learn to look to ourselves as ancestors, not merely descendants.[1]

Another favorite of mine is the final chapter, in which Hook presents his criteria for a good teacher. He includes intellectual competence, patience toward beginners, the ability to plan a lesson without mechanically imposing it on the class, knowledge of human beings, sympathy, a vision that inspires students with a passion for excellence, and, finally, a sense of humor, not taking oneself too seriously. The discussion is a masterful account of teaching by a masterful teacher.

Through his teaching Hook is connected to education in a second way, for he was a devoted undergraduate instructor. Like his lifelong friend Ernest Nagel, also a distinguished teacher, Hook began teaching in secondary school, where the essentials of good teaching were stressed. Throughout more than forty years of working with undergraduates, Hook never lost his passion for the give-and-take of an undergraduate class. These days a common way to attract notable academics to a faculty position is reducing their teaching as much as possible, preferably eliminating it entirely. But for Hook, a promise to eliminate his teaching would have been not an incentive but a deterrent.

A third connection between Hook and education is his effort to

172

see his educational ideals put into practice. In _Education for Modern Man_ he offers a detailed description of an ideal liberal arts curriculum and sums it up thus: "[T]he answer to the question _what should we teach?_ is selected materials from the fields of mathematics and the natural sciences, social studies, including history, language and literature; philosophy and logic; art and music. The knowledge imparted by such study should be acquired in such a way as to strengthen the skills of reading and writing, of thinking and imaginative interpretation, of criticism and evaluation."[2]

How might such an ideal be put into practice? Suppose every candidate for a liberal arts degree had to meet the following requirements: a course in English composition, a course in the history and literature of Greece and Rome, a course in European literature, a course in the history of European civilization from the decline of Rome to the present, a course in philosophical analysis, a course in the history of art or music, a course in foreign literature, a course in sociology, a course in psychology, a course in government, a course in economics, a course in mathematics, and a course in a laboratory science. Such a curriculum would have notable merits, but would any college faculty institute it?

In fact, as late as the academic year 1965, such were the requirements for a bachelor's degree at Washington Square College of New York University. And Sidney Hook played a crucial role in developing and supporting that curriculum.

It was abandoned during the late 1960s, but on one occasion when it was under attack, I heard Hook take to the floor of a faculty meeting and speak in its defense. I remember from that day the brilliance and passion of Hook's presentation. I also recall an amusing incident that followed. After he had finished, a noted political scientist of Marxist persuasion arose to speak in opposition to the requirements. He began, however, by praising Hook for his contribution to Marxist scholarship and went on to emphasize that in certain respects he agreed with some of what Hook had said. At that moment from the back of the auditorium came Hook's voice: "If you're agreeing with me, I better rethink my position."

In sum, Hook was a profound educational philosopher, a great teacher, and a courageous and effective champion of ideas. I consider myself fortunate to have known him.

NOTES

1. Sidney Hook, *Education for Modern Man: A New Perspective* (New York: Humanities Press, 1973), pp. 126, 133.

2. Ibid., p. 155.

CHAPTER 7

Flexibility and Revolution

Christopher Phelps

*T*he paradox of Sidney Hook's thought is that although by conventional measurements—renown, prestige, influence, and power—he reached his apex in the 1950s and '60s, his writings from that period taken as a whole now seem rote, formalistic, and predictable—of far less interest than the creativity and boldness he displayed as a young upstart in the 1930s.

As one might expect, Hook did not acknowledge this decline. Not only that, he denied *any* change in his thought. He preferred to think of himself as, across his life, a consistently independent thinker—*Out of Step,* as his memoir's title put it.

But was Hook really out of step in 1972, when he called publicly for a vote for Richard M. Nixon? In 1980, when voting for Ronald Reagan? Was Hook really of the same independent cast of mind in the

175

1950s when calling for stripping Communist teachers of their professional positions on the basis of party membership alone, regardless of classroom conduct, as he was in the 1930s when helping form and lead a revolutionary socialist organization, the American Workers Party?

Consider two forgotten movements in the Hook adagio: first, *The Fail-Safe Fallacy* (1963), one of Hook's less-remembered books. A refutation of the popular novel positing a computer-generated nuclear nightmare, containing a vigorous defense of Strangelovean thermonuclear strategist Herman Kahn, *The Fail-Safe Fallacy* concludes with a crescendo of guilt by association that brands *Fail-Safe*'s writers suitable candidates for the Lenin Peace Prize. *The Fail-Safe Fallacy* illustrates how the later Hook tended to find those who disagreed with him not merely erroneous or misguided, but guilty of ignorance, naïveté, or bad faith. It shows how, on the verge of the Vietnam debacle, he treated any fundamental criticism of US foreign policy as tantamount to pro-Communist apologetics. If Hook was an independent thinker, he was an independent thinker in the service of the national security state.[1]

Second, a political hearing that took place in 1958. For ten years the Independent Socialist League (ISL), led by Max Shachtman, and its predecessor organization, the Workers Party—a small group through which had passed Gertrude Himmelfarb, Irving Kristol, Irving Howe, and many other New York intellectuals—fought against their inclusion on the attorney general's "subversive" list. Asked to testify on behalf of the ISL before the Justice Department's appeals board, Hook refused. The issue at stake could not possibly be construed as Stalinism or "conspiracy." The ISL was devotedly opposed to the Soviet state and the Communist Party. Its members were as anti-Stalinist as they come. At issue was the right of democratic radicals to express themselves without government harassment. How feeble the appreciation for heresy left in the author of *Heresy, Yes—Conspiracy, No* (1953). Hook's anti-

Stalinism had transmogrified. His revolutionary opposition to Stalinism of the 1930s had been replaced in the 1950s by a liberal-conservative centrism. Even though Hook claimed to support democracy and freedom, he would not risk a finger to help remove the lingering Truman-McCarthy stigmata from independent socialists who were, in some cases, his former comrades. When the ISL won its case, it was with testimony by Dwight Macdonald, Norman Thomas, and Daniel Bell—and no thanks to Sidney Hook.[2]

To reclaim what is of value in Hook we must reach back farther in time to the decisive decade in his thinking, 1927–38. This was the period of his philosophical synthesis or blending of pragmatism and Marxism, in which he cast Marxism as a revolutionary method of action, *practice*. It was the phase of his greatest intellectual creativity and brilliance, in which he wrote *Towards the Understanding of Karl Marx* (1933) and *From Hegel to Marx* (1936), as well as such crucial articles as "On Worker's Democracy" (1934) and "Communism without Dogmas" (1934).[3] It was the pinnacle of his left-wing political engagement, including sustained cooperation with socialist groups (in part derived from a favorable reading of Lenin on socialist organization) and his defense of Leon Trotsky against the Moscow Trial fabrications.

Hook's thought of this period had a double-sided quality, conveyed by the rubrics—*rubric* I offer as a more pragmatist word than *principle*—of *flexibility* and *revolution*. To combine flexibility and revolution may seem paradoxical; revolutionaries are often thought unyielding, flexibility to imply compromise. To Hook, however, they were complementary. *Revolutionary socialist conviction seasoned by flexibility* describes the political method guiding Hook at the pinnacle of his youthful intellectual attainment.

Permit me to elaborate on these rubrics in turn. The writings of the young Hook often invoked the term *flexible*. By this he meant an experimental intellectual method holding knowledge to be hypothetical, fallible, and provisional. Ideas, he held, are only true insofar as verified in experience or practice. Knowledge is created and obtained, not received as sense-impression, as in prior empiricisms. These pragmatist themes derived from Hook's training under John Dewey but equally, however, from Karl Marx—as in the "Theses on Feuerbach." Historical materialism to Hook *was* experimental naturalism. Writing in the short-lived *Marxist Quarterly* of 1937, he defined Marxism as "critical, historical, and experimental" and wrote, "Socialism, democracy, and scientific method . . . are indissolubly connected. Neither one can fully come into its own without the others."[4]

Flexibility, experimentalism, and revision according to the dictates of experience were intended by Hook as a challenge to reductive, schematic, dogmatic versions of Marxist theory. In the first half of the twentieth century, these came in a variety of forms: economic determinism, Stalinist and social democratic positivisms holding Marxism to be an infallible science, and fatalistic postulations of historical inexorability and inevitability.

Today such theoretical matters may seem passé. American intellectuals and the Left are almost wholly free of the dogmas Hook pilloried. Who here today needs to be disabused of a belief in the inexorability of Communism? Social democracy, likewise, is hardly given to fatalistic forms of Marxism—indeed, hardly to leftist impulses of any sort. The triumph of neoliberalism worldwide in the 1980s and '90s meant that as bureaucratic Communism vanished from the scene, social democracy was pulled rightward, stripped even of its commitment to basic social welfare provision.

If the objects of Hook's original criticism have faded, however, the general method informing Hook's early polemics remains quite relevant. Admission of fallibility and celebration of experimentation—in a word, *flexibility*—remain essential to intelligent action and moral wisdom in politics and social action. They are useful guides to action for a new generation of anticapitalists and antiwar activists seeking to change the world, overturn exploitation, and challenge

178

injustice, if they wish to ensure that their own dreams of a better future are not distorted by some new version of cancer within the Left.

Our situation, however, is not for the most part that of a misguided Left, but rather the collapse of any meaningful Left. The novelty of Hook's thought of 1930s today is not in its chastened and experimental disposition or its emphasis on flexibility so much as in its radicalism.

This brings me to revolution. It is a word to which many fantastic meanings attach. Hook's thought of the 1930s was uncompromisingly radical; he was a revolutionary. Marxism, Hook wrote, is a "theory of social revolution" if nothing else, and Hook held classless society a prerequisite to human emancipation.[5]

It may seem curious today, but Hook had *pragmatist* grounds for this radicalism. What society, he asked, would best permit the widest use of free and critical intelligence? Socialism. Class society, capitalist society, blocked genuine community of inquiry. Social experimentation was stunted under capitalism because ruling classes would block any proposal that made significant inroads on their prerogatives of property and profit.

To extrapolate to the present, Hook's thinking explains why, despite compelling scientific knowledge of global warming, measures are not being taken with sufficient rapidity to reorient the advanced economies toward sustainability. Detroit, Houston, and Riyadh, not the established conclusions of the community of inquirers, drive energy policy.

Hook's revolutionary outlook was defined in opposition to two competing perspectives, Stalinism and liberalism. Long before the Khrushchev revelations, Hook recognized that the road to barbarism can be paved with Communist intentions. Stalinist malignance, however, was not the consequence of socialism, Marxism, or Leninism; it was a repudiation of communist egalitarianism. As Hook wrote in 1934, "the only valid criticism of the Communist Party is that it is not communist enough."[6] His was a far-reaching criticism of Stalinism, beyond what even Trotskyists were willing to make. In the mid-1930s, he was among the first to challenge concepts of the Soviet Union as a "workers' state." State property is insufficient, he held. The baseline of revolutionary judgment is whether power is accorded to working people.

With regard to liberalism, Hook's admiration for his teacher John Dewey was tremendous. They shared liberal values of free inquiry, free expression, and individual personality. But Hook jousted with political liberalism across the 1930s. The pursuit of reforms was desirable, he held, but reformism, or gradualism, as a strategy was inadequate. In the *New Republic* in 1931, Hook faulted Dewey for "failure to appreciate the instrumental value of *class struggle* rather than class collaboration in effecting the transition from Corporate America to Collective America."[7] Ultimately, he posited, social movements will fall short of socialism and fail even to win and defend reforms successfully if confined to the horizons of capitalist politics. Hook also had differences with liberal conceptions of democracy: "actual power," not mere "registration of consent," had to be considered the heart of democracy, he wrote in 1934.[8]

The central concept of Hook's revolutionary thinking was *workers' democracy*. Socialism, he argued, was impossible without popular power: democracy. Workers must forge their own liberation, and the aim must be workers' control (i.e., direct rule in factories, offices, and workplaces).[9]

Many difficult theoretical issues followed. What should be the relationship between necessary representative forms and direct democracy? What allowances should be made for expertise, skill, and experience? How can complex institutions be administered without some degree of organizational structure comparable to what we call bureaucracy? Hook had only begun to explore these before his revolutionary thinking was cut short. He had no total plan.

But the evaporation of workers' liberation as the central basis for his political judgment helps unlock the riddle of Hook's life. The

Moscow Trials of the late 1930s unmoored Hook, sent him on a rightward trajectory. Hook called himself a social democrat, but by the 1950s he had adopted a politics of the conventional center, absent any concern for workers' control, lacking any objection to capitalism. Despite a nominal attachment to pragmatism and socialism later in life, without recourse to revolutionary intellectual method, without the ultimate objective of workers' democracy, Hook's political thought narrowed, his social experimentalism withered.

He came unmoored from allegiance to the interests of the working class, hard in any circumstance for an intellectual to sustain. He ceased to pay attention to ownership, property forms, or the social and economic system, the very issues that confront us again in an age of profit slowdown, Gilded Age distinctions of wealth and poverty, and corporate scandal. The democratic ideal shrank in his thought from power to consent, from a consistent commitment to the expansion of popular participation and rule to a liberal formalism that looked upon representative institutions as sufficient in themselves.

The thought of the young Hook is no Rosetta stone for the present. But it has more to offer than Hook's end point. In his later work, the occasional valuable idea or essay is overshadowed by the cumulative effect of a sustained cold war polemic. Irving Howe was correct to write, "Within that first-rate mind, there had formed a deposit of sterility, like rust on a beautiful machine."[10] A revival of "cultural freedom"—that catchphrase of the 1950s—today requires sources other than the old saws of the cold war. As Philip Rahv warned in 1952, anti-Stalinism alone cannot provide a "total outlook on life . . . or even a philosophy of history."[11]

The Hook who fused experience, action, revolution, and practice; the Hook who recognized capitalism as class society, stunting of equality and democracy; the Hook whose idea of cultural freedom extended to the problem of work and the promise of the working class; the Hook who called democracy, socialism, and scientific method "indissolubly connected" and meant it—that, I submit, is the Sidney Hook whose thought is most likely to serve as a resource for cultural and political renewal in our own time.

NOTES

1. Sidney Hook, *The Fail-Safe Fallacy* (New York: Stein and Day, 1963).

2. Hook's refusal to testify was a topic of an interview by the author with B. J. Widick, former Workers Party and Independent Socialist League member and United Auto Workers staff member, October 23, 2002; see also Alan Wald, *The New York Intellectuals* (Chapel Hill: University of North Carolina Press, 1987), p. 277.

3. Sidney Hook, "On Workers' Democracy," *Modern Monthly* 8 (October 1934): 529–44; Sidney Hook, "Communism without Dogmas," in *The Meaning of Marx*, ed. Sidney Hook (New York: Farrar & Rinehart, 1934), pp. 101–144.

4. Sidney Hook, "Marxism and Values," *Marxist Quarterly* 1 (January–March 1937): 38–45.

5. Sidney Hook, *Towards the Understanding of Karl Marx* (New York: John Day, 1933), p. 9.

6. Hook, "Communism without Dogmas," p. 118.

7. Sidney Hook, "John Dewey and His Critics," *New Republic* 67 (June 3, 1931): 74.

8. Hook, "On Workers' Democracy," p. 541.

9. For extensive evidence and analysis of this general outlook as one of the primary themes in Hook's early political philosophy, consult Christopher Phelps, *Young Sidney Hook: Marxist and Pragmatist* (Ithaca, NY: Cornell University Press, 1997).

10. Irving Howe, *A Margin of Hope* (San Diego: Harcourt Brace Jovanovich, 1982), p. 211.

11. Quoted in Wald, *The New York Intellectuals*, p. 276.

CHAPTER 8

Sidney Hook, Higher Education, and the New Failure of Nerve

Edward Shapiro

n his column of December 27, 1938, Walter Lippmann argued that the study of the liberal arts was largely responsible for the political freedom characteristic of Western civilization. Unfortunately, the arts no longer reigned supreme in the university, and freedom in the United States and Europe was imperiled. "Men are ceasing to be free," he wrote, "because they are no longer being educated in the arts of free men. We have emptied education of rigorous training in the arts of thought . . . and having done that, we are no longer able to read in any language, the classic masterpieces of the human mind. Between ourselves and the sources from which our civilization comes we have dropped an iron curtain of false progress that leaves us to the darkness of our whims, our vagrant opinions, and our unregulated passions."

Fortunately, however, the picture was not completely bleak. "Here in this country and abroad," Lippmann noted, "there are men who see that the onset of barbarism must be met not only by programs of rearmament but by another revival of learning."[1] He mentioned the tentative efforts of educators at Columbia University, the University of Virginia, and the University of Chicago to restore the classic liberal arts curriculum. But more than these were the developments at St. John's College in Annapolis, Maryland, where, as a result of curriculum changes instituted in 1937, a small group of students were immersed in the study of the classics of Western civilization. "I venture to believe," Lippmann concluded, "that in the future men will point to St. John's College and say that there was the seedbed of the American Renaissance."[2] Some people, however, believed that the educational experiment at St. John's signified not a renaissance but a descent into medievalism, intolerance, and superstition. Among them was Sidney Hook.

Hook's antagonism to St. John's stemmed from what he perceived to be the pernicious efforts by Robert Maynard Hutchins and Mortimer J. Adler to impose an authoritarian and religious-based curriculum on US higher education. One offshoot of Hutchins's and Adler's efforts was the introduction at St. John's College in 1937 of a new curriculum revolving around the reading of the "great books" of Western civilization. Hutchins and Adler were personally involved in the changes at St. John's: both had advised those planning the new curriculum, and Hutchins had been offered the presidency of the college. Hutchins served on the St. John's board of trustees, and he sent a monthly check of one hundred dollars to the college. It was rumored during the late 1930s that both Adler and Hutchins would be relocating to Annapolis because of opposition at the University of Chicago to their proposed educational reforms. They did not; instead, the trustees of St. John's appointed Stringfellow Barr as its president and Scott Buchanan as its dean,

184

two men who had been brought to the University of Chicago by Hutchins and who agreed with him on the need to reform undergraduate education. Little wonder then that St. John's exemplified for Hook the threat hanging over US higher education. He viewed St. John's as a manifestation of "the new failure of nerve" of secular US intellectuals, against which he warned in his famous *Partisan Review* essay of 1943.[3]

Hutchins, the former dean of Yale Law School, became president of the University of Chicago in 1929. He came to the Windy City on a crusade to purge undergraduate education of its vocationalism, anti-intellectualism, empiricism, and emphasis on athletics, which he saw as permeating the US academy. In 1930 Hutchins brought his friend Adler, a Thomistic philosopher and an instructor at the Columbia University Law School, to Chicago. Despite his lack of scholarly publications, Adler's Chicago salary was almost three times what he had received at Columbia and one thousand dollars higher than that of full professors in Chicago's philosophy department. He was appointed to the rank of associate professor, even though he had only received his PhD in 1929. Adler further alienated many of the university's faculty because of his combative temperament, open contempt of the university's social scientists and philosophers, and indiscreet pronouncements as to how he intended to reform the university's undergraduate education and to show his colleagues, some of whom were twice his age, the errors of their ways. Mary Ann Dzuback, a biographer of Hutchins, noted that Adler's ideas "might have been laughable as the grandiose plan of a self-inflated upstart," except for the fact that he was a close friend of Hutchins.[4]

The educational objectives of Adler and Hutchins were outlined in the latter's brief book, *The Higher Learning in America*. Here Hutchins declared that the sole purpose of the university is "the single minded pursuit of the intellectual virtues" and that its underlying principle should be "the pursuit of truth for its own sake." Opposed to this was vocational education, which threatened to transform the university into a trade school. This would be "bad for the universities, bad for the professions, and bad for the students." Vocational education conflicted with the idea of the university as a "haven where the search for truth may go unhampered by utility or pressure for 'results.'" Because truth is the same everywhere, Hutchins said, then education should be the same everywhere. "The heart of any course of study designed for the whole people," he wrote, "will be the same at any time, in any place, under any political, social, or economic conditions." But what is the truth that the university should pursue? Hutchins (and Adler) believed that the role theology had played in the medieval university must necessarily be played by "metaphysics" in the modern university, since there was no other alternative.

In a bit of syllogistic legerdemain, Hutchins argued that the aim of higher education is wisdom; wisdom involves knowledge of principles and causes; and metaphysics deals with principles and causes. Therefore metaphysics is "the highest science, the first science, and as first, universal," sentiments that did not endear him to social and natural scientists, particularly when he never defined in his book what he meant by metaphysics or set down the specifics of his educational goals. Order in higher education, Hutchison maintained, can be achieved only "by removing from it the elements which disorder it today, and these are vocationalism and unqualified empiricism. If when these elements are removed we pursue the truth for its own sake in the light of some principle of order, such as metaphysics, we shall have a rational plan for a university." Since no US college at the time devoted itself to the type of education recommended by Hutchins, he argued that it was necessary to create such an institution. "The times call for the establishment of a new college or for an evangelistic movement in some old ones which shall have for its object the conversion of individuals and finally the teaching profession to a true conception of general education."[5]

The major foil of *The Higher Learning in America* was progressive education, and John Dewey, the major spokesperson of progressive education, vigorously responded to Hutchins's manifesto. Dewey rejected the assumption that one type of education was appropriate for all; he did not share Hutchins's disdain for the social sciences; he did not believe the university could or should separate itself from daily life; he argued that the type of education proposed by Hutchins was ill suited for an age of democracy, technology, and science; and he rejected the notion that there were timeless and unchanging truths that teachers should inculcate into their charges. Truth, Dewey said, was relative and evolutionary, and it was best discovered through scientific method and not metaphysics. Dewey concluded that the educational views of Adler and Hutchins reflected an authoritarianism derived from Roman Catholicism, even though neither Adler nor Hutchins was a Catholic. Hook agreed with Dewey regarding Hutchins and Adler, and the eagerness with which he took up their challenge to US educators reflected not only his combative nature but also his deep affection for Dewey, his revered mentor and friend.[6]

The educational experiment at St. John's College began the year after the publication of *The Higher Learning in America*. The college's curriculum did not include elective courses, and every student was expected to study everything taught at the college. Teaching primarily involved a close reading and discussion of approximately 120 "great books." The new curriculum, Stringfellow Barr told the college's board, "is not the introduction of another 'experiment' into an educational system already disorganized by expediency and complacency. It is the restoration of St. John's to the great and ancient tradition of liberal education." Barr hoped the college would serve as a model for other US institutions. Hutchins was equally enthusiastic. He suggested that the college might represent "a turning point in American educational history."[7]

Hook initially was rather open-minded about the St. John's curriculum and eager to learn more about it. In October 1938 he invited Scott Buchanan to speak at a symposium on higher education to be held in November at the New School for Social Research in New York. Hook told Buchanan that the participants in the conference were very interested in what was taking place at St. John's and wished to explore with him the nature of scientific method. Buchanan agreed to speak at the conference, although he recognized that he would be entering hostile territory. He told Hook that he was "very glad that the time seemed to have arrived when our vicarious battles by magazine articles can give place to hand to hand combats in discussion." He also told Hook that he intended to defend the proposition that metaphysics and religion were rational and scientific, sentiments unlikely to be welcomed by Hook, an atheist and Deweyite.[8]

The watershed event in Hook's relationship with St. John's occurred on September 10, 1940, when Adler delivered a controversial talk at the Conference on Science, Philosophy, and Religion in Their Relation to the Democratic Way of Life, held at the Jewish Theological Seminary in New York City. The conference was the brainchild of Rabbi Louis Finkelstein, the seminary's chancellor, who saw it as a means to strengthen the country's democratic defenses in the struggle against totalitarianism. Finkelstein invited Adler to help plan the conference, and he suggested that Adler deliver a paper outlining his views on the relationship between science, philosophy, and religion. Adler later admitted that it had been a mistake to speak at the conference. His language, he said in his 1977 autobiography, "could not have been more misguided or inept," and some of his propositions went far beyond what "could be reasonably held or rationally defended." But Adler had not come to New York to win friends or to influence his listeners but to defend the reforms that he and Hutchins had tried to institute at Chicago.[9]

"God and the Professors" was delivered after the fall of France, during the London Blitz, and while Americans were debating their country's stance on the European war. Adler's view of the major threat facing the United States was idiosyncratic, to say the least. According to him, US democratic culture was being undermined by positivist and naturalist professors, who deny that religion is "the supreme human discipline, because it is God's discipline of man." Democracy, Adler maintained, "has much more to fear from the mentality of its teachers than from the nihilism of Hitler. It is the same nihilism in both cases, but Hitler's is more honest and consistent, less blurred by subtleties and queasy qualifications, and hence less dangerous. . . . It is probably not from Hitler, but from the professors, that we shall ultimately be saved."

Adler attempted to demonstrate this eccentric assertion by examining sixteen supposedly irrefutable propositions about philosophy and religion. These included the claims that philosophical knowledge is superior to scientific knowledge; that metaphysics can demonstrate the existence of God; that it is impossible for anyone claiming to be a philosopher to deny the rational knowledge of God; that religious faith is more certain than scientific knowledge; that religion, resting as it does on supernatural knowledge, is superior to both philosophy and science; that religion is the supreme human discipline; and that "just as there are no systems of philosophy, but only philosophical knowledge less or more adequately possessed by different men, so there is only one true religion, less or more embodied in the existing diversity of creeds." Adler's conclusion shocked his listeners. "Until the professors and their culture are liquidated," he said, "the resolution of modern problems—a resolution which history demands should be made—will not even begin."[10]

Hook was deeply angered by Adler's talk and by the claims of other speakers at the conference that secularism, humanism, and naturalism were incompatible with democracy. He promised to boycott all future meetings of the conference, and he declared that conference participants who did not follow his lead would be aiding "theological reactionaries," "neo-Thomist authoritarianism," and "anachronistic medievalism." Hook feared that the conference indicated that US intellectuals were losing their nerve and "being swept away on a tidal wave of irresponsibility, bad logic, and obscurantism." The US democracy, Hook avowed, was threatened more by the antidemocratic tendencies of religionists than by the influence of naturalists and humanists. Such attacks on the nonreligious, he said, undermined the forces opposed to totalitarianism.[11]

Hook's criticisms of the conference itself were mild compared to his response to Adler's speech, which he described as "pontifical and arrogant." For personal and ideological reasons, Hook had not been friendly with Adler for over a decade. But he had a grudging admiration for Adler's mind and debating skills, and he viewed him as a worthy, although at times dogmatic and uniformed, foe. After "God and the Professors," however, Hook's relationship with Adler took on the character of a vendetta.[12]

Hook was the respondent to Adler's paper, and his comments were published by the *New Republic* under the title "The New Medievalism." Here Hook accused Adler of duplicity, intellectual irresponsibility, and shoddy philosophic thinking. All of Adler's philosophical propositions were "false," Hook wrote, while his theological propositions led logically to religious intolerance, a new Inquisition, and state religion. Hook denied that metaphysics and theology could provide certain and immediate knowledge; he rejected the subordination of science and philosophy to sacred theology; and he argued that scientific knowledge was the most reliable form of learning. But for Hook the most disturbing part of Adler's speech was his comment about the liquidation of intellectuals. Hook did not understand this metaphorically, and he continually mentioned it after September 1940 when discussing Adler. In 1941, for example, Hook denied that Adler's words were simply a "harmless jest": "At a time when intelligent believers in democracy must unite on a limited program against the greatest evil," Hook wrote, Adler fashions "the ideological premises which would unleash overt religious conflicts within the land." In his autobiography, published two years before his death, Hook argued that Adler's speech was the equivalent of "an *auto-da-fe* in American education."[13]

Perhaps the most notable event in the Hook-Adler confrontation occurred in March 1951, when *Time* magazine ran a favorable cover story on Adler titled "Mortimer Adler: Should Professors Commit Suicide?" Hook was incensed by *Time*'s praise of Adler, its claim that John Dewey had prevented Adler from doing graduate work in philosophy at Columbia, and its comments about pragmatism. The pragmatists, *Time* charged, had done great harm to US education by creating "an intellectual universe without fixed truth, where right and wrong swirl through time and space, always dependent on local interpretation and individual desire." Particularly odious to Hook was a photograph of Dewey over the caption "More dangerous than Hitler?" Hook immediately wrote to Henry Luce, *Time*'s publisher, in protest. He denied that Dewey blackballed Adler, denounced the caption, and stated that his mentor had done more to alert the West to the dangers of totalitarianism than any other person. Furthermore, Hook said, the article failed to mention that Adler had defended the death sentence for heresy. "This portrait of Dewey as feuding with and persecuting a student," Hook wrote a year after the *Time* article, "could not be anything but wildly absurd to everyone who knew Dewey. Dewey disliked Adler's exhibitionism and what he believed was a lack of serious respect for truth about fact. He never gainsaid his dialectical talents, but thought that in his relation to others he was too much like a pushy young college debater in training, ready to refute what others said no matter what they believed, and even before they had spoken."[14]

The imbroglio over Adler influenced Hook's view of St. John's College because of Adler's praise of and association with the school. One year after delivering "God and the Professors," Adler noted that St. John's was the only US college "working for the revival of a liberal curriculum. . . . If in some way the spiritual union of St. John's and Chicago could be consummated, we might hope for the blessed event of a cultural rebirth." Such praise tainted St. John's in Hook's mind. His previous openness and curiosity regarding the college disappeared, and he now perceived it as an ally of reactionary educational ideologues and religious fundamentalists who opposed pragmatism, secularism, the scientific method, and democracy. For Hook, the debate over the St. John's educational experiment had become part of a much larger and more significant controversy regarding the direction of US culture.[15]

In several articles of the early 1940s and then in his 1946 book, *Education for Modern Man*, Hook highlighted what he perceived as St. John's educational fallacies. Indeed, during these years Hook appeared more concerned with the direction of higher education than with the threat of Communism. In his correspondence with Scott Buchanan, Hook claimed that St. John's was following in the path of Hutchins and Adler in their efforts to purge higher education of naturalists, secularists, pragmatists, and positivists. Hutchins and Adler, he noted, were Scholastics and thus unfriendly to academic freedom, while St. John's had fallen under the influence of reactionary elements, particularly Roman Catholics. During the 1930s and '40s, Hook perceived the Roman Catholic church as a totalitarian organization opposed to liberalism and academic freedom. Buchanan was incensed by Hook's accusations, which in fact were based on no firsthand knowledge of the workings of the college or of the biographies of the architects of the St. John's program, none of whom were Roman Catholics. He told Hook that he was obviously ignorant of what was taking place at the college. Buchanan vehemently denied that he was a member of any "Thomist gang" or that the college was part of a Catholic-fascist clique opposed to academic freedom and progressive education. St. John's, Buchanan said, was simply a modest educational experiment.[16]

By July 1944 Buchanan had run out of patience with Hook's criticisms about St. John's. In a letter terminating any further discussion with Hook regarding the college, he wrote that his colleagues at St. John's believed that Hook should not be taken seriously and should be ignored. Buchanan told Hook that when it came to the college, he seemed possessed by demons and that he was apparently more concerned with leading a witch hunt against the school and scoring sophomoric debating points than learning what the school was really about. Until Hook became interested in knowing the truth (and Buchanan was skeptical that this would ever occur), there was no sense in continuing their correspondence. In his parting words, Buchanan urged Hook to visit Annapolis, after which he would realize that those running St. John's were acting in good faith.[17]

Hook refused to take him up on this challenge. Indeed, Hook argued during the next four decades that it had been unnecessary for him to visit St. John's in order to make categorical statements about the school because he was merely analyzing the educationally dubious arguments put forth by the architects of its curriculum. Thus there was no need to investigate firsthand what was actually occurring in Annapolis. Hook, in other words, resorted to a priori thinking in order to refute what he saw as the a priori presupposition of the St. John's people. This is not an argument one would expect from a disciple of John Dewey. This tendency to substitute dogmatism for empirical evidence would also appear in the 1950s, when Hook maintained on a priori grounds that Communists should not be allowed to teach in a university because their affiliation with a totalitarian movement made it virtually impossible for them to be open-minded.[18]

The anger of St. John's supporters toward Hook came to a head as a result of his two-part series of articles in the *New Leader* titled "Ballyhoo at St. John's College." Here Hook exaggerated the influence of Hutchins and Adler over St. John's and claimed that the college's defenders exhibited "not only a lamentable deficiency in logic and scientific method, but the disingenuousness of a purveyor of patent medicines and other universal nostrums." Hook's fundamental criticism of the college's curriculum was its concentration on that Western tradition that began with the Greeks and continued into the Christian era. Only two of the 120 books read by the students of St. John's were from the twentieth century, he pointed out, and the only US author included who lived after the Civil War was William James. There were also no non-Western books on the reading list.

Hook found it bizarre that at St. John's the social problems of classical Greece and medieval and Renaissance Europe were studied but not those of the twentieth-century United States and Europe. The college evidently believed that there was no need to study contemporary difficulties since the works of Aristotle, Aquinas, and Hobbes provided central truths for perennial issues. And for that same reason there was no need to include in the St. John's canon books from Hindu, Far Eastern, Islamic, and other non-Western cultures. Hook disagreed. Propositions believed to be eternally true, even those derived from the Greeks or the church, he noted, were either false or had a limited historical validity. The St.

John's people refused "to dip into the fresh seas of contemporary experience to test and amplify their stock of 'eternal truths.'"[19]

For Hook the debate over St. John's transcended mere educational matters, and this accounted for the dogmatic fervor with which he attacked the college's curriculum. Despite the disclaimers of Buchanan and others at the college, Hook continued to argue that the refusal of St. John's to focus its liberal arts curriculum on contemporary cultural problems and its neglect of the study of modern languages stemmed from a "neo-Thomist" abhorrence of modernity, which it shared with Hutchins and Adler. The neo-Thomists, Hook avowed, viewed education as a means to preserve the power of "dogmatic theology or political religions." For them the past was "a weapon in a present struggle over a present issue which should be frankly brought into the light." This struggle and this issue involved secularization.

If the neo-Thomists triumphed, Hook feared, religion would permeate the public schools and separation of church and state would end. By contrast, he suggested that redirecting education from the so-called eternal truths to contemporary problems would not only enable students to better appreciate the distinctive elements of their own culture but would also provide them with the knowledge and values that "have a definite relevance to the perennial task of making life better here and now." Among these values were secularism, intellectual freedom, and scientism. In all of his writings on St. John's, Hook's ultimate target was never the college. Rather, it was those he called "the great panjandrums of the anti-Dewey parade, who are convulsed with fury at what they call progressive education." This particularly included Mortimer J. Adler. Little wonder, then, that the college's representatives found Hook's criticisms of the school to be mean-spirited, misdirected, and inaccurate.[20]

For over half a century Hook's shifting attitude toward St.

John's reflected what he saw as the major challenges facing US higher education. In his mind, the college's curriculum was always subsidiary to more important concerns. Thus in a letter to J. Winfree Smith, a St. John's official, in November 1981, Hook denied that he had ever had a feud with or been unfriendly toward the college. In fact, he said, he admired the manner in which the college weathered the academic turmoil in the 1960s. By this time, of course, Hook's concern for US higher education had long shifted from the influence of Adler, St. John's, and desecularization to the impact of the New Left and affirmative action. These latter fears were more justified than those of the 1940s.[21]

Hook's criticisms of St. John's in the 1940s and his attacks on the New Left in the 1960s and 1970s stemmed from the same source: his abhorrence of authoritarianism and the threat it posed to academic freedom. If during World War II Hook believed the major menace to academic freedom in the United States came from Thomists, Roman Catholics, and other proponents of authoritarian religion, in the 1960s and 1970s he saw it coming from a mélange of feminists, political radicals, and the racist demagogues who sought to politicize the academy to conform to their pet prejudices. The response of the faculty during this time, he wrote, even in the face of violence, "was initially one of complacency, then of compromise to avoid the necessity of firm adherence to principle and to possible disciplinary action, and finally in most cases retreat and craven capitulation." What accounted for this failure of nerve, a failure that was far greater than that of the 1940s? Hook argued that the culprit was fear. But in contrast to the fear of the 1940s, which stemmed from the intimidation of intellectuals by Adler and his ilk, the fear of the 1960s and 1970s had its source in the intimidation by students and their faculty allies. The fright of professors, Hook argues, was "not of violence to themselves but, incredibly, fear of being criticized in the student press—invariable in the hands of the student extremists—fear of being denounced at student meetings as reactionaries, fear of being unpopular with the student body." The moral cowardice of professors and administrators had allowed lawlessness to run rampant on America's college campuses.[22]

This focus on the New Left as the major threat to academic freedom also stemmed from Hook's more discriminating view of the Roman Catholic church. After World War II, Hook did not display the reflexive antagonism toward the church that he had exhibited during the controversy with Adler and St. John's College. The church and Thomism, he now believed, were not the authoritarian danger he had previously imagined it to be, nor were Catholics necessarily enemies of democracy, liberty, and academic freedom. In his autobiography, Hook recalled his response to a conference of philosophers in Holland in 1948 at which, much to his surprise, some of the strongest proponents of intellectual freedom were Roman Catholic clerics. Indeed, he recounted, "on every issue that involved intellectual and political freedom, these philosophical priests lined up solidly with the democratic forces." Hook attributed this to "a new awareness of the dangers of authoritarian institutional controls to the integrity of the philosophical life." He noted wryly that when he wrote about this in the *Partisan Review* he was attacked by Irving Howe for having sold out to the Catholic church. One year later he was amazed by the claim of some of the attendees at the famous Cultural and Scientific Conference for World Peace (the Waldorf Conference) that the Vatican was a bigger menace to peace and freedom than the Kremlin. Indeed, after World War II Hook welcomed the support of Catholics in their common struggle against Communist totalitarianism, and he regretted that the Catholic colleges seemed to be as vulnerable as secular institutions to academic terrorists and to those demanding the dilution of academic standards.[23]

For Hook, the threat to academic freedom once posed by Mortimer Adler and St. John's College paled when compared to that presented by the Black Panthers and Students for a Democratic Society. The transgressions of Adler and St. John's involved philosophical and academic issues, and these could be countered by essays and books. Adler had remained a lonely voice within academia, and the reforms instituted at St. John's had little effect nationwide. The actions of the SDS and the Black Panthers, by contrast, required police intervention, and their effects were more widespread. These actions included "the ransacking of administrative offices, the torching of libraries and other acts of vandalism, the bombing of research facilities, the assaults against faculty, administrators, and other students, which in one or two cases actually resulted in murder." But Hook's defense of reason and academic freedom resonated less strongly in the academy in the 1960s than in the 1940s, and his disgust with the failure of nerve and cowardice within the university deepened. Little wonder, then, that he prematurely left New York University in 1972 and took up residence at the Hoover Institution.[24]

NOTES

1. Walter Lippmann, "The St. John's Program," *New York Herald Tribune*, December 27, 1938.

2. Ibid.

3. Sidney Hook, "The New Failure of Nerve, Part 1," *Partisan Review* 10 (January–February 1943): 2–23, and "Part 2: The Failure of the Left," *Partisan Review* 10 (March–April 1943): 165–77.

4. Mary Ann Dzuback, *Robert M. Hutchins: Portrait of an Educator* (Chicago: University of Chicago Press, 1991), pp. 94–99; William H. McNeill, *Hutchins' University: A Memoir of the University of Chicago, 1929–1950* (Chicago: University of Chicago Press, 1991), pp. 33–40.

5. Robert Maynard Hutchins, *The Higher Learning in America*

(New Haven: Yale University Press, 1936), pp. 31, 52–57, 66, 81, 97–99, 108, 117. For a brief analysis of Hutchins's thinking, see Charles C. Alexander, *Nationalism in American Thought, 1930–1945* (Chicago: Rand McNally, 1969), pp. 148–52.

6. Alan Ryan, *John Dewey and the High Tide of American Liberalism* (New York: W. W. Norton, 1995), pp. 39, 276–83, 338–39; James Sloan Allen, *The Romance of Commerce and Culture: Capitalism, Modernism, and the Chicago-Aspen Crusade for Cultural Reform* (Chicago: University of Chicago Press, 1983), pp. 92–93.

7. J. Winfree Smith, *A Search for the Liberal College: The Beginning of St. John's Program* (Annapolis, MD: St. John's College Press, 1983), pp. 1–5, 22–23.

8. Sidney Hook, letter to Scott Buchanan, October 8, 1938; Buchanan to Hook, October 18 and November 10, 1938; available at the Scott Buchanan-Sidney Hook correspondence file, St. John's College Archives, Annapolis, Maryland.

9. Mortimer J. Adler, *Philosopher at Large: An Intellectual Autobiography* (New York: Macmillan, 1977), pp. 185–90.

10. Mortimer J. Adler, "God and the Professors," *Vital Speeches of the Day* 7 (December 1, 1940): 98–103. For Hutchins's similarly negative attitude toward the secular US intelligentsia, see Allen, *The Romance of Culture and Commerce*, pp. 95–96.

11. Sidney Hook, "Theological Tom-Tom and Metaphysical Bagpipe," *Humanist* 2 (Autumn 1942): 96–102; see also Sidney Hook, "National Unity and 'Corporate Thinking,'" *Menorah Journal* 30 (January 1942): 61–68; and Sidney Hook, "Metaphysics, War, and the Intellectuals," *Menorah Journal* 28 (October 1940): 326–37.

12. Sidney Hook, "National Unity and 'Corporate Thinking,'" p. 67; Sidney Hook, "The Baptism of Aristotle and Marx," *New Republic* 147 (April 9, 1938): 415–17. For Dewey's response to Adler's piece, see Robert Westbrook, *John Dewey and American Democracy* (Ithaca, NY: Cornell University Press, 1991), pp. 520–23.

13. Sidney Hook, "The New Medievalism," *New Republic* 103 (October 28, 1940): 602–606; Sidney Hook, "Two Views on Mortimer Adler and Milton Mayer," *New Leader* 25 (May 16, 1942): 5; Sidney

Hook, "The Counter-Reformation in Higher Education," *Antioch Review* 1 (Spring 1941): 336–37; Sidney Hook, letter to Edward Shils, November 9, 1940; Hook to H. A. Overstreet, October 26, 1942; Hook to Joseph Epstein, March 6, 1985; available in the Hook Papers, Hoover Institution, Stanford University.

14. "Mortimer J. Adler: Should Professors Commit Suicide?" *Time*, March 17, 1952, pp. 76–84; Sidney Hook, letter to Henry Luce, April 1, 1952, Hook Papers. Hook's comments about Adler and Dewey appeared in his essay "Some Memories of John Dewey," *Commentary*, September 1952, and were reprinted in his book *Pragmatism and the Tragic Sense of Life* (New York: Basic Books, 1974), pp. 105–106. Adler claimed that Hook misunderstood his attitude toward Dewey. See Adler, *Philosopher at Large*, pp. 49–50.

15. Mortimer J. Adler, "The Chicago School," *Harper's Magazine* 183 (September 1941): 388.

16. Sidney Hook, letter to Scott Buchanan, January 15, 1943; Buchanan to Hook, January 18, 1943; Buchanan to Hook, June 25, 1944; Hook to Buchanan, June 30, 1944; Hook Papers. For Hook's continuing skepticism about the Hutchins-Adler-St. John's approach to higher education, see Sidney Hook, "General Education: The Minimum Indispensables," *The Philosophy of the Curriculum: The Need for General Education*, ed. Sidney Hook, Paul Kurtz, and Miro Todorovich (Amherst, NY: Prometheus Books, 1975), p. 31.

17. Scott Buchanan, letter to Sidney Hook, July 10, 1944, Hook Papers.

18. Sidney Hook, letter to J. Winfree Smith, November 18, 1981, Hook Papers.

19. Sidney Hook, "Ballyhoo at St. John's College: I. Education in Retreat," *New Leader* 27 (May 1944): 8–9; Sidney Hook, "Ballyhoo at St. John's: II. The 'Great Books' and Progressive Teaching," *New Leader* 27 (June 3, 1944): 8–10; Sidney Hook, "An Apologist for St. John's College: Hook Answers *The Saturday Evening Post*," *New Leader* 27 (November 25, 1944): 3. For a critique of Hook's views of St. John's, see Smith, *A Search for the Liberal College*, pp. 55–57.

20. Sidney Hook, "God, Geometry, and Good Society," *Partisan*

Review 11 (Spring 1944): 161–67; Sidney Hook, review of Algo D. Henderson, *Vitalizing Liberal Education: A Study of the Liberal Arts Program, Nation* 158 (March 11, 1944): 312–14; Sidney Hook, "The Ends of Education," *Journal of Educational Sociology* 18 (November 1944): 1–10; Sidney Hook, *Education for Modern Man: A New Perspective* (New York: Knopf, 1963), p. 15; Sidney Hook, *Out of Step: An Unquiet Life in the 20th Century* (New York: Knopf, 1985), pp. 338–46; Sidney Hook, "Thirteen Arrows against Progressive Education," *Humanist* 4 (Spring 1944): 1–10. For a response by Adler to Dewey and Hook, see Mortimer J. Adler and Milton Mayer, *The Revolution in Education* (Chicago: University of Chicago Press, 1958), pp. 152–73.

21. Sidney Hook, letter to J. Winfree Smith, November 30, 1981, Hook Papers.

22. Hook, *Out of Step*, pp. 548–51; see also Sidney Hook, *Academic Freedom and Academic Anarchy* (New York: Cowles, 1970).

23. Hook, *Out of Step*, pp. 346–50, 389, 409–10.

24. Ibid., p. 590.

CHAPTER 9

From Dewey to Hook
World War II and the Crisis of Democracy

Gary Bullert

$\mathcal{D}$uring World War II, Sidney Hook served as the major defender of Deweyan pragmatism both philosophically and politically. This daunting responsibility was inaugurated by his publication of *John Dewey: An Intellectual Portrait* (1939) and was reaffirmed by editing Dewey's ninetieth-birthday Festschrift, *John Dewey: Philosopher of Science and Freedom* (1949).[1] In the immediate aftermath of the Trotsky Trial, Hook emancipated himself from the residue of revolutionary Marxism and embraced a fervent Deweyan defense of democracy. By establishing with Dewey the Committee for Cultural Freedom in May 1939, Hook prioritized the struggle between democracy and totalitarianism as the preeminent issue of the times. Though accused by some of souring into a "Johnny One-Note," Hook collaborated with Dewey on a variety of projects in addition to vigilance over the threat of Communism.[2] These projects included the defense of academic freedom, promotion of civil liberties during wartime, answering the full-throated attacks on pragmatic liberalism from both secular and religious critics, and responding to the pedagogical offensive launched by Robert Maynard Hutchins and his disciples. Although Dewey and Hook did not maintain a regimented Leninist conformity on every conceivable issue, their positions were overwhelmingly congruent. Sidney Hook should be properly recognized as the major advocate of Dewey's pragmatic liberal legacy.

I.

Dewey and Hook experienced personally the debilitating effects of the Communist infiltration of the labor movement, particularly teachers' unions. As early as 1935, Dewey endeavored to revoke the charters of American Federation of Teachers (AFT) locals that had been captured by Communist operatives.[3] He was initially rebuffed. Dewey joined Paul Blanshard's Liberal and Labor Committee to Safeguard the American Labor Party.[4] In early 1941, Dewey and Hook actively promoted the successful ouster of two New York locals from the American Federation of Teachers.[5] Hook initiated a petition to form a new organization, the New York Federation of College Teachers, which would send delegates to the AFT national convention to replace the College Teachers' Union locals that were expelled.[6] Dewey served on at least two committees that investigated Communist subversion of labor unions.[7] He sent a message to the AFT convention: "If I were present in person, I should want to pay especial regards to old friends with whom I was associated in the past and who never yielded the least ground in their battles for teachers, for the labor movement in association with teachers and for the freedom of unionism from subjection to foreign political influences."[8] When Sidney Hook later elicited an academic maelstrom when he called for the dismissal of Communist Party members from university faculty (subject to peer review and due process), he was arguably applying longstanding policy advocated by Dewey himself.[9]

Dewey rejected efforts to mobilize teachers on a "class" rather than "social" basis. Democratic freedom of inquiry and not class struggle was the proper frame of reference. Otherwise, Dewey feared that the schools would be co-opted as a tool of propaganda and indoctrination.[10] Scientific method must not be poisoned by a preordained ideological bias. By 1939, Sidney Hook adopted the Deweyan position.[11] In the debate with Trotsky over "means and ends," Dewey charged that Trotsky fanatically asserted that class struggle was both a scientific law of historical change and a necessary means to bring about the desired change. This precluded a scientific examination of whether the violent means employed would actually promote the betterment of mankind.[12] Persuaded by Dewey's argument for experimental intelligence, Hook gravitated toward social democratic reformism. However, rather by acquiescing to the status quo, Dewey insisted that his position was the most radically democratic.[13]

In 1934 Dewey explained why he wasn't a Communist. He declared, "as an unalterable opponent of Fascism in every form, I can not be a Communist."[14] Communism and fascism were twin species of totalitarianism that were largely identical in practice. He predicted that they might well become aligned militarily.[15] Dewey and Hook collaboratively founded the Committee for Cultural Freedom (CCF) in 1939, mounting a direct attack on the Popular Front by including the Soviet Union among totalitarian states. After the *Nation* published an infamous letter (August 26, 1939) signed by over four hundred intellectuals denouncing the Committee for

Cultural Freedom, it is notable that only two of the signers recanted their position after the Nazi-Soviet pact. This renders ever more implausible the contention that party members and fellow travelers were simply politically innocent progressives energized by a more authentic, resolute attachment to the laboring masses.[16] In actuality, the CCF functioned effectively as a means to awaken gullible sympathizers by unmasking party tactics and its various front group operations. During this period, Hook engaged numerous Stalinist apologists in public debate, including Corliss Lamont, Freda Kirchwey, Upton Sinclair, George Soule, and Frederick Schuman. He claimed that Lenin's legacy resulted in a Russia that was less free than it was under the czars.[17] After the Nazi-Soviet pact, Dewey ostensibly resigned from the CCF, wrongly believing that the Popular Front had self-destructed and therefore the Committee had fulfilled its original purpose. However, in May 1940 he still referred to himself as a member of the Committee for Cultural Freedom in the *New York Times*.[18] Far from renouncing Sidney Hook's hard anti-Communism, Dewey contemporaneously became a contributing editor of the staunchly anti-Communist *New Leader.*

After US belligerency, Dewey and Hook both fought the surfacing of a New Popular Front. In January 1942, Dewey wrote a letter to the *New York Times* indicting Joseph Davies' book, *Mission to Moscow*, as vicious propaganda crafted to cultivate a myopic love affair with Stalinism. Dewey stated that "it is possible to rejoice in Russian victories over a common enemy without idealizing a reign of terror. Never before have democratic peoples been asked to idealize despotism because its political interests happened to coincide with theirs."[19] This theme was reiterated by Hook's article, "Russia's Military Successes Do Not Whitewash Crimes at Home."[20] When the book was reincarnated into a major Warner Brothers movie in 1943, Dewey charged that it was worse than the book in its gross historical distortions. It amounted to totalitarian propaganda for mass consumption.[21] Corliss Lamont, chairman of the National Council of American-Soviet Friendship, held a New York rally that gave an award to the producers while identifying critics of the film as unpatriotic purveyors of "anti-Soviet propaganda" who were undermining Allied morale. Following Dewey's lead, Sidney Hook signed a letter denouncing the film.[22] Despite his courageous out-of-step stance as leader of the anti-Stalinist Left, Hook has been maligned for "losing his nerve."[23] Meanwhile, Dewey emerged as a radical icon who became alienated from Hook's "obsession" with Communist totalitarianism. The evidence weighs heavily against this contention.

II.

After the outbreak of belligerency in Europe, Hook initially advocated US neutrality. Along with Dewey, he held that emphasis should be placed upon preserving and extending democracy "here at home." During the 1930s, Hook opposed the collective security arrangements associated with the Popular Front while voicing fears of the potential effects of military mobilization on life in the United States. In October 1939 he proclaimed, "Personally, I believe that the cause of democratic socialism will suffer if we become involved in war. But support or opposition to war is not the acid test of differentiation among socialists but rather the method we have used in reaching our conclusion."[24] In an address that also celebrated Dewey's eightieth birthday, Charles Beard reiterated Dewey's assertion that the future of the United States should be constructed by its own distinctive civilization, not European ideologies or commitments.[25] Hook identified the preservation of civil liberties and enhanced, informed political participation as the most critical priorities. Both Dewey and Hook attacked the Dies House

Un-American Activities Committee investigation of alleged "subversive" influences in US textbooks.[26] This stance was particularly valorous because Dewey himself was publicly vilified as "un-American."[27] With Dewey, the Committee for Cultural Freedom defended Bertrand Russell's right to teach at the City College of New York.[28] The CCF even supported Communist Earl Browder's right to speak at Harvard University. John Dewey condemned Nicholas Murray Butler, Columbia University president, when Butler proposed that all faculty who disagreed with his position on the war should resign.[29] Instead of promoting a moratorium upon criticisms of governmental policy, Dewey and Hook persisted in defending essential freedoms.

On the labor and race issue, Dewey protested racial segregation in the US military, terming it "an insurmountable barrier to human decency."[30] He called for compliance of companies receiving defense orders with the National Labor Relations Board Act. Over five hundred AFL union officers also signed the petition.[31] Hook was attacked by Max Shachtman's Workers Party as a "social-patriot" because of Hook's advocacy of US belligerency. The Trotskyite line consisted of conducting a civil war within countries trying to defeat Hitler. Hook characterized this as a "criminal absurdity."[32] During the war, Hook articulated his prescription for socialists: work for an independent labor party, maintain critical autonomy from the Roosevelt administration, unambiguously support the war while championing democratic liberties, and promote social democratic labor parties in Europe as a means of postwar reconstruction.[33] By contrast, James Cannon (of the Socialist Workers Party) advocated election of officers by rank-in-file soldiers, worker control of war industries, military training by "working-class" organizations, and enforcement of labor's right to strike during wartime.

Another component of Hook's initial war policy was support for the Ludlow Amendment.[34] A national referendum on war had long been part of the agenda of the antiwar Left. Robert LaFollette's presidential platform in 1924 advocated the war referendum measure.[35] During the 1930s, it was packaged with other neutrality legislation as a failsafe device to keep the United States out of war.[36] Large majorities of the US public supported this legislation.[37] Norman Thomas supported this measure, urging that eighteen-year-olds also be allowed to vote.[38] Thomas would continue to lobby for the war referendum up to Pearl Harbor.[39] What prompted Hook to endorse this national referendum? First, it would provide a litmus test to determine which politicians actually desired to keep the United States out of war. Second, a national public debate on the critical issue of war could be a robust exercise of democracy. Third, Hook maintained the Deweyan position that democratic ends required democratic means for their realization. Hook's theory of democracy entailed that citizens, through consent and majority rule, determine by which laws they ought to be governed. He trusted the fallible will of majorities more than that of "expert" elites. In fact, Hook maintained that a democratically enfranchised citizenry must have ultimate authority over the policy prescriptions of the experts. Earlier, advocating the outlawing of war proposal, Dewey remarked, "The world has suffered more from leaders and authorities than from the masses."[40] The classical antidemocratic argument, dating back to Plato, perpetually consigned the population to a childlike servility; they were simply too ignorant to be capable of self-government. Hook argued that minorities were no more reliable historical depositories to protect individual rights than majorities; indeed, they were probably less reliable. His proposal insisted upon educating a more enlightened majority and more accountable elected officials. By contrast, Reinhold Niebuhr opposed the war referendum, claiming that war was the policy area where pure democracy was "most perilous and least applicable."[41]

Hook applied logically the principle of popular control to judicial review. He cited Felix Frankfurter as recognizing that "judicial review is a deliberate check upon democracy through an organ of government not subject to democratic control."[42] Hook charged that the court maintains that pretense of knowing the will of the legislature better than the legislature itself. Although he provided an extended historical analysis of the Constitution, his most substantive argument was an analytical application of the theory of democracy. Hook's test of the democratic process entailed how resolutely citizens accepted the legitimacy of the majority outcome even if it was contrary to their specific position. He reiterated that "the cure for the evils of democracy is better democracy."[43] Government by consent does not claim omniscience but is self-corrective. Hook should be characterized as a "radical democrat."

III.

Both Hook and Dewey supported Norman Thomas for president in 1940.[44] By then Thomas had argued that (1) the European war consisted of a morally ambiguous clash between rival imperialisms, (2) US participation in the war was a graver threat to democratic freedoms than Adolf Hitler, (3) Roosevelt was disingenuously leading an unwilling people into full belligerency, and (4) socializing the economy would ameliorate the conditions that incubated totalitarianism. During 1940, a schism emerged in socialist ranks over the war issue. The Social Democratic Federation of New York announced, "unless the totalitarian regimes are crushed, civilization can not be preserved—this is the issue now. As Social Democrats, true to our tradition, we abhor war. But there is one thing that is far worse than war and that is slavery. The preservation of our own liberties depends on the defeat of Hitler's Germany."[45] As president of the League for Industrial Democracy (1940–41), John Dewey presided over a conference in which Norman Thomas insisted that war would surely lead to fascism in the United States. Thomas also opposed military conscription.[46] Both sides on the war were represented, which typified Dewey's ambivalence. Dewey opposed the draft, along with Norman Thomas.[47] However, in May 1940 he wrote to William Ernest Hocking that "a policy of 'appeasement' will not work any better in my judgment with the old totalitarian institution than it has with newer ones. Every weakening will be a signal for new attacks."[48] Dewey propounded the theme of preserving the US way of life "here at home" and providing a model of democracy for the rest of the world.[49] In early 1941 he would gravitate toward intervention.

After the fall of France, Hook directly attacked the Thomas pacifist-isolationist stance on the war. The defeat of capitalist democracies would be disastrous for the socialist movement. Independent labor organizations and political liberties would be obliterated. Hook crystallized the issue to the following alternatives for socialists: either devote their energies to help the democracies win or to oppose them and thus undermine their struggle against fascism. The first *may* lead to totalitarianism; the second *will* lead to totalitarianism.[50] Hitler possessed the intent, and with the mobilization of the resources of a nazified Europe and a few technological inventions, he could acquire the capability of attacking the United States. Why wait until a direct attack on US territory, when the margin of security is further eroded, before addressing the threat? Hook advocated sending immediate military and economic aid to Britain. He acknowledged that this policy could lead to full belligerency. But why should socialists oppose this? Can one argue that British socialists are in no better position than French socialists? Is there a "moral equivalence" between Hitler and Roosevelt? Hook responded with a "so what" to the charge that this was a policy of the "lesser of evils." Political policy stances that fail to scrutinize the likely consequences are an exercise in doctrinal fanaticism. In this specific instance, they are suicidal. Nonetheless, Hook indicated that the war policy was his only disagreement with the Socialist Party and voiced his intention to vote for Norman Thomas.[51]

In January 1944, Hook warned that the postwar world would be shaped by the location of Stalin's armies and not pretentious diplomatic declarations. He accused the liberal press in the United States of a "will to illusion."[52] Hook called upon social democrats to maintain a constant criticism of the betrayal of democratic aspirations. Likewise, Dewey protested the effort to sell out Poland. Dewey and Hook detected the hypocrisy of those who castigated any appeasement of Hitler but were now thumping for appeasement of Stalin. Avoidance of war became the fashionable diplomatic mantra.[53] Dewey and Hook were among the earliest formulators of the postwar policy of containment.

IV.

The rise of Nazism, coupled with the ever-darkening clouds of war, led many to ask about the root cause of the failure of Western society to confront decisively this menace to democratic civilization. From a variety of directions, pragmatic liberalism was targeted as the parasitic influence that had enervated the West's will to resist. This was expanded into critiques of Dewey's alleged pernicious influence over public education. Reinhold Niebuhr and Lewis Mumford opportunistically capitalized upon the war climate to mount their assault upon "pragmatic liberalism."[54] Meanwhile, Mortimer Adler and Robert Maynard Hutchins linked Dewey's scientific secularism to relativism, materialism, and fascism. Collectively, this assault, according to Hook, had placed liberalism everywhere on the defensive.[55] Despite some collaborative essays by Hook and Dewey, Hook assumed the formidable task of answering these attacks.[56]

On September 10, 1940, the Jewish Theological Seminary held a Conference on Science, Philosophy, and Religion in Their Relation to the Democratic Way of Life. This conference would be held annually throughout the war. Over five hundred academics participated in the 1940 event, including Harold Lasswell, Pitirim Sorokin, Robert MacIver, Henry Overstreet, Jacques Maritain, Albert Einstein, Mortimer Adler, and Sidney Hook.[57] Organized by Rabbi Louis Finkelstein, the conference endeavored to mount a common defense of democracy against the rise of totalitarianism. Not surprisingly, ideological fault lines surfaced over whether religion or science offered the proper foundation for democracy. Einstein further roiled the meeting by advocating a Spinozistic religion without a personal God. Dr. Finkelstein responded by accusing Einstein of making pedestrian "absolute" judgments outside of his specific area of expertise. Jacques Maritain warned ominously that an education that prioritized science over philosophy and theology contained the seeds of fascism.[58] The conference midwifed a bland statement of nonoverlapping magisterial authority: scientists established truth based upon experimental proof while allowing theologians to speculate in areas that transcended empiricism. However, the scientists refused to concede that such speculations provided any verifiable knowledge. Both sides congratulated each other on the capacity to model democratic tolerance.[59]

The spirit of decorum was shattered by two former students of Dewey, Mortimer Adler and Sidney Hook. In his manifesto, "God and the Professors," Adler charged, "the most serious threat to democracy is the positivism of the professors, which dominates every aspect of modern education and is the central corruption of modern culture. Democracy has much more to fear from the mentality of its teachers than from the nihilism of Hitler. It is the same nihilism in both cases, but Hitler's is more earnest and consistent, less slurred by subtleties and queasy qualifications and hence less dangerous." Though Adler was a war interventionist (unlike Robert Maynard Hutchins), he recycled Hutchins's charge that the United States' major enemy was within, a secular-scientific "fifth column."[60] Hook termed Adler's invective as "not only false but irresponsible." He replied that Adler's set of absolute metaphysical propositions would ultimately liquidate the academic freedom of those that disagreed with them.[61] In addition, Adler attacked the conference itself for nurturing an attitude of tolerance, which betrayed an "indifference about the truth." The battle between the perennialists and the pragmatists would rage throughout the war.

At the second annual conference, participants at the Columbia University session were able to draft a common credo. It announced that all civilized government rested upon "the dignity and worth of the human personality."[62] Furthermore, even scientific agnostics conceded that "American democracy may accurately be described as having roots in the Jewish and Christian religious traditions, both of which have clearly and forcefully stressed the principle of human dignity and worth."[63] With Dewey as honorary chairman, Hook organized the Scientific Spirit and Democratic Faith conference as a counterinitiative.[64] Its statement warned of the political and ideological threats against democracy internally. At its second annual conference, Dewey attacked Hutchins's effort to bifurcate vocational and liberal arts education. Not only was it a return to feudalism but an authoritarian attempt to capture public education.[65] Meanwhile, Sidney Hook wrote a critical commentary on the national radio broadcast, aired by the Mutual Broadcast System, promoting the Adler-Hutchins agenda.[66] On a higher level of civility, Hook and Maritain exchanged views on the foundations of the democratic faith.[67] Throughout his career, Hook defended vigorously the secular humanist perspective.[68]

While Dewey privately voiced objections to criticisms from the Mumford-Niebuhr-MacLeish-Frank circle, Sidney Hook engaged the battle publicly.[69] Mumford's strident attack on "pragmatic liberalism" and the scientific temper leveled the irresponsible charge that this outlook was responsible for the rise of fascism. In addition to abetting the irrationalist cultural forces that he claimed to be fighting, Mumford proposed a comprehensive program for suppressing the civil liberties of those whom he suspected of disagreeing with him. Hook dissected the flaws inherent in Reinhold Niebuhr's theology but generously credited Niebuhr with more enlightened political positions. Though they shared many common political causes, Niebuhr's theory of democracy was radically at odds with the Hook-Dewey position.[70] Niebuhr praised Roosevelt's Machiavellian tactics in maneuvering the United States into the war despite overwhelming public opposition. Niebuhr maintained that democratic ends required undemocratic means for their realization.[71] It might be to Hook's credit that neither Mumford nor Niebuhr actually responded in print to Hook's critique.

V.

During World War II, Dewey's and Hook's outlooks converged both philosophically and politically. This shared vision included (1) advocacy of experimental intelligence as the means to knowledge; (2) a critical defense of imperfect democracy against totalitarianism; (3) an embrace of socialist reforms, not revolution; (4) opposition to Communist Party subversion in the teaching profession; (5) rejection of the Popular Front and Stalinist apologetics; (6) vigorous protection of freedom of inquiry and civil liberties; (7) the battle against religious influences in US public life; (8) eventual support for intervention in World War II; (9) legitimating public policies upon a "social," not a "class" basis; (10) a critique of elitism and procedural democracy in lieu of an active, informed citizenry; and (11) promotion of anti-Communist labor movements, both at home and abroad, as a bulwark of democracy. Though some forage ceaselessly to decipher a distance between Dewey and Hook, these are more the effect of temperament than differences over first principles. As a public intellectual and academic statesman who applied the pragmatic liberal perspective of problems of men, Hook transmitted the Deweyan legacy with passion, brilliance, and courage.

NOTES

1. Sidney Hook, *John Dewey: An Intellectual Portrait* (New York: John Day, 1939). I am grateful for the cooperation of the Hoover Institute in forwarding me materials from the Sidney Hook Papers.

2. See William Barrett, *The Truants* (New York: Doubleday, 1982), p. 85. In response to Philip Rahv's remark, Barrett immediately added that "it has to be said now with the clarity of hindsight that the one note at which he was perpetually hampering away was a momentous one."

3. John Dewey, "Teachers and Labor," *Social Frontier* 2 (October 1935): 7; John Dewey, "Class Struggle and the Democratic Way," *Social Frontier* 2 (May 1936): 241–42; Heywood Broun, "Dewey Finds Communists in the CIO," *New Republic* 93 (January 12, 1938): 280. On espionage carried out by Communist Party members, see John Earl Haynes and Harvey Klehr, *Venona: Decoding Soviet Espionage in America* (New Haven: Yale University Press, 1999), p. 487.

4. "Blanshard Scores Labor Left Wing," *New York Times*, March 7, 1940, p. 11. Hereafter referred to as *NYT*.

5. "25 Educators Back Union Ouster from American Federation of Teachers," *NYT*, February 28, 1941, p. 21.

6. "Anti-Red Teachers Lining Up Quickly," *NYT*, June 16, 1941, p. 17; see Sidney Hook, "The Basic Values and Loyalties of Communists," *American Teacher* 25 (May 1941): 4–6; "Red Teacher Purge Is Hailed by Union," *NYT*, May 9, 1941, p. 25; "Teachers Uphold Ouster of 'Reds,'" *NYT*, August 24, 1941, p. 18; "Teachers Seen Tied to Red Party," *NYT*, March 4, 1941, p. 25.

7. See Gary Bullert, *The Politics of John Dewey* (Amherst, NY: Prometheus Books, 1983), pp. 130–31.

8. "Teachers Uphold Ouster of 'Reds.'"

9. The literature on this issue is immense, though in the final analysis the differences seem rather minimal. Dewey maintained that fellow travelers, instead of avowed Communists, were a greater threat to the process. See John Dewey, "Communists as Teachers," *NYT*, June 21, 1949, p. L24.

10. John Dewey, "Class Struggle and the Democratic Way," *Social Frontier* 2 (May 1936): 241–42; John Childs, "Democracy, Education, and Class Struggle," *Social Frontier* 2 (June 1936): 274–78.

11. Sidney Hook, "John Dewey at Eighty," *New Leader* 22 (October 28, 1939): 5.

12. See John Dewey, "Means and Ends," in *Their Morals and Ours: Marxist versus Liberal Views on Morality*, ed. George Novack (New York: Pathfinder Press, 1973), pp. 70–73. Christopher Phelps, *Young Sidney Hook: Marxist and Pragmatist* (Ithaca, NY: Cornell University Press, 1997), p. 189, claims that Hook assisted in formulating Dewey's response.

13. John Dewey, "Democracy Is Radical," *Common Sense* 6 (January 1937): 10–11; "Dewey Rebukes Those Liberals Who Will Not Look into Facts," *New Leader* 20 (May 14, 1937): 4, 7.

14. John Dewey, "Why I Am Not a Communist," *Modern Monthly* 7 (April 1934): 135.

15. See Agnes Meyer, "The Significance of the Trotsky Trial: Interview with John Dewey," *International Conciliation* (February 1938): 57.

16. See Bullert, *The Politics of John Dewey*, p. 140.

17. Sidney Hook, "Russia's Democracy Denied," *NYT*, December 28, 1939, p. 20. On a related note, Dewey offered sympathy and support

217

for Nationalist China. He supported a boycott of Japan while serving on an advisory board headed by Madam Chiang Kai-shek: "Butler, Dr. Dewey Honored by China," *NYT*, December 26, 1939, p. 20; "Open Cultural Institute," *NYT*, February 23, 1939, p. 10. After the war, a trip was arranged for Dewey by the Chinese premier to serve as a catalyst for anti-Communist forces: T. V. Soong, letter to John Dewey, November 15, 1945. Dewey, letter to Sidney Hook, September 6, 1950, revealed that he supported Chiang as a "lesser of evils." Letters cited available in the John Dewey Papers, Morris Library, Southern Illinois University, Carbondale.

18. John Dewey, "Investigating Education," *NYT*, May 6, 1940, p. 12.

19. John Dewey, "Russia's Position," *NYT*, January 11, 1942, p. E7; Arthur Pope, "Dewey Disputed," *NYT*, January 18, 1942; John Dewey and John Childs, "Can We Work with Russia?" *Social Frontier* 8 (March 15, 1942): 79–80. Dewey proposed that the time to discuss war aims with Stalin was when Stalin was most vulnerable. Childs, "Dr. Dewey on Our Relations with Russia," *Social Frontier* 8 (April 15, 1942): 194, was shocked when Dewey implied that a war against Stalinism might be mandated before a genuine peace could emerge. See Bullert, *The Politics of John Dewey*, pp. 192–94.

20. Sidney Hook, "Russia's Military Successes Do Not Whitewash Crimes at Home," *New Leader* 25 (June 1942): 5.

21. John Dewey and Suzanne LaFollette, "Several Faults Are Found in 'Mission to Moscow' Film," *NYT*, May 9, 1943, p. E8.

22. "A National Scandal—Critics Hit 'Submission to Moscow,'" *New Leader* 26 (May 29, 1943): 5, 7; "Davies' 'Mission to Moscow' Praised at Rally," *NYT*, May 21, 1943, p. 4. See Arthur Pope, letter to the editor, *NYT*, May 11, 1943, p. E14, which verged on indicting Dewey for treason.

23. See Phelps, *Young Sidney Hook*, pp. 218–28; Robert Westbrook, *John Dewey and American Democracy* (Ithaca, NY: Cornell University Press, 1991), p. 494; Robert Westbrook, "Stream of Contentiousness," *Nation* 244 (May 27, 1987): 726–30. On calculating the militancy of Dewey's anti-Communism, see Bullert, *The Politics of John Dewey*, pp. 127–45, 191–203. Also resisting the popular tide, Dewey and Hook worked to promote a democratic Germany with Reinhold Niebuhr and

Paul Tillich. They protested the deportation of Sudeten Germans from Czechoslovakia. Rex Stout vilified their efforts as another "German trap." He charged, "The 'Salvage Germany' propagandists dare to come out with the warning that we should not 'base the reconstruction of Europe on the enslavement of the German people.' There is no better proof that these propagandists have not faintest idea about the American concepts of justice and morals." "Council for Democratic Germany Found by Refugee Leaders Here," *NYT*, May 3, 1944, p. 10; Sidney Hook, "Hitler's Spirit Still Lives: Czechoslovaks Perpetuate Atrocities against Sudeten Germans," *New Leader* 28 (October 6, 1945): 8; Sidney Hook, "Total Condemnation: Denunciation of All Germans Unfair to Anti-Nazis," *NYT*, June 10, 1945, p. 8. Louis Finkelstein, "Religion Need for Germany," *NYT*, August 11, 1945, p. 12, argued that only a religious revival could salvage Germany after the war: "The whole world knows and will long remember that the only institutions in Germany which offered effective resistance to the Nazis were those of religion. The fact was well understood by the Nazis themselves as is evidenced by the rapidity with which Catholic priests and Protestant ministers joined Jewish rabbis in concentration camps."

24. Hook, "Dewey at Eighty," p. 5. For an account of the Left's movement from nonintervention to war, see "Neutralism and the Depression," in Bullert, *The Politics of John Dewey*, pp. 147–70.

25. "Beard Warns U.S. to Guard Heritage," *NYT*, October 22, 1939, p. 17. Scant evidence exists to validate the notion that Randolph Bourne's critique of Dewey's support for World War I provided a major catalyst for Dewey's initial neutrality toward World War II. Dewey's position was predicated upon the consequences of a German victory and not a naive faith that Allied war aims were harmonious with US democratic ideals. In "What America Will Fight For," *New Republic* 12 (August 15, 1917): 66–67, he proclaimed, "Not until the almost impossible happens, not until the Allies are fighting on our terms for democracy and civilization will that [end of hesitation] happen." On the contrary, Bourne, *War and the Intellectuals* (New York: Harper and Row, 1965), p. 5, argued that "all that can be done is to try to keep your country out of situations where such expressive releases occur." Bourne contended that the "war tech-

nique" was inexorable and escaped human effort at rational control. Robert Westbrook, *John Dewey and American Democracy*, p. 208, insisted that Bourne, not Dewey, provided the authentic pragmatic analysis of the war. Bourne was more Deweyan than Dewey himself. Bourne's argument was "grounded not in mere 'amiable sentiment' but a hardheaded, empirical criticism." Where does Bourne offer a strategic-political analysis? For a debate on Dewey's alleged "pacifism," see Gary Bullert, "John Dewey on War and Fascism: A Response," *Educational Theory* 39 (Winter 1989): 71–80; Charles Howlett, "'Twilight of Idols' Revisited: A Reply to Gary Bullert's 'John Dewey on War and Fascism: A Response,'" *Educational Theory* 39 (Winter 1989): 81–84. See also John Diggins, *The Promise of Pragmatism* (Chicago: University of Chicago Press, 1994), pp. 253–56.

26. Sidney Hook, "Fight for Civil Liberties Can Balk 'Totalitarianites,'" *New Leader* 22 (October 7, 1939): 5; "Liberals Ask Dies for 'Front' Inquiry," *NYT*, February 26, 1940, p. 5; John Dewey, "Investigating Education," *NYT*, May 6, 1940, p. 12.

27. See "John Dewey's Aims Held Un-American," *NYT*, October 22, 1939, p. 18.

28. John Dewey, "The Case of Bertrand Russell," *Nation* 150 (June 1940): 732–33; "Educators Protest Ouster of Russell," *NYT*, April 5, 1940, p. 21.

29. "Dr. Butler's Edict Scolded in Senate," *NYT*, October 5, 1940, p. 1.

30. John Dewey, "The Case of Odell Waller," *NYT*, May 19, 1942, p. 18; "A Hearing for Odell Waller," *NYT*, June 11, 1942, C22. In addition to taking up the cause of black discrimination in the South, see "317 Leaders Assail Racial Segregation," *NYT*, December 16, 1943, p. 22. Phelps, *Young Sidney Hook*, p. 210, charges that the CCF failed to defend the rights of US blacks; however, this certainly wasn't true of Dewey.

31. "Demand Labor Act Compliance," *NYT*, October 27, 1940, p. 39.

32. Sidney Hook, "Socialism, Common Sense, and the War," *New Leader* 23 (August 31, 1940): 7; Sidney Hook, "Socialists Face Need of Unified Action," *New Leader* 23 (March 9, 1940): 7; Sidney Hook, "A Rehash of Social-Patriotism," *The Call* (November 25, 1940): 2.

33. Sidney Hook, "The New Failure of Nerve," *Partisan Review* 10

220

(March–April 1943): 167–77. By contrast, Phelps, *Young Sidney Hook*, p. 219, characterizes James Cannon's war policy as "creative." For an examination of the sectarian infighting among various Marxist labor groups, see Alan Wald, *The New York Intellectuals* (Chapel Hill: University of North Carolina Press, 1987), pp. 164–217.

34. "Hook Urges Inclusion of Ludlow Clause in Neutrality Act," *New Leader* 22 (November 4, 1939): 8.

35. "The LaFollette Program," *World Tomorrow* (June 1924): 181.

36. Two treatments of the politics surrounding this issue are Manfred Jonas, *Isolationism in America, 1935–1941* (Ithaca, NY: Cornell University Press, 1966), pp. 159–67; and Robert Divine, *The Illusion of Neutrality* (Chicago: Quadrangle Press, 1962), pp. 219–22.

37. "Referendum on War Is Favored in Survey with 68 Per Cent of Replies for Voting Plan," *NYT*, October 2, 1938, p. 38; "Peace Group Asks Firmer Neutrality," *NYT*, July 18, 1938, p. 3.

38. See Norman Thomas and Bertram Wolfe, *Keep America Out of War* (New York: Frederick Stokes, 1939), p. 11.

39. See *Social Frontier* 7 (November 15, 1941): 43.

40. Quoted in Joseph Ratner, ed., *Characters and Events* (New York: Holt, 1929), 2:623.

41. *Social Frontier* 7 (November 15, 1941): 43. For a comparison of Niebuhr and Dewey on the war, see Gary Bullert, "Dewey and Niebuhr: World War II and the Crisis of Pragmatic Liberalism," *World & I* (June 1987): 669–82; see also Gary Bullert, "Reinhold Niebuhr and *The Christian Century*: World War II and the Eclipse of the Social Gospel," *Journal of Church and State* 44 (Spring 2002): 271–90.

42. Sidney Hook, "Democracy and Judicial Review," in *The Paradoxes of Freedom* (Berkeley and Los Angeles: University of California Press, 1962), p. 67. During the war, Hook discussed the issue of majority rule in "Charles Beard's Political Testament," *Nation* 157 (October 23, 1943): 474–76; and "The Perpetual Debate," *Nation* 159 (December 11, 1943): 709–10.

43. See Robert Talisse, "Sidney Hook Reconsidered," The Pragmatism Cybrary, http://www.pragmatism.org/genealogy/hook.htm (accessed March 24, 2004), on Hook's theory of democracy. See also John Dewey,

"Democratic Ends Need Democratic Means for Their Realization," *New Leader* 22 (October 21, 1939): 3.

44. See "New Group Backs Thomas," *NYT*, August 25, 1940, p. 33; "For Thomas and Krueger," *Nation* 151 (September 28, 1940): 283.

45. "'Right' Socialists Uphold the Allies," *NYT*, April 22, 1940, p. 6.

46. "See Fascism Here if We Enter War," *NYT*, June 17, 1940, p. 8.

47. "Declaration against Conscription," *NYT*, July 9, 1940, p. 4.

48. Bertrand Russell, *The Autobiography of Bertrand Russell, 1914–1945* (Boston: Little, Brown, 1968), p. 355.

49. "Dr. Dewey Pleads for a Better World," *NYT*, November 29, 1940, p. 16.

50. Sidney Hook, "Socialism, Common Sense, and the War," *New Leader* 23 (August 31, 1940): 8.

51. This posture was prefigured by Hook's call for unified action while allowing for open differences of opinion; see Sidney Hook, "Socialists Face Need for Unified Action," *New Leader* 23 (March 9, 1940): 6. Reinhold Niebuhr resigned from the Socialist Party in disgust; see Niebuhr, "An End to Illusions," *Nation* 150 (June 2, 1940): 778–79. Thomas would maintain his nonintervention stance up to Pearl Harbor; see "Split on Going to War," *NYT*, December 6, 1941, p. 4. Both Niebuhr and Hook called upon Stalin to dissolve the American Communist Party as a condition for securing US aid. How could a government expect aid while subsidizing foreign agents? See Sidney Hook, "Moscow Order Dissolving Communist Party in U.S. Would Swing Public Support for Aid for USSR," *New Leader* 24 (October 11, 1941): 4.

52. Sidney Hook, "Appeasement Imperils Peace," *New Leader* 28 (July 21, 1945): 1, 6.

53. Sidney Hook, "The Rebirth of Political Credulity," *New Leader* 27 (January 1, 1944): 4–5; John Dewey, letter to Sidney Hook, March 8, 1945, Sidney Hook Collection, Center for Dewey Studies, Carbondale, Illinois.

54. Gary Bullert, "Dewey's Critics: The Revolt against Scientific Reason," in *The Politics of John Dewey*, pp. 171–90.

55. Hook, "The New Failure of Nerve," reprinted in *The Quest for Being* (New York: Dell, 1963), p. 74.

56. See Dewey, "Anti-Naturalism in Extremis," *Partisan Review* 10 (January–February 1943): 24–39; "Penning-In of Natural Science," *Humanist* 4 (Summer 1944): 157–59; "Challenge to Liberal Thought," *Fortune*, August 1944, pp. 155–57.

57. "Union of Science and Democracy for Betterment Is Urged," *NYT*, September 12, 1940, p. 24.

58. "Religion of Good Urged by Einstein," *NYT*, September 11, 1940, p. 27. Dr. Finkelstein's colleague, Rabbi Mordecai Kaplan, held a naturalistic revisionist outlook strikingly close to that of John Dewey.

59. "Unit of Thinking Termed Bid Task," *NYT*, September 13, 1940, p. 22. A dispute also arose over whether the conference should be titled "Conference of Science, Philosophy, and Religion" or "Conference of Religion, Philosophy, and Science." Diplomacy prevailed when scientists claimed that first mention implied "leadership," whereas theologians asserted that being last in theological processions signified being the "highest dignitary."

60. Mortimer J. Adler, "God and the Professors," *Vital Speeches* 7 (December 1, 1940): 98.

61. Sidney Hook, "The New Medievalism," *New Republic* 103 (October 24, 1940): 602–606.

62. "Personal Ideal Democracy's Key," *NYT*, September 16, 1941, p. 19. See also Lyman Bryson and Louis Finkelstein, eds., *Science, Philosophy, and Religion* (New York: Conference on Science, Philosophy, and Religion, 1943).

63. President Roosevelt also praised the Jewish Theological Seminary's effort to establish the "intimate relationship between Judeo-Christianity and the democratic ideals for which the current war is fought." Roosevelt noted the ecumenical work done during the war that had produced "national solidarity." Finkelstein was a major voice in the National Conference of Christians and Jews, which staunchly supported the war effort. See "Roosevelt Hails Jewish Seminary," *NYT*, November 12, 1942, p. 23. Hook participated in a conference with Eleanor Roosevelt, who feared that antitotalitarian sentiment could lead to persecution of Communists; see "Forum Will Open Its Session Today," *NYT*, October 25, 1939, pp. 1, 2.

64. "Scientists to Confer," *NYT*, May 29, 1943, p. 24.

65. "Educators Attack Hutchins' Theories," *NYT*, May 28, 1944, p. 35.

66. Sidney Hook, "Thirteen Arrows against Progressive Education," *Humanist* 4 (Spring 1944): 1–10; Sidney Hook, letter to the editor, *Humanist* 3 (Spring 1943): 32–38.

67. Jacques Maritain, "The Foundations of Democracy," *Nation* 160 (April 21, 1945): 440–47; Sidney Hook, "The Autonomy of the Democratic Faith," *American Scholar* 15 (December 7, 1945): 105–109.

68. In Adler's autobiography, *Philosopher at Large* (New York: Macmillan, 1977), pp. 185–90, he argued that Hook had never acknowledged how Adler's views had shifted over the years from Dewey being labeled "Public Enemy No. 1" to Adler acknowledging the "genuine worth of Dewey's thought." Both Dewey and Adler's ethical views converge toward Aristotelian naturalism. When reviewing Bloom's *The Closing of the American Mind*, Hook, *Convictions* (Amherst, NY: Prometheus Books, 1990), p. 120, conceded that he would find his own academic freedom more secure under Bloom's followers than his adversaries. The proposed curricula of Bloom and Hook contain major areas of overlap.

69. John Dewey, letter to Max Otto, September 16, 1940, Max Otto Collection, Wisconsin Historical Society, Madison, Wisconsin, confided that he found the possibilities of meaningful dialog with Mumford to be quite remote. See Bullert, "Lewis Mumford: Prophet of the New Age," *South Atlantic Quarterly* 84 (Autumn 1986): 339–50; and Sidney Hook, "Metaphysics, War, and the Intellectuals," *Menorah Journal* 28 (October 1940): 330–31.

70. See Hook, "The New Failure of Nerve."

71. Reinhold Niebuhr, "Christmas Light on History," *Christianity and Crisis* 1 (December 29, 1941): 2.

CHAPTER 10

Polemics, Open Discussion, and Tolerance

Neil Jumonville

s the work of philosopher and public intellectual Sidney Hook still relevant? That is a reverberating question that underlay discussions during the observance of the centennial of his birth. By reviewing his career as a polemicist, I want to suggest that in the age of terrorism, especially in the wake of 2001, Hook is now more relevant than he has been for the last quarter of a century—and maybe longer.

Beginning in the autumn of 2001, after the attacks on New York and Washington, one of the first questions that faced Americans is whether they were obligated to be tolerant of their assailants. This was not a question confronting Americans in December 1942, after the Japanese attack on Pearl Harbor, nor was it a doubt in the 1940s and '50s with respect to adversaries such as the Germans and

Soviets. In the late twentieth century, however, tolerance of "the other" grew from the lessons of the civil rights and other related movements in the 1960s. The value of tolerance was wed to the virtue of cultural diversity, and together they received their own three-day weekend holiday in January. In the increasingly relativistic and anthropological atmosphere of the past few decades, where differences are to be respected instead of judged, tolerance became a justifiably respected pillar of US civil religion, perhaps even eclipsing democracy itself.

But what does it mean for Americans to tolerate their adversaries? That is a lesson that has not yet been taught, and as a result even many adroit intellectuals avoid rather than analyze this puzzle. Americans in their founding documents, if not always in their hearts, honor free speech and dissent, but they are rarely encouraged to honor violent acts. Yet Americans value those people, often in the past considered "others," who have been mistreated by the dominant culture and who have legitimate grievances against mainstream society—grievances that in the past have sometimes boiled over into a violence that might almost be considered excusable. With this lesson in mind, should Americans try to understand—perhaps tolerate—those in the Islamic world who have attacked them?

In the world of terrorism that Americans now face, the work of the philosopher and public intellectual Sidney Hook—whether he was right or wrong—is more relevant than it has been in several decades. As Hook did in the 1940s and '50s, we again are trying to balance a globe scattered with opposing ideologies and are living in a world where some ideologies want to bury others. Hook, as a storied proponent of pragmatism, never had trouble balancing the toleration required to embrace free speech while at the same time defending what in US culture he supported. Whereas Hook's own formula might not be a balance some would want to replicate, others will find it useful.

226

I.

Sidney Hook was part of the talented and contentious group known as the New York Intellectuals, about which much has been written over the past few decades.[1] This collection of scholars, critics, journalists, and editors sported such intellectual sharpshooters as Irving Howe, Philip Rahv, Harold Rosenberg, and Dwight Macdonald. Like many of them, Hook learned the art of polemical battle in the sectarian leftist groups to which they belonged in their youth, in their working-class New York neighborhoods, and at the campus of City College.

Yet the precocious Hook was brash even at Boys High School in Brooklyn during World War I. He once responded to a class proposition on the importance of love of country with the retort, "I have another version," which was that love of country could be a detriment to civilization. His teacher, livid, ordered him out of the classroom. Often, at this young age, he contradicted his instructors with Marxist logic, and, after one such episode, "[T]he teacher punched out a series of zeroes as my grade with such a forceful pencil that he punctured his marking book."[2]

At City College, Hook practiced the art of intellectual combat with fellow leftist students eager to establish ideological leadership credentials by embarrassing each other in lunchtime debates.[3] But he also learned his debating lessons at the knee of philosopher Morris Raphael Cohen, whose courses he took. In class, Hook witnessed Cohen dispatching his students "with a rapier or a sledgehammer—and usually with a wit that delighted those who were not being impaled or crushed at the moment." As Hook later explained, "We became logical hygienists and terrorized our friends and families and especially other teachers with the techniques, and sometimes the pungent expressions, that we picked up observing Cohen in action."[4] The New York Intellectuals grew into a group that cherished dispute, and they contested ideas as one might conceive a hockey game: mixing graceful, fast, and smooth flourishes with bouts of less refined pummeling of each other.

Hook's colleagues saw this combative nature in him. William Barrett, for example, said that once Hook had made up his mind about a subject, "he was aggressive and vocal about it, no matter how unpopular a figure he might cut." William Phillips, phrasing it diplomatically, reported that Hook "never let social considerations stand in the way of his intellectual principles." Irving Howe realized that he and Hook shared this style. Hook "had an amusing need always to have the last word," Howe remembered. "I found it amusing because I wasn't exactly free of it myself."[5]

Others outside the New York Intellectuals also noticed Hook's enthusiasm for dispute. Max Eastman, who had a noted exchange with him, remarked that "Sidney Hook can wield the blackjack, not to mention the rapier, with the best of them."[6] Historian John Patrick Diggins, who first wrote of Hook in *Up from Communism* (1975), later claimed that "Hook was one of the most gifted polemicists of his age," with an "image of intellectual pugnacity" that forever clung to him. Hook, Diggins noted, "seemed to have been born for disputation, and he could seldom resist the urge to annihilate his opponents." Witness the rest of Diggins's description: "A raging rationalist, scrappy, aggressive, and witty, he was the Jake LaMotta of American philosophy, who went the rounds with the best of them (Trotsky, Russell, Einstein) and was never knocked out."[7]

Self-aware, Hook recognized this disputatious trait in himself. He believed it had its roots in his youth, understood that it prompted his choice to become a pragmatist instead of an idealist philosopher, and realized that becoming a pragmatist in turn completed the circle by magnifying his pugnacity. Individuals with a temperament that likes peace and calm, he once said, endorse philosophies of stability, eternity, and theology. "The temperament which enjoys battle," he continued, "for which variety is a genuine good, which values the perplexities that attend the pursuit of incompatible goods as the opportunities for creative action, is likely to follow the vital option of experimentalism."[8] Someone with a personality such as Hook's, that is, could be expected to find pragmatism, experimentalism, and intellectual dispute congenial. In addition, Hook was large enough to make fun of himself. In the midst of a serious article on the theologian Paul Tillich, for example, Hook commented that "on the many occasions on which I have polemized against him, with my usual mildness and restraint," Tillich had always been gracious.[9]

Hook could be a kind and gentle man, very gracious and generous, especially when he wasn't being attacked. William Barrett, a former student and fellow member of the New York Intellectuals, remembered that Hook had a "kindly and paternal regard" for the younger Delmore Schwartz. Daniel Bell said Hook served as a father figure for him, because Hook knew that Bell's father had died when he was young. Even Hook's adversaries admitted he had a warm character.[10] Howe, one of Hook's constant political foes, conceded that Sidney "was amiable, even avuncular." Once, when Howe was in a deep depression, Hook worried that Howe wasn't eating enough and Hook's wife brought chicken soup to Howe, which moved him "to speechlessness."[11] There was nothing like a couple of good, mutual antagonists to make each other feel wanted. Hook's relationship with Howe, as with other of his adversaries, is reminiscent of one of Finley Peter Dunne's stories of his character Mr. Dooley. Dooley declares to his friend Hennessy that "life'd not be worth livin' if we didn't keep our inimies," and Dooley decides about his main enemy, Dorsey, that "wan that hates ye ha-ard an' that ye'd take th' coat off yer back to do a bad tur-rn to, is a luxury that I can't go without in me ol' days." Dooley concludes, "I'll swear off on annything but Dorsey. He's a good man, an' I despise him. Here's long life to him."[12]

229

Occasionally Hook maintained that he didn't seek out battles but that they were thrust on him because no one else was willing to defend important values.[13] Other times he insisted that intellectual battles over principles were necessary in order to understand, preserve, and choose the correct public policies and choices, and he usually was willing to serve as sheriff to make sure the right ideas won.[14] Yet, no matter what he said of his motives for arguing, it is obvious that he relished a fight. An indication of his enthusiasm is that once, when he was explaining the difference between a mere discussion and a real dispute, Hook declared that "fighting, real fighting, is when someone insults you and you kick them in the balls."[15]

Of course the way Hook kicked someone in the balls was verbally. His essays were filled with epithets, many of them deserved. In his opponents' articles and positions Hook found superficiality and ignorance, bare-faced lies, and vulgar self-interest.[16] His antagonists were apologists, sympathizers, subverters, or slavish concealers; they were quislings, or cowardly, or they were posers.[17] They were disingenuous and extreme and irresponsible, or they were fools or betrayers.[18] Some of his adversaries promoted intellectual treason, or capitulation, or appeasement; others demonstrated a failure of nerve; still others were fanatics.[19]

Could dispute be so strident and yet not limit open discussion? It is no surprise that Hook thought so. The example of Morris Cohen, whom Hook felt had been too rough, showed him that when being strident one needed to be courteous as well. One could be tough if the importance of the argument justified it, so long as one was mannerly in the process. "Over the years, I suppose I have acquired a reputation as a polemicist," Hook admitted, "but my polemics have always been in response to criticism or in defense of the causes in which I was involved. I have never wittingly done gratuitous hurt to anyone." It is fine to inflict pain so long as it isn't more than is required.

230

Other rules of rough engagement include that one should win an argument through debate, not by the repression of your opponent's speech.[20] In addition, one should not use physical force in an argument unless it is to stop the force used by an adversary. Hook deplored the violence and disruption used by the student radicals of the 1960s and warned them that "a blow never communicates properly."[21] But he thought that to use force to stop the unwarranted use of violence by an opponent is an intelligent decision, so he recommended that university administrators ask police to stop disruption by student groups. In selected contexts, that is, Hook believed force is permitted by the ethics of dispute and is a smart move.[22]

Zealotry, however, is a trait Hook never welcomed in any dispute. It is not too grand to say that Hook made a career of opposing absolutism. He saw no place in a discussion for a fanatic.[23] The most important role of open discussion in liberal society is to preserve the freedom of future choice and continuing options. Pragmatists, like democrats, can only operate in an open universe of possibilities. So absolutists, whether Communist, Islamic, or Christian, should never be allowed, even by free choice, to put a society in a position that it no longer has free speech or free choice or the ability to reverse its own choice. If the free speech at the heart of the liberal society is used by some absolutists to promote a condition in which free speech or free choice is no longer a continuing option from which to choose, then the continuing grant of free speech to those absolutists is not an absolute right in itself and needs to be weighed in the context of the situation pragmatically.

Another rule of polemics, Hook reported, is that consequences alone can't be a fair test of intentions. Because a person's proposal turns out badly is not evidence that the person was trying to hurt someone. Nor is a good result proof of a good will. According to Hook, both Senator Joseph McCarthy and his opponents engaged in this logic. "One of Senator McCarthy's favorite techniques of argument," he explained, "is to insinuate that, since a policy has been followed by the Kremlin, or approved by the Kremlin, anyone else who advocates such a policy is therewith suspect of being a Soviet agent." Actually, Hook was even more worried that "anti-anticommunist" critics of his, such as Irving Howe at *Dissent*, were using the same tactics on him for allegedly being too close to McCarthy. "Unfortunately," Hook complained, "some of those who are critical of Senator McCarthy's methods do not hesitate to use some of his techniques of argument against those who disagree with them: Because Senator McCarthy says that the Communist party is a conspiracy, therefore anyone who says that the Communist party is a conspiracy is suspect of McCarthyism."[24]

Similarly, poisoned polemical methods such as Lenin used could not be permitted in disputes. These tactics were described by Lenin in the following way: "Such a formulation is calculated not to convince, but to break up the ranks of an opponent, not to correct the mistakes of an opponent but to destroy him. . . . This formulation is indeed of such a nature as to evoke the worst thought, the worst suspicions about the opponents, and indeed, as contrasted with formulation that convinces and corrects, it 'carries confusion into the ranks of the proletariat.'"[25] In the 1950s, when Hook wrote "The Ethics of Controversy" in the *New Leader* magazine, he thought that critics should refrain from tactics such as assuming guilt by association. Yet on this matter he walked a wiggly tightrope line above New York City, because he also believed that guilt by association was a proper tactic if the right evidence existed. Those who opposed all use of guilt by association, he felt, were "failing to distinguish between legal and moral guilt, and between degrees and quality of association—for example, between association by membership and by accidental proximity."[26]

II.

Sidney Hook was also an active proponent of open dialogue. Given his professional values as a pragmatist, it is natural that he should value the free exchange of ideas. Even considering Hook's pronouncements and reassurances about the ethics of polemics, one might wonder whether dispute such as he engaged in—kicking an opponent in the balls and launching epithets—could be this strident and yet still be consistent with encouraging open democratic dialogue. From the vantage of early in the twenty-first century, when speech codes on campus encourage individuals to create a welcome atmosphere for the exchange of ideas, Hook's aggressive approach might seem to muffle free speech by frightening unpopular or weak voices out of the public town hall. Would the plea for a tolerance of others, in the wake of the terrorist attacks of 2001, be drowned out by Hook's aggressive debating style?

Hook's pragmatism actually has much in common with an open-market system of choice. The economic concept of improving products and choices through unhindered competition has its counterpart in the pragmatists' reliance on the free competition of hypotheses as well as the freedom of observers to judge the worth of such hypotheses by their consequences in action. May the best hypothesis, judged by its effects, win. As Paul Kurtz has pointed out, Hook "has descended to the marketplace of ideas and action, and he has not considered it demeaning, or degrading, or any less philosophical to do so."[27] This pragmatic process of competition is based on the scientific method (Charles Peirce was a scientist, after all) of open dialogue utilizing explicit and documented methods, as well as a cooperative rivalry for the best results. This market model is also a feature of the free exchange of ideas, as in the marketplace of ideas analogy often associated with the writings of Thomas Jefferson.

Yet, for all of Hook's enthusiasm for open dialogue, free speech

233

in his opinion was neither a natural right nor an all-or-nothing prospect. Instead, speech should be weighed in the context of the situation pragmatically. The Constitution and the Bill of Rights cover a "complex of freedoms" that must be balanced against each other. As he put it, "Intelligent political life in a democracy consists in resolving conflicts of freedoms in such a way as to strengthen the security of the entire structure of our freedoms." So when one right (a fair trial) clashes with another (freedom of the press) then we need to prioritize them in the context of the circumstances. "It is absurd," he warned, "to speak as if any particular right is absolute or unlimited or can be exercised independently of its effects on social welfare and the whole complex of freedoms."[28]

A right to free speech, for example, does not give a person a right to engage in conspiracy.[29] Not all speech should be free. If it incites to violence or triggers illegal action it should be forbidden. "One may legally advocate repeal of the conscription law or denounce the ban on racial segregation," Hook cautioned, "but one may not urge conscripts to refuse to serve or to desert, or incite a crowd to lynch or riot."[30] Rules must be enforced intelligently, and sometimes even broken. As Hook explained, intelligence involves "the courage to make the new decision, even if it means breaking a rule. *Sometimes* it is necessary to pass a red light to avoid a disastrous accident, and to fight fire with fire." The Bill of Rights is to be considered composed of strategic rights that shouldn't be violated easily. "This is the rule. But here, too," he says, "the rule must be enforced intelligently." These constitutional rights are of first importance but are not absolute. Otherwise it would be "inviting intelligence to abdicate in favor of a few formulas to be mechanically applied." This is a precarious stand to take, but "it is sometimes more dangerous and harmful not to make exceptions." Broad ethical principles lead to a much better legal and moral climate than rigid formulas.[31]

An example of Hook adhering to this logic in practice is found in his battle with the sponsors of the Waldorf Conference in New York in March 1949.[32] It was very representative of Hook's interests (a defense of intellectual freedom and independent thinking) and his style of combat (making sure that all sides were permitted to speak and roughing them up when he thought he should). Cultures and ideas only remained free, he believed, if people fought for them hard, as though those ideas made a difference.

A further connection of Hook's pragmatism to the issue of intellectual freedom is evident in what he once told Max Eastman: "More important than any belief a man holds is the *way* he holds it. Any fool or fanatic can embrace a doctrine. Even if true, it remains *dogma* unless evaluated in light of its alternatives, and the relevant evidence for them. The whole enterprise of intelligence consists in envisaging alternatives before embarking on action."[33] This was important to the way that Hook saw the problems of the Waldorf Conference.

The Waldorf Conference was actually named the Cultural and Scientific Conference for World Peace. The sponsoring agency was the National Council of the Arts, Sciences, and Professions, and Harlow Shapley, a Harvard professor of astronomy, was chairman of the conference. Americans, Soviets, and Western Europeans had been invited. Hook and many members of the New York Intellectuals believed that it was simply a Communist-front conference, which constituted an intellectual hoax. As Hook saw it, the alleged free and intellectual nature of the conference meant that he had an individual right to address the conference as a participant. He asked for but was refused a chance to address the conference, which seemed to confirm his suspicions. Shapley invited Hook to ask a question of a speaker in the three-minute period allotted afterward for questions. But Hook said that didn't constitute a discussion but instead an intellectual fraud. The conference's rigging of the speakers "made honest discussion impossible."[34] And if the conference leaders wouldn't let Hook address the conference, then they were not behaving as responsible intellectuals who were allowing a free exchange of opinions. They were undermining the intellectual vocation by supporting a party-line meeting.

Hook cast his antagonism with the Waldorf Conference as an issue of independent thinking. The main responsibility of a good thinker was to maintain the integrity of his or her opinion. A person needed the freedom to speak honestly, candidly, and heretically. One's analysis had to be untainted from official pressure from outside—such as from the authority of the church or the party. That is, a person had to make up his own mind instead of simply being an unthinking promoter of an official doctrine. Again, as a pragmatist Hook believed that intellectuals needed constantly to test their convictions against their effects in the real world.

As Hook wrote to Einstein years after the conference, "I am old-fashioned enough to believe that truth is the best answer to the propaganda of the lie—not counter-propaganda. But I have learned enough from modern psychology to know that silence is no answer at all."[35] Thus Hook and some others created an opposition group named Americans for Intellectual Freedom and held their own counterconference at Freedom House, near Bryant Park.

Hook said that the real failure of the Waldorf participants was not their endorsement of Communism but "their renunciation of the vocation to think," by which he meant thinking independently. A thinker needed to experiment with ideas and might support incorrect ideas occasionally, so "one should not reproach intellectuals for thinking their way to conclusions which turn out to be false." But "the sin of the intellectuals who fell under Communist domination was that they yielded to this demand and stopped thinking."[36] In Hook's parlance they became absolutists or zealots or fanatics.

When the State Department refused to issue visas to almost all of the Western European delegates to the conference, Hook told the press, "That contrast between our way of life and theirs becomes blurred when our Government refuses entry to foreign nationals of any political persuasion."[37] This statement clearly underlines Hook's commitment to open dialogue. The New York Intellectuals thought the Waldorf participants were not functioning as true, free thinkers because they were blinded by a party line. They were a danger to society and to the life of the mind. But if the State Department refused them entry, then freedom of expression would be hurt even more. Hook's idea was that he should work hard to guarantee the rights of foreigners to enter the country and speak at the conference, but then he could also speak up to oppose and refute everything they had to say.

The Waldorf sponsors, Hook thought, had a duty as intellectuals to make distinctions about the kind of leftism that was free enough to be supported. But at the same time many observers felt that he failed to make the necessary distinctions himself—because he branded all associates of the Waldorf Conference as equally guilty. Hook did not acknowledge that a person could support the Waldorf Conference with hope and integrity. One of Hook's colleagues at NYU in educational philosophy, Theodore Brameld, complained of him, "By the kind of philosophic test which they themselves usually employ to settle important problems—the test of practical consequences—it is entirely plausible to argue that the consequence of their own tactics may turn out to be vastly more injurious to the cause of democracy than any which could possibly follow from sponsorship."[38] Brameld, it seems, believed that Hook's style of polemics and action closed off rather than encouraged open discussion.

Hook answered in his stinging style, "Those who, like Dr. Brameld, remained as sponsors and did nothing whatsoever to prevent Communist domination of the program became accomplices in the perpetration of an intellectual fraud upon the public" but now aim their criticism at people like Hook. "This," he said, "testifies to a bad conscience." In return, Brameld accused Hook of shifting the discussion "from an impersonal level to that of one's own integrity," and Brameld claimed Hook had accused him of "guilt by association."[39]

Freda Kirchwey, editor of *The Nation*, thought that there was nothing wrong with leftists trying to get together at a conference to prevent war. As she said, "If we do not want to fight communism, the only alternative is to deal with it, try to work out ways of accommodation. Most anti-Communists of the Hook school insist that neither they nor this country desire war with Russia. If they are sincere, and I think they are, then they should be wary of rejecting as a frame-up every attempt to talk to Russians or other Communists."[40] Like Brameld, Kirchwey was convinced that Hook's approach derailed rather than furthered open discussion.

Kirchwey asked whether it would have been so bad if Hook actually *had* been denied participation in the conference. Excluding him would not have proved fraud or Communist duplicity. Besides, Kirchwey pointed out, Hook's Americans for Intellectual Freedom (AIF) had an ideological narrowness at its Freedom House counter-conference, too. But Hook wondered how Kirchwey and *The Nation* could presume to speak about intellectual diversity: "As anyone knows who listened to our speakers, especially the noted pacifist A. J. Muste, more differences on foreign policy were expressed than have ever been voiced at the dinner forums of *The Nation* since the days of Oswald Garrison Villard." During their exchange, Hook also accused Kirchwey of a "totalitarian liberalism" that was blind to "red totalitarianism." Furthermore, he charged that her writing during the previous decade had been "a record of intellectual and moral double-dealing."[41]

Again, could Hook's style of argument be this strident and yet be consistent with encouraging open dialogue? Was it compatible with an open marketplace of ideas? As Hook's example in the Waldorf controversy reveals, his tough debating style did not close off open dialogue, and in fact it might have prompted these exchanges. Hook's Waldorf performance shows that the intellectual marketplace requires neither quiet discussion nor lack of commitment on the part of its participants. All figures and opinions need to be able to enter the market, but if that condition is met, there is no hazard in them fighting against each other for priority within that marketplace. Hook felt that when one was convinced of a tentative truth, especially when it was important to the future of humanity, then one should fight as a citizen and empiricist for the right outcome with all one's power—while at the same time being attentive to arguments that might disprove one's convictions. Hook lived for the exchange of ideas. But he didn't feel as though the open exchange of ideas should stop him from hitting his opponent with everything he could possibly muster in a debate. In fact, toughness in debate and openness in debate—although they might seem at odds with each other—went together to help ideas and culture stay free and independent.

III.

The ideas of Sidney Hook about polemics, fighting, and tolerance are now more relevant than ever, although many people will not like what he has to say. What is the lesson of Hook's polemical career for the world in the current age of terrorism?

The cold war, which Hook addressed, and the current struggle of the West with terrorism are very different situations. But the lessons about polemics, open discussion, and tolerance apply equally to each. Talking about the cold war, Hook proclaimed that one might have to decide to fight and lose one's life, because "the best way of saving one's life is sometimes to be prepared to lose it."

239

Fighting for freedom is important. "There is no substitute for intelligence" in an argument, Hook acknowledged. "But intelligence may not be enough," and thus "sometimes intelligence requires the use of force."[42] He was clear that we cannot wish conflict away. Once, Hook told Karl Popper that "pious thoughts cannot turn away flying missiles." He advised Popper that "it is one of the principles of any sane view of politics to *disbelieve* that everything is possible in human affairs."[43] If we do fight, there needs to be a pragmatic and tentative approach such as Reinhold Niebuhr suggested. Niebuhr recommended using a "historical pragmatism" so that we are not "tempted to bring the whole of modern history to a tragic conclusion by one final and mighty effort to overcome its frustrations."[44] Small steps should be taken in conjunction with the enemy through negotiations.

At the end of 2002 the *New York Times* ran an article on tolerance that asked, "Must we be tolerant of those who are intolerant of us?"[45] The piece perfectly echoed some of Hook's concerns forty years earlier. In 1960, Hook had cautioned that "tolerance always has its limits—it cannot tolerate what is itself actively intolerant." A decade later he ridiculed the belief that "true tolerance requires that we tolerate the actively intolerant."[46]

What does the term *tolerance* signify? Even the most tolerant person would not accept incorrect answers to math questions, or stand for genocide, or perhaps even endure a noisy neighbor or the practice of polygamy. If this is the case, is current tolerance only the acceptance of those with whom we feel comfortable—blacks, Buddhists, or gays? Canadian ethicist Mark Wexler asks whether people should be willing to tolerate those who believe terrorism may be "a way to give a voice to the powerless." His response is, "I don't want to be killed by my own liberality," a sentiment that Hook would have endorsed.[47]

As Hook counseled, we need to respect the right of others to

240

talk, but we also have the freedom to be tough in our discussions. We need to understand our adversaries, but, as in the case of Hitler, hatred might be justified even if we comprehend them. We are not obligated to allow perfect freedom or tolerance to madmen. Some differences should be tolerated because variety is good. "But," Hook urged, "a distinction must be made between difference and conflict. Some differences are complementary to each other; some are compatible with each other; some are incompatible."[48] We do not need to tolerate those who are fanatics or zealots and don't tolerate others. Toleration is important to freedom, but it is not as important as freedom itself.

In 1929, when Hook was in Berlin, he concluded that one of the causes of the collapse of the Weimar regime was a liberalism that believed democracy required a tolerance of the intolerant. Hook later quoted Kurt Lewin on this: "It has been one of the tragedies of the German Republic that the democratically minded people who were in power immediately after [World War I] . . . did not know that 'intolerance against the intolerant' is as essential for maintaining, and particularly for establishing a democracy, as 'tolerance for the tolerant.'"[49]

NOTES

1. Alexander Bloom, *Prodigal Sons* (New York: Oxford University Press, 1986); Neil Jumonville, *Critical Crossings* (Berkeley and Los Angeles: University of California Press, 1991); Alan Wald, *The New York Intellectuals* (Chapel Hill: University of North Carolina Press, 1987).

2. Sidney Hook, *Out of Step: An Unquiet Life in the 20th Century* (New York: Carroll & Graf, 1987), pp. 17–23.

3. Irving Howe, *A Margin of Hope* (New York: Harcourt Brace Jovanovich, 1982); Irving Kristol, *Reflections of a Neoconservative* (New York: Basic Books, 1983).

4. Hook, *Out of Step*, pp. 55–58.

5. William Barrett, *The Truants* (Garden City: Doubleday, 1982), p. 84; Howe, *A Margin of Hope*, p. 211; William Phillips, *A Partisan View* (New York: Stein and Day, 1983), p. 134.

6. Sidney Hook, *Political Power and Personal Freedom* (New York: Criterion Books, 1959), p. 349.

7. John Patrick Diggins, "The Man Who Knew Too Much," *New Republic* 203 (December 3, 1990): 27–34.

8. Milton Konvitz, "Sidney Hook: Philosopher of Freedom," in *Sidney Hook and the Contemporary World*, ed. Paul Kurtz (New York: John Day Company, 1968), p. 19.

9. Sidney Hook, *Pragmatism and the Tragic Sense of Life* (New York: Basic Books, 1974), p. 193.

10. Barrett, *The Truants*, p. 214; Jumonville, *Critical Crossings*, p. 215.

11. Howe, *A Margin of Hope*, pp. 211–12.

12. Finley Peter Dunne, *Mr. Dooley in Peace and War* (Boston: Small, Maynard, 1898), p. 99.

13. Hook, *Out of Step*, p. 347.

14. Sidney Hook, "The Ethics of Controversy," in *Philosophy and Public Policy* (Carbondale: Southern Illinois University Press, 1980), pp. 117–18.

15. Jumonville, *Critical Crossings*, pp. 214–15; Neil Jumonville, interview with Sidney Hook, July 15, 1985.

16. Hook, *Out of Step*, pp. 248–49, 579.

17. Ibid., pp. 251, 54, 55.

18. Hook, *Political Power*, pp. 185, 271, 392, 98.

19. Sidney Hook, *Academic Freedom and Academic Anarchy* (New York: Cowles, 1969), pp. 91, 89, 137, 71.

20. Hook, *Out of Step*, pp. 57, 349, 428.

21. Hook, *Academic Freedom and Academic Anarchy*, pp. 85, 142.

22. Hook, *Pragmatism and the Tragic Sense of Life*, p. 23.

23. Ibid., pp. 6, 77; Jumonville, *Critical Crossings*.

24. Hook, "The Ethics of Controversy," p. 121.

25. Ibid.

26. Hook, *Academic Freedom and Academic Anarchy*, p. 33; see also Hook, *Political Power*.

27. Paul Kurtz, ed., *Sidney Hook and the Contemporary World* (New York: John Day, 1968), p. 12.

28. Hook, *Political Power*, p. 270.

29. Hook, *Academic Freedom and Academic Anarchy*, p. 40.

30. Hook, *Pragmatism and the Tragic Sense of Life*, p. 92.

31. Ibid., pp. 68, 91, 93, 96–97.

32. Jumonville, *Critical Crossings*, pp. 1–48.

33. Hook, *Political Power*, pp. 363–64.

34. Sidney Hook, "Waldorf Aftermath—Dr. Hook Protests," *Nation* 168 (April 30, 1949): 511–13.

35. Quoted in Sidney Hook, "My Running Debate with Einstein," *Commentary* 74 (July 1982): 48.

36. Sidney Hook, "Myths of Marx," *Saturday Review*, May 15, 1954, p. 12.

37. Charles Grutzner, "New Protest Sent to Acheson on Ban of Cultural Delegates," *New York Times*, March 23, 1949, pp. 1, 18.

38. Theodore Brameld, "Conference Defended," *New York Times*, April 3, 1949, section 4, p. 8.

39. Sidney Hook, "Stand of the Liberals," *New York Times*, April 3, 1949, p. 28; Theodore Brameld, "Lessons of Cultural Meeting," *New York Times*, April 19, 1949, p. 24.

40. Freda Kirchwey, "Waldorf Aftermath—Miss Kirchwey Replies," *Nation* 168 (April 30, 1949): 512.

41. Freda Kirchwey, "Battle of the Waldorf," *Nation* 168 (April 2, 1949): 377–78; Kirchwey, "Waldorf Aftermath—Miss Kirchwey Replies"; Hook, "Waldorf Aftermath—Dr. Hook Protests."

42. Hook, *Pragmatism and the Tragic Sense of Life*, pp. 25, 23.

43. Ibid., p. 163.

44. Ibid., p. 70; Reinhold Niebuhr, *The Irony of American History* (New York: Charles Scribner's Sons, 1952), pp. 143, 46.

45. Serge Schmemann, "The Burden of Tolerance in a World of Division," *New York Times*, December 29, 2002.

46. Hook, *Academic Freedom and Academic Anarchy*, p. 243; Hook, *Pragmatism and the Tragic Sense of Life*, p. 23.

47. Quoted in Douglas Todd, "The 'Irksome Other,'" *Times Colonist* (Victoria, BC), March 1, 2003.

48. Hook, *Academic Freedom and Academic Anarchy*, p. 137; Hook, *Political Power*, p. xii; Hook, *Pragmatism and the Tragic Sense of Life*, pp. 85, 74.

49. Hook, *Political Power*, p. xv.

PART 3.

REMINISCENCE

CHAPTER 11

Concerning Sidney Hook

Nathan Glazer

f we consider Sidney Hook today, it is almost inevitable that our major interest will be in his role in the long conflict in US intellectual life between, on the one hand, Communists and those sympathetic to Communism and, on the other hand, those who could see no redeeming features in Communism, in Communists, or in Communist sympathizers and saw only confusion or deceit in those who defended Communists or Communist sympathizers. In the wake of the collapse and disintegration of the Soviet Union and the fall of Communism almost everywhere outside the citadels of North Korea and Cuba [as well as China—Ed.], his leadership in this effort may not seem, at the present, the worthy and important enterprise it appeared to those of us engaged in it in the second half of the twentieth century. Almost everyone here is, I assume, younger than two of the members of this panel. Communism defeated and discredited may not appear the threat it was when it controlled half the world or more. The issue of what kind of a threat Communism was and what did it justify in the effort to counter it is still a question with some legs. Some scholars and analysts today have raised what they call "the lesser evil" question, most prominently perhaps the expert on Soviet Russia and Communism Martin Malia: Was Communism, they ask, any lesser an evil than Nazism? And if it was no lesser an evil, how do we explain the general tolerance in intellectual, scholarly, and academic circles for those who look with some sympathy on Communism, as against the complete withdrawal of tolerance from anyone who showed any sympathy with Nazism or collaborated with it in any way? I don't know where Sidney Hook would stand today on this issue, but the reason he becomes controversial and we talk about his heritage is because of the possibility he would stand with Martin Malia on this issue and might assert, yes, Communism was no lesser an evil.

I was associated with Sidney Hook in this conflict and did not fully agree with all the stands he took, but on the whole I insist that he played a key role in a very important issue, the most important issue that the world and we faced in the second half of the twentieth century. Hardly anyone disputes today that Communism in practice simply turned countries into prison houses—as North Korea still is today—and denied any iota of freedom, political or intellectual or academic. For decades, however, it was seen by many intellectuals as an enlightened and progressive system, something to be supported, spread, and protected. From today's perspective, with new issues engaging us, it may be hard to recognize how important this fight was. It had to be waged in intellectual life generally, in colleges and universities, in publishing houses and magazines, in unions and community organizations. Much of our current scholarly work on this issue is subsumed under the rubric of

McCarthyism, and this quite distorts the nature of this struggle. Excesses and political opportunism, as exemplified by McCarthyism, did characterize a good part of the fight against Communism. Today our repugnance to McCarthyism—and Sidney Hook found it as repugnant as any liberal or leftist scholar—tends to color the account given in textbooks in US history and in much of the scholarship of the entire spectrum of opinions and attitudes that saw Communism as abhorrent and as a threat. Even if one disagrees with Sidney Hook's positions on specific issues that came up in this long, decades-old struggle in many venues, one has to first make it clear where one stood. I stood with Sidney Hook, something like a soldier in the ranks, on this key issue. I was part of that varied group of ex-Communists, ex-Trotskyists, ex-socialists, as well as many still-committed socialists, who saw the fight against Communism, Communist influence in US intellectual life, and sympathy with Communist influence as a very important one, indeed perhaps the most important one in maintaining integrity, decency, and common rationality in intellectual life.

I will concentrate in this essay on one issue in this extended conflict into which I was drawn by Sidney Hook, as well as on one point of disagreement. I first heard Sidney speak as a teenager, when an older brother took me to Cooper Union for a public talk on, I assume, Marxism or socialism. This must have been in the late 1930s or early '40s. I first began to have contact with Sidney when I began to work on the new magazine *Commentary* in 1945 and met some of the people around *Partisan Review*, with which he was linked. The inner circle of *Partisan Review* had traveled the road from adherence to Communism through Trotskyism and left socialism to a thoroughgoing anti-Communism, but one in which some still considered themselves Marxists and in which all certainly considered themselves—at that time—at the least, socialists.

In those early days at *Commentary* I edited a column titled "The

Study of Man," which dealt with developments in the social sciences. We were once pleased and honored to get a contribution from John Dewey. I never met Dewey—the contribution came by way of Sidney Hook, a friend and contributor to *Commentary*. I recall I was somewhat taken aback to find in the manuscript that Sidney brought us long inserts in his handwriting. I had the impression that Sidney had carte blanche to edit and elaborate on what John Dewey wrote as he, Sidney, thought best. Perhaps I was wrong. Perhaps John Dewey had instructed Sidney to make these additions. No matter. We published the article—there may have been more than one—as Sidney gave it to us, and we never heard any protest from Dewey. Sidney had persuaded John Dewey to chair the commission that went to Mexico to clear Trotsky, in Mexico, of the wild and imaginary charges made against him in the Moscow trials. After the war Sidney was a key figure in organizing the Congress for Cultural Freedom and the American Congress for Cultural Freedom, and I would meet him at the meetings and events the American Congress organized.

There came a time when he asked me to do more than come to meetings and sign statements. In 1955 and 1956 there occurred one of those recurrent upsurges of agitation over the Rosenberg case. The Rosenbergs had already been executed. Morton Sobell, who was convicted with them, was in jail. A new book on the Rosenberg case, arguing that they were innocent, had just appeared. Many such have been published over the years. There were meetings and demonstrations in Europe, new appeals here, on the basis of purported new evidence, for Morton Sobell. Justice in the United States, it was charged, was no better than Nazi or fascist justice, in which the innocent were convicted of crimes they did not commit and were put to death. Of course this became a major point in the Communist effort to persuade intellectuals that the United States was not worthy of support in the conflict with the Soviet Union.

Sidney Hook remembered I had been involved in a correspondence in the *New York Times* with Harold Urey, the Nobel Prize–winning scientist who had written a letter to the *Times* arguing that the Rosenbergs were innocent. I had also been troubled by the case, had read the transcript, was convinced they were guilty, and so wrote to the *Times*. In those days, letters to the *Times* could be quite extended—they were not simply, as they are today, mere assertions of opinion. Hook recalled the correspondence, and said, "Nat, this is a big thing in Europe; you must write an article." In a sense, he was acting like a general, deploying his troops for the struggle against Communism, Communist influence, and the lies and distortions used to expand Communist influence.

I read the mass of material that had been presented to the Court in various appeals that had been made to reopen the case of Morton Sobell and read through the transcript of a related case, and my original conviction that yes, the Rosenbergs were guilty, was reaffirmed. I wrote a long article that was published as a supplement to the *New Leader.* I doubt that it had much influence on the way people thought about the case, though many years later, Ronald Radosh, in his authoritative book on the case, did commend my prescience in pointing to obscure details in the trial that would in time, I asserted, strengthen the evidence that pointed to involvement in espionage.

I tell this story because it raises the questions, Did we go too far? Was this fight worth fighting? Yes, the Rosenbergs had committed espionage for Soviet Russia. They had done so out of belief and conviction. They had done so at a time when Soviet Russia was an ally. Their penalty was horribly out of line with the measure of their guilt. Klaus Fuchs, the German atomic scientist at Los Alamos who had done so much more than they had and who was in a position to do so much more, got, as I recall, fourteen years in the United Kingdom and then went off scot-free to do further research on atomic weapons or something related in Communist East Germany. Another scientist at Los Alamos, an American, aided the Russians, was never indicted, skipped the country to pursue research in physics in the United Kingdom, and returned to the United States after the statute of limitations had expired. Others who had done much more than the Rosenbergs were able to escape trial or penalty.

So the case, and our concern to demonstrate their guilt against those who we thought were only concerned to defend Communism and Communists, raises questions as to the Sidney Hook style of anti-Communism. Why were we busy arguing for the guilt of the Rosenbergs, when, some might say, we should have been arguing against the grossly unfair death sentence? I would make two points on that. Sidney Hook was not for the death sentence, I was not for the death sentence. But to us the issue was the use of the Rosenberg case to paint the United States as a cruel and near-fascist state and to obscure the reality that yes, there was a world conflict between a totalitarian system that deprived men of freedom and an opposing group of nations, led by the United States, that defended freedom and democracy and stood for a more humane and decent society. Those who argued for the innocence of the Rosenbergs were defending the interests of Communism in this conflict. That seemed to us at the time to be the first issue to make clear: that they were truly guilty.

Upon thinking of Sidney Hook's centennial, I looked up what Sidney Hook had to say about the Rosenberg case in his autobiography. I assumed he was against the death sentences but I did not recall whether he had made any public statement on the matter, expressed himself on the matter. There are a few references to the Rosenberg case in *Out of Step,* and in almost every one Hook makes clear that yes, they were guilty, but no, they did not deserve the death sentence. Indeed, the Congress for Cultural Freedom sent a message to President Eisenhower asking for clemency for the Rosenbergs.

We did not disagree about the Rosenbergs. Later, when I was asked to contribute to a Festschrift for Sidney Hook, I went back to the case and explored at length an issue that was tangential in my original article, that is, the death sentence, around which there are many issues that must ever be troubling.

The issue on which Sidney Hook gained a reputation for an unbending and inhuman logic was that of whether Communists should be allowed to teach in colleges and universities. Sidney's argument was that if one became a Communist, a party member, with all the commitment that party membership required, one gave up one's intellectual freedom and was obligated to follow the party line, regardless of what one thought. But a teacher in a college or a university, to deserve academic freedom, has to be able to exercise independence of thought; ergo, he or she did not have a right to teach. This is the way Sidney's position was generally summarized. But there were many qualifications to this rather crude logic; Sidney spells them out in his autobiography. I have not been able to check back to the writings at the time to see if some of these nuances and qualifications were as marked as they are in his later account. But he writes in his autobiography, "I defended the rights of teachers and scholars to hold any views at all, including Communism and fascism. I have always opposed federal or state investigations of teachers and teaching in our academic institutions. . . . I have argued that the faculties themselves must uphold the standards of professional ethics and must move against those who violate them only under the rules of due process. I have refused to appear before any Congressional committees investigating Communists and from the outset vigorously criticized the exaggerated and irresponsible claims and behavior of Senator Joseph McCarthy."[1] He writes that when he was subpoenaed before the Rapp-Coudert committee in New York State in 1940 or 1941, he was asked two questions. The first was whether he could identify, through personal knowledge,

253

any member of the teaching staff of City College who was a member of the Communist Party (CP). He answered no. The second question was, "What is dialectical materialism?" Sidney's response was that one could be a dialectical materialist without being a Communist, but the converse was not possible.

And, further detailing his position, he writes, "Even though I believed that membership in the CP rendered an individual unfit, because of his violation of professional ethics, to be a member of the teaching staff, I did *not* believe that the mere fact of membership should result in automatic dismissal. Faculty committees on professional ethics should not undertake any investigations except in the face of evidence of CP cell activities."[2] This is a respectable position, but the way it came out in practice was not as a defense of the rights of Communist teachers but as giving some legitimacy to their dismissal. The trap the Communists had put us in, as their opponents, was that they denied they were Communists, they insisted they were liberals, and if we argued—as we did—in public, that that was ridiculous, X or Y was clearly a Communist, in his writings, his teaching, his political and union activities on campus, were we not objectively supporting the dismissal that was, in the atmosphere of the times, inevitable? It was a dilemma. I think Sidney's concern for the truth against lying meant inevitably a downgrading of compassion. For Sidney, it was first necessary to establish the truth. To concern ourselves first with compassion—that this man was going to lose his job—inevitably meant that we shoved aside the responsibility to the truth. Had the Communists openly asserted that yes, we are Communists, we believe thus and so, it would have been easier for us to defend them. In the end it seemed that Sidney and our group of committed anti-Communists were defending the firing of Communist teachers, despite the host of considerations and qualifications that we believed distinguished us from congressional investigators.

Whether it was out of softness or softheadedness on my part, I did not find the matter simple. After all, there were Communists who taught mathematics and physics and Latin—was their teaching affected by Communist Party membership? Yes, Communist Party membership in theory meant giving up one's freedom to think as one wished—but in practice is that what happened? Did E. J. Hobsbaum, whose autobiography is now being reviewed and who maintained his Communist Party membership until the end, think differently or write differently or teach differently because he was a CP member? He thought, wrote, and taught the way he did because he was a Marxist and would have been one even if he had become a Labor Party member.

Sidney, the son of a friend once remarked, both in fear and in awe, had a steel-trap mind. So he did. Sometimes it led to a conclusion that would have been modified had he taken into account more the actual confusions and contradictions of the world. But I will not end on that note. For my generation, he first taught us about Marxism, where it came from, and what it asserted; then he taught us what was wrong with it. And most important, he was unbending in organizing intellectuals to fight the strange intellectual influence exercised by the states that claimed to be based on and to be realizing Marxism in practice but who had actually instituted regimes of inhuman cruelty. To be on the right side of that issue, when so many leading intellectuals were not, is heritage enough.

NOTES

1. Sidney Hook, *Out of Step: An Unquiet Life in the 20th Century* (New York: Harper and Row, 1987), p. 503.
2. Ibid., p. 504.

CHAPTER 12

Sidney Hook's Prescience

Tibor R. Machan

t is not that Sidney Hook was the only one who recognized the vile directions of the Soviet Union early in the twentieth century: certain various Russians saw through the Leninist ruse—for example, Yevgeny Zamyatin, author of the famous dystopian novel *We*, and, of course, Ayn Rand, whose own *We the Living* and *Anthem* made clear note of the horrors of collectivism and whose unabashed defense of capitalism and egoism alienated her from most US intellectuals for the rest of her life.

Sidney Hook, however, was of the US Left. For him to have raised cautionary notes about the Soviet Union was troublesome and difficult. Indeed, even today some famous people remember him not for his courage and prescience but for some alleged capitulation to right-wing sentiments or some alleged obsession with Communism.

How exactly Sidney Hook could be faulted for not regarding Joe McCarthy as an equal to Joseph Stalin is one of those puzzles that will always baffle me, coming as they do from otherwise competent intellectuals and historians.[1] It was Victor Navasky, publisher and one-time editor of the consistently, persistently, and unapologetically left-wing magazine *The Nation*, who articulated one prominent rationalization for treating the Soviets with kid gloves. He did this most explicitly in his well-known book, *Naming Names*—which vehemently attacked the 1950s anti-Communist crusade in the United States while spending hardly any ink on the vicious tyranny that Marxism-Leninism spawned in the Soviet Union—"[There is] the profound difference between Marxists, who identified with the weak and spoke the language of social justice, and fascists, who identified with an elite and spoke the language of racism and violence."[2]

Many intellectuals, among them some who are still hostile to Sidney for his astuteness of seeing the enormous difference between the evils of the two Joes, still hold this not only bizarre but morally quite appalling view. They do not even qualify it by noting that the Soviet Marxists only "spoke" some of the language of social justice but did virtually nothing about it at all, apart from taking some very costly wealth redistribution and social security measures that were highly selectively applied. Furthermore, those who hold to this position about the moral dissimilarity between the Nazis and the Soviets do not notice that, of course, the Nazis spoke the language of a supposedly higher humanity and culture, not entirely unlike many people who today regard with contempt those who do not lead a pure, healthful, politically correct one-size-fits-all life.[3] These are the intellectuals and celebrities who righteously and indignantly advocate living by regimes of various kinds and who eagerly promote government measures against tobacco smoking, driving SUVs, fast-food eating, and any exhibition of tastes and preferences not their own. Some go so far as to condemn industrial civilization on such grounds as that it removes us all from the pristine natural—or more accurately, wild and organically grown and fed—life we should be living. These and similar attitudes they share with the Nazis, even as they eschew their more brutal practices. But that is just what they did as far as the Soviets were concerned—selectively endorsed their particularly conceived, visionary, one-size-fits-all ideology.

One interesting way the differential treatment toward leftist tyrannies can be detected today—aside from the fact that most of those who have been sympathetic to the Soviets still lie low and remain intransigent and unapologetic about their grievous oversight or evasion—is how many people treat with considerable respect the culture of the Soviets versus that of the Nazis. This may be illustrated by imagining that one is sitting on a plane browsing through the *SkyMall* catalog and finding a nice old U-boat clock shown, with a swastika displayed on it prominently, offered at a reasonable price of $80. Or how about a nice hat that proudly carried on its front the Iron Cross of the Third Reich for a modest $150 or, if made of fine fur, for $450? I am not certain, but I doubt *SkyMall*'s management would be hailed for its sensitivity—a little like illustrating its pages with little Sambo figures from the deep south, no?

Now place yourself in the shoes of a refugee from some Soviet bloc country, as am I and are millions of other Americans, who run across the clock from a Soviet submarine in *SkyMall*, and a mouton and mink ushankas, promoted as memorabilia from the worst tyranny in human history.

But that isn't all. What if National Public Radio offered up some of the wonderful performances of Beethoven or Brahms from, well, the National Socialist Symphony Orchestra of the Third Reich, for its listeners to enjoy some of the performances of the great music of the past? Or what if some film festival, on, say, a classic movie cable channel were to feature, without comment and as simple film art, the works of some German director, such as Leni Riefenstahl, who just did what she was told by Hitler but did it beautifully?

Many of us know well and good that nothing like that could happen. The Nazis had no redeeming social value to offer up, period, and quite understandably so. Their regime was so vile, so horrible, and so inhumane that any thought of enjoying some part of it, even if in principle distinguishable from what the Nazis as Nazis did, is itself nearly unbearable. And this is so despite the currently fashionable babble in some circles to the effect that whether we disapprove of a regime or approve of it is simply a matter of where we happen to stand.[4]

Sidney Hook's struggles and legacy are clearly topical for us, what with such evidence of neglect toward political decency and humanity still very much evident on the part of very prominent representatives of the Left. Here we are; in thousands of airline back-seat pockets around the United States people are able to contemplate purchasing for themselves memorabilia from the Soviet era and hundreds of university radio stations, getting their programming from NPR, presenting to all their loyal, elite listeners classical tunes from the various orchestras of the Soviet Union. What is the not-so-hidden message here, anyway?

It is, quite unambiguously, that a great many of those people who call the shots in what counts as palatable, unobjectionable thinking in recent human history seem to believe that whereas the Nazis were a categorically nasty lot—never mind that they may have made some movies and played some classical music well enough—the butchers of the Soviet era don't qualify for such contempt. And why is this? Because for most of these folks who tell us what counts as culturally palatable, the Soviet era was merely a somewhat rough experiment, a good thing that sadly didn't quite work out. Or, alternatively, perhaps because the very idea of rational contempt is now beyond the pale, given that "rational" itself is deemed by many to be a culturally bound concept and procedure.

Stalin, and Lenin before him—and the rest of who followed, and all their lackeys, all those little helpers of history who carried out the murder of roughly twenty million innocent human beings within about fifty years, with a good deal of moral support from the intellectual and cultural elite of the rest of the globe—were, well, just misguided, off a bit, nothing to get all excited about. In contrast, Hitler and his gang, maybe because we just do not like them so much—because they were not embarking on launching the international socialist revolution but a national socialist program and because they murdered about 6 millions Jews, Romanys, homosexuals, and others—were clearly contemptible. They were not aiming for the liberation of the workers of the world as they perpetrated their mass murder, their genocide, so they cannot be embraced in any shape or form, at least not by those who have taken their stand on the Left. The Soviets—well, at any rate, some of them—meant well. And isn't it the thought that counts or some such neo-Kantian concept?

This, of course, is indefensible. The Nazis, as I have already noted, had some fine enough goals, like preserving high culture, reinvigorating Germany and molding the people into an excellent specimen of humanity, goals shared by many respectable people in history who, however, wouldn't go about getting there the way the Nazis tried. The plain truth is that both the Soviets and the Nazis had some ideals, more or less worthy, but then deployed means that left those ideals essentially in total disgrace.

Anyone like Hook—who didn't take Joseph McCarthy and McCarthyism to be the worst thing in the United States, comparable to nothing less than slavery itself, but thought that McCarthy was a relatively small nuisance compared to Stalin and his supporters—just did not and still doesn't deserve respect from these politically correct people. Maybe their early blindness to just how vicious, how vile the Soviets were makes it very difficult for these folks to confess their misjudgments even now, guided as they are by a theory that precludes serious, objective assessment of political merit.

The consequence of such bias and noncommitment may, however, be more serious than lots of folks think: it may encourage a perpetuation of the idea that the Soviet horrors were not much to fret about and that remembering those who stood by the side of these butchers is sort of cute, even nostalgic.

There is much more to Sidney Hook, however, than his resistance to leftist tolerance of, ambivalence about, and perhaps even occasional admiration for the Soviets. So, let me move now to some personal recollections of Sidney Hook.

I met Sidney back in 1970, when at a political philosophy conference he and I debated various issues at some length. What was notable about this event is how utterly absent had been any condescension from him toward much younger and less experienced interlocutors. Later, in the mid-1970s, Sidney and I were both at the Hoover Institution, he as a senior and I as a national fellow. Both of us worked mainly in philosophy, although we both had interests beyond the strict academic version of the discipline. Sidney Hook was an occasional mentor to me, although we had different ideas on many subjects, from metaphysics to politics.

I had the privilege of interviewing him during that time for *Reason* magazine, which I helped found in 1969 and for the pages of which I had been assigned to interview several prominent intellectuals (Friedman, Hayek, Szasz, Teller, Buckley, and others). This was a fascinating exchange, no holds barred and yet the most civil and often quite exploratory, despite the firm contrasting convictions held by all parties involved. What seemed to underlie the civility of it was a common expectation that a rational, feet-firmly-planted-on-the-ground approach ought eventually to lead to resolutions of human problems. An example of this will suffice to illustrate Hook's style and substance. We had been discussing socialism versus capitalism, and Sidney raised the following point:

> I must confess that I've taken my economic history for granted. I was very much impressed by an argument—I don't know how valid the evidence is—made by one of my colleagues at Hoover, Dr. Robert Hessen, some years ago. He asserted that despite the hardships resulting from the industrial revolution, which we were all brought up to regard as unmitigated evils, the only historical alternative to the factory system at the time was mass starvation. If that was truly the case, then it seems to me that on moral grounds we would have to accept the factory system as the lesser evil. But not all the evils of the factory system were necessary to its continuance.[5]

The entire tone of the discussion was nonconfrontational, despite the very serious disagreements between interviewers and interviewee—for example, on the origins of basic human rights, the mutual compatibility of valid rights claims, etc.

At this point, however, let me turn to some anecdotes from this and later periods of our interaction that help to illustrate the character and personality of Sidney Hook.

I believe it was the 1969 American Philosophical Association meeting at which Sidney had it out with Kai Nielsen about whether the APA ought to send a letter to the White House opposing the Vietnam War. What was so puzzling about this is that Nielsen—one of my teachers at New York University back in 1965–66 (where Sidney was then chair of the Division of Philosophy and Psychology in the graduate school)—was an avowed moral skeptic. He wrote a very prominently published essay skeptical about human rights for the *Philosophical Review* in 1965 in which he contended that one simply had no justification for concluding that human beings have any rights, based on his endorsement of G. E. Moore's naturalist fallacy argument. Yet Nielsen had no compunction about urging the membership of the APA to issue moral declarations about the war. Sidney, who was willing to make moral judgments from his pragmatic stance, objected to Nielsen on the grounds that it wasn't the function of a professional association such as the APA to make declarations on such matters in the name of its entire membership.

In a less serious vein, I recall that while at the Hoover Institution, Sidney noticed on one occasion that I dealt somewhat unmercifully with a famous economist. This famous economist had announced rather smugly to a sizable gathering of scholars, "Truth doesn't matter; utility does." I spoke up after thinking about this a bit, by asking the eminent man, a bit slyly, whether what he said is true. Afterwards Sidney, who had heard the exchange while standing some distance away, took me aside and said to me (and I paraphrase only a little), "However much you may be tempted, you shouldn't put people in corners from which they cannot escape when you argue with them. It kills the dialogue."

On another occasion I was going to ask the head of my program at Hoover to let me see a journal in which a piece of mine would soon appear—he had had something published there and I hadn't seen a recent copy. Sidney advised that I ask to see the article by this person that had been published in the journal, thus accomplishing two valuable ends! Was this the "applied" pragmatist at work?

Sidney and I later, in 1986, made a television pilot for a proposed series on political philosophy that didn't seem to please the panels at the appropriate government agency, since they turned it down. The pilot, produced by Robert Chitester—who would later produce Milton Friedman's television program *Free to Choose*, dealt with Karl Marx and was called "For the Love of Work." (What appears to have killed the project is my own participation, not Sidney's. According to a report in the *Wall Street Journal*, some NEH panelists had objected to the program being hosted by "a mere popularizer of libertarianism.")

In the course of making this one-hour program Sidney, the crew, and I traveled to England, Germany, New York, and the San Francisco Bay area to do a good deal of shooting, including a now lost day-long exchange of ideas at the Waldorf Astoria Hotel in New York. In addition to what went on the record, we also argued a good deal off camera, mainly about Marxism and the proper scope of democracy.

Our major dispute on camera occurred at the Berlin Wall, where Sidney advanced the idea that Marx would have wanted to be on the Western side; I replied that although that may well be so, Marx's ideas did, intentionally or not, give support to the Eastern side, regardless of his personal preferences. There was no doubt in Sidney's mind that the Soviets were politically vile and that East Germany was a hellhole for the bulk of its citizens. (This, incidentally, contrasted sharply with how others, identified as radical pragmatists, would later characterize the difference between the East and the West at that time; more on that shortly.) Despite our disagreements, we had many very cordial, even friendly on-camera exchanges, as the one shot in Winston Churchill's home where we talked about Sidney's famous book *The Hero in History: A Study in Limitation and Possibility* (Beacon Press, 1955), with reference to Marx's position of historical determinism.

We did, however, focus mainly on disagreements. For me Sidney's social-democratic views seemed too unconstrained by prospective constitutional principles that would protect individual rights, something we argued about at length on camera. He, however, argued that democracy is all we have, no matter how strict a constitutionalism one might like, since even the most unambiguous constitution is subject to democratic adjustment, amendment.

Around the same period Sidney and I had some exchanges in the pages of *Encounter* magazine. Among other things, we disputed about whether Marx's thought lent any support to Soviet imperialism. He didn't think so, but I did. In particular, we differed on how to interpret some remarks of Marx in the 1883 introduction to the Russian edition of *The Communist Manifesto*. Marx said there that in order for Russia to be able to advance toward socialism, it would have to annex the West, as it were, since Russia had never gone through capitalism, a must according to Marx, for advancing toward socialism. Marx wrote, "Now the question is, can the Russian *obshchina* ['community, organization'], though greatly undermined, yet a form of primeval common ownership of land, pass directly to the higher form of Communist common ownership? Or, on the contrary, must it first pass through the same process of dissolution as constitutes the historical evolution of the West?" Marx's reply was the point of contention between Sidney and me: "The only answer to that possible today is this: If the Russian Revolution becomes the signal for a proletarian revolution in the West, so that both complement each other, the present Russian common ownership of land may serve as the starting-point for a communism development."

I contended that this gave evidence that Marx envisioned the future Russian Communist state to embark upon serious imperialist efforts, so as to manage to integrate the West and its development through capitalism into its own social-economic development. Sidney disputed my interpretation, claiming that I read into Marx something that wasn't there. In general, Sidney gave Marx the benefit of the doubt, as against those who in his view illegitimately appropriated him.

Sidney's thesis that Karl Marx championed freedom sounded

odd to this refugee from Communist Hungary, even shocking; but his conception of Marxism as a form of democratic socialism—which I disputed—made sense of this to some extent, since the form of freedom important to those enslaved by the Soviets, namely, "negative liberty," isn't the form that Marx was stressing, namely what has come to be called "positive freedom."

Sidney often discussed ethics in a way that clearly illustrated his pragmatic bent in philosophy, as having to do with difficult, even intractable, choices from among competing goods and right conduct, to be evaluated, ultimately, by reference to the consequences that would flow from pursuing one or another good, doing one or another right thing. In reply to Sidney, I used to argue that consequences themselves require evaluation, and for that we need standards that cannot then be evaluated once again by consequences, because an infinite regress would ensue. Of course, Sidney had responses to these and related arguments, and we continued our discussions and debates until very late into his life.

Concerning Sidney's version of pragmatism, the most important point for me was his realist metaphysics and his confidence that human reason is a reliable means for understanding reality and reaching agreement about it if one is but vigilant. Pragmatism, as I understood it, was one understandable reaction to the Cartesian and neo-Cartesian/Kantian ambition for human knowledge. Earlier, Plato's idealism entertained such an ambition, namely, to know whatever we know finally, perfectly, timelessly. This is a chimera, and pragmatism recognized it as such. The alternative that had been introduced by Charles Peirce, William James, Dewey, and Hook was more a contextualist criterion for what knowledge must be. The practical dimensions of such knowledge took the place of its unrealistic rationalist foundations in philosophers such as Descartes. And that certainly recovered for us the confidence that we, human beings with our kind of cognitive capacities, can reach

267

an understanding of things even if such an understanding will not issue in finality, frozen or petrified definitions and theories.

Yet, as I saw it, this was still a bit apologetic, as if the dream of the idealist school of achieving final truth were still the admittedly impossible but desirable goal. (Popperian fallibilism was another such tip of the hat to the idealists.) Because practices are, after all, highly varied and often quite possibly misguided and ill conceived, their function as criteria for knowledge would not, it seemed to me, suffice to secure the prospect of objectivity and prevent subjectivism and relativism, in the last analysis, when pushed to the extreme implications.[6]

Sidney Hook would, I think, share Susan Haack's resistance to Rorty's version of pragmatism, given his realism and confidence in human reason. Yet, I am convinced, something more than practice is necessary to assure us that we can indeed know things as they are. This would, I believe, involve a conception of what knowledge must be that is contextualist and pluralist. For example, some facts we know may well be unchanging, such as Aristotle's laws of being; some universal enough, say the laws of nature, and others more temporal than those, such as the character of one's best friend.

In any case, the debates Sidney and I had about the various central and not-so-central topics of philosophy were most productive for me and showed me just how it is possible for someone to be firmly convinced of, even passionate about, various ideas yet still not dogmatic, not closed off to arguments about them.

It was very sad that Sidney didn't live long enough to witness the collapse of the Soviet Union. He would have been not only happy for all the victims of this tyranny who became free as a result but perhaps even a little bit triumphant.

Sidney Hook was certainly vindicated, on a historical scale—especially by all the revelations of Lenin's and Stalin's tyrannical and brutal conduct—vis-à-vis his many critics on the Left who held out nearly blind faith in the Soviet Union (in contrast to Sidney's understanding that such a system is vicious and shouldn't be supported even if it laid claims to being socialist and even if some of its foes were uncivil, dangerous cads like Joe McCarthy).

Sidney's critical mind could see past the shallow and naive hopefulness of many of his colleagues on the Left and recognize that in such a utopian ideology there was far less evidence of goodwill toward other people than the intention to dominate them and to impose one's own vision on all, regardless of how they saw fit to live their lives. Only George Orwell seems to me to have attained such understanding while remaining loyal to at least some kind of leftist conception of political justice.

NOTES

1. Hook's autobiography, *Out of Step: An Unquiet Life in the 20th Century* (New York: Harper & Row, 1987), chronicles all of his ideological battles in considerable detail and shows clearly that he agreed with Norman Thomas, who wrote to Albert Einstein, "I am thoroughly persuaded, as I think you are, that the test of freedom in America and indeed among thoughtful men everywhere is a capacity to oppose both Communism and the thing that in America we call McCarthyism. These two movements interact to help each other" (quoted on p. 486).

2. Victor Navasky, *Naming Names* (New York: Viking Press, 1980), p. 411.

3. It is notable that once again this missionary zeal to impose a health regime on society is experiencing a resurgence. Not only has smoking been banned all over California and New York, but various pious groups are targeting various unhealthy foods and the customers who prefer them for possible legal action. Few make note of the similarity between these allegedly noble efforts and the goals of the Nazis.

4. All this is déjà vu for me, given that when I chose my topic for my doctoral dissertation, "Human Rights, A Meta-Ethical Inquiry," I was

motivated in part by having read Margaret Macdonald's paper "Natural Rights," in *Philosophy, Politics and Society*, ed. Peter Laslett and W. G. Runciman (London: Blackwell, 1967), pp. 35–55, where she lays out exactly that idea, now being reaffirmed by Richard Rorty, among others, concerning political differences. Compare the following two quotes, the first from Macdonald, the second from Richard Rorty, "The Seer of Prague," *New Republic* 205 (July 1, 1991): 35–40: "To assert that 'Freedom is better than slavery' or 'All men are of equal worth' is not to state a fact but to *choose* a *side*. It announces *This is where I stand*." Rorty: "Non-metaphysicians [such as Rorty proposes we all be] cannot say that democratic institutions reflect a moral reality and that tyrannical regimes do not reflect one, that tyrannies get something wrong that democratic societies get right."

5. Tibor R. Machan and Davis Keeler, "Challenge from a Social Democrat: An Interview with Sidney Hook," *Reason* 9 (May 1977): 29–30.

6. That is, I believe, what has happened with the emergence of Richard M. Rorty's version of radical pragmatism, wherein the quest for objectivity is abandoned and instead, some kind of epistemology of democracy or community is championed. See Richard M. Rorty, *Objectivity, Relativism, and Truth* (Cambridge: Cambridge University Press, 1991).

CHAPTER 13

Sidney Hook
Teacher and Public Philosopher

Bruce Wilshire

*M*y first encounter with Sidney Hook was in a graduate class in social philosophy at New York University, spring 1958. It changed my life. Because in his electric aura I could believe that I could become who I am—I, too, could be a philosopher.

I came to the encounter far from sanguine about my chances. Already twenty-six, I had several abandoned careers behind me—fairly early abandoned, thank goodness. I had lasted two weeks at Berkeley, failing to be ignited by a seminar on Kant, "How Are Propositions Synthetic A Priori Possible?" I had not yet learned why I should care. Nor was I ignited by a huge class in symbolic logic in which the professor was barely aware that we were there in the same room with him. Rattling from coast to coast, I learned that Hook presided at NYU and, as luck would have it, was offering a seminar that spring. I recalled the verve with which he had written *The Metaphysics of Pragmatism*, which I had read as an undergraduate, and I signed up to take this one course as an experiment, a somewhat desperate one.

I had heard that when Toscanini emerged from the wings to conduct, it was as if he would scurry across the space, as if he didn't want to be seen before he stood on the podium, appearing there as if in epiphany. Likewise with Hook. Hardly an imposing figure physically in any case, he would slip into his chair before we could fairly notice his entry into the room. But once seated, his eyes would sparkle, he would adjust the rubber bands around his wrists—reminders to do things—and all present would barely breathe. We were down to business in some text.

But it wasn't ordinary business; it was some very special business. Over the years I have tried to put words to it. The closest I have come are words from Ralph Waldo Emerson—though Hook himself seldom alluded to Emerson, that I can remember: "The true thinker is the person delegated by humanity to think for it as a way of life."[1] In Emerson's words, he or she is Humanity thinking. It is more than any particular person's obvious self-interest; it is thinking that is as necessary for us all as is the air in which we are immersed. It is thinking as a gift that all of us in the room, we saw, could, with struggle, learn to give.

I can't imagine Sidney Hook using the word *sacred* with a straight face. But as I look back on it now, that is the word that seems most appropriate to describe his presence and his behavior. He acted as if he had inherited a sacred trust. We were to think as if our lives depended upon it, and we saw, by God, that they did. He would often say to us, "Think—or off with your heads!"

We had to think intelligently if we were to survive and maybe thrive. Hook's authority resided in his being deputized to convey this imperative. Sometimes it was tough love that he gave us. After

272

my first venture at expositing John Dewey, he said, "All right, enough of the headlines, let's get down to work."

Yes, I do believe that there was a dimension we students entered that was more than the crassly secular, more than the solution of clearly formulable problems, more than consumerism, more than comfort and convenience. Hook was not just another analytic philosopher opening his conceptual tool box with the same emotional flatness and detachment with which he would repair a drain pipe. Something spoke to him from beyond the easily visible horizon. Later in my graduate career, he confided in me that in certain moments (as a student in high school I think it was) he felt as if a hand behind him had gripped him by the neck, raised him up, and propelled him to the front of the classroom to deliver some speech or other.

Ego was certainly not absent from Hook, but there was something more than ego. There was an imperative to think, come what may, let the chips fall where they may. For Hook, the only unforgivable sin was to refuse to talk. Thus the faculty occupied double desks in the philosophy office, one professor facing another: say, existentialist William Barrett facing positivist Paul Edwards (pardon, please, the labels). They could refuse to talk, but it was difficult, and as far as I know they didn't refuse.

Along with Emerson's presence there was Charles Peirce's— that strangely blessed and cursed man who spoke of our obligation to keep on talking when all seemed to be hopeless impasse and intractable difficulty. Those hours in the philosophy department— it was all a lesson in what I would later read in Peirce, Hook in his single chairman's desk wheeling to pass papers to the secretary at her single desk. Peirce's words: "[Reasoning] inexorably requires that our interests shall not be limited. They must not stop at our own fate, but must embrace the whole community. . . . He who would not sacrifice his own soul to save the whole world, is, it seems to me, illogical in his inferences, collectively. Logic is rooted in the social principle."[2]

I left the department prepared to grasp something of William James in the same vein. That philosopher, refusing the initial invitation to join the fledgling American Philosophical Association in 1901 (and probably to be elected president), replied curtly, "I don't foresee much good from a philosophical society. Philosophy discussion proper only succeeds between intimates who have learned how to converse by months of weary trial and failure. The philosopher is the beast dwelling in his individual burrow. Count me out."[3]

Hook's, Dewey's, Peirce's, Emerson's, and James's legacies are hard to keep alive. How the world has changed, all across the board, in the last fifty years or so! Then the learned public could be caught up in a debate on the issue of Communism—better dead or red? Bertrand Russell opted for better red than dead. Hook opted for better dead than red. People listened. Hook's arguments emerged directly from the great US pragmatic tradition, particularly from Peirce. If the road of inquiry were to be blocked, dissent quashed, our intellectual freedoms and obligations unrealizable, then the heart of ourselves—the de facto sacred core of ourselves—would be violated. It would be better to be dead.

Much has conspired to break the continuity of the tradition. First, perhaps, is the incredible acceleration of technological change, and since we are thinking organisms, the incredible change in modes of thinking. To refer to anything sacred—tacit or manifest—seems more than retrograde and reactive, it amounts to an affront, perhaps pardonable. "You know, the old folks." Second, perhaps, is the incredibly rapid acceleration of the professionalization of everything, even philosophy. From what I can see, only the fewest newly minted PhDs from the "best" graduate schools would have any idea of how to argue Hook's points. Future shock: they are stunned without knowing it.

Indeed, so deracinated are the best products of the best schools that most have never thought seriously about Emerson, Dewey, Hook, et al. To cite that the APA membership has more than doubled in a few years is utterly uninformative. We are left in the Kafkaesque situation in which philosophical issues and perplexities fairly crowd us off the stage but are not recognized as philosophical issues. Thus in September's *New Republic* (2002) a learned historian from Yale reviews at length two weighty volumes on science, technology, and government and closes with the advice that we need the experts to assemble and discuss issues of commercialized and commodified university research ("how corrupting is it?"), the patenting of human and nonhuman genes ("does it serve the public interest?"), etc. But those are the questions, not the answers. Who are the experts in these issues? Could more empirical research conceivably answer these questions? Or is it a matter of truly fundamental research, a matter of thorough conceptual construction and reconstruction? The word *philosophy* is never mentioned by the learned historian.

Contributing to the befuddlement is what I've intimated. Analytic-academic philosophers have not systematically developed any critique of technology. Most are totally caught up, at least tacitly, in Cartesian dualism: mind is not essentially, in its very concept, embedded in bodily comportment, skills, perceptual attitudes, physical instruments. Most cannot distinguish phenomenalism from phenomenology. Many do try to wriggle out of Cartesian assumptions, and most are exhausted by their efforts, I think.

The words most generative of the great tradition are Emerson's in "Nature": "Miller owns this field, Locke that, and Manning the woodland beyond. But none of them owns the landscape. There is a property in the horizon that no man has but he whose eye can integrate all the parts. . . . This is the best part of these men's farms, yet to this their warranty deeds give no title."[4] Into this horizon that no

275

person can own is where Hook was in fact conducting us in his classrooms. The horizon presents itself as pointing inward toward everything it includes visually around us and toward ourselves. But simultaneously—if we really engage the phenomenon and look and think—it points outward toward everything else.

Of course, we cannot know what all this is, but the fact that there is something that escapes our whats can be made evident. And we do get a meaning, one that Emerson, James, and Peirce make explicit: it is the mysterious "more" that we bump up against in religious experience, say, or in art, or in what Peirce calls "musement." Again, Hook did not speak of the sacred or of the mysterious. But looking back on it, that's the best way of explaining our rapt attention in his classrooms. Emerson, in "Nature" again: the horizon is "something as beautiful as our own nature," and we belong to nature before anything can belong to us. Nature says, "You belong to me, and maugre all your impertinent griefs, you shall be glad with me." Hook: "Think—or off with your heads!" You must think and give back to be worthy of yourselves and of the gifts that have been given to you. You may patent technical devices, but if you patent your insights and discoveries, you rot at the core. You pull out your roots from the continent of humanity.

It's hard to overestimate the loss of intellectual culture in the United States in the last fifty years or so. It's hard even to imagine it, so caught up and captured by the loss are we. The patient labor between intimates trying to understand each other—James. What could that be in our driven, workaholic, sexaholic, generally addictive culture? Our thirty-second sound bite, McLaughlin, *Hardball*, generally violent culture? We try to manage everything, but I think we secretly long to be moved by what lies beyond our scientific and technical modes of understanding. James: There is something wild and heroic at the heart of us. Emerson in "Circles":

The one thing we seek with insatiable desire is to forget ourselves, to be surprised out of our propriety . . . to do something
without knowing how or why. . . . Nothing great was ever accomplished without enthusiasm. The way of life is wonderful; it is by
abandonment. . . . Dreams and drunkenness, the use of opium
and alcohol are the semblance and counterfeit of this oracular
genius, and hence their dangerous attraction for men. For the like
reason they ask the aid of wild passions, as in gaming and war, to
ape in some manner these flames and generosities of the heart.[5]

When this longing for spontaneous responsiveness and heroic
initiative is repressed, it emerges in addictive short-circuiting of
the regenerative cycles of nature in which we were formed during
the 99 percent of genus *Homo*'s existence as hunters and gatherers.
The short-circuitings are explosive or deadening eruptions of dis-
appointment and wrath. As one observer at Ground Zero recently
observed, when the terrible mess was finally cleaned up and a nice
rectangular hole appeared, a strange sadness descended on the
scene. The arena for heroism was closed. Many who had worked
in the cleanup had destroyed their lungs. But would they perhaps
die happy?

Anything to be done? I seem to hear Sidney Hook saying,
enough of the headlines, back to the text. This command takes me
to the internal books of *Experience and Nature*, in which Dewey
describes just how screwed up the subconscious minding of "civilized" humans is, cluttered as it is with half-baked meanings. He
means abortive means of "adjustment" that have never really been
tested in actual engagement with a chancy and dangerous but, of
course, a potentially supportive nature:

There then occur systematized withdrawals from intercourse and
interaction . . . ; carefully cultivated and artificially protected fantasies of consolation and compensation; rigidly stereotyped

beliefs not submitted to objective tests; habits of learned ignorance or systematized ignorings of concrete relationships; organized fanaticisms; dogmatic traditions which socially are harshly
intolerant and which intellectually are institutionalized paranoic
systems; idealizations which instead of being immediate enjoy-
ments of meanings cut man off from nature and his fellows.[6]

At the close of *Experience and Nature*, Dewey enjoins us to do
the desperately needed work of philosophy. This is the criticism of
criticism. It is the struggle not to be consumed in the foreground
squabbles and misunderstandings of what passes as critical thought
in our culture but to place our predicaments against the background
of the big picture. He means the use of the most general concepts
at our disposal, the categories of the stable and the precarious, for
example. What is stable in the body of humanity? What do we share
with 1.2 billion Muslims, for a timely example? What longings for
vitality, fulfillment, self-respect as human organisms? Can some of
the frightened, half-baked means and meanings be shrunk out of
our big-brained heads without losing our *elan*, our vitality?

There is no quick fix. No New Age spirituality, I am afraid, will
work. For it is caught in psychophysical dualisms: "Rise out of the
darkness of the body into the light," etc. But the roots of our
behavior dive deep into the fertile darkness that we ignore at our
peril. I am afraid that much the same applies to Teilhardian evolu-
tionism, which believes that inevitably the world strives for a noos-
phere, a unification of everything through mind. But what unifica-
tions we actually see are too often ecstatic fusings in cultures hys-
terically threatened by other culture's modes of constructing an
experienced world. Genocide: Get 'em all, kill 'em. What can
change this horrendous propensity? We are incredibly vulnerable
bodily beings who engage, often very faultily, in mindings. There
is no quick fix for the fear that is "wired" into us.

In the fertile darkness lies a sense of the sacred, and of the wild and heroic, repressed and mangled as it often is. It's a question of how to live with it. It's a question of how to live without it—or without acknowledging it. How do we fully account for Hook's zeal to root out Communists unless we suppose it in some form? This zeal has earned him the undying hatred of many people. I can only say that he was and is a greatly important teacher in my life, from whom I have learned in many, many ways.

NOTES

1. Ralph Waldo Emerson, "The American Scholar."
2. Charles Peirce, "The Doctrine of Chances," third article of a series, *Popular Science Monthly* 12 (1878): 604–15.
3. Quoted in E. I. Pitts, "Ideals and Reality: The Early Years of the APA," excerpted from his PhD dissertation (Pennsylvania State University, 1979); see also Bruce Wilshire, "The Ph.D. Octopus: William James' Prophetic Grasp of the Failures of Academic Professionals," in *Fashionable Nihilism: A Critique of Analytic Philosophy* (Albany: State University of New York Press, 2002).
4. Larzer Ziff, ed., *R. W. Emerson: Selected Essays* (London: Penguin Books, 1982), p. 38.
5. Ibid.
6. John Dewey, *Experience and Nature* (New York: Dover, 1958), pp. 299–302; see also Bruce Wilshire "Body-Mind and Subconsciousness: Dewey and Tragedy," in *The Primal Roots of American Philosophy: Pragmatism, Phenomenology, and Native American Thought* (University Park: Pennsylvania State University Press, 2000).

Afterword

Richard Rorty

Reading David Sidorsky's comprehensive and informative narrative of Hook's career made me realize how difficult it is to get a synoptic view of his achievements. As Sidorsky shows, each stage in his career led naturally to the next, and at each he did something important. But his achievements were so various that there is little point in trying to see them as facets of a single project, or to pick out one of them as central.

Hook's early effort to place Marx in the context of nineteenth-century German philosophy was just as important to him as his later attempt (doomed, in my opinion) to reconcile the philosophical outlooks of Dewey and Russell. His polemics against Reinhold Niebuhr and Mortimer Adler, illuminatingly discussed by Edward Shapiro, Gary Bullert, and others in this volume, were no less heartfelt than his criticisms of the people he called "anti-anti-Com-

281

munists." Hook was a person of great intensity, for whom nothing was just a sideshow or a diversion. His mind and his emotions were fully engaged whenever he sat down at the typewriter. His energy lasted for many decades. Throughout a long life, his arguments were always worth considering, even when one laid down his latest piece convinced that he was just plain wrong. I emphatically disagree with Christopher Phelps's judgment that Hook's writings of the 1950s and '60s are "of far less interest than the creativity and boldness he displayed as a young upstart in the 1930s," even though I agree with many of Phelps's criticisms of *The Fail-Safe Fallacy* and of *Heresy, Yes—Conspiracy, No*.

Though one cannot usefully divide Hook's writings into those that were central and those that were peripheral, one can nevertheless easily specify those that were most influential. I entirely agree with Nathan Glazer that, at the present time (if perhaps not forever) our major interest in Hook will be in his crusade against the influence of Stalinism on US intellectual and political life. Glazer is also right that readers whose memories do not stretch back to World War II may find it hard to appreciate how necessary that crusade was.

Because Stalin is now routinely bracketed with Hitler, we have trouble remembering that in the 1940s that bracketing was deeply shocking and offensive to a majority of Americans who thought of themselves as on the political Left. These were people who had been persuaded by living through the Great Depression that the capitalist system probably could not be made to work, had learned a lot from Marx, and were loath to believe Trotsky's claim that Stalin had betrayed the Bolshevik Revolution. Leftists of this sort thought they saw a big difference between what they saw as the Soviet Union's flawed but still praiseworthy attempt to create a socialist society and the German regime that had murdered six million Jews and plunged the world into war. For five years or so after the Nazi camps were opened, it was as hard for the majority of US leftists to admit the existence of the gulag as it was for their counterparts in countries such as Italy and France.

I am somewhat younger than Glazer, but, having entered my teens in the closing years of the war and having being raised in a household in which leftist politics mattered more than anything else, I was well placed to appreciate the intensity of the conflict that raged, in the 1940s and '50s, between those who agreed with Henry Wallace that the cold war could and should be avoided and those who agreed with President Truman that Stalin had to be contained and, if possible, pushed back. The anti-Communism of the opening years of the cold war is often thought of as a series of attempts by dishonest and ruthless politicians (such as Martin Dies, Richard Nixon, and Joseph McCarthy) to acquire political power by victimizing innocent Hollywood actors and college professors. But the activities of those contemptible opportunists had little to do with the change of mind that was occurring on the Left—the gradual realization that Wallace had been wrong, and the consequent conversion of the vast majority of US leftist intellectuals into what are now called "cold war liberals."

These intellectuals were not swayed by propaganda, nor did they succumb to intimidation. Their conversion was a result of rational persuasion—the result of pondering the arguments of people like Hook. Glazer is right that effecting this conversion was necessary in order to maintain "integrity, decency, and common rationality in intellectual life." Leftist intellectual life in the United States between 1946 and 1956 (the year Soviet tanks rolled into Budapest) had much more of those qualities than leftist intellectual life in France in the same period. Raymond Aron and his friends pretty much failed, but Hook and his largely succeeded.

Glazer is also right, unfortunately, that "Sidney's concern for the truth against lying inevitably meant a downgrading of compassion." Many of the contributors to this volume make clear that, like

Glazer and myself, they wish that Hook had not argued that membership in the American Communist Party was prima facie cause for dismissal from academic positions. Many others wish, as I also do, that Hook had eventually joined leftists such as Irving Howe and Arthur Schlesinger in urging the country to concede defeat, pull out of Vietnam, and stop the killing. But the momentum of his anti-Communism was too strong, as it was for many other leftist intellectuals (such as James T. Farrell) who had been fighting the good fight against Stalinism for thirty years. They supported the Vietnam War to the end, and wound up urging us to vote for Nixon and defeat McGovern.

As far as I can see, there is no interesting connection between these political controversies and the disputes that Hook conducted with his fellow philosophy professors about such topics as the nature of truth, the nature of knowledge, and the nature of morality. I have argued in the past and would still maintain that one can follow James in giving up on the correspondence theory of truth, agree with Dewey about the means-end continuum, and applaud Peirce's devastating critique of the Cartesian notion of "immediate knowledge" without thereby being led to adopt any particular political position. Sartre, for example, could have cheerfully agreed with the pragmatists on all three of these topics without then being impelled to reconsider his conviction that anti-Communists like Hook were scum.

My belief that academic philosophy is one thing and politics another makes me dubious about Michael Eldridge's account of the "eclipse of pragmatism and the rise of analytic philosophy in the midtwentieth century." All that happened was that the philosophy professors got bored with James and Dewey and latched on to something that looked new and promising. Dewey's ideas had been around for a long time. Many of them had become part of US common sense, and all of them were old hat. Something fresh was needed. Carnap and Quine supplied it, just as, when the New Criticism had reached senescence, de Man and Derrida supplied the English departments with something new to do.

But such changes in academic fashion do not matter greatly to society or culture. Intellectual life in the United States did not move off in a new direction when philosophy students began reading A. J. Ayer, any more than it did when literature students began reading Derrida. Secularism, what Sidorsky calls "Enlightenment Naturalism," and a social-democratic politics—all the things closest to Dewey's heart—were the conventional wisdom of US philosophy departments in 1970 just as much as they had been in 1940. Few nonphilosophers noticed that the philosophy professors were now writing in a different manner. The fad for "logical analysis" that Carnap and Quine imported into the United States lasted only a few decades; what we now call "analytic philosophy," for want of a better name, is something quite different. The idea that Carnap was a more "precise and rigorous" thinker than Hook is just wrong; the change in style did not bring about an improvement in intellectual quality. Carnap and Hook were equally able, but they were interested in different things.

The transformation of US philosophy departments between 1950 and 1970 was just an example of the normal rhythm of academic life, one of those generational shifts that keep disciplines from freezing over. The absurd overprofessionalization of the discipline that accompanied the fad for "analysis"—the phenomenon that William James foresaw when he wrote "The Ph.D. Octopus"— was not due to philosophers having discovered new and sharper tools with which to chisel concepts but simply to the explosive expansion of US higher education in the 1950s and '60s. If that expansion had occurred earlier, US philosophy departments would have been filled with thousands of absurdly overprofessionalized pragmatists, most of whose work would have been as of little interest to nonphilosophers as most analytic philosophy is now.

I remember vividly the controversy in the *Journal of Philos-*

ophy between Hook and Victor Lowe that Eldridge describes, but I think that he may overestimate its importance. I suspect that most of the philosophers who followed that controversy were on Lowe's side but that it never occurred to them for a minute that Hook, by arguing as he did, was selling the pass to the analytic philosophers. Nor were philosophers who had been brought up on Dewey hoping that Hook, or somebody, would come up with "a precise, rigorous alternative to the analytic approach." Carnap's writings were not more "intellectually demanding" (in Eldridge's phrase) than Hook's, any more than those of Derrida and de Man were more demanding than those of T. S. Eliot and Cleanth Brooks. Carnap and Derrida were simply a little harder to understand on first reading. All Carnap and Quine did was to make it briefly fashionable for US philosophers to try to give "analyses"—that is, necessary and sufficient conditions for the truth of certain philosophically problematic sentences. No such conditions were ever discovered, and Hook was wise not to go haring after them.

Getting US leftists who had been drawn to Marxism to wise up to the fact that Stalinism had nothing to do with the pursuit of social justice was a far more important contribution to US intellectual life than getting philosophy students to learn symbolic logic and start reading Frege. Hook knew, and regretted, that he was regarded as a dinosaur by the bright young philosophers of the postwar period. But the scorn of the rising generation should not have caused him the concern it did. He and Dewey did a great deal to change the way US intellectuals thought about what was going on in the twentieth century and about what needed to be done. Historians of the twentieth-century United States will have to read both men's books.

A Complete Bibliography of Sidney Hook's Published Work

Compiled by Jo-Ann Boydston
and Kathleen Poulos
Updated by Matthew J. Cotter

1922

"The Philosophy of Non-Resistance." *Open Court* 36 (Jan. 1922): 1–5.
"A Philosophical Dialogue." *Open Court* 36 (Oct. 1922): 621–26.

1926

Review of Rebecca Cooper, *The Logical Influence of Hegel on Marx.*
    Journal of Philosophy 23 (18 Feb. 1926): 106–8.
"The Metaphysics of Leading Principles." *Journal of Philosophy* 23 (1
    Apr. 1926): 169–83.
"Methodological Considerations in Primitive Art." *Open Court* 40 (June
    1926): 328–39.

1927

The Metaphysics of Pragmatism. Chicago: Open Court Pub. Co., 1927.
Collected Works of Vladimir Ilyich Lenin, trans. Sidney Hook and David Kvitko. New York: International Publishers, 1927.
"The Ethics of Suicide." *International Journal of Ethics* 37 (Jan. 1927): 173–88.
"Freedom." *Open Court* 41 (Feb. 1927): 65–73.
"Categorial Analysis and Pragmatic-Realism." *Journal of Philosophy* 24 (31 Mar. 1927): 169–87.
"The Metaphysics of the Instrument, Part 1." *Monist* 37 (July 1927): 335–56. "Part 2: Thinking as Instrumental." Ibid. 37 (Oct. 1927): 601–19. "Part 3: The Ethics of the Instrument." Ibid., pp. 620–23.
"The Irrationality of the Irrational." *Journal of Philosophy* 24 (4 Aug. 1927): 421–37.

1928

"Marx and Freud: Oil and Water." *Open Court* 41 (Jan. 1928): 20–25. See Max Eastman, "Karl Marx Anticipated Freud." *New Masses* 3 (July 1927): 11–12.

The final version of Boydston and Poulos's bibliography, originally published in *Sidney Hook: Philosopher of Democracy and Humanism*, ed. Paul Kurtz (Amherst, NY: Prometheus Books, 1983), pp. 311–55, was compiled with the assistance of editors from the Center for Dewey Studies, Southern Illinois University at Carbondale, and the cooperation of Dale Reed, Assistant Archivist, Library of the Hoover Institution on War, Revolution and Peace. The compilers are indebted to John Dennis Crowley, S.J., for his work on the "Bibliography of Sidney Hook," in *Sidney Hook and the Contemporary World*, ed. Paul Kurtz (New York: John Day Co., 1968), pp. 429–71. Cotter's update begins with the year 1979 for Hook's works, 1980 for reviews of Hook's works.

"The Philosophy of Dialectical Materialism, Parts 1 and 2." Review of Vladimir I. Lenin, *Materialism and Empirio-Criticism. Journal of Philosophy* 25 (1 Mar. 1928): 113–24; ibid. 25 (15 Mar. 1928): 141–55.

    Reply by Max Eastman, ibid. 25 (16 Aug. 1928): 475–76.

    Rejoinder by Hook, ibid. 25 (11 Oct. 1928): 587–88.

"Marxism, Metaphysics, and Modern Science." Review of Max Eastman, *Marx, Lenin, and the Science of Revolution. Modern Quarterly* 4 (May–Aug. 1928): 388–94.

    For the debate that ensued, see:

        Eastman, "As to Sidney Hook's Morals." Ibid. 5 (Nov. 1928–Feb. 1929): 85–87.

        Hook, "As to Max Eastman's Mentality." Ibid., pp. 88–91.

        Eastman, "Excommunication and Exorcism as Critical Methods, Part 1." Ibid. 7 (May 1933): 210–13.

        Hook, "The Engineering Conception of Marxism." Review of Max Eastman, *Karl Marx's "Capital" and Other Writings*. Ibid., pp. 248–50.

        Eastman, "A Master Magician, Part 2." Ibid. 7 (June 1933): 290–93, 307.

        Eastman, letter in reply to Hook's review of *Karl Marx's "Capital."* Ibid., p. 320.

        Eastman, "Man and History." Ibid. 7 (July 1933): 348–50.

        Hook, "A Note from Sidney Hook." Ibid., pp. 350–51.

        Eastman, letter in reply. Ibid. 7 (Aug. 1933): 447–48.

        Hook, response. Ibid. 7 (Sept. 1933): 510–11.

        V. F. Calverton, "To Max Eastman and Sidney Hook." Ibid., pp. 511–12.

        Eastman, letter. Ibid. 7 (Oct. 1933): 576.

"Freedom." *Archiv für systematische Philosophie und Soziologie* 31 (1928): 17–26. [Concluding chapter of *The Metaphysics of Pragmatism*, 1927.]

1929

"What Is Dialectic? Part 1." *Journal of Philosophy* 26 (14 Feb. 1929): 85–99. "Part 2." Ibid. 26 (28 Feb. 1929): 113–23.

Review of Julius Löwenstein, *Hegels Staatsidee. Journal of Philosophy* 26 (12 Sept. 1929): 526–30.

"A Pragmatic Critique of the Historico-Genetic Method." In *Essays in Honor of John Dewey*, pp. 156–74. New York: Henry Holt and Co., 1929.

1930

"A Critique of Ethical Realism." *International Journal of Ethics* 40 (Jan. 1930): 179–210. [Reprinted, with slight changes, in *Pragmatism and the Tragic Sense of Life*, 1974.]

"A Personal Impression of Contemporary German Philosophy." *Journal of Philosophy* 27 (13 Mar. 1930): 141–60.

    Reply by Dorion Cairns, "Mr. Hook's Impression of Phenomenology." Ibid. 27 (17 July 1930): 393–96.

    Rejoinder by Hook, "In Defence of an Impression." Ibid. 27 (6 Nov. 1930): 635–37.

"The Revolt against Dualism." Review of Arthur O. Lovejoy, *The Revolt against Dualism. New Republic* 63 (18 June 1930): 129–30.

"Husserl's Phenomenological Idealism." Review of Edmund Husserl, *Formale und transzendentale Logik. Journal of Philosophy* 27 (3 July 1930): 365–80.

"Contemporary American Philosophy." Review of *Contemporary American Philosophy: Personal Statements*, ed. George P. Adams and William P. Montague. *New Republic* 63 (16 July 1930): 237–39.

"The Philosophy of Morris R. Cohen." *New Republic* 63 (23 July 1930): 278–81.

"Capitalism and Protestantism." Review of Max Weber, *The Protestant Ethic and the Spirit of Capitalism. Nation* 131 (29 Oct. 1930): 476–78.

Review of George S. Counts, *The American Road to Culture. Current History* 33 (Oct. 1930): x–xiii.

"The Meaning of Marxism." *Modern Quarterly* 5 (Winter 1930–31): 430–35. [Part of a symposium on "Marxism and Social Change."]

"The Non-Sense of the Whole." Review of Waldo Frank, *The Re-Discovery of America: An Introduction to a Philosophy of American Life. Modern Quarterly* 5 (Winter 1930–31): 504–13.

Reply by Frank, ibid., pp. 514–16.

Encyclopaedia of the Social Sciences, ed. Edwin R. A. Seligman. New York: Macmillan Co., 1930–35.

Contributions:

"Bauer, Bruno." Vol. 2, 1930, p. 481.

"Büchner, Ludwig." Vol. 3, 1931, p. 30.

"Determinism." Vol. 5, 1931, pp. 110–14.

"Dietzgen, Joseph." Vol. 5, 1931, p. 139.

"Engels, Friedrich." Vol. 5, 1931, pp. 540–41.

"Feuerbach, Ludwig Andreas." Vol. 6, 1931, pp. 221–22.

"Materialism." Vol. 10, 1933, pp. 209–20.

"Ruge, Arnold." Vol. 13, 1934, pp. 462–63.

"Violence." Vol. 15, 1935, pp. 264–67.

1931

Review of Henri DeMan, *The Psychology of Socialism. Current History* 33 (Jan. 1931): xxi–xxiii.

"The New Individualism." Review of John Dewey, *Individualism Old and New. Current History* 33 (Mar. 1931): xxii–xxiv.

"The Soviet Challenge." Review of George S. Counts, *The Soviet Challenge to America. Current History* 34 (May 1931): xiii–xiv.

"John Dewey and His Critics." *New Republic* 67 (3 June 1931): 73–74.

"Marx and Darwinism." *New Republic* 67 (29 July 1931): 290.

Reply by Robert Morss Lovett, ibid., pp. 290–91.

"Towards the Understanding of Karl Marx." *Symposium* 2 (July 1931): 325–67.

Review of Willy Moog, *Hegel und die Hegelsche Schule. Journal of Philosophy* 28 (27 Aug. 1931): 497–500.

"Experimental Logic." *Mind* 40 (Oct. 1931): 424–38.

Review of Edmund Husserl, *Ideas—General Introduction to Pure Phenomenology. Symposium* 2 (Oct. 1931): 531–40.

"The Metaphysics of Experience." Review of John Dewey, *Philosophy and Civilization. New Republic* 68 (4 Nov. 1931): 330–31.

"From Hegel to Marx, Part 1." *Modern Quarterly* 6 (Winter 1931): 46–62. "Part 2: Hegel and Marx in Continuity." Ibid. 6 (Summer 1932): 33–43. "Part 3: Dialectic in Hegel and Marx." Ibid. 6 (Autumn 1932): 58–67.

1932

"Reason and Nature: The Metaphysics of Scientific Method." Review of Morris Cohen, *Reason and Nature. Journal of Philosophy* 29 (7 Jan. 1932): 5–24.

Review of Theodor L. Haering, *Hegel, Sein Wollen und Sein Werk*, vol. 1. *Philosophical Review* 41 (Jan. 1932): 75–77.

"An Epic of Revolution." Review of Leon Trotsky, *The Overthrow of Tzarism. The History of the Russian Revolution*, vol. 1. *Saturday Review of Literature* 8 (27 Feb. 1932): 549–51.

"Pictures of the Past." Review of Michael N. Pokrovsky, *History of Russia*, vol. 1. *Saturday Review of Literature* 8 (30 Apr. 1932): 700.

Review of Dewitt H. Parker, *Human Values. International Journal of Ethics* 42 (Apr. 1932): 348–53.

Review of *Principles of Philosophy. Collected Papers of Charles Sanders Peirce*, ed. Charles Hartshorne and Paul Weiss, vol. 1. *Symposium* 3 (Apr. 1932): 248–56.

Review of *Principles of Philosophy. Collected Papers of Charles Sanders Peirce*, ed. Charles Hartshorne and Paul Weiss, vol. 1. *Current History* 36 (May 1932): 4–5.

"The Contemporary Significance of Hegel's Philosophy." *Philosophical Review* 41 (May 1932): 237–60.

"Half-baked Communism." Review of Robert Briffault, *Breakdown: The Collapse of Traditional Civilisation*. *Nation* 134 (8 June 1932): 654–55.

> Replies by M. F. Ashley-Montagu, Nelson Morris, and Briffault, ibid. 135 (13 July 1932): 36–37.

> Hook, "Rejoinder to Mr. Ashley-Montagu." Ibid. 135 (24 Aug. 1932): 170–71.

"Hegel's Phenomenology of Mind." Review of *Hegel's Phenomenology of Mind*, 2d rev. ed., trans. J. B. Baillie. *Journal of Philosophy* 29 (23 June 1932): 361–62.

"Myth, Fact, and Poetry of Soviet Russia." Review of Waldemar Gurian, *Bolshevism: Theory and Practice*; Joseph Freman, *The Soviet Worker*; Waldo Frank, *Dawn in Russia*; George S. Counts, Luigi Villari, Malcolm Rorty and Newton D. Baker, *Bolshevism, Fascism, and Capitalism*. *Nation* 135 (14 Sept. 1932): 237–38.

Review of Vladimir I. Lenin, *What Is To Be Done? American Journal of Sociology* 38 (Sept. 1932): 315–17.

1933

Towards the Understanding of Karl Marx: A Revolutionary Interpretation. New York: John Day Co., 1933.

"Karl Marx and the Young Hegelians." *Modern Monthly* 7 (Feb. 1933): 33–44.

"Marxism—Dogma or Method?" *Nation* 136 (15 Mar. 1933): 284–85. Letter in reply by Leon Trotsky, with response by Hook, ibid. 137 (5 July 1933): 18–19.

"The Marxian Dialectic." *New Republic* 74 (22 Mar. 1933): 150–54.

"Russia in Solution." Review of Leon Trotsky, *The History of the Russian Revolution*, vols. 2 and 3, trans. Max Eastman. *Saturday Review of Literature* 9 (8 Apr. 1933): 521–22.

Review of August Faust, *Der Möglichkeitsgedanke Systemgeschichtliche Untersuchungen*. *Journal of Philosophy* 30 (13 Apr. 1933): 221–23.

"Against the Fascist Terror in Germany." *New Masses*, Apr. 1933.

"Karl Marx and Bruno Bauer." *Modern Monthly* 7 (Apr. 1933): 160–74.

"Education and Politics." Review of *The Educational Frontier*, ed. William Heard Kilpatrick. *New Republic* 75 (24 May 1933): 49–50.

"Why the German Student Is Fascist." *Student Outlook* 1 (May 1933): 4–6, 20.

"Science and the Crisis." Review of H. L. Levy, *The Universe of Science*, and *Science and the Changing World*, ed. Mary Adams. *Nation* 136 (21 June 1933): 705–6.

"Revolutionist's Symposium." Review of *Recovery through Revolution*, ed. Samuel D. Schmalhausen. *Nation* 136 (28 June 1933): 733–34.

"Kant and Political Liberalism," by Karl Marx, trans. Sidney Hook. *Modern Monthly* 7 (July 1933): 352–54.

"Arnold Ruge and Karl Marx, Part 1." *Modern Monthly* 7 (Aug. 1933): 409–21, 431; "Part 2." Ibid. 7 (Sept. 1933): 480–86.

"De Libris: Disputatio." *City College Alumnus*, Sept. 1933.

"On Hegel's 'Concrete Universal'," by Karl Marx, trans. Sidney Hook. *Modern Monthly* 7 (Sept. 1933): 496–97, 501.

"Karl Marx and Max Stirner." *Modern Monthly* 7 (Oct. 1933): 547–55, 569.

"Psychology: The Social Bias." Review of Edna F. Heidbreder, *Seven Psychologies*. *New Republic* 77 (29 Nov. 1933): 81–82.

"Social Psychology—Marxian Style." Review of Leon Samson, *Towards a United Front: A Philosophy for American Workers*. *Modern Monthly* 7 (Nov. 1933): 637–39.

"Theories of Social Determinism." *Scientia* 54 (Dec. 1933): 437–49.

1934

The Democratic and Dictatorial Aspects of Communism. Part 2. Worcester, Mass.: Carnegie Endowment for International Peace, 1934. [Part 1: Joseph Stalin, *The Political and Social Doctrine of Communism*.]

"The Meaning of Marx." In *The Meaning of Marx*, ed. Sidney Hook, pp.

47–82. New York: Farrar and Rinehart, 1934. [Symposium by Bertrand Russell, John Dewey, Morris R. Cohen, Sherwood Eddy, and Sidney Hook.]

"Towards the Understanding of Karl Marx." In Max Eastman, *Art and the Life of Action*, pp. 121–33. New York: Alfred A. Knopf, 1934.

"Is Marxism Compatible with Christianity?" *Christian Register* 113 (15 Feb. 1934): 103–6.

> Reply to Francis A. Henson, "The Challenge of Marxism to Christianity." Ibid. 113 (18 Jan. 1934): 35–38.

> Reply to Henry P. Van Dusen, "The Challenge of Christianity to Marxism." Ibid. 113 (1 Feb. 1934): 71–73.

"A Shot in the Dark." Review of Ralph Fox, *Lenin: A Biography. Saturday Review of Literature* 10 (24 Feb. 1934): 503.

"The Philosophy of Technics in the U.S.S.R." *Modern Monthly* 8 (Feb. 1934): 31–36.

"The Nature of Discourse." Review of Alfred Korzybski, *Science and Sanity: An Introduction to Non-Aristotelian Systems and General Semantics. Saturday Review* 10 (10 Mar. 1934): 546–47.

"Dewey on Thought and Action." Review of John Dewey, *How We Think. New Republic* 78 (21 Mar. 1934): 165.

"The Mythology of Class Science." *Modern Monthly* 8 (Mar. 1934): 112–17.

"What Is Materialism?" *Journal of Philosophy* 31 (26 Apr. 1934): 235–42.

> Reply by R. W. Sellars, "Is Naturalism Enough?" Ibid. 41 (28 Sept. 1944): 533–44.

> Rejoinder by Hook, "Is Physical Realism Sufficient?" Ibid., pp. 544–51.

"A Symposium on Communism: Why I Am a Communist (Communism without Dogmas)." *Modern Monthly* 8 (Apr. 1934): 143–65.

> Bertrand Russell, "Why I Am Not a Communist." Ibid., pp. 133–34.

> John Dewey, "Why I Am Not a Communist." Ibid., pp. 135–37.

> Morris R. Cohen, "Why I Am Not a Communist." Ibid., pp. 138–42.

295

"Marxism and Democracy: Some Notes on the Draft Program of the A.W.P." *Labor Action*, 1 May 1934.

"Sidney Hook Replies." *Commonwealth College Fortnightly* 10 (15 June 1934): 2–3.

> Reply to William Cunningham, "Misunderstanding Marxian Economics." Ibid. 10 (15 Feb. 1934): 2–3.

> Response by Paul Evans, "On Sidney [sic] Hook's Reply." Ibid. 10 (15 July 1934): 2–3.

"Socialism at the Crossroads." Review of *Socialism, Fascism and Communism*, ed. Joseph Shaplen and David Shub. *Saturday Review of Literature* 11 (21 July 1934): 1–2.

"The Fallacy of the Theory of Social Fascism." *Modern Monthly* 8 (July 1934): 342–52.

"The Challenge of the Social Order to the Curriculum of the Liberal Arts College." In *Report of the 11th Annual Meeting of the Fellows of the National Council on Religion in Higher Education*, Colgate-Rochester Divinity School, Rochester, N.Y., 4–10 Sept. 1934.

"An Open Letter to Lincoln Steffens." *Modern Monthly* 8 (Sept. 1934): 486–92.

Review of *Systematic Sociology on the Basis of the Beziehungslehre and Gebildelehre of Leopold von Wiese*, adapted by Howard Becker. *Philosophical Review* 43 (Sept. 1934): 532–35.

Review of Theodore B. Brameld, *A Philosophic Approach to Communism. American Economic Review* 24 (Sept. 1934): 548–49.

"A Demonstration for Relief." *New Republic* 80 (31 Oct. 1934): 340. Letter, also signed by J. B. S. Hardman, James Burnham, Louis F. Budenz, and A. J. Muste.

"On Workers' Democracy." *Modern Monthly* 8 (Oct. 1934): 529–44.

> Replies by Will Herberg: "Workers' Democracy or Dictatorship?: On Hook's Revival of Kautsky's Theories." *Workers Age* 3 (15 Dec. 1934): 3, 8; "Parties under Workers' Rule: An Answer to Sidney Hook's Concept of Parties in a Dictatorship." Ibid. 4 (4 May 1935): 5; "As to a Multi-Party Dictatorship: Hook Confuses Dictatorship with Bourgeois Democracy." Ibid. 4 (11 May 1935): 3.

Response by Hook, "Manners and Morals of Apache-Radicalism." *Modern Monthly* 9 (June 1935): 215–21.

Reply by Herberg, "Professor Hook Loses His Temper: Concluding Remarks on Hook's Misconception of Dictatorship." *Workers Age* 4 (6 July 1935): 3.

"The Importance of a Point of View, Part 1." *Social Frontier* 1 (Oct. 1934): 19–22. "Part 2." Ibid. 1 (Nov. 1934): 17–19.

"The Democratic and Dictatorial Aspects of Communism." *International Conciliation* 305 (Dec. 1934): 452–64.

"Karl Marx and Moses Hess." *New International* 1 (Dec. 1934): 140–44.

1935

"Experimental Naturalism." In *American Philosophy Today and Tomorrow*, ed. Sidney Hook and Horace M. Kallen, pp. 205–25. New York: L. Furman, 1935.

"Hegel and Marx." In *Studies in the History of Ideas*, vol. 3, pp. 329–404. New York: Columbia University Press, 1935.

"Marx's Criticism of 'True Socialism'." *New International* 2 (Jan. 1935): 13–16.

"A Philosophic Pathfinder." Review of George H. Mead, *Mind, Self and Society. Nation* 140 (13 Feb. 1935): 195–96.

"Interpreting Soviet Russia." Review of Julius Hecker, *Moscow Dialogues*; *Russian Sociology*; *Religion and Communism*; and *The Communist's Answer to the World's Needs*; James Bunyan and H. H. Fisher, *The Bolshevik Revolution, 1917–1918*; Maurice Parmelee, *Bolshevism, Fascism, and the Liberal-Democratic State. Saturday Review* 11 (16 Feb. 1935): 494–95.

"Marxism and Religion." *Modern Monthly* 9 (Mar. 1935): 29–35.

"Our Philosophers." *Current History* 41 (Mar. 1935): 698–704.

"Literature of Revolt: A Reply to Professor Cohen–II." *Student Outlook* 3 (May 1935): 11–13.

"Philosophical Burlesque." *Modern Monthly* 9 (May 1935): 163–72.

"What Happened in Russia." Review of William Henry Chamberlin, *The Russian Revolution, 1917–1921. Saturday Review* (1 June 1935): 40–41.

"Pareto's Sociological System." Review of Vilfredo Pareto, *The Mind and Society. Nation* 140 (26 June 1935): 747–48.

"Saint Stalin." Review of Henri Barbusse, *Stalin. Saturday Review of Literature* 13 (16 Nov. 1935): 7.

"A Triumph of Scholarship." Review of *Encyclopaedia of the Social Sciences. Saturday Review of Literature* 13 (7 Dec. 1935): 38, 42.

"William James." Review of Ralph Barton Perry, *The Thought and Character of William James. Nation* 141 (11 Dec. 1935): 684–86.

"Ludwig Feuerbach." Part 1. *Modern Monthly* 9 (Dec. 1935): 357–69; Part 2: "Feuerbach's Psychology of Religion." Ibid. 9 (Jan. 1936): 430–36; Part 3: "Feuerbach's Philosophy of Anthropomorphism." Ibid. 9 (Mar. 1936): 493–501.

1936

From Hegel to Marx: Studies in the Intellectual Development of Karl Marx. New York: John Day Co., 1936; New York: Reynal and Hitchcock, 1936.

"Plato without the Legend." Review of Warner Fite, *The Platonic Legend. New Republic* 82 (27 Feb. 1936): 81.

"Revolutionary Mythology." Review of August Thalheimer, *Introduction to Dialectical Materialism. Nation* 142 (4 Mar. 1936): 288–90.

"The Faith of a Scientist." Review of Bertrand Russell, *Religion and Science. New Republic* 86 (1 Apr. 1936): 227.

"Marx's Life and Thought." Review of Franz Mehring, *Karl Marx: The Story of His Life. Saturday Review of Literature* 13 (18 Apr. 1936): 18–19.

"Radicals and War." A debate with Ludwig Lore. *Modern Monthly* 10 (Apr. 1936): 12–17.

"Ethereal Politics." Review of Richard Rothschild, *Three Gods Give an Evening to Politics. Nation* 142 (20 May 1936): 653–54.

"Social Masks and Social Facts." Review of Thurman Arnold, *The Symbols of Government*. *New Republic* 87 (20 May 1936): 51–52.

"On Rereading Veblen." Review of *What Veblen Taught*, ed. Wesley Clair Mitchell. *New Republic* 87 (17 June 1936): 182.

"Man behind Marx." Review of Gustav Mayer, *Friedrich Engels*. *Saturday Review of Literature* 14 (27 June 1936): 10.

"The Prophetic Trotsky." Review of Leon Trotsky, *The Third International after Lenin*. *Saturday Review* 14 (11 July 1936): 10.

"New Trend in Philosophy." Review of George H. Mead, *Movements of Thought in the Nineteenth Century*. *Nation* 143 (22 Aug. 1936): 220–21.

"The Uses of Opposition." *Modern Monthly* 10 (Aug. 1936): 13–15.

"Marxism as a Living Philosophy." *New Republic* 88 (30 Sept. 1936): 233–34.

> Reply to Herman Simpson's review of *From Hegel to Marx*, ibid., pp. 232–33.
>
> Rebuttal by Simpson, ibid. 89 (18 Nov. 1936): 75–76.
>
> Rejoinder by Hook, ibid., p. 76.

"Philosophy in Action." Review of Horace M. Kallen, *The Decline and Rise of the Consumer*. *Opinion* 7 (Dec. 1936): 25, 27.

1937

"The Philosophical Implications of Economic Planning." In *Planned Society: Yesterday, Today and Tomorrow*, ed. Findlay Mackenzie, pp. 663–77. New York: Prentice-Hall, 1937.

Introduction to Richard Lowenthal, *What Is Folksocialism?* New York: League for Industrial Democracy, 1937.

"Marxism and Values." *Marxist Quarterly* 1 (Jan.–Mar. 1937): 38–45.

Review of Karl Joël, *Wandlungen der Weltanschauung*. *Journal of Philosophy* 34 (4 Mar. 1937): 131–33.

"Dialectic and Nature." *Marxist Quarterly* 1 (Apr.–June 1937): 253–84.

"A Philosopher on Movie Censorship." Review of Mortimer Adler, *Art and Prudence: A Study in Practical Philosophy. Saturday Review* 16 (15 May 1937): 17.

"Both Their Houses." *New Republic* 91 (2 June 1937): 104.

"History in Swing Rhythm." Review of Pitirim Sorokin, *Social and Cultural Dynamics. Nation* 145 (10 July 1937): 48–49.

"Socialism for a Democracy." Review of Harry W. Laidler, *American Socialism. Saturday Review* 16 (28 Aug. 1937): 20.

"Fantasia on the Left." Review of Albert Weisbord, *The Conquest of Power: Liberalism, Anarchism, Syndicalism, Socialism, Fascism, and Communism. Nation* 145 (11 Sept. 1937): 270–71.

"Discussion: Totalitarianism in Education." *Social Research* 4 (Sept. 1937): 401–4.

"Seeking Truth about Trotsky." Review of Preliminary Commission of Inquiry, *The Case of Leon Trotsky: Report of Hearings on the Charges Made against Him in the Moscow Trials. New York Herald Tribune Books*, 10 Oct. 1937.

"Worlds of Chance." Review of Edward Gleason Spaulding, *A World of Chance. Nation* 145 (23 Oct. 1937): 451–53.

"Promise without Dogma: A Social Philosophy for Jews." *Menorah Journal* 25 (Oct.–Dec. 1937): 273–88.

> Reply by Alvin Johnson, "A Social Philosophy for Jews." Ibid. 26 (Jan.–Mar. 1938): 1–6.
>
> Response by Hook, "A Note on Alvin Johnson's Article." Ibid. 26 (Winter 1938): 103–4.

"The Sociology of Knowledge." Review of Karl Mannheim, *Ideology and Utopia. Marxist Quarterly* 1 (Oct.–Dec. 1937): 450–54.

"The Technique of Mystification." Review of Kenneth Burke, *Attitudes Toward History. Partisan Review* 4 (Dec. 1937): 57–62.

> Reply by Burke, ibid. 4 (Jan. 1938): 40–44.
>
> Response by Hook, "Is Mr. Burke Serious?" Ibid., pp. 44–47.

"Ends and Means." Review of Aldous Huxley, *Ends and Means. Nation* 145 (11 Dec. 1937): 656–58.

"Liberalism and the Case of Leon Trotsky." *Southern Review* 3 (1937–38): 267–82.

Correspondence by Hook, Frederick, Schuman, Carleton Beals, and James T. Farrell, ibid., pp. 406–16.

1938

"Violence As a (Marxist) Professor Sees It." *Common Sense* 7 (Jan. 1938): 22–23.

"The Ways of Philosophy." Review of Irwin Edman, *Four Ways of Philosophy. Nation* 146 (8 Jan. 1938): 48–49.

"Storm Signals in American Philosophy." *Virginia Quarterly Review* 14 (Winter 1938): 29–43.

"Zweiter Entfer oyf der Frage: Zie Leybt in sich Izt die Sowietische Arbeiter Besser, wie die Arbeiter in andere Lender?" *Der Tag*, 7 Feb. 1938.

"Broun v. Dewey." *New Republic* 94 (16 Feb. 1938): 48.

Letter in reply to Heywood Broun, "Dr. Dewey Finds Communists in the C.I.O." Ibid. 93 (12 Jan. 1938): 280–81.

"Metaphysics and Social Attitudes: A Reply." *Social Frontier* 4 (Feb. 1938): 153–58.

Reply to Brand Blanshard, "Metaphysics and Social Attitudes." Ibid. 4 (Dec. 1937): 79–81.

Response by Porter Sargent, "Metaphysics and Social Attitudes: Some Forgotten Facts." Ibid. 4 (Mar. 1938): 178–79.

Reply by Pitirim A. Sorokin, ibid., pp. 179–80.

Rejoinder by Blanshard, "Metaphysics and Social Attitudes, A Rejoinder." Ibid. 4 (Apr. 1938): 219–21.

Response by Hook, "Relevant Issues Restated." Ibid., pp. 221–23.

"Logic, Politics, and Plain Decency." *Social Frontier* 4 (Mar. 1938): 190–92.

Response to Earl Browder, "Toward the American Commonwealth: 2. The Present Communist Position." Ibid. 4 (Feb. 1938): 161–64.

"Corliss Lamont: 'Friend of the G.P.U.'" *Modern Monthly* 10 (Mar. 1938): 5–8.

"The Baptism of Aristotle and Marx." Review of Mortimer J. Adler, *What Man Has Made of Man. Nation* 146 (9 Apr. 1938): 415–17.

"Some Social Uses and Abuses of Semantics." *Partisan Review* 4 (Apr. 1938): 14–25.

"The Politician's Handbook." Review of Thurman Arnold, *The Folklore of Capitalism. University of Chicago Law Review* 5 (Apr. 1938): 341–49.

> Reply by Arnold, "The Folklore of Mr. Hook—A Reply." Ibid., pp. 349–53.

> Rejoinder by Hook, "Neither Myth nor Power—A Rejoinder." Ibid., pp. 354–57.

"Thoughts in Season." *Socialist Review* 6 (May–June 1938): 6–7, 16.

"Democracy as a Way of Life." *Southern Review* 4 (Summer 1938): 45–57.

> Revised as "The Democratic Way of Life." *Menorah Journal* 26 (Oct.–Dec. 1938): 261–75.

"Science and the New Obscurantism." *Modern Quarterly* 11 (Fall 1938): 66–85.

"An Effective Logic." Review of Paul Weiss, *Logic: The Theory of Inquiry. New Republic* 97 (23 Nov. 1938): 79–80.

"Eduard Heimann on the 'Revolutionary Situation'." *Social Research* 5 (Nov. 1938): 464–71.

> Response to Heimann, "The 'Revolutionary Situation' and the Middle Classes." Ibid. 5 (May 1938): 227–36.

> Reply by Heimann, ibid. 5 (Nov. 1938): 471–73.

"The Tragedy of German Jewry." *New Leader* 21 (26 Nov. 1938): 8.

"Whitehead's Latest Phase." Review of Alfred North Whitehead, *Modes of Thought. Nation* 147 (10 Dec. 1938): 632–33.

"Critical Analysis as a Method of Radio Education." *School and Society* 48 (31 Dec. 1938): 858–59.

1939

John Dewey: An Intellectual Portrait. New York: John Day Co., 1939.

"Democracy as a Way of Life." In *Tomorrow in the Making*, ed. J. N. Andrews and C. A. Marsden, pp. 31–36. New York: McGraw-Hill, 1939.

"A Challenge to the Liberal-Arts College." *Journal of Higher Education* 10 (Jan. 1939): 14–23, 58.

"The Fetishism of Power." Review of Gaetano Mosca, *The Ruling Classes*. *Nation* 148 (13 May 1939): 562–63.

Letter by Hook introducing the Manifesto of the Committee for Cultural Freedom. Manifesto signed by Hook et al. *Nation* 148 (27 May 1939): 626.

    Reply by Freda Kirchwey, "Red Totalitarianism." Ibid., pp. 605–6.

    Response by Hook with rebuttal by Kirchwey, ibid. 148 (17 June 1939): 710–11.

"The Anatomy of the Popular Front." Essay review of Max Lerner, *It Is Later Than You Think. Partisan Review* 6 (Spring 1939): 29–45.

"Soviet Union a Totalitarian Dictatorship Just as Is Germany." Letter to the editor. *New York Post*, 7 June 1939.

"Hook Warns against Forgery Tactics of Totalitarian Agents." Letter to the editor. *New Leader*, 24 June 1939.

"Dialectic in Social and Historical Inquiry." *Journal of Philosophy* 36 (6 July 1939): 365–78.

"'The Totalitarian Mind'—and Those Who Hew to the 'Line'." *New York Post*, 2 Sept. 1939, p. 12.

"Salute to John Dewey!" *Call*, 27 Oct. 1939.

"John Dewey at Eighty." *New Leader*, 28 Oct. 1939.

"The Importance of John Dewey in Modern Thought." *Modern Quarterly* 11 (Fall 1939): 30–35.

"Upton Sinclair vs. Sidney Hook: The Debate on Russia Grows Warmer." *Call*, 18 Nov. 1939.

"Academic Freedom and 'The Trojan Horse' in American Education."

American Association of University Professors Bulletin 25 (Dec. 1939): 550–55.

"Reflections on the Russian Revolution." Review of Leon Trotsky, *The Revolution Betrayed*. *Southern Review* 4 (Winter 1939): 429–62.

Review of Ernest Nagel, *Principles of the Theory of Probability*. *Philosophic Abstracts* 1 (1939–40): 8.

Review of Folke Leander, *The Philosophy of John Dewey, A Critical Study*. *Philosophic Abstracts* 1 (1939–40): 21–22.

"Abstractions in Social Inquiry." *Illinois Law Review* 34 (1939–40): 15–29.

1940

Reason, Social Myths and Democracy. New York: John Day Co., 1940.

"Unreconstructed Fellow-Travelers." *Call*, 13 Jan. 1940, p. 2.

Review of Theodor L. Haering, *Hegel: Sein Wollen und sein Werk*, vol. 2. *Philosophical Review* 49 (Jan. 1940): 87–88.

"An Attack on Freedom." *New York Herald Tribune Books*, 9 Mar. 1940, p. 14.

"Socialists Face Need of Unified Action." *New Leader* 23 (9 Mar. 1940): 7.

"Conceptions of Human Motivation: Socialism and the Motives of Men." *Frontiers of Democracy* 6 (15 Mar. 1940): 167.

"On Ideas." Review of Max Lerner, *Ideas Are Weapons. Partisan Review* 7 (Mar.–Apr. 1940): 152–60.

"What Stalin Wrote." Review of *Stalin's Kampf*, ed. M. R. Werner. *New York Herald Tribune Books*, 7 Apr. 1940, p. 6.

"Prof. Hook to Prof. Schuman." *Saturday Review* 21 (20 Apr. 1940): 9. Reply to Frederick L. Schuman's review of *Stalin's Kampf*, ed. M. R. Werner, ibid., 6 Apr. 1940.

"What Is Living and What Is Dead in Marxism?" *Frontiers of Democracy* 6 (15 Apr. 1940): 218–20.

"The Integral Humanism of Jacques Maritain." Review of Jacques Maritain, *True Humanism. Partisan Review* 7 (May–June 1940): 204–29.

"Is Nazism a Social Revolution?" *New Leader* 23 (20 July 1940): 4, 6.

"How Has John Strachey Changed His Mind?" Review of John Strachey, *A Programme for Progress*. *New York Herald Tribune Books*, 21 July 1940, p. 5.

"Socialism, Common Sense and the War." *New Leader* 23 (31 Aug. 1940): 7.

"Alexander Goldenweiser: Three Tributes." With Ruth Benedict and Margaret Mead. *Modern Quarterly* 11 (Summer 1940): 31–32.

Review of James K. Feibleman, *Positive Democracy*. *Journal of Philosophy* 37 (26 Sept. 1940): 557–59.

"Thinkers Who Prepared for Revolution." Review of Edmund Wilson, *To the Finland Station: A Study in the Writing and Acting of History*. *New York Herald Tribune Books*, 29 Sept. 1940.

"Engels as Scientist." Review of Friedrich Engels, *Dialectics of Nature*. *Nation* 151 (5 Oct. 1940): 308.

"Planning—and Freedom." Review of Karl Mannheim, *Man and Society in an Age of Reconstruction*. *Nation* 151 (26 Oct. 1940): 398–99.

"The New Medievalism." *New Republic* 103 (28 Oct. 1940): 602–6. Hook's comments on Mortimer Adler's "God and the Professors." A paper delivered at the National Conference on Science, Philosophy, and Religion in Their Relation to the Democratic Way of Life. Jewish Theological Seminary, New York City, 10–11 Sept. 1940. Adler's and Hook's papers reprinted in a special issue of the *Daily Maroon* (University of Chicago), 14 Nov. 1940, along with papers by Frank Knight, Quincy Wright, and Milton Mayer.

"Metaphysics, War, and the Intellectuals." Review of Waldo Frank, *Chart for Rough Water*; Archibald MacLeish, *The Irresponsibles*; and Lewis Mumford, *Faith for Living*. *Menorah Journal* 28 (Oct. 1940): 326–37.

"Despair on Mt. Olympus." Review of George Santayana, *The Realm of Spirit*. *Nation* 151 (2 Nov. 1940): 423–24.

"A Democratic Survival." Review of Emil Lederer, *State of the Masses*. *New York Herald Tribune Books*, 1 Dec. 1940, p. 38.

1941

"'Out of the Night' Uncovers Underworld of a Rotted Religion." Review of Jan Valtin, *Out of the Night. New Leader* 24 (15 Feb. 1941): 5.

"The Counter-Reformation in American Education." *Antioch Review* 1 (Mar. 1941): 109–16.

"The Basic Values and Loyalties of Communism." *American Teacher* 25 (May 1941): 4–6.

"Reason and Revolution." Review of Herbert Marcuse, *Reason and Revolution: Hegel and the Rise of Social Theory. New Republic* 105 (21 July 1941): 90–91.

"Moscow Order Dissolving Communist Party in U.S. Would Swing Wide Public Support to Aid for U.S.S.R." *New Leader* 24 (11 Oct. 1941): 4.

"Social Change and Original Sin: Answer to Niebuhr." Review of Reinhold Niebuhr, *The Nature and Destiny of Man* and Charles Sherrington, *Man and His Nature. New Leader* 24 (8 Nov. 1941): 5, 7.

"The Philosophical Presuppositions of Democracy." Abstract. *Journal of Philosophy* 38 (4 Dec. 1941): 685–86. Printed in full in *Ethics* 52 (Apr. 1942): 275–96.

"The Late Mr. Tate." *Southern Review* 6 (1941): 840–43.

1942

"Salvation by Semantics." Review of S. I. Hayakawa, *Language in Action: A Guide to Accurate Thinking. Nation* 154 (3 Jan. 1942): 16.

"Crisis of Our Culture." Review of Pitirim A. Sorokin, *The Crisis of Our Age: The Social and Cultural Outlook. New York Herald Tribune Books*, 11 Jan. 1942, p. 10.

"Russia's Military Successes Do Not Whitewash Crimes at Home." *New Leader* 25 (31 Jan. 1942): 5.

"National Unity and 'Corporate Thinking'." *Menorah Journal* 30 (Jan. 1942): 61–68. Comments on *Science, Philosophy and Religion: A Symposium* (New York: 1941).

"Milton Mayer: Fake Jeremiah." *New Leader* 25 (4 Apr. 1942): 5.

"Whitehead's Final Views." Review of *The Philosophy of Alfred North Whitehead*, ed. Paul Arthur Schilpp. Library of Living Philosophers, vol. 3. *Nation* 154 (4 Apr. 1942): 401–3.

"Two Views on Mortimer Adler and Milton Mayer." With Francis McMahon. *New Leader* 25 (16 May 1942): 5, 7.

"Sidney Hook Analyzes a New 'Faith' for the Businessman: A Review of Hocking's New 'Philosophical Healing'." Review of William Ernest Hocking, *What Man Can Make of Man*. *New Leader* 25 (5 Sept. 1942): 2, 7.

"The Function of Higher Education in Postwar Reconstruction." *Journal of Educational Sociology* 16 (Sept. 1942): 43–51.

"Theological Tom-Tom and Metaphysical Bagpipe." *Humanist* 2 (Autumn 1942): 96–102.

1943

The Hero in History: A Study in Limitation and Possibility. New York: John Day Co., 1943.

"The New Failure of Nerve, Part 1." *Partisan Review* 10 (Jan.–Feb. 1943): 2–23; "Part 2: The Failure of the Left." Ibid. 10 (Mar.–Apr. 1943): 165–77.

> Response by David Merian, "The Nerve of Sidney Hook." Ibid. 10 (May–June 1943): 248–57.
>
> Replies by Hook, "The Politics of Wonderland." Ibid., pp. 258–62; "Faith, Hope, and Dialectic: Merian in Wonderland." Ibid. 10 (Sept.–Oct. 1943): 476–81.
>
> Response by Malcolm Cowley, "Marginalia." *New Republic* 109 (12 July 1943): 50.
>
> Response by Isaac Rosenfeld, "The Failure of Verve." Ibid. 109 (19 July 1943): 80–81.
>
> Reply by Hook, "Experience and Intelligence." Ibid. 109 (6 Sept. 1943): 336–37.
>
> Responses by Cowley and Rosenfeld, ibid., pp. 337–38.

"Education for the New Order." Review of Alexander Mieklejohn, *Education between Two Worlds*. *Nation* 156 (27 Feb. 1943): 308, 310, 312. Response by Mark Van Doren, with reply by Hook, ibid. 156 (20 Mar. 1943): 430–31.

"Tribute to Carlo Tresca." *Il Martello* 28 (28 Mar. 1943): 44.

"Philosophy of Art and Culture." Review of Horace M. Kallen, *Art and Freedom*. *New York Herald Tribune Weekly Book Review*, 11 Apr. 1943, p. 20.

"Illusions of Our Time." Review of Harold Laski, *Reflections on the Revolution of Our Time*. *Partisan Review* 10 (Sept.–Oct. 1943): 442–47.

"Charles Beard's Political Testament." Review of Charles A. Beard, *The Republic: Conversation on Fundamentals*. *Nation* 157 (23 Oct. 1943): 474–76.

"The Perpetual Debate." Review of Henry Steele Commager, *Majority Rule and Minority Rights*. *Nation* 157 (11 Dec. 1943): 709–10.

1944

"Naturalism and Democracy." In *Naturalism and the Human Spirit*, ed. Y. H. Krikorian, pp. 40–64. New York: Columbia University Press, 1944.

"The Rebirth of Political Credulity." *New Leader* 27 (1 Jan. 1944): 4–5.

"Humanism and the Labor Movement." *New Europe*, Feb. 1944.

"Progressive Liberal Education." Review of Algo D. Henderson, *Vitalizing Liberal Education*. *Nation* 158 (11 Mar. 1944): 312–14.

"Hitlerism: A Non-Metaphysical View." Review of Konrad Heiden, *Der Fuehrer*. *Contemporary Jewish Record* 7 (Apr. 1944): 146–55.

"Ballyhoo at St. John's College—Education in Retreat." Part 1. *New Leader* 27 (27 May 1944): 8–9.

"Ballyhoo at St. John's—The 'Great Books' and Progressive Teaching." Part 2. *New Leader* 27 (3 June 1944): 8–10.

"God, Geometry and the Good Society." Review of Mark Van Doren, *Liberal Education*. *Partisan Review* 11 (Spring 1944): 161–67.

"Thirteen Arrows against Progressive Liberal Education." *Humanist* 4 (Spring 1944): 1–10.

"Is Physical Realism Sufficient?" *Journal of Philosophy* 41 (28 Sept. 1944): 544–51.

> See Hook, "What Is Materialism?" Ibid. 31 (26 Apr. 1934): 235–42; and R. W. Sellars, "Is Naturalism Enough?" Ibid. 41 (28 Sept. 1944): 533–44.

"Heroic Vitalism." Review of Eric Bentley, *A Century of Hero-Worship*. *Nation* 159 (7 Oct. 1944): 412–14.

"If Only . . ." Review of Ludwig von Mises, *Omnipotent Government*. *Nation* 159 (28 Oct. 1944): 530.

"Planned Diversity." Review of Karl Mannheim, *Diagnosis of Our Time*. *Nation* 159 (11 Nov. 1944): 596.

"An Apologist for St. John's College." *New Leader*, 25 Nov. 1944.

"Schooling for Democrats." Review of Marie Syrkin, *Your School, Your Children*. *Nation* 159 (18 Nov. 1944): 621–22.

"The Ends of Education." *Journal of Educational Sociology* 18 (Nov. 1944): 173–84.

"Road to Freedom." Review of Bronislaw Malinowski, *Freedom and Civilization*. *New Europe*, Dec. 1944.

1945

The Authoritarian Attempt to Capture Education. By John Dewey, Sidney Hook, Arthur Murphy, Irwin Edman, and others. New York: King's Crown Press, 1945.

What Is the Future of Socialism? London, 1945.

"Proletariat." In *Encyclopaedia Britannica*. Chicago: Encyclopaedia Britannica, 1945.

"The Dilemma of T. S. Eliot." *Nation* 160 (20 Jan. 1945): 69–71.

"The Degradation of the Word." *New Leader* 28 (27 Jan. 1945): 7.

"Freedom and Socialism: Reply to Max Eastman." *New Leader* (3 Mar. 1945): 4–5.

"Democratic Faith and Puritan Piety." Review of Ralph Barton Perry, *Puritanism and Democracy*. *Nation* 160 (26 May 1945): 603–5.

"Total Condemnation: Denunciation of All Germans Held Unfair to Anti-Nazis." Letter by Hook et al. *New York Times*, 10 June 1945, p. 8.

"Man and the Universe of Symbols." Review of Ernst Cassirer, *An Essay on Man*. *Kenyon Review* 7 (Spring 1945): 335–38.

"The Case for Progressive Education." *Saturday Evening Post* 217 (30 June 1945): 28–29, 39, 41.

"A Discussion of the Theory of International Relations." *Journal of Philosophy* 42 (30 Aug. 1945): 493–95.

"Are Naturalists Materialists?" With Ernest Nagel and John Dewey. *Journal of Philosophy* 42 (13 Sept. 1945): 515–30.

> Reply to Wilmon Henry Sheldon, "A Critique of Naturalism." Ibid. 42 (10 May 1945): 253–70.

> For a continuation of the discussion, see Rudolph Allers, "Does Human Nature Change?" *Catholic University Bulletin* 14, no. 2 (1946): 6–9.

"Education for Vocation." *Antioch Review* 5 (Fall 1945): 415–28.

"The Signs of Aldous Huxley." Review of Aldous Huxley, *The Perennial Philosophy*. *Saturday Review of Literature* 28 (3 Nov. 1945): 12–13.

"Reflections on the Nuremberg Trial." *New Leader* 28 (17 Nov. 1945): 8, 14.

"Bertrand Russell among the Sages." Review of Bertrand Russell, *A History of Western Philosophy*. *Nation* 161 (1 Dec. 1945): 586, 588, 590.

"The Autonomy of Democratic Faith." *American Scholar* 15 (Winter 1945–46): 105–9.

> Part 3 of a forum on "The Future of Religion." For parts 1 and 2, see Raphael Demos, "The Need for Religion and Its Truth," pp. 97–102; and Paul Tillich, "Vertical and Horizontal Thinking," pp. 102–5. See rejoinders by Demos and Tillich, pp. 109–12, and by Hook, pp. 11–13.

1946

Education for Modern Man. New York: Dial Press, 1946.

"Illustrations." In *Theory and Practice in Historical Study: A Report of the Committee on Historiography*, pp. 108–30. New York: Social Science Research Council (Bulletin 54), 1946.

"Introduction." In *Social Democracy versus Socialism*, by Karl Kautsky, ed. David Shub, trans. Joseph Shaplen, pp. 7–20. New York: Rand School Press, 1946.

"Problems of Terminology in Historical Writing." With Charles A. Beard. In *Theory and Practice in Historical Study: A Report of the Committee on Historiography*, pp. 105–8. New York: Social Science Research Council (Bulletin 54), 1946.

"Role of Science in Determination of Democratic Policy, A Symposium." In *Papers: Science for Democracy*, ed. Jerome Nathanson, pp. 109–70. New York: King's Crown Press, 1946.

"Fin du Mondisme: The Birth of a New World Mood in Face of Atom-bomb." *New Leader*, 23 Feb. 1946, pp. 8–9.

"Toward Intellectual Teamwork: Notes on the Evolution of a Conference." *Commentary* 1 (Feb. 1946): 81–85.

"What Is Philosophy?" Review of Brand Blanshard, Curt J. Ducasse, Charles Van Hendel, Arthur E. Murphy, and Max C. Otto, *Philosophy in American Education: Its Tasks and Opportunities. Nation* 162 (30 Mar. 1946): 375–77.

"Moral Values and/or Religion in Our Schools." *Progressive Education* 23 (May 1946): 256–57, 278–79.

"The Philosophic Scene: Scientific Method on the Defensive." *Commentary* 1 (June 1946): 85–90.

"Russia's Foreign Policy." Letter to the editor. *New York Times*, 17 Oct. 1946, p. 22.

"The Laws of Dialectic." *Polemic* no. 6 (Nov.–Dec. 1946): 9–29.

"Synthesis or Eclecticism?" *Philosophy and Phenomenological Research* 7 (Dec. 1946): 214–25.

The National council of Jewish women on the present–day Jewish scene. New York, 1946.

1947

"Intelligence and Evil in Human History." In *Freedom and Experience: Essays Presented to Horace M. Kallen*, ed. Sidney Hook and Milton R. Konvitz, pp. 24–45. Ithaca: Cornell University Press, 1947.

"Education for Vocation." In *American Thought*, with an introduction by Philip Wylie, pp. 133–47. New York: Gresham Press, 1947.

"The Future of Socialism." *Partisan Review* 14 (Jan.–Feb. 1947): 23–36.

"Philosophy and the Police." Review of John Somerville, *Soviet Philosophy: A Study of Theory and Practice. Nation* 164 (15 Feb. 1947): 188–89.

> Reply by Somerville with Hook's response, ibid., 10 May 1947, pp. 550–52.

"Totalitarian Liberalism." *Time* 49 (17 Feb. 1947): 28.

"What Exactly Do We Mean by 'Democracy'?" *New York Times Magazine*, 16 Mar. 1947, pp. 10, 48, 49.

"Intelligence and Evil in Human History." *Commentary* 3 (Mar. 1947): 210–21.

"From Question to Assertion: A Rejoinder to Professor Demos." *Philosophy and Phenomenological Research* 7 (Mar. 1947): 439–45.

"Mr. Fly's Web of Confusions: A Problem of Contemporary Liberalism." *New Leader* 30 (18 Oct. 1947): 8, 9, 15.

> Reply by James Lawrence Fly, "On the Befuddlement of Sidney Hook." Ibid. 30 (22 Nov. 1947): 8.
>
> Rejoinder by Hook, "Mr. Fly Entangles Himself More Deeply." Ibid., pp. 9, 15.

"Is the U.S. a Republic or Democracy?" *New York Times Magazine*, 19 Oct. 1947, pp. 17, 49, 50, 51.

"The U.S.S.R. Views American Philosophy." *Modern Review* 1 (Nov. 1947): 649–53. Foreword to M. Dynnik, "Contemporary Bourgeois Philosophy in the U.S."

"The Source of Value." Review of Clarence I. Lewis, *An Analysis of Knowledge and Valuation. New York Times Book Review*, 16 Nov. 1947, p. 16.

"Moral und Politik." *Amerikanische Rundschau* 3 (1947): 3–18.

"An Unanswered Letter to the American Jewish Congress." *New Leader* 30 (1947): 15.

"Portrait . . . John Dewey." *American Scholar* 17 (Winter 1947–48): 105–10.

Letter to the editor. *Philosophical Review* 56 (1947): 608–9.

1948

"The Autonomy of Democratic Faith." In *Living, Reading, and Thinking*, ed. J. R. Chamberlain, W. B. Pressey, and R. E. Watters, pp. 649–60. New York: Scribners, 1948.

"Humanism and the Labor Movement." In *European Ideologies*, ed. Feliks Gross, pp. 1057–63. New York: Philosophical Library, 1948.

"Meeting of Logic and the Arts." Review of F. S. C. Northrup, *The Logic of the Sciences and the Humanities. New York Times*, 11 Jan. 1948, p. 7.

"On the Casting Out of Devils." Review of Norman Angell, *The Steep Places. New York Times Book Review*, 25 Jan. 1948, pp. 1, 33.

"The Communist Manifesto 100 Years After." *New York Times Magazine*, 1 Feb. 1948, pp. 6, 36, 38.

"On Historical Understanding." *Partisan Review* 15 (Feb. 1948): 231–39.

"The State—Servile or Free?" *New Leader* 31 (13 Mar. 1948): 1, 12.

"Academic Freedom." Letter to the editor. *New York Times*, 23 Mar. 1948, p. 24.

"Why Democracy Is Better." *Commentary* 5 (Mar. 1948): 195–204.

"Mr. Toynbee's City of God." Review of Arnold Joseph Toynbee, *Civilization on Trial. Partisan Review* 15 (June 1948): 691–99.

> Replies by C. Roland Wagner and E. G. Gallagher, ibid. 15, Aug. 1948, pp. 940–41.
>
> Response by Hook, Ibid., pp. 941–42.

Letter to the editor. *American Scholar* 17 (Summer 1948): 360–61.

"Russia's Slave Labor." Letter to the editor, by Sidney Hook et al. *New York Times*, 2 Nov. 1948, p. 24.

"Drei Grundzüge westlichen Denkens." *Der Monat* 1 (Nov. 1948): 8–17.

1949

"Academic Freedom and Communism." In *People Shall Judge*, by the Social Science Staff, pp. 705–14. Chicago: University of Chicago Press, 1949.

"Nature and the Human Spirit." In *Proceedings: 10th International Congress of Philosophy*, pp. 153–55. Amsterdam: North Holland Publishing Co., 1949.

"Should Communists Be Permitted to Teach?" *New York Times Magazine*, 27 Feb. 1949, pp. 7, 22, 24, 26, 28, 29.

"Communism and the Intellectuals." *American Mercury* 68 (Feb. 1949): 133–44.

"Die Zukunft der demokratischen Linken." *Der Monat* 1 (Feb. 1949): 13–17.

"International Communism." *Dartmouth Alumni Magazine* 41 (Mar. 1949): 13–20.

"John Dewey: Ein Porträt." *Der Monat* 1 (Mar. 1949): 40–46.

"The Philosophy of Democracy as a Philosophy of History." *Philosophy and Phenomenological Research* 9 (Mar. 1949): 576–87.

"On the Battlefield of Philosophy." *Partisan Review* 16 (Mar. 1949): 251–68.

"Stand of the Liberals." With George S. Counts. *New York Times*, 13 Apr. 1949, p. 28.

"The Fellow-Traveler: A Study in Psychology." *New York Times Magazine*, 17 Apr. 1949, pp. 9, 20, 21, 22, 23.

"Dr. Hook Protests." *Nation* 168 (30 Apr. 1949): 511.

"Reflections on the Jewish Question." Review of Jean–Paul Sartre, *Anti-Semite and Jew*. *Partisan Review* 16 (May 1949) 463–82.

"Science, Freedom and Peace." *New Leader* 32 (25 June 1949): 6.

"A Gallant American Rebel." Review of Ray Ginger, *The Bending Cross: A Biography of Eugene Victor Debs*. *New York Times Book Review*, 17 July 1949, p. 7.

"Report on the International Day Against Dictatorship and War." *Partisan Review* 16 (July 1949): 722–32.

"What Shall We Do about Communist Teachers?" *Saturday Evening Post* 222 (10 Sept. 1949): 33, 164–68.

"The Literature of Political Disillusionment." *American Association of University Professors Bulletin* 35 (Autumn 1949): 450–67.

"John Dewey at Ninety: The Man and His Philosophy." *New Leader* 32 (22 Oct. 1949): S-3, S-8.

"Academic Integrity and Academic Freedom." *Commentary* 8 (Oct. 1949): 329–39.

> Reply by Helen Lynd, ibid. 8 (Dec. 1949): 594–95.
>
> Response by Hook, "Professor Hook Replies." Ibid., pp. 598–601.

"U.S.S.R. Distorts Theories to Fit 'Party Truth'." *New York Times*, 18 Nov. 1949, p. 28.

"Academic Freedom—Academic Confusions." *Journal of Higher Education* 20 (Nov. 1949): 422–25.

1950

From Hegel to Marx. With a new introduction by Hook. Ann Arbor: University of Michigan Press, 1950.

"The Desirable and Emotive in John Dewey's Ethics." In *John Dewey: Philosopher of Science and Freedom*, ed. Sidney Hook, pp. 194–216. New York: Dial Press, 1950.

"John Dewey and His Critics." In *Pragmatism and American Culture*, ed. Gail Kennedy, pp. 92–94. Boston: D. C. Heath and Co., 1950.

"The Place of John Dewey in Modern Thought." In *Philosophic Thought in France and the United States*, ed. Marvin Farber, pp. 483–503. Buffalo: University of Buffalo Press, 1950.

Contribution in *Religion and the Intellectuals*. A symposium with John Dewey, Hook, and others. New York: Partisan Review, 1950.

"Democracy—Minus the Rhetoric." Review of R. M. MacIver, *The Ramparts We Guard. New York Times Book Review*, 26 Feb. 1950, pp. 3, 31.

"Religion and the Intellectuals." *Partisan Review* 17 (Mar. 1950): 225–32.

Reply by Ernest van den Haag, ibid. 17 (July–Aug. 1950): 607–12.

Rejoinder by Hook, ibid., pp. 612–16.

"Mr. Hook Replies." *Commentary* 9 (Mar. 1950): 286–87.

"The Scientist in Politics." *New York Times Magazine*, 9 Apr. 1950, pp. 10, 25, 27, 28, 30.

"Communists in the Colleges." *New Leader* 33 (6 May 1950): 16–18.

"Lenin—oder Die Rolle des Einzelnen." *Der Monat* 2 (May 1950): 174–89.

"Heresy, Yes—But Conspiracy, No." *New York Times Magazine*, 9 July 1950, pp. 12, 38–39.

"The Berlin Congress." Letter to the editor on comments by H. R. Trevor-Roper on the Congress for Cultural Freedom. *Manchester Guardian Weekly*, 7 Sept. 1950.

"Past and Present of the Case That Shook the Nation." Review of Alistair Cooke, *A Generation on Trial: U.S.A. v. Alger Hiss. New York Times Book Review*, 24 Sept. 1950, p. 7.

"The Berlin Congress for Cultural Freedom." *Partisan Review* 17 (Sept.–Oct. 1950): 715–22.

"The University of California and the Non-Communist Oath." Review of George R. Stewart, *The Year of the Oath. New York Times Book Review*, 1 Oct. 1950, p. 6.

"Encounter in Berlin." *New Leader* 33 (14 Oct. 1950): 16–19.

"How to Stop Russia without War." Review of Boris Shub, *The Choice. New York Post*, 22 Oct. 1950.

"Why They Switch Loyalties." *New York Times Magazine*, 26 Nov. 1950, pp. 12, 26, 28, 30.

"U.N. Stand on Korea." Letter to the editor. *New York Times*, 15 Dec. 1950, p. 30.

1951

"Bertrand Russell's Philosophy of History." In *Philosophy of Bertrand Russell*, ed. Paul A. Schilpp, pp. 643–78. New York: Free Press, 1951.

"General Education: Its Nature and Purpose." In *General Education in Transition*, ed. Horace T. Morse, pp. 68–82. Minneapolis: University of Minnesota Press, 1951.

"Nature and the Human Spirit." In *Freedom and Reason*, ed. Salo Baron, Ernest Nagel, and K. S. Pinson, pp. 142–56. New York: Free Press, 1951.

"The Danger of Authoritarian Attitudes in Teaching Today." *School and Society* 73 (20 Jan. 1951): 33–39.

"Communists: Authoritarians in the Schools." *Socialist Call*, 26 Jan. 1951, pp. 3, 5.

"Prof. Hook and the Loyalty Oaths." *Socialist Call*, 26 Jan. 1951, p. 3.
    Reply to S. M. Lipset, ibid., 12 Jan. 1951.

"Coverage of Rousset Trial." Letter to the editor, by Sidney Hook et al. *New York Times*, 15 Feb. 1951, p. 30.

"To Counter the Big Lie—A Basic Strategy." *New York Times Magazine*, 11 Mar. 1951, pp. 9, 59, 60, 61, 62, 63, 64.

"A Case Study in Anti–Secularism." Review of Eliseo Vivas, *The Moral Life and the Ethical Life*. *Partisan Review* 18 (18 Mar. 1951): 232–45.

"Liberty, Society and Mr. Santayana." Review of George Santayana, *Dominations and Powers*. *New York Times Book Review*, 6 May 1951, pp. 1, 20.

"Academic Freedom." Letter to the editor. *New York Times*, 27 May 1951, p. 8.

"Interpreting the Madison Incident." Letter to the editor. *New York Times*, 21 Aug. 1951, p. 26.

"Bread, Freedom, and Businessmen." *Fortune* 44 (Sept. 1951): 117, 176–88.

"The Dangers in 'Cultural Vigilantism'." *New York Times Magazine*, 30 Sept. 1951, pp. 9, 44, 46, 47.

"The Use and Abuse of Words." Review of *Democracy in a World of Tensions*, ed. Richard Mckeon. *New Leader* 34 (15 Oct. 1951): 20–21.

"Russia by Moonshine, Part 1." *New Leader* 34 (12 Nov. 1951): 15–18.
    "Part 2." Ibid. 34 (19 Nov. 1951): 12–14.
    Reply. Ibid. 34 (26 Nov. 1951): 28–29.
    Reply. Ibid. 34 (3 Dec. 1951): 28.

1952

Democracy and Desegregation. New York: Tamiment Institute, 1952.

Heresy, Yes—Conspiracy, No. New York: American Committee for Cultural Freedom, 1952; New York: John Day Co., 1953.

"Academic Freedom and Its Values for Higher Education." In *Current Issues in Higher Education,* by the National Conference on Higher Education, pp. 70–75. Washington, D.C.: Association for Higher Education, 1952.

"Atheism." In *Collier's Encyclopedia,* vol. 2, p. 418. New York: P. F. Collier and Son, 1952.

"The Philosophical Basis of Marxian Socialism in the United States." In *Socialism and American Life,* ed. Donald Drew Egbert and Stow Persons. Princeton: Princeton University Press, 1952.

"Why Democracy Is Better." In *My Life, My Country, My World,* ed. H. M. Gloster, W. E. Farrison, and N. Tillman, pp. 514–33. Englewood Cliffs, N.J.: Prentice-Hall, 1952.

"Kann man die Freiheit essen?" *Der Monat* 4 (Jan. 1952): 339–44.

"Perennial and Temporal Goals in Education." *Journal of Higher Education* 23 (Jan. 1952): 1–12.

"Mindless Empiricism." *Journal of Philosophy* 49 (14 Feb. 1952): 89–100.

> See Victor Lowe, "A Resurgence of 'Vicious Intellectualism'." Ibid. 48 (5 July 1951): 435–47.
>
> Response by A. O. Lovejoy, "On a Supposed Resurgence of Vicious Intellectualism." Ibid. 49 (14 Feb. 1952): 85–89.
>
> Reply by Lowe, "In Defense of Individualistic Empiricism: A Reply to Messrs. Lovejoy and Hook." Ibid., pp. 100–111.
>
> Rejoinder by Lovejoy, "Rejoinder to Mr. Lowe." Ibid., pp. 111–12.
>
> Rejoinder by Hook, "Not Mindful Enough." Ibid., pp. 112–21.

"Is America in the Grip of Hysteria?" *New Leader,* 3 Mar. 1952.

"Cultural Freedom and Starving Men: A Case for Democracy." *Bharat Jyoti,* 16 Mar. 1952.

"Degrees of Soviet Scholars." Letter to the editor. *New York Times*, 28 Apr. 1952, p. 18.

"The Faiths of Whittaker Chambers." Review of Whittaker Chambers, *Witness*. *New York Times Book Review*, 25 May 1952, pp. 1, 34–35.

   Letters by Herman F. Reissig et al., ibid., 22 June 1952, p. 17.

   Hook reply to Reissig letter, ibid.

"Russland im Mondenschein." *Der Monat* 4 (May 1952): 172–78.

"Academic Manners and Morals." *Journal of Higher Education* 23 (June 1952): 323–26, 342–43.

"One Hit, One Miss." Review of Paul Blanshard, *Communism, Democracy and Catholic Power*. *Twentieth Century* 152 (July 1952): 45–48.

"Our Country and Our Culture." *Partisan Review* 19 (Sept. 1952): 569–74.

"Some Memories of John Dewey." *Commentary* 14 (Sept. 1952): 245–53.

"Letter to an English Friend." *New Leader* 35 (13 Oct. 1952): 16–18.

"The Fall of the Town of Usher." *New Leader* 35 (27 Oct. 1952): 16–19.

"John Dewey and Dr. Barnes." *Commentary* 14 (Nov. 1952): 504.

"Lattimore on the Moscow Trials." *New Leader* 35 (10 Nov. 1952): 16–19.

"What Is 'Guilt by Association'?" *American Mercury* 75 (Nov. 1952): 37–43.

   Reply to James Burnham, "The Case against Adlai Stevenson." Ibid. 75 (Oct. 1952): 11–19.

   Response by Burnham, ibid. 75 (Nov. 1952): 69.

"A Trans-Atlantic Dialogue." *New Leader* 35 (8 Dec. 1952): 15–20.

"The Job of the Teacher in Days of Crisis." *New York Times Magazine*, 14 Dec. 1952, pp. 9, 62, 63, 65.

1953

"Philosophy of Democracy as a Philosophy of History." In *Vision and Action*, ed. Sidney Ratner, pp. 133–47. New Brunswick: Rutgers University Press, 1953.

"The Ethics of Academic Freedom." In *Academic Freedom, Logic and Religion*, 1953. Symposium with George Boas.

"The Quest for Being." In *Proceedings of the 11th International Congress of Philosophy*, Brussels, 1953. Amsterdam: North Holland Publishing Co., 1953.

Letter to the editor. *Life* 34 (12 Jan. 1953): 7. On Communism in the United States.

"Soviet Anti-Semitism." Letter to the editor. *New York Times*, 30 Jan. 1953, p. 20.

"Does the Smith Act Threaten Our Liberties?" *Commentary* 15 (Jan. 1953): 63–73.

> "Mr. Hook Replies." Ibid. 15 (Mar. 1953): 308–9.

"Education: Campuses Unlimited." *New York Times Magazine*, 1 Feb. 1953, p. 70.

"Sidney Hook Replies to British Critic of United States Foreign Policy." *New Leader* 36 (2 Feb. 1953): 27.

"The Place of the Public School in American Life." Review of James Conant, *Education and Liberty*. *New York Times Book Review*, 15 Feb. 1953, p. 3.

"Should We Stress Armaments or Political Warfare?" *New Leader* 36 (23 Feb. 1953): 17–19.

"Indoctrination and Academic Freedom." *New Leader* 36 (9 Mar. 1953): 2–4.

"A Reply to the Editors' 'In Justice to Mr. Conant'." *New York Times Book Review*, 15 Mar. 1953, p. 28.

"Science et materialisme dialectique." In *Science et Liberté*, pp. 22–30. A supplement to *Preuves*, no. 37, Mar. 1954.

"Freedom in American Culture." *New Leader* 36 (6 Apr. 1953): S3–S16.

"Can We Trust Our Teachers?" *Saturday Review* 36 (18 Apr. 1953): 11, 12, 45–47.

> Replies by Gwynne Nettler, William Couch, and Stanley Cooperman, ibid. 36 (23 May 1953): 21.

"Mr. McCarthy Criticized." *New York Times*, 8 May 1953, p. 24.

"The Words Came Easily." Review of Kingsley Martin, *Harold Laski (1893–1950)*. *New York Times Book Review*, 17 May 1953, pp. 7, 33.

"The Party Line on Psychology." Review of Brian H. Kirman, *This Matter of Mind. New Leader* 36 (25 May 1953): 23–24.

"Firing Teachers for Communist Membership." *New Leader* 36 (5 Oct. 1953): 27–29.

"The Fifth Amendment—A Moral Issue." *New York Times Magazine*, 1 Nov. 1953, pp. 9, 57, 59, 60, 62, 64, 66.

"The Quest for 'Being'." *Journal of Philosophy* 50 (19 Nov. 1953): 709–31.

>   Reply by J. H. Randall, Jr., "On Being Rejected." Ibid. 50 (17 Dec. 1953): 797–805.

1954

"Modern Education and Its Critics." In *American Association of Colleges Yearbook*, pp. 139–60. Oneonta, N.Y.: American Association of Colleges, 1954.

"The Problem of the Individual in a Totalitarian Society." In *The Contemporary Scene*. Symposium by the Metropolitan Museum of Art, 28–30 Mar. 1952. New York: New York Metropolitan Museum of Art, 1954.

"The Ethics of Controversy." *New Leader* 37 (1 Feb. 1954): 12–14.

"Symposium: Are Religious Dogmas Cognitive and Meaningful?" *Journal of Philosophy* 51 (4 Mar. 1954): 165–68.

"The Techniques of Controversy." *New Leader* 37 (8 Mar. 1954): 15–18.

"Articles of the Bolshevik Faith." Review of Nathan Leites, *A Study of Bolshevism. New York Times Book Review*, 28 Mar. 1954, p. 10.

"Reply to A. J. Muste." *New Leader* 37 (5 Apr. 1954): 29–30.

"Robert Hutchins Rides Again." *New Leader* 37 (19 Apr. 1954): 16–19.

"Rigors of Heresy." Review of Norman Thomas, *The Test of Freedom. Saturday Review* 37 (24 Apr. 1954): 16–17.

"Myths of Marx." Review of Granville Hicks, *Where We Came Out. Saturday Review* 37 (15 May 1954): 11–12.

"Unpragmatic Liberalism." Review of Henry Steele Commager,

Freedom, Loyalty and Dissent. New Republic 130 (24 May 1954): 18–21.

"The Substance of Controversy: A Reply." *New Leader* 37 (24 May 1954): 18–19.

"Uncommon Sense about Security and Freedom." *New Leader* 37 (21 June 1954): 8–10.

"Security and Freedom." *Confluence* 3 (June 1954): 155–71.

"The Problem of the Ex-Communist." *New York Times Magazine*, 11 July 1954, pp. 7, 24–27.

"Should Our Schools Study Communism?" *New York Times Magazine*, 29 Aug. 1954, pp. 9, 24, 26.

    Response by Howard Selsam, ibid., 26 Sept. 1954, p. 6.

    Reply by Hook, ibid., 10 Oct. 1954, p. 6.

"Why Some Sign Up." Review of Gabriel A. Almond et al., *Appeals of Communism. New York Times Book Review*, 19 Sept. 1954, pp. 3, 28, 29.

"Sikkerhed og Frihed." *Det Danske Magasin* 2 (1954): 441–58.

1955

Dialectical Materialism and Scientific Method. Manchester, England, 1955.

Marx and the Marxists: The Ambiguous Legacy. Princeton, N.J.: Van Nostrand, 1955.

"Science and Dialectical Materialism." In *Science and Freedom*, pp. 182–95. Boston: Beacon Press, 1955.

"Historical Determinism and Political Fiat in Soviet Communism." *Proceedings of the American Philosophical Society* 99 (1955): 1–10.

"Fallacies in Our Thinking about Security." *New York Times Magazine*, 30 Jan. 1955, pp. 15, 33, 35.

"A Question of Means and Ends in a World Threatened by Evil." Review of Bertrand Russell, *Human Society in Ethics and Politics. New York Times Book Review*, 30 Jan. 1955, p. 3.

"Marx in Limbo." *New Leader* 38 (2 May 1955): 14–17.

"Tyranny through the Ages." Review of George W. Hallgarten, *Why Dictators? New Leader* 38 (6 June 1955): 18–19.

"A Steady Light." Review of *John Dewey: His Contribution to the American Tradition*, ed. Irwin Edman. *New York Times Book Review*, 24 July 1955, pp. 3, 20.

"The Grounds on Which Our Educators Stand." Review of Richard Hofstadter and Walter P. Metzger, *The Development of Academic Freedom in the United States* and Robert M. MacIver, *Academic Freedom in Our Time. New York Times Book Review*, 30 Oct. 1955, pp. 6, 28.

"The Teaching and the Taught." Review of E. Merrill Root, *Collectivism on the Campus. New York Times Book Review*, 6 Nov. 1955, p. 58.

"A Reply." *New York Times Book Review*, 27 Nov. 1955, pp. 52–53.

"Introduction" to *Communism's Postwar Decade. New Leader* 38 (19 Dec. 1955): S2–S4.

"A Reply." *New York Times Book Review*, 25 Dec. 1955, p. 12.

1956

"Naturalism and First Principles." In *American Philosophers at Work*, ed. Sidney Hook, pp. 236–58. New York: Criterion Books, 1956.

"The Ethics of Controversy Again." *New Leader* 39 (16 Jan. 1956): 16–18.

"Prophet of Man's Glory and Tragedy." Review of *Reinhold Niebuhr— His Religious, Social, and Political Thought*, ed. Charles Kegley and Robert W. Bretall. *New York Times Book Review*, 29 Jan. 1956, pp. 6, 7, 22.

"The Strategy of Truth." *New Leader* 39 (13 Feb. 1956): 21–24.

"Six Fallacies of Robert Hutchins." *New Leader* 39 (19 Mar. 1956): 18–28.

> Responses, ibid. 39 (2 Apr. 1956): 28–29; ibid. 39 (9 Apr. 1956): 22; ibid. 39 (16 Apr. 1956): 29; ibid. 39 (23 Apr. 1956): 28–29; ibid. 39 (14 May 1956): 29.

Replies by Hook, ibid. 39 (16 Apr. 1956): 29–30; ibid. 39 (23 Apr. 1956): 28–29.

"Exposing Soviet Purges." *New York Times*, 1 Apr. 1956, p. 8.

"Prospects for Cultural Freedom." *New Leader* 39 (7 May 1956): Sec. 2, p. 5.

"The AAUP and Academic Integrity." *New Leader* 39 (21 May 1956): 19–21.

Response by Cormac Philip, ibid. 39 (4 June 1956): 29.

Rejoinder by Hook, ibid., p. 29.

Response by Ralph F. Fuchs, ibid. 39 (25 June 1956): 28–29.

Rejoinder by Hook, ibid., pp. 29–31.

Responses by Pierre Aubeuf and Arthur O. Lovejoy, ibid. 39 (2 July 1956): 21–22.

Response by William Edel, ibid. 39 (16 July 1956): 13.

Response by Sam Lambert, ibid. 39 (13 Aug. 1956): 22.

"Portrait and Definition of Academic Freedom." *Time* 67 (11 June 1956): 69.

"Education and Creative Intelligence." *School and Society* 84 (7 July 1956): 3–8.

"Wanted, an Ethics of Employment for Our Time." Review of John Cogley, *Report on Blacklisting*. *New York Times Book Review*, 22 July 1956, pp. 6, 14.

Letters in response with Hook's reply, ibid., 19 Aug. 1956, p. 22.

"The Jurisdiction of Intelligence." *School and Society* 84 (4 Aug. 1956): 35–39.

"Common Sense and the Fifth Amendment." Review of Erwin N. Griswold, *The Fifth Amendment*. "Logic and the Fifth Amendment." *New Leader* 39 (1 Oct. 1956): 12–22; "Psychology and the Fifth Amendment." Ibid. 39 (8 Oct. 1956): 20–24; "Ethics and the Fifth Amendment." Ibid. 39 (15 Oct. 1956): 16–24; "Politics and the Fifth Amendment." Ibid. 39 (22 Oct. 1956): 16–23.

Reply by Griswold, "The Individual and the Fifth Amendment." Ibid. 39 (29 Oct. 1956): 20–23.

Rejoinder by Hook, "Logic, History and Law: A Rejoinder to Dean Griswold." Ibid. 39 (5 Nov. 1956): 12–15.

"Philosophy Must Provide Synthesis of Thought and Action." *Indian Express*, 11 Oct. 1956.

"Right to Equal Treatment." Letter to the editor. *New York Times*, 7 Nov. 1956, p. 30.

"Sense and Salvation." Review of Cohn Wilson, *The Outsider*. *Commentary* 22 (Nov. 1956): 479–80, 82.

"Man as a Whole." Letter to the editor. *Listener* 56 (27 Dec. 1956): 1076–77.

> Reply to John Nef, "Man as a Whole." Ibid. 56 (29 Nov. 1956): 875–76.

> Reply by John Nef, "Man as a Whole." Ibid. 57 (7 Feb. 1957): 233, 235.

"Filosofien i den moderne verden." *Perspektiv* 4 (Dec. 1956): 28–30.

"A Joint Statement on a Matter of Importance." With Ralph F. Fuchs. *AAUP Bulletin* 42 (Dec. 1956): 692–95.

"Scope of Philosophy of Education." *Harvard Educational Review* 26 (1956): 145–48.

1957

Common Sense and the Fifth Amendment. New York: Criterion Books, 1957.

"Outlook for Philosophy." In Arnold Toynbee et al., *New Frontiers of Knowledge*, pp. 18–21. Washington: Public Affairs Press, 1957.

"The Monolithic State." Review of Carl J. Friedrich and Zbigniew K. Brzezinski, *Totalitarian Dictatorship and Autocracy*. *New York Times Book Review*, 20 Jan. 1957, pp. 3, 36.

"Liberalism and the Law." Review of Zechariah Chafee, *The Blessing of Liberty*. *Commentary* 23 (Jan. 1957): 46–56.

> Response by C. Rajagopalachari, ibid. 23 (Apr. 1957): 380.

"From Opera Bouffe to Treason." Review of Theodore Draper, *The Roots of American Communism*. *Saturday Review of Literature*, 16 Mar. 1957, pp. 14–15.

"Abraham Lincoln, American Pragmatist." *New Leader* 40 (18 Mar. 1957): 16–18.

> Reply by Max Eastman, "Lincoln Was No Pragmatist." Ibid. 40 (23 Sept. 1957): 19–20.
>
> Response by Hook, "Marx, Dewey and Lincoln." Ibid. 40 (21 Oct. 1957): 16–18.
>
> Responses by Bernard Herman and Martin Gardner, ibid. 40 (18 Nov. 1957): 28–29.
>
> Reply by Hook, "Pragmatism." Ibid. 40 (9 Dec. 1957): 29–30.
>
> Response by Eastman, "A Debate on Pragmatism: Marx, Dewey and Hook." Ibid. 41 (10 Feb. 1958): 16–18.
>
> Reply by Hook, "Marx, Dewey and Eastman." Ibid., pp. 18–19.

"The Fifth Amendment: A Crucial Case." *New Leader* 40 (22 Apr. 1957): 18–20.

"Use of Fifth Amendment Discussed." *New York Times*, 10 May 1957, p. 26.

> Reply by Irving Mariash, ibid., 17 May 1957, p. 24.

"A Fateful Chapter of Our Times." Review of Alger Hiss, *In the Court of Public Opinion. New York Times Book Review*, 12 May 1957, pp. 1, 28, 29.

"Scientific Knowledge and Philosophical 'Knowledge'." *Partisan Review* 24 (Spring 1957): 215–34.

"The Atom and Human Wisdom." *New Leader* 40 (3 June 1957): 8–10.

"The Old Liberalism and the New Conservatism." *New Leader* 40 (8 July 1957): 7–10.

"The Affair Hiss." *Encounter* 9 (July 1957): 81–84.

"Moral Judgment and Historical Ambiguity." *New Leader* 40 (19 Aug. 1957): 16–19.

"Socialism and Liberation." *Partisan Review* 24 (Fall 1947): 497–518.

"The Red Lodestar." Review of Raymond Aron, *The Opium of the Intellectuals. Saturday Review* 40 (23 Nov. 1957): 18–20.

"Justice Black's Illogic." *New Leader* 40 (2 Dec. 1957): 17–20.

1958

"Necessity, Indeterminism and Sentimentalism." In *Determinism and Freedom in the Age of Modern Science*, ed. Sidney Hook, pp. 180–93. First Symposium, New York University Institute of Philosophy, 9–10 Feb. 1957. New York: New York University Press, 1958.

"The Missing Link in American Science." *New Leader* 41 (6 Jan. 1958): 16–19.

> Replies by Susan Bodan, Sol Feinstone, Edward Rozek, E. Burton, and A. M. Wallach, ibid. 41 (3 Feb. 1958): 28–29.

"Befreiung durch Evolution." *Der Monat* 10 (Feb. 1958): 10–25.

"A Foreign Policy for Survival." *New Leader* 41 (7 Apr. 1958): 8–12.

> Response by Bertrand Russell, "World Communism and Nuclear War." Ibid. 41 (26 May 1958): 9–10.

> Reply by Hook, "A Free Man's Choice." Ibid., pp. 10–12.

"Democracy and Desegregation." *New Leader* 41 (21 Apr. 1958): Sec. 2, pp. 3–19.

"A Look at the Evidence in a Famous Case." Review of Fred J. Cook, *The Unfinished Story of Alger Hiss. New York Times Book Review*, 4 May 1958, pp. 4, 20.

> Letters in response, ibid., 1 June 1958, p. 14.

"Bureaucrats Are Human." *Saturday Review* 41 (17 May 1958): 12–14, 41.

"Moral Freedom in a Determined World." *Commentary* 25 (May 1958): 431–43.

"Bertrand Russell Retreats." *New Leader* 41 (7–14 July 1958): 25–28.

"Brotherhood Aim Held Impractical." *New York Times*, 15 July 1958, p. 27.

"Die letzte Entscheidung: Ein Streitgespräch über die Atombombe." *Der Monat* 10 (July 1958): 11–16.

> Reply by Bertrand Russell, "Keine Despotie währt ewig." Ibid., pp. 16–18.

> Response by Hook, "Grenzen der Nachgiebigkeit." Ibid., pp. 18–21.

Response by Russell, "Die Freiheit zu überleben." Ibid. 10 (Sept. 1958): 81–84.

Reply by Hook, "Mehr als zu überleben." Ibid., pp. 84–89.

"Socialism and Democracy." *New Leader* 41 (3 Nov. 1958): 17–18.

"Education in Japan." *New Leader* 41 (24 Nov. 1958): 8–11.

1959

John Dewey: His Philosophy of Education and Its Critics. New York: Tamiment Institute, 1959.

Political Power and Personal Freedom: Critical Studies in Democracy, Communism, and Civil Rights. New York: Criterion Books, 1959.

"Science and Mythology in Psychoanalysis." In *Psychoanalysis, Scientific Method and Philosophy*, ed. Sidney Hook, pp. 212–25. Second Symposium, New York University Institute of Philosophy, 28–29 Mar. 1958. New York: New York University Press, 1959.

"John Dewey, 1859–1952." In *Philosophy in Mid–Century*, vol. 4, ed. Raymond Klibansky, pp. 210–14. International Institute of Philosophy, 1958–1959. Florence: La Nuova Italia, 1959.

"The Philosophical Basis of Education." In *Proceedings of the Summer Conference*, ed. Western Washington College of Education, pp. 13–15. Bellingham: Western Washington College of Education, 1959.

"Philosophy for a Time of Crisis." In A. Koch, *Naturalism and Democracy*, pp. 302–19. New York: E. P. Dutton and Co., 1959.

"The Philosophy of Reading." In *Science and the Philosophy of Reading*, pp. 20–34. Newark: University of Delaware Press, 1959.

"Proletariat." In *Encyclopaedia Britannica*, 14th ed., p. 576. Chicago: Encyclopaedia Britannica, 1959.

"The Psychological Basis of Education." In *Proceedings of the Summer Conference*, ed. Western Washington College of Education, pp. 22–36. Bellingham: Western Washington College of Education, 1959.

"The Social Basis of Education." In *Proceedings of the Summer Conference*, ed. Western Washington College of Education, pp. 39–50. Bellingham: Western Washington College of Education, 1959.

"What Is Education?" In *Education in the Age of Science*, ed. Brand Blanshard, pp. 1–52. New York: Basic Books, 1959.

"Conscience and Consciousness in Japan." *Commentary* 27 (Jan. 1959): 59–66.

"Which Way Japan?" *New Leader* 42 (9 Feb. 1959): 3–7.

"The Impact of Ideas." Review of H. Stuart Hughes, *Consciousness and Society: The Reorientation of European Social Thought, 1890–1930*. *New York Times Book Review*, 29 Mar. 1959, p. 22.

"The Philosophy of Reading." *Proceedings of the 41st and 42nd Annual Education Conferences*, University of Delaware School of Education 8 (Mar. 1959): 20–34.

"Grim Report: Asia in Transition." *New York Times Magazine*, 5 Apr. 1959, pp. 11, 104, 106, 108.

"J. H. Randall, Jr., on American and Soviet Philosophy." *Journal of Philosophy* 56 (23 Apr. 1959): 416–19.

Reply to Randall, "The Mirror of U.S. Philosophizing." Ibid. 55 (6 Nov. 1958): 1019–28.

"Man and Nature: Some Questions for Mr. Mitin." *Journal of Philosophy* 56 (23 Apr. 1959): 408–16.

"A Talk with Bhave." *New Leader* 42 (4 May 1959): 10–13.

"A Talk with Vinoba Bhave." *Encounter* 12 (May 1959): 14–18.

"Hannah Arendt's Reflections." Letter to the editor. *Dissent* 6 (Spring 1959): 203.

Reply by Arendt, "Hannah Arendt Replies." Ibid., pp. 203–4.

"What's Left of Karl Marx?" *Saturday Review* 42 (6 June 1959): 12–14, 58.

"Pragmatism and Existentialism." *Antioch Review* 19 (Summer 1959): 151–68.

"'Common Sense' in Japan." *New Leader* 42 (5 Oct. 1959): 10–12.

"John Dewey: His Philosophy of Education and Its Critics." *New Leader* 42 (2 Nov. 1959): Sec. 2.

"What Is Education?" *Science Teacher* 26 (Nov. 1959): 462–67, 516–21.

"John Dewey: Philosopher of Growth." *Journal of Philosophy* 56 (17 Dec. 1959): 1010–1018.

"The Ends and Content of Education." *Daedalus* 88 (Winter 1959): 7–24.

"Two Types of Existentialist Religion and Ethics." *Partisan Review* 26 (Winter 1959): 58–63.

1960

"A Pragmatic Note." In *Dimensions of Mind*, ed. Sidney Hook, pp. 202–11. Third Symposium, New York University Institute of Philosophy, 15–16 May 1959. New York: New York University Press, 1960.

"The Centrality of Method." In *The American Pragmatist*, ed. Milton R. Konvitz and Gail Kennedy, pp. 360–69. New York: Meridian Books, 1960.

"To Free Gold and Sobell." *New York Times*, 16 Feb. 1960, p. 36. [Letter with Nathan Glazer, Irving Kristol, and Dwight Macdonald.J

"Of Tradition and Change." Review of F. A. Hayek, *The Constitution of Liberty. New York Times Book Review*, 21 Feb. 1960, pp. 6, 28.

"Modern Knowledge and the Idea of God." *Commentary* 29 (Mar. 1960): 205–16.

"A Handbook for the Years Ahead." Review of Robert L. Heilbroner, *The Future as History. Saturday Review* 43 (2 Apr. 1960): 22–23.

"Distrust of Soviet." *New York Times*, 5 Apr. 1960, p. 36.

"A New Ism for Socialism." *New York Times Magazine*, 10 Apr. 1960, pp. 13, 62, 64, 66, 69.

"Second Thoughts on Peace and Freedom." *New Leader* 43 (11 Apr. 1960): 8–12.

"Carte-Blanche Legislative Authority." Review of Charles L. Black, Jr., *The People and the Court. Saturday Review* 43 (30 Apr. 1960): 19–20.

"Bertrand Russell's Political Fantasies." *New Leader* 43 (9 May 1960): 15–17.

"Pragmatism and the Tragic Sense of Life." *Commentary* 30 (Aug. 1960): 139–49.

Letter by George Kimmelman with Hook's reply, ibid. 30 (Dec. 1960): 536.

"A Recollection of Berthold Brecht." *New Leader* 43 (10 Oct. 1960): 22–23.

"Scapegoat for Tyranny." Review of Clinton Rossiter, *Marxism: The View from America. Saturday Review* 43 (12 Nov. 1960): 25–26.

"'Welfare State'—A Debate That Isn't." *New York Times Magazine*, 27 Nov. 1960, pp. 27, 118–19.

> Response by Marjorie H. Schefler, ibid., 11 Dec. 1960, p. 4.
>
> Reply by Hook, ibid.

"Philosophy and Human Conduct." *Kenyon Review* 22 (Fall 1960): 648–66.

"Visionary or Man of Vision?" *New Leader* 43 (12 Dec. 1960): 22–23.

"Political Pretenders and How to Tell Them." *Saturday Review* 43 (31 Dec. 1960): 6–8, 29.

"Was hat uns Karl Marx heute noch zu sagen?" *Politische Studien* 11 (1960): 364–70.

1961

The Quest for Being, and Other Studies in Naturalism and Humanism. New York: St. Martin's Press, 1961.

"The Atheism of Paul Tillich." In *Religious Experience and Truth: A Symposium*, ed. Sidney Hook, pp. 59–65. Fourth Symposium, New York University Institute of Philosophy, 21–22 Oct. 1960. New York: New York University Press, 1961.

"Diderot's Great Legacy." Review of *A Diderot Pictorial Encyclopedia of Trades and Industry. New Leader* 44 (2 Jan. 1961): 25–26.

"In Memoriam: S. M. Levitas." *New Leader* 44 (16 Jan. 1961): 3–4.

"The Ethics of Controversy: Rejoinder to Julius Stone." *Observer*, 18 Mar. 1961.

"The Death Sentence." *New Leader* 44 (3 Apr. 1961): 18–20.

> Reply by Hugo Adam Bedau, ibid. 44 (8 May 1961): 28.

Review of Ayn Rand, *For the New Intellectual: The Philosophy of Ayn Rand. New York Times Book Review*, 9 Apr. 1961, p. 3. Correction, ibid., 23 Apr. 1961, p. 44.

> Letters in response with Hook's reply, ibid., 7 May 1961, p. 35.

"The Couch and the Bomb." *New Leader* 44 (24 Apr. 1961): 6–9.

> Replies by Zbigniew Brzezinski, Bernard Herman, and Paul Lauter, ibid. 44 (8 May 1961): 27–28.
>
> Reply by Erich Fromm, ibid. 44 (29 May 1961): 10–12.
>
> Response by Hook, "Escape from Reality." Ibid., pp. 12–14. [Correction to Hook's "Escape from Reality" appears in ibid. 44 (5 June 1961): 22.]
>
> Response by Maximilien Rubel, ibid. 44 (12 June 1961): 30.
>
> Reply by Hook, ibid., p. 30.
>
> B. K. Harper in response to Fromm, ibid. 44 (19 June 1961): 29.
>
> Response by Maximilien Rubel, ibid. 44 (31 July–7 Aug. 1961): 29.
>
> Response by Hook, ibid., p. 29.

"Growth of Pacifism Noted." *New York Times*, 2 May 1961, p. 36.

"In League with the Kremlin." Review of Sandor Voros, *American Commissar. Saturday Review* 44 (20 May 1961): 38–39.

"Split Decisions." Review of Wallace Mendelson, *Justices Black and Frankfurter. New York Times Book Review*, 23 July 1961, pp. 6, 26.

"For Stand at West Berlin." Letter to the editor. *New York Times*, 28 Aug. 1961, p. 24.

> Reply to letter by Erich Kahler, ibid., 18 Aug. 1961, p. 20.

"Enlightenment and Radicalism." *Encounter* 17 (Aug. 1961): 44–50.

"The New Revisionism." Review of John Lukacs, *The History of the Cold War. East Europe* 10 (Aug. 1961): 19, 48–49.

> Letter by Hook, ibid. 10 (Oct. 1961): 39.

"Symposium on Capital Punishment." *New York Law Forum* 7 (Aug. 1961): 249–319. [Hook's contribution, pp. 278–83, 296–99, 300.]

"Questions of Conformity." Letter to the editor. *New Republic* 145 (21 Aug. 1961): 30–31.

"Unless We Resist." *Time*, 8 Sept. 1961, p. 22.

"Western Values and Total War." *Commentary* 32 (Oct. 1961): 277–304.

[A panel with H. Stuart Hughes, Hans J. Morganthau, and C. P. Snow.]

> See William F. Rickenbacker, "Schism of the Left." *National Review* 11 (15 July 1961): 8.

"After Berlin—What Next?" *Nation's Business* 49 (Oct. 1961): 59–60.

"Marx and Alienation." *New Leader* 44 (11 Dec. 1961): 15–18.

1962

Paradoxes of Freedom. Berkeley: University of California Press, 1962.

Political Power and Personal Freedom: Critical Studies in Democracy, Communism and Civil Rights. Collier Macmillan paperback, 1962.

World Communism, ed. Sidney Hook. Princeton, N.J.: Van Nostrand, 1962.

"Enlightenment and Radicalism." In *History and Hope*, pp. 59–67. Congress for Cultural Freedom, Berlin, 1960. New York: Praeger, 1962.

"Hegel and the Perspective of Liberalism." In *A Hegel Symposium*, ed. Don C. Travis, pp. 39–62. Austin: University of Texas, 1962.

"The Humanities and the Taming of Power." In *The Role of the Humanities in Ordering a Peaceful World*, pp. 5–21. New Britain: Central Connecticut State College, 1962.

"The Import of Ideological Diversity." In *Problems of Communism: Russia under Khrushchev*, ed. Abraham Brumberg, pp. 554–70. New York: Praeger, 1962.

Introduction to R. R. Abrahamovich, *The Soviet Revolution.* New York: International University Press, 1962.

"Philosophy and Human Culture." In *Philosophy and Culture—East and West*, ed. C. A. Moore, pp. 15–32. Honolulu: University of Hawaii Press, 1962.

"Better Red Than Dead, or Lord Russell's Guide to Peace." Review of Bertrand Russell, *Has Man a Future? New York Times Book Review*, 14 Jan. 1962, p. 44.

> Letters in response with Hook's reply, ibid., 18 Feb. 1962, pp. 42–43.

"Revisionism at Bay." *Encounter* 19 (Sept. 1962): 63–67.

"Communism: What Lies Ahead." *Nation's Business* 50 (Oct. 1962).

"The Map Was Redrawn to Make Man's Agony a Part of the Geography." Review of Martin Heidegger, *Being and Time*. *New York Times Book Review*, 11 Nov. 1962, pp. 6, 42.

"The Politics of Science Fiction." Review of Eugene Burdick and Harvey Wheeler, *Fail-Safe*. *New Leader* 45 (10 Dec. 1962): 12–15.

"The Impact of Expanding Research Support on the Universities." *Journal of Medical Education* 37 (Dec. 1962): 230–46.

"The Cold War and the West." *Partisan Review* 29 (Winter 1962): 20–27.

1963

Education for Modern Man: A New Perspective. New York: Alfred A. Knopf, 1963.

The Fail-Safe Fallacy. New York: Stein and Day, 1963.

"Objectivity and Reconstruction in History." In *Philosophy and History*, ed. Sidney Hook, pp. 250–75. Fifth Symposium, New York University Institute of Philosophy, 11–12 May 1962. New York: New York University Press, 1963.

"Democracy and Equality." In *Quest of Value*, ed. Frederick C. Dommeyer, pp. 60–70. San Francisco: Chandler Publishing Co., 1963.

"Heresy and Conspiracy." In *Quest of Value*, ed. Frederick C. Dommeyer, pp. 485–99. San Francisco: Chandler Publishing Co., 1963.

"Intelligence and Human Rights." In *Memorias del XIII Congreso Internacional de Filosofía*, VII, pp. 101–2. México: Universidad Nacional Autónoma de México, 1963.

"Philosophy and Social Welfare." In *Health-Care Issues of 1960*. New York: Group Health Insurance, Inc., 1963.

Introduction to Eric Hoffer, *The True Believer*. New York: Time-Life Books, 1963.

"'Lord Monboddo' and the Supreme Court." Review of *One Man's Stand for Freedom*, ed. Irving Dilliard. *New Leader* 46 (13 May 1963): 11–15.

"Do the People Rule and Can They?" Review of Walter Lippmann, *The Essential Lippmann*. *New York Times Book Review*, 14 July 1963, pp. 1, 24, 25.

 Letters in response with Hook's reply, ibid., 8 Sept. 1963, p. 32.

"Why the U.S. Needs a Freedom Academy." *Think* 29 (Sept. 1963): 6–9.

"Challenging Study: Challenge of Communism." *New York Times Magazine*, 13 Oct. 1963, pp. 25, 33, 34, 38, 41.

 Reply by Louis Fischer and response by Hook, ibid., 27 Oct. 1963, p. 12.

"Accused Assassin Belied Tenets of Marxism, Experts Here Agree." *New York Times*, 27 Nov. 1963, p. 21.

"Religious Liberty from the Viewpoint of the Open Society." *Cross Currents* 13 (Winter 1963): 65–75.

"American Philosophy Today." *America* 68 (1963): 27–34.

1964

"Law, Justice and Obedience." In *Law and Philosophy*, ed. Sidney Hook, pp. 55–60. Sixth Symposium, New York University Institute of Philosophy, 10–11 May 1963. New York: New York University Press, 1964.

"Conversations by Professors Hook, Dallin and Bell." In *World Politics*, ed. Mahir Nasim. Cairo: Dar Al-kurrnek, 1964.

"The Death Sentence." In *The Death Penalty in America*, ed. Hugo Adam Bedau, pp. 146–54. Chicago: Aldine, 1964.

"Historical Determinism and Political Fiat in Soviet Communism." In *Political Thought since World War II*, ed. W. J. Stankiewicz, pp. 159–74. New York: Free Press, 1964.

Introduction to Walter Lippmann, *A Preface to Morals*, new ed. New York: Time-Life Books, 1964.

"Religious Liberty from the Viewpoint of a Secular Humanist." In Earl Rabb, *Religious Conflict in America*, pp. 138–51. Garden City, N.Y.: Doubleday, 1964.

"Liberalism and the Negro." With James Baldwin, Nathan Glazer, and Gunnar Myrdal. *Commentary* 37 (Mar. 1964): 25–42.

"Fulbright's Rights Stand." *New York Times*, 8 Apr. 1964, p. 42.

Reply by J. A. Fabro, ibid., 13 Apr. 1964, p. 28.

"Pornography and the Censor." *New York Times Book Review*, 12 Apr. 1964, pp. 1, 38–39.

Response and Hook's reply, ibid., 10 May 1964, pp. 32–33.

"The Cunning of History." Review of Isaac Deutscher, *The Prophet Outcast*. *New Leader* 47 (11 May 1964): 15–18.

"Common Sense and Disarmament." *Yale Political* 3 (Spring 1964): 16, 29–30.

"There's More Than One Way to Teach." *Saturday Review* 47 (18 July 1964): 48–49, 59.

"Thinking about Thinkers of the Unthinkable." Review of Anatol Rapoport, *Strategy and Conscience*. *New York Times Book Review*, 19 July 1964, pp. 6, 25.

Responses and Hook's reply, ibid., 6 Sept. 1964, p. 18.

"A Search Here and Beyond." Review of Whittaker Chambers, *Cold Friday*. *New York Times Book Review*, 8 Nov. 1964, pp. 3, 32.

"Faces of Betrayers." Review of Rebecca West, *The New Meaning of Treason*. *New York Times Book Review*, 29 Nov. 1964, pp. 1, 60–61.

"Hegel e le prospettive del liberalismo." *De Homine*, nos. 9–10 (1964): 115–40.

Review of John F. Boler, *Charles Peirce and Scholastic Realism: A Study of Peirce's Relation to John Duns Scotus*. *Bibliography of Philosophy* 11 (1964): 100.

Review of Sören Halldén, *True Love, True Humour and True Religion: A Semantic Study*. *Bibliography of Philosophy* 11 (1964): 208.

Review of Emil L. Fackenheim, *Metaphysics and Historicity*. *History and Theory* 3 (1964): 389–92.

1965

Reason, Social Myths and Democracy. With a new introduction by Hook. New York: Harper and Row, 1965.

"Academic Freedom and the Right of Students." In Seymour Martin Lipset, *The Berkeley Student Revolt*, pp. 432–42. Garden City, N.Y.: Anchor Books, 1965.

"The Political Aspects of General and Complete Disarmament." In *The Prospects for Arms Control*, ed. James E. Dougherty and John F. Lehman, Jr., pp. 153–63. Philadelphia: Macfadden Books, 1965.

"Second Thoughts on Berkeley." In *Revolution at Berkeley*, ed. Michael V. Miller and Susan Gilmore, pp. 116–59. New York: Dial Press, 1965.

Introduction to Paul Edwards, *The Logic of Moral Discourse.* New York: Free Press of Glencoe, 1965.

Introduction to Rebecca West, *The New Meaning of Treason*, new ed. New York: Time-Life Books, 1965.

"Hegel Rehabilitated?" *Encounter* 24 (Jan. 1965): 53–58.

> Reply by Shlomo Avineri, "Hook's Hegel." Ibid. 25 (Nov. 1965): 63–66.
>
> Letters in reply by Paul Goodman, Lawrence D. Hochman, Harold Leitenberg, and Kay Boyle, ibid., 17 Jan. 1965, pp. 6, 21.
>
> Response by Hook, ibid., p. 21.

"Defends Protests to Russia on Jews." *New York Times*, 13 Feb. 1965, p. 20.

> Response to Stephen P. Dunn, "Anti-Semitism in Soviet." Ibid., 25 Jan. 1965, p. 36.

"Changing Values in Higher Education in a Changing Society." *New York State Education* 52 (Feb. 1965): 7–9.

"Reply to Dr. Oppenheimer." *Denver Post*, 27 July 1965, p. 19.

> Reply to Frank Oppenheimer's letter on U.S. policy toward Communism, ibid., 6 June 1965, p. 51.

"The Philosophy of American Pragmatism." *Span* 6 (Aug. 1965): 21–28.

"Friends and Enemies." Review of Haakon Chevalier, *Oppenheimer*. *New York Times Book Review*, 22 Aug. 1965, pp. 3, 28.

>   Reply by Chevalier and response by Hook, ibid., 19 Sept. 1965, pp. 52–53.

"Radicalism in America." *New Leader* 48 (27 Sept. 1965): 34–35.

"Second Thoughts on Berkeley." *Teachers College Record* 67 (Oct. 1965): 32–63.

"The Conflict of Freedoms." *Common Factor* 1 (Autumn 1965): 36–42.

"Thoughts after Knopfelmacher." *Minerva* 4 (Winter 1965): 279–85.

1966

"Are There Universal Criteria of Judgments of Excellence in Art?" In *Art and Philosophy*, ed. Sidney Hook, pp. 49–55. Seventh Symposium, New York University Institute of Philosophy, 23–24 Oct. 1964. New York: New York University Press, 1966.

"The Content of Education." In *The Education of Modern Man*, ed. Margaret Starkey, pp. 138–43. New York: Pitman Publishing Corp., 1966.

"Man's Quest for Security: A Philosopher's View." In *Man's Quest for Security*, ed. E. J. Faulkner, pp. 3–17. Lincoln: University of Nebraska Press, 1966.

"Marxism in the Western World: From 'Scientific Socialism' to Mythology." In *Marxist Ideology in the Contemporary World—Its Appeal and Paradoxes*, ed. Milorad M. Drachkovitch, pp. 1–36. Palo Alto, Calif.: Stanford University Press, 1966.

"Pragmatism and the Tragic Sense of Life." In *Moderns on Tragedy*, ed. Lionel Abel, pp. 227–49. New York: Fawcett Publishers, 1966.

"Pragmatism and the Tragic Sense of Life," and "Naturalism and First Principles." In *American Philosophy in the Twentieth Century*, ed. Paul Kurtz, pp. 522–44. New York: Macmillan, 1966.

"In Reply to Dr. Hutchins." Letter to the editor. *Santa Barbara News-Press*, 27 Feb. 1966.

"U.S. Policy and Communism." Letter to the editor. *Santa Barbara News-Press*, 20 Mar. 1966.

"Writer Buttresses His Previous Criticism of Tax-Exempt Center." Letter to the editor. *Los Angeles Times*, 4 Apr. 1966, pt. 2, p. 4.

"Liberal Catholic Thought." Review of Michael Novak, *Belief and Unbelief. Commentary* 41 (Apr. 1966): 94–100.

"Speaking of Books: Karl Marx's Second Coming." *New York Times Book Review*, 22 May 1966, pp. 2, 44–45.

> Response by L. Marcus, ibid., 10 July 1966, p. 50.
>
> Reply by Hook, ibid., pp. 50–51.

"Hegel and His Apologists." *Encounter* 26 (May 1966): 1–8.

"Neither Blind Obedience nor Uncivil Disobedience." *New York Times Magazine*, 5 June 1966, pp. 52–53, 122–28.

"Lord Russell and the War Crimes 'Trial'." *New Leader* 49 (24 Oct. 1966): 6–11.

> Reply by Ralph Schoenman, "Lord Russell's 'Tribunal'." Ibid. 49 (19 Dec. 1966): 27–28.
>
> Response by Hook, ibid., p. 28.

"Liberties in Conflict." Review of Thomas I. Emerson, *Toward a General Theory of the First Amendment. Book Week*, 6 Nov. 1966, pp. 5, 10.

"Some Educational Attitudes and Poses." *Harvard Educational Review* 36 (Fall 1966): 496–504.

1967

Religion in a Free Society. Lincoln: University of Nebraska Press, 1967.

"Basic Values and Economic Policy." In *Human Values and Economic Policy*, ed. Sidney Hook. Eighth Symposium, New York University Institute of Philosophy, 13–14 May 1966. New York: New York University Press, 1967.

"The Outlook for Philosophy." In Arnold Toynbee et al., *New Frontiers of Knowledge*, pp. 18–21. Washington, D.C.: Public Affairs Press, 1967.

"On the Couch." Review of Meyer A. Zeligs, *Friendship and Fratricide. New York Times Book Review*, 5 Feb. 1967, pp. 4, 40, 41.

Response by Zeligs with Hook's reply, ibid., 19 Mar. 1967, pp. 59–60.

Response by Marshall A. Best, ibid., 2 Apr. 1967, p. 44.

"Le Deuxième avénement de Marx." *Le Contrat Social* 11 (Mar.–Apr. 1967): 91–94.

"Whither Russia? Fifty Years After." *Problems of Communism* 16 (Mar.–Apr. 1967): 76–79.

"Lessons of the Hungarian 'October'." *Scope*, Spring–Autumn 1967.

"Crisis for White, Negro Leadership." *Los Angeles Times*, 28 July 1967, Part 2, p. 5.

"Cruel Deception." Letter to the editor. *New Leader* 50 (14 Aug. 1967): 26–27.

"Is There a Legal 'Right' to Revolt?" *Los Angeles Times*, 15 Aug. 1967, Part 2, p. 5.

"Fluff on the Sleeve of History." Review of C. P. Snow, *Variety of Men*. *New Leader* 50 (28 Aug. 1967): 16–18.

"Fulbright's Colossal Gall." *Providence Journal*, 4 Sept. 1967.

Letter to the editor. *New Republic* 50 (25 Sept. 1967): 27.

Response to comments by M. S. Arnoni on the Vietnamese conflict, ibid., pp. 26–27.

Reply by Arnoni, ibid. 50 (23 Oct. 1967): 34.

Rejoinder by Hook, ibid., pp. 34–35.

"Liberal Anti-Communism Revisited: A Symposium." With Lionel Abel et al. *Commentary* 44 (Sept. 1967): 44–48.

"Social Protest and Civil Disobedience." *Humanist* 27 (Sept.–Dec. 1967): 157–59, 192–93.

"The Human Cost [of Soviet Industrialization following the 1917 Revolution]." *New Leader* 50 (6 Nov. 1967): 16–20.

"Does Philosophy Have a Future?" *Saturday Review* 50 (11 Nov. 1967): 21–23, 62.

"A Right Way to Remedy a Wrong, a Wrong Way to Remedy a Right." *New York Times Magazine*, 26 Nov. 1967, pp. 124, 126.

1968

Contemporary Philosophy. Chicago: American Library Association, 1968.

"Experimental Naturalism." In *American Philosophy Today and Tomorrow*, ed. Sidney Hook and Horace M. Kallen, pp. 205–25. Freeport, N.Y.: Books for Libraries Press, 1968.

"In Defense of 'Justice' (A Response)" and "Reflections on Human Rights." In *Ethics and Social Justice*, ed. Howard E. Kiefer and Milton K. Munitz, pp. 75–84, 252–81. Vol. 4 of *Contemporary Philosophic Thought: The International Philosophy Year Conferences at Brockport*. Albany: State University of New York Press, 1968.

"The Democratic Challenge to Communism." In *Fifty Years of Communism in Russia*, ed. M. M. Drachkovitch, pp. 284–92. Hoover Institution Publication no. 77. University Park: Pennsylvania State University Press, 1968.

"Human Rights and Social Justice." In *Social Justice and the Problem of the Twentieth Century*, ed. Sidney Hook, Tom Wicker and C. Van Woodward. Raleigh, N.C., 1968.

"The University Law School." In *The Law School of Tomorrow*, ed. D. Haber and J. Cohen. New Brunswick: Rutgers University Press, 1968. [Speech by Robert M. Hutchins with comment by Sidney Hook.]

"Ethics of Political Controversy (and Discussion)." In *Proceedings of the First Annual Symposium on Issues in Public Communications*, June 1968, pp. 50–85.

"The Enlightenment and Marxism." *Journal of the History of Ideas* 29 (Jan.–Mar. 1968): 93–108.

"The Human Costs of Revolution." *Survey* 66 (Jan. 1968): 129–37.

"Public Strikes." *New York Times*, 9 Feb. 1968, p. 26.

"Student Revolts Could Destroy Academic Freedom." *New York University Alumni News*, May 1968, pp. 8–9.

"America Must Erase the Cult of Violence." *Newsday*, 6 June 1968.

"Civil Liberties Issue in Appointment." *New York Times*, 1 Aug. 1968, p. 30.

Reply by Donald D. Schack, "Academic Freedom Called Issue." Ibid., 6 Aug. 1968, p. 36.

"Political Thinking beyond Politics." Review of Leszek Kolakowski, *Toward a Marxist Humanism. New York Times Book Review*, 1 Sept. 1968, pp. 8, 25.

"Hook Favors Bigger Role for Faculty." *New York Times*, 29 Sept. 1968, p. 52.

"N.Y.U. vs. Hatchett." *New York Times*, 28 Oct. 1968, p. 46.

"Marcusian Values." *New York Times Magazine*, 10 Nov. 1968, p. 22.

Reply to Herbert Marcuse, "Marcuse Defines His New Left Line." Ibid., 27 Oct. 1968.

Letters by others, ibid., 17 Nov. 1968, p. 12.

"Sidney Hook Replies." Letter to the editor. *New York Post*, 19 Nov. 1968.

1969

The Essential Thomas Paine, ed. Sidney Hook. New American Library, Mentor paperback, 1969.

"Empiricism, Rationalism, and Innate Ideas." In *Language and Philosophy: A Symposium*, ed. Sidney Hook, pp. 160–67. Ninth Symposium, New York University Institute of Philosophy, 1968. New York: New York University Press, 1969.

"Absolutism and Human Rights." In *Philosophy, Science, and Method: Essays in Honor of Ernest Nagel*, ed. Sidney Morgenbesser, Patrick Suppes, and Morton White, pp. 382–99. New York: St. Martin's Press, 1969.

"Social Protest and Civil Disobedience." In Paul Kurtz, *Moral Problems in Contemporary Society*, pp. 161–72. Englewood Cliffs, N.J.: Prentice-Hall, 1969.

"Brecht." *New Leader* 52 (3 Feb. 1969): 34.

Reply to Eric Bentley's review of Robert Conquest, *The Great Terror*. Ibid. 51 (2 Dec. 1968): 6–8.

Reply by Robert Conquest, ibid. 52 (3 Mar. 1969): 35.

Rebuttal by Eric Bentley, ibid. 52 (17 Mar. 1969): 34–35.

Responses by Hook and Henry M. Pachter, ibid. 52 (28 Apr. 1969): 34–35.

"Prof. Hook Replies to His Critics." *Connecticut Daily Campus*, 4 Feb. 1969. Letter to the editor relating to comments by Jerome Shaffer and others on Hook's speech "The Trojan Horse in American Higher Education."

"Professor Hook Replies." *Connecticut Daily Campus*, 24 Feb. 1969. Letter to the editor relating to comments by Jerome Shaffer and others on Hook's letter to the editor "Prof. Hook Replies to His Critics."

"The War against the Democratic Process." *Atlantic* 223 (Feb. 1969): 45–49.

"Reason and Violence: Some Truths and Myths about John Dewey." *Humanist* 29 (Mar.–Apr. 1969): 14–16.

"Who Is Responsible for Campus Violence?" *Saturday Review* 52 (19 Apr. 1969): 22–25, 54–55.

"Help Wanted—Superman." Review of Herbert Marcuse, *An Essay on Liberation. New York Times Book Review*, 20 Apr. 1969, p. 8.

"Mr. Hook Replies." *Atlantic* 223 (Apr. 1969): 46–47.

"Barbarism, Virtue, and the University." *Public Interest*, no. 15 (Spring 1969): 23–39.

"The Real Crisis on the Campus: A Noted Educator Sounds a Warning—Exclusive Interview." *U.S. News and World Report*, 19 May 1969, pp. 40–44.

"Democracy's Survival Problematic." *Antioch College Record*, 23 May 1969.

"The Barbarism of Virtue." *PMLA* 84 (May 1969): 465–75.

"*Modern Quarterly*, A Chapter in American Radical History: V. F. Calverton and His Periodicals." *Labor History* 10 (Spring 1969): 241–49.

"Labor Sit-Ins and University Sit-Ins: The Crucial Differences." *Measure*, June 1969.

"John Dewey and the Crisis of American Liberalism." *Antioch Review* 29 (Summer 1969): 218–32.

"The Crisis of Our Democratic Institutions." *Humanist* 29 (July–Aug. 1969): 6–7.

"The Architecture of Educational Chaos." *Phi Delta Kappan* 51 (Oct. 1969): 68–70.

Review of Henri Lefebvre, *The Sociology of Marx*. Trans. from French by N. Guterman. *American Historical Review* 75 (Oct. 1969): 148–49.

"The Trojan Horse in American Higher Education." *Educational Record* 50 (Winter 1969): 21–29.

"Some Reflections on the Encyclopedia of Philosophy." *Religious Humanism* 3 (Winter 1969): 4–7.

"Harold Taylor's Evasions." *Phi Delta Kappan* 51 (Dec. 1969): 197–98.
Response to Harold Taylor, "Students, Universities, and Sidney Hook." Ibid., pp. 195–97.

1970

American Freedom and Academic Anarchy. New York: Cowles Book Co., 1970.

"Conflict and Change in the Academic Community." In *Papers of the Fifty-second Annual Conference*, National Association of Student Personnel Administrators, 1970.

"Paradise Lost: The Tragedy of Whittaker Chambers." Review of Whittaker Chambers, *Odyssey of a Friend: Whittaker Chambers' Letters to William F. Buckley, Jr., 1954–1961. Chicago Sun-Times*, 1 Feb. 1970.

"Justice Douglas." *New York Times*, 19 Apr. 1970, p. 17.

"The Ideology of Violence." *Encounter* 34 (Apr. 1970): 26–29, 31–38.

"What Student Rights in Education?" *Current*, no. 117 (Apr. 1970): 21–27.

"Philosophy and Public Policy." *Journal of Philosophy* 67 (23 July 1970): 461–70.

"A Plan to Achieve Campus Peace." *Los Angeles Times*, 30 Aug. 1970.

"From the Platitudinous to the Absurd." *Philosophic Exchange* (Summer 1970): 21–30.

"Hook's Views on Riots." *New York Times*, 30 Sept. 1970, p. 42.

"Points of Confusion." *Encounter* 35 (Sept. 1970): 45–53.

"The Survival of the Free University." *Humanist* 30 (Sept.–Oct. 1970): 26–28.

Contribution to a symposium on William O. Douglas, *Points of Rebellion. Brooklyn Law Review* 37 (Fall 1970): 16–22.

Panel Discussion, ibid., pp. 22–32.

"Corporate Politics on Campus." *Freedom at Issue*, Sept.–Oct. 1970.

"Campus Terror: An Indictment." *New York Times*, 22 Oct. 1970, p. 47.

Reply by Lipman Bers, ibid., 30 Oct. 1970, p. 40.

"The Political Fantasies of Noam Chomsky." *Humanist* 30 (Nov.–Dec. 1970): 26–29.

1971

In Defense of Academic Freedom, ed. Sidney Hook. New York: Pegasus, 1971.

"Academic Freedom and the Supreme Court: The Court in Another Wilderness." In *On Academic Freedom*, ed. Valerie Earle. Washington: American Enterprise Institute for Public Policy Research, 1971.

"How Democratic Is America? A Response to Howard Zinn." In *How Democratic Is America? Responses to the New Left Challenge*, ed. Robert A. Goldwin. Chicago: Rand McNally, 1971.

"Ideals and Realities of Academic Tenure." In *Proceedings of the Twenty-eighth Annual Utah Conference on Higher Education*. Logan: Utah State University, 1971.

"Ideologies of Violence and Social Change." In *Peaceful Change in Modern Society*, ed. E. B. Tompkins, pp. 112–27. Stanford, Calif.: Stanford University Press, 1971.

"The Place of John Dewey in Modern Thought." In *Philosophical Thought in France and the United States*, pp. 483–503. Buffalo: University of Buffalo Publications in Philosophy, 1971.

"The Knight of the Double Standard." *Humanist* 31 (Jan.–Feb. 1971): 29–34.

    Response by Noam Chomsky, ibid., pp. 23–29.

"Knight Comes a Cropper." *Humanist* 31 (Mar.–Apr. 1971): 34–35.

"A Sentimental View of Crime." Review of Ramsey Clark, *Crime in America*. *Fortune* 83 (Feb. 1971): 140–41.

"Comments on Professor Nelson's Address." *Personalist* 52 (Spring 1971): 335–42.

"The Snare of Definitions." *Humanist* 31 (Sept.–Oct. 1971): 10–11.

"An American Verdict on Star–Spangled Australia." *Sunday Australian*, 31 Oct. 1971.

"Discrimination, Color Blindness and the Quota System." *Measure*, Oct. 1971.

"Discrimination against the Qualified?" *New York Times*, 5 Nov. 1971, p. 43.

    Reply by Martha Burke–Hennessy and Myra L. Skluth, ibid., 24 Nov. 1971, p. 34.

    Response by J. Stanley Pottinger, "Come Now, Professor Hook." Ibid., 18 Dec. 1971, p. 29.

    Response by Frank Askin, ibid., 19 Dec. 1971, p. 10.

"John Dewey and His Betrayers." *Change* 3 (Nov. 1971): 22–26.

    Discussed by Albert Shanker in his weekly column, "Where We Stand," *New York Times*, 3 Oct. 1971, p. 9.

"Authority and Democracy in the University." *Quadrant*, Nov.–Dec. 1971, pp. 42–48.

"Epilogue: Democracy and the Open Society." *Humanist* 31 (Nov.–Dec. 1971): 29–31.

"HEW Regionals—A New Threat to Educational Integrity." *Freedom at Issue*, no. 10 (Nov.–Dec. 1971): 5–7.

1972

Introduction to Marvin Zimmerman, *Contemporary Problems of Democracy*. New York: Humanities Press, 1972.

"The Freedom Shouters." *New York Times*, 17 Jan. 1972, p. 30.

> Reply by Barry Commoner, ibid., 28 Jan. 1972, p. 44.

Preface to Ernest van den Haag, "Civil Disobedience." *National Review* 24 (21 Jan. 1972): 29.

"Illich's De-Schooled Utopia." Review of Ivan Illich, *De-schooling Society. Encounter* 38 (Jan. 1972): 53–57.

"Democracy and Genetic Variation." *Humanist* 32 (Mar.–Apr. 1972): 9.

"The Road to a University 'Quota System.'" *Freedom at Issue*, no. 12 (Mar.–Apr. 1972): 2, 21–22.

> Response by Jack Hirshleifer, ibid., p. 23.

"The Rights of the Victims." *Encounter* 38 (Apr. 1972): 11–15.

"Adrienne Koch: Student and Colleague." *Maryland Historian* 3 (Spring 1972): 5–8.

"HEW's Faculty 'Quotas' Inspire Semantic Evasions." *Freedom at Issue*, no. 14 (July–Aug. 1972): 12–14.

"An Open Letter to Senator George McGovern." *Los Angeles Times*, 15 Oct. 1972.

"Uncertain Progress." *Measure*, no. 20 (Oct. 1972): 1–2.

1973

Education and the Taming of Power. La Salle, Ill.: Open Court Pub. Co., 1973.

Education for Modern Man: A New Perspective. New Enlarged Edition. Atlantic Highlands, N.J.: Humanities Press, 1973.

Heresy, Yes—Conspiracy, No. With new introduction. Westport, Conn.: Greenwood Press, 1973.

Foreword to *Radical School Reform, Critique and Alternatives*, ed. Cornelius J. Troost. Boston: Little, Brown and Co., 1973.

> See also Hook, "John Dewey and His Betrayers," pp. 57–66; "Illich's De-Schooled Utopia," pp. 67–73; "The Teaching of Values," pp. 190–95.

"Higher Education and Morality." In *Private Higher Education: The Job*

Ahead. Papers delivered by Ernest van den Haag et al. of the American Association of Presidents of Independent Colleges and Universities, Annual Conference, Scottsdale, Ariz., Dec. 1972. [c 1973].

"Marxism." In *Dictionary of the History of Ideas*, ed. Philip P. Wiener, vol. 3, pp. 146–61. New York: Charles Scribner's Sons, 1973.

"The Relevance of John Dewey's Thought." In *The Chief Glory of Every People*, ed. Matthew Bruccoli, pp. 53–75. Carbondale: Southern Illinois University Press, 1973.

"Lenin and the Communist International." Review of Branko Lazitch and Milorad M. Drachkovitch, *Lenin and the Comintern*, vol. 1. *Russian Review* 32 (Jan. 1973): 1–14.

"The Politics of Irresponsibility." Review of Richard King, *The Party of Eros: Radical Social Thought and the Realm of Freedom. Virginia Quarterly Review* 49 (Spring 1973): 274–82.

"Make the Punishment Fit the Criminal." *New York Times*, 6 Apr. 1973, p. 40.

"The Academic Mission and Collective Bargaining." *Proceedings of the First Annual Conference*, National Center for the Study of Collective Bargaining in Higher Education, New York City, Apr. 1973.

"Myth and Fact in the Marxist Theory of Revolution and Violence." *Journal of the History of Ideas* 34 (Apr.–June 1973): 271–80.

"Semantics and Politics." *Measure*, May 1973.

"Solzhenitsyn and the Western Liberals." *New York Times*, 19 Sept. 1973, p. 46.

"John Reed, the Romantic." Review of Barbara Gelb, *So Short a Time. New Republic* 169 (29 Sept. 1973): 23–25.

"Have We Reached Shore?" *Measure,* no. 24 (Sept. 1973): 1–3.

"Humanist Manifesto II," by Sidney Hook et al. *Humanist* 33 (Sept.–Oct. 1973): 4–9.

"Materials for a Biography." Review of George Dykhuizen, *The Life and Mind of John Dewey. New Republic* 169 (27 Oct. 1973): 38–39.

"For Louis Althusser." Review of Louis Althusser, *For Marx. Encounter* 41 (Oct. 1973): 86–92.

"William James and George Santayana." *ICarbS* 1 (Fall–Winter 1973): 34–39.

"Professing the Truth: An Exchange." *Columbia Forum*, Winter 1973.
"The Attack on Objectivity." *Measure*, no. 26 (Dec. 1973): 1–2.

1974

Pragmatism and the Tragic Sense of Life. New York: Basic Books, 1974.
"Democracy and Higher Education." In *The Idea of a Modern University*,
    ed. Sidney Hook, Paul Kurtz, and Miro Todorovich, pp. 33–40. Buf-
    falo, N.Y.: Prometheus Books, 1974.
"The Modern Quarterly: Baltimore and New York, 1923–1932,
    1938–1940. The Modern Monthly: New York, 1933–1938." In *The
    American Radical Press*, vol. 2, ed. Joseph R. Conlin, pp. 596–605.
    Westport, Conn.: Greenwood Press, 1974.
"A Dawning Light—Belated but Welcome." *Measure*, no. 27 (Jan. 1974):
    4.
"Reflections on the Disorder of Our Times." *Alternative* 7 (Jan. 1974):
    5–7.
"Humanism and the Human Experience." *Humanist* 34 (Jan.–Feb. 1974):
    6–7.
"Violence Usually Frustrates or Delays Reform." *Los Angeles Times*, 27
    Feb. 1974, p. 7.
"Letter from New York." *Encounter* 42 (Feb. 1974): 44–45.
"Anyone for Objectivity?" *Encounter* 42 (Mar. 1974): 94–95.
"The Education of an Auto–Didact." Review of James D. Koerner,
    Hoffer's America. *Change* 6 (Mar. 1974): 60–61.
"John Dewey's *Democracy and Education*." *New York University Educa-
    tion Quarterly* 5 (Spring 1974): 26–29.
"Stalin—Mystery and Legacy." Review of Ronald Hingley, *Joseph
    Stalin: Man and Legend*; Robert Tucker, *Stalin as Revolutionary*; and
    Adam B. Ulam, *Stalin: The Man and His Era*. *New Republic* 171 (20
    July 1974): 21–24.
"The Bias in Anti-Bias Regulations." *Measure*, no. 30 (Summer 1974):
    1–2, 4–6.

"Congressional Testimony: On Discrimination." *Measure*, no. 31 (Sept. 1974): 1, 2, 5, 6.

"A Quota Is a Quota Is a Quota." *New York Times*, 12 Nov. 1974, p. 39.
    Reply by Peter J. Wilson, ibid., 27 Nov. 1974, p. 36.
    Reply by Nancy Alderman Ransom, ibid., 2 Dec. 1974, p. 32.

"Will to Illusion." Review of Ernest Fisher, *An Opposing Man*. *New Republic*, 16 Nov. 1974, pp. 27–28.

"A Bolshevik Reconsidered: The Case of Comrade Bukharin." Review of Stephen Cohen, *Bukharin and the Bolshevik Revolution, 1888–1938*. *Encounter* 43 (Dec. 1974): 81–92.

1975

Revolution, Reform, and Social Justice—Studies in the Theory and Practice of Marxism. New York: New York University Press, 1975.

The Philosophy of the Curriculum: The Need for General Education, ed. Sidney Hook, Paul Kurtz, and Miro Todorovich. Buffalo, N.Y.: Prometheus Books, 1975.

"Higher Education and Morality." In *Private Higher Education: The Job Ahead*, vol. 4, pp. 1–6. American Association of Presidents of Independent Colleges and Universities Annual Meeting Talks, Scottsdale, Arizona, 1975.

Preface to John Dewey, *Moral Principles in Education*. Carbondale and Edwardsville: Southern Illinois University Press, Arcturus Books, 1975.

"For An Open Minded Naturalism." *Southern Journal of Philosophy* 13 (1975): 127–36.

"In the Forefront." *New York Post*, 1 Feb. 1975.
    Response to Carl Rowan, "The War on Quotas," ibid., 20 Jan. 1975.

"Education: The Wrong Affirmative Action." Letter by Sidney Hook et al. *New York Times*, 29 Mar. 1975, p. 22.

"What the Cold War Was About." *Encounter* 44 (Mar. 1975): 62–67.

"A Humanist Philosophy of Life." Review of Paul Kurtz, *The Fullness of Life*. *Humanist* 35 (Mar.–Apr. 1975): 36–37.

"University Women: An Exchange." *New York Review of Books*, 3 Apr. 1975, pp. 36–37.

    Reply by Gertrude Ezorsky, ibid., pp. 37–38.

"The Issue Redefined." *Freedom at Issue*. May–June 1975, pp. 17–19.

"America Now: A Failure of Nerve?—A Symposium." *Commentary* 60 (July 1975): 41–43.

"The Hiss Ruling's Contradictions." *Wall Street Journal*, 25 Aug. 1975, p. 6.

    Response by John F. Burke, ibid., 29 Sept. 1975, p. 11.

    Reply by Hook, ibid.

"The Promise of Humanism." *Humanist* 35 (Sept.–Oct. 1975): 41–43.

    Response to Jerome Frank, "The Limits of Humanism." Ibid., pp. 38–40.

    Reply by Albert Ellis, "Comments on Frank's 'The Limits of Humanism'." Ibid., pp. 43–45.

    Response by Frank, ibid. 35 (Nov.–Dec. 1975): 34.

    Rejoinder by Hook, ibid., pp. 34–35.

"In Defense of Terminological Sobriety: A Reply to Professor Kellner." *Journal of Politics* 37 (Nov. 1975): 912–16.

    See Menachem Marc Kellner, "Democracy and Civil Disobedience." Ibid., pp. 899–911.

"The Tyranny of Reverse Discrimination." With Miro Todorovich. *Change* 7 (Dec. 1975–Jan. 1976): 42–43.

1976

Ethics, National Ideology, Marxism and Existentialism: Discussions with Sidney Hook. Ed. Harsja W. Bachtiar. Jakarta, Indonesia: Djambatan, 1976. In Indonesian and English.

Foreword to James Gouinlock, *The Moral Writings of John Dewey*. New York: Macmillan Co., Hafner Press, 1976.

Introduction to *The Middle Works of John Dewey, 1899–1924*, ed. Jo Ann Boydston, vol. 2. Carbondale and Edwardsville: Southern Illinois University Press, 1976.

"The Strange Case of Whittaker Chambers." *Encounter* 46 (Jan. 1976): 78–89.

Review of John P. Diggins, *Up from Communism*. *New Republic* 174 (21 Feb. 1976): 24–27.

    Reply by Diggins, ibid. 174 (12 June 1976): 31–32.

    Response by Hook, ibid., p. 32.

"Alger Hiss: The Continuing Whitewash." Review of John Chabot Smith, *Alger Hiss: The True Story*. *Wall Street Journal*, 22 Mar. 1976, p. 14.

"Intelligence, Morality and Foreign Policy." *Freedom at Issue*, no. 35 (Mar.–Apr. 1976): 3–6.

    Condensed in New York Times, 1 May 1976, p. 23.

"The Legacy of 1776—and a New Call for Freedom." *American Views* 1 (5 July 1976): 1–2.

"Bertrand Russell the Man." *Commentary* 62 (July 1976): 52–54.

Review of Michael Harrington, *The Twilight of Capitalism: A Marxian Epitaph*. *New Republic* 175 (7 and 14 Aug. 1976): 34–37.

"Morris Cohen—Fifty Years Later." *American Scholar* 45 (Summer 1976): 426–36.

    Reply by Diggins, ibid. 174 (12 June 1976): 31–32.

    Response by Hook, ibid., p. 32.

"The Social Democratic Prospect." *New America* 13 (Aug.–Sept. 1976): 8–9, 14.

"The Big Casino in the Sky." *New York Times*, 3 Sept. 1976.

"It's All in the Cards, My Dear. (Luck plays important role in life.)" *Fort Worth Star-Telegram*, 19 Sept. 1976.

"Can the University Survive Equal Access?" Review of *On The Meaning of the University*, ed. Sterling M. McMurrin. *Change* 8 (Sept. 1976): 59–61.

"A Symposium: What Is a Liberal—Who Is a Conservative?" *Commentary* 62 (Sept. 1976): 69–70.

"Is Secular Humanism a Religion?" *Humanist* 36 (Sept.–Oct. 1976): 5–7.

"The Hero and Democracy." *Gandhi Marg* 21 (Oct. 1976): 226–34.

"A Voice from Another Shore." Review of Lev Navrozov, *The Education of Lev Navrozov*. *Humanist* 36 (Nov.–Dec. 1976): 47, 50.

"An Interview with Sidney Hook." *Forum* (Austin, Texas) 1 (Dec. 1976): 6–7.

"Letters from George Santayana." *American Scholar* 46 (Winter 1976–77): 76–84.

Letter to editor. *American Scholar* 46 (Winter 1976–77): 142–43.

1977

"Academic Freedom and Professional Responsibility." In *The Ethics of Teaching and Scientific Research*, ed. Sidney Hook, Paul Kurtz, and Miro Todorovich, pp. 117–23. Buffalo, N.Y.: Prometheus Books, 1977.

"Dr. Hibbs and the Ethics of Discussion." *The Ethics of Teaching and Scientific Research*, ed. Sidney Hook, Paul Kurtz, and Miro Todorovich, pp. 187–90. Buffalo, N.Y.: Prometheus Books, 1977.

"How Democratic Is America? A Response to Howard Zinn." In *How Democratic Is America? Responses to the New Left Challenge*, ed. Robert A. Goldwin, pp. 61–75. Chicago: Rand McNally & Co., 1977.

"The Books That Shape Lives: Book Choices of Henry David Aiken and Sidney Hook." *Christian Century* 94 (5–12 Jan. 1977): 20.

"The New Religiosity." *Humanist* 37 (Jan.–Feb. 1977): 38–39.

Part of a symposium entitled "The Resurgence of Fundamentalism."

"Lillian Hellman's *Scoundrel Time*." *Encounter* 48 (Feb. 1977): 82–91.

"Racial and Sexual Quotas: They're Not Only Illegal, They're Immoral." *New York Daily News*, 27 Mar. 1977.

"To Teach the Truth without Let or Hindrance." *Chronicle of Higher Education* 14 (4 Apr. 1977): 40.

Reply by Leonard Marsak, ibid., 2 May 1977, p. 16.

Response by Hook, ibid., 23 May 1977.

"Marxists and Non-Marxists." *Times Literary Supplement* 88 (29 Apr. 1977): 522.

Reply to Ghita Ionescu review, ibid., 8 Apr. 1977, p. 427.

"An Outstanding Symbol of Free Trade Unions." *New America* 14 (May 1977): 8.

"Fanaticism and Absolutism." *Intellect* 105 (May 1977): 387–88.

"Marxism and Crypto-Marxism." *New York Times*, 26 Oct. 1977, p. 27.

"The Bias in Public Media Programs." *Measure*, no. 44 (Oct. 1977): 3–5.

"Socialism Means Freedom." *New America*, Oct. 1977.

"Reflections on the Metaphysics of John Dewey: *Experience and Nature.*" *Revue Internationale de Philosophie* (*La Pensée Philosophique Américaine 1776–1976*), no. 121–22 (1977): 313–28.

1978

The Hero in History: Myth, Power, or Moral Ideal? Stanford University: Hoover Institution on War, Revolution and Peace, 1978.

The University and the State, ed. Sidney Hook, Paul Kurtz, and Miro Todorovich. Buffalo, N.Y.: Prometheus Books, 1978.

"Bernstein's Contribution to Social Democracy." *New America* 15 (Jan. 1978): 2, 8.

"Of I.Q. Tests and the Desire to Succeed." Letter to the editor. *New York Times*, 3 Mar. 1978, p. 24.

"Politics on the Obituary Page." *National Review* 30 (28 Apr. 1978): 514.

"Capitalism, Socialism and Democracy." *Commentary* 65 (Apr. 1978): 48–50.

"Civil Discourse and Editorial Responsibility." *Measure*, no. 46 (Apr.–May 1978): 3, 8.

"Above All, Freedom." *Time*, 26 June 1978, p. 22.

> Response to speech by Alexander Solzhenitsyn, Harvard Yard, June 1978.

Review of John G. Gurley, *Challengers to Capitalism: Marx, Lenin, and Mao*. *Slavic Review* 37 (June 1978): 307–8.

Review of Eugen Loebl, *My Mind on Trial*. *Slavic Review* 37 (June 1978): 323–25.

"Beyond Freedom Lies Terror." *Business and Society Review*, no. 26 (Summer 1978): 15.

"Imaginary Enemies, Real Terror." Review of James Atlas, *Delmore Schwartz: The Life of an American Poet*. *American Scholar* 47 (Summer 1978): 406–12.

Review of Kostas Axelos, *Alienation, Praxis, and Techne in the Thought of Karl Marx. Journal of Economic History* 38 (Summer 1978): 744–46.

"The Case of Alger Hiss." Review of Allen Weinstein, *Perjury: The Hiss-Chambers Case. Encounter* 51 (Aug. 1978): 48–55.

> Reply to Eric Jacobs and Margaret Stern, ibid., Mar. 1979, pp. 85–90.

"Letter to the editor." *Contemporary Sociology*, Sept. 1978. On review by Jerome H. Skolnick of Ernest van den Haag, *Punishing Criminals.*

"Home Truths." Review of Yvonne Kapp, *Eleanor Marx. Commentary* 66 (Sept. 1978): 82–86.

"*Bakke*—Where Does It Lead? The Triumph of Racism?" *Freedom at Issue*, no. 47 (Sept.–Oct. 1978): 3–6.

> Reply by Nathaniel R. Jones, "Marshall Points the Way." Ibid., pp. 3–6.

> Rejoinders by Hook and Jones, ibid., pp. 7, 12.

"Solzhenitsyn and Secular Humanism: A Response." *Humanist* 38 (Nov.–Dec. 1978): 4–6.

1979

"Solzhenitsyn and Western Freedom: How Serious a Challenge?" In *Conference on Issues in Liberal Education*, University of Oklahoma, Norman, 28 Mar. 1979.

"Are There Alternatives to Collective Bargaining?" In *Landmarks in Collective Bargaining in Higher Education,* ed. Aaron Levenstein, pp. 150–54. Proceedings of the Seventh Annual Conference on Collective Bargaining in Higher Education, 24 Apr. 1979. New York: National Center for the Study of Collective Bargaining in Higher Education, 1979.

"Cosmology and Ethics." Letter to the editor. *New Republic* 180 (5 May 1979): 7.

> Reply to Henry Fairlie, "By Jupiter!" Ibid. 180 (7 Apr. 1979): 18–21.

"Hook vs. Wills." Letter to the editor. *Time*, May 21, p. 5.

    Reply to R. Z. Sheppard's review of Garry Wills, *Confessions of a Conservative. Time*, 23 Apr. 1979, pp. 86–87.

"Solzhenitsyn and Western Freedom." *World Literature Today*, Autumn 1979, pp. 573–78. Reprinted in *Marxism and Beyond*, 1983.

"The Weber Case." Letter to the editor. With Miro Todorovich. *Commentary* 68 (Sept. 1979): 21.

    Reply to Carl Cohen, "Justice Debased: The Weber Decision." Ibid., pp. 43, 53.

    Reply by Cohen, ibid., p. 21.

1980

Philosophy and Public Policy. Carbondale and Edwardsville: Southern Illinois University Press, 1980.

"A World Split Apart." Comment on Aleksandr I. Solzhenitsyn, in *Solzhenitsyn at Harvard*, ed. Ronald Berman, pp. 3–20. Washington, D.C.: Ethics and Public Policy Center, 1980.

"Spectral Marxism." Essay review of Leszek Kolakowski, *Main Currents of Marxism: Its Rise, Growth, and Dissolution: The Founders; The Golden Age; The Breakdown. American Scholar* 49 (Spring 1980): 250–71. Reprinted in *Marxism and Beyond*, 1983.

"Marx for All Seasons." Review of Robert L. Heilbroner, *Marxism: For and Against. Commentary* 70 (July 1980): 78–80. Reprinted in *Marxism and Beyond*, 1983.

    Reply by Seymour Yellin, "Marx & Marxists." *Commentary* 70 (Sept. 1980): 24.

    Response by Hook, ibid.

"Bertrand Russell's 'Reserve.'" *Midstream* 26 (Aug.–Sept. 1980): 64.

    Reply to Harry Ruja's "Bertrand Russell on the Jews." Ibid. 26 (Feb. 1980): 50–52.

    Response by Ruja, Ibid. 26 (Aug.–Sept. 1980): 64.

Review of Norman Podhoretz, *The Present Danger. American Spectator*, Sept. 1980, pp. 32–33.

Reply by Frank O'Connell, "An Inordinate Fear of Labor?" Part 1. Ibid., Jan. 1981, pp. 25, 36.

Reply by Paul Gottfried, "An Inordinate Fear of Labor?" Part 2. Ibid., p. 36.

Rejoinder by Hook, ibid., pp. 36–37.

"Disremembering the Thirties." Review of Malcolm Cowley, *The Dream of the Golden Mountain: Remembering the Thirties. American Scholar* 49 (Autumn 1980): 556–60. Reprinted in *Marxism and Beyond*, 1983.

"Righting Marx." *American Spectator*, Oct. 1980, p. 36.

Reply to Arnold Beichman's review of *Philosophy and Public Policy*. Ibid., Aug. 1980, pp. 40–41.

"Misread 'Secular Humanist Declaration.'" Letter to the editor. With Paul Kurtz. *New York Times*, 7 Nov. 1980, p. A26.

Reply to Kenneth A. Briggs, "Secular Humanists Attack a Rise in Fundamentalism." Ibid., 15 Oct. 1980, p. A18; and Samuel A. Turk, ibid., 25 Oct. 1980, p. 22.

"Books for Christmas." *American Spectator*, Dec. 1980, p. 23.

1981

Afterword to Bertram D. Wolfe, *A Life in Two Centuries*, pp. 714–16. New York: Stein and Day, 1981.

"Jacobo Timerman." Letter to the editor. *New York Times Book Review*, 2 Aug. 1981, p. 24.

Reply to Anthony Lewis's review of Jacobo Timerman, *Prisoner without a Name, Cell without a Number*. Ibid., 10 May 1981, pp. 1, 30–32.

"'The Future Danger.'" *Commentary* 72 (Aug. 1981): 4.

Reply to Norman Podhoretz, "The Future Danger." Ibid. 71 (Apr. 1981): 29–47.

"So schön war's früher mal in Kalten Krieg." *Die Welt*, 12 Sept. 1981, Geistige Welt section, p. 1.

"A Million-Dollar Gift's Forbidding Proviso." Letter to the editor. *New York Times*, 10 Oct. 1981, p. 24.

> Reply to Dudley Clendinen, "Gift to Amherst College Requiring Black Professor Stirs Debate." Ibid., 14 Sept. 1981, p. 16.

"The Worldly Ways of John Kenneth Galbraith." Review of Galbraith, *A Life in Our Times. American Spectator*, Oct. 1981, pp. 7–12. Reprinted in *Marxism and Beyond*, 1983.

> Response by John Lukacs, "Galbraith Unhooked." *American Spectator*, Feb. 1982, pp. 29, 40–41.

> Reply by Hook, "Lukacs Hooked." Ibid., pp. 41–44.

"Communism and the American Intellectuals from the Thirties to the Eighties." *Free Inquiry* 1 (Fall 1981): 11–15.

> Reply by Lawrence Cranberg, "Is Marx Refutable?" Ibid. 2 (Winter 1981–82): 5, 44.

1982

"General Education in a Free Society." In *Freedom, Order, and the University*, ed. James R. Wilburn, pp. 31–41. Malibu, Calif.: Pepperdine University Press, 1982.

"Soviets Won't Honor Freeze." *Stanford Daily*, 23 Apr. 1982, p. 4.

> Comment by Hook, "Key Omission?" Ibid., 30 Apr. 1982.

> Reply by Joe Walder, "Anti-Soviet Propaganda Falsely Accepted." Ibid., 4 May 1982.

> Comments by Joe Walder, ibid., 13 May 1982.

> Response by Hook, "Verifying a Nuclear Freeze." Ibid., p. 4.

"Out of the Depths." Review of Anton Antonov-Ovseyenko, *The Time of Stalin: Portrait of a Tyranny. American Scholar* 51 (Spring 1982): 291–95. Reprinted in *Marxism and Beyond*, 1983.

"My Running Debate with Einstein." *Commentary* 74 (July 1982): 37–52.

> Replies by Maynard Kniskern and Otto Nathan, ibid. 74 (November 1982): 16–17.

Response by Hook, ibid., pp. 17–18.

Reply by Stephen Siteman, ibid. 74 (December 1982): 76–77.

Response by Hook, ibid., pp. 77–78.

"A Dissent on Kohrmon." *Brattleboro* (Vt.) *Reformer*, 4 Aug. 1982, p. 4.

Reply to Katherine Kohrmon, ibid., 31 July 1982, p. 4.

"The First Amendment vs. the Rest of the Constitution." *Denver Post*, 26 Sept. 1982, p. 3B.

"An Interview with Sidney Hook at Eighty." *Free Inquiry* 2 (Fall 1982): 4–10. [Interviewed by Paul Kurtz.]

Comment by Edwin H. Wilson, ibid. 3 (Summer 1983): 3.

Reply by Hook, ibid., pp. 3–4.

Editorial comment, ibid., p. 4.

"The Soviet Threat to Peace and Freedom." *Washington Times*, 9 Dec. 1982, p. 18A.

"A Symposium: The Bishops and the Arms Race." Hook et al. *New York Times*, 26 Dec. 1982, p. E3.

"Living with Deep Truths in a Divided World." *Free Inquiry* 3 (Winter 1982–83): 30–31.

1983

Marxism and Beyond. Totowa, N.J.: Rowman and Littlefield, 1983.

Foreword to Gary Bullert, *The Politics of John Dewey*, pp. 3–5. Amherst, N.Y.: Prometheus Books, 1983.

"Ominous Rumblings in the Academy." *Measure*, no. 61 (March 1983): 1, 8.

"Hook: The Test Is Always the Quality, Not Quantity, of Scholarly Works." *Campus Report* (Stanford), 11 May 1983, p. 11.

"The Morality of Survival in a Nuclear Face-Off: People with Courage to Fight for Freedom Have the Best Chances of Avoiding Misery." *Los Angeles Times*, 11 May 1983, Part II, p. 5. (Commentary adapted from *Marxism and Beyond.*)

"Edging towards Disaster?" *Measure*, no. 62 (May 1983): 1, 8.

"What Can Be Done?" *Measure*, no. 62 (May 1983): 4, 7–8.

"An Open Letter to the U.S. Senate." *Washington Times*, 26 July 1983, p. 1C.

"Cold Warrior." *Encounter* 61 (July–Aug. 1983): 12–16.

"The Incredible Story of Michael Straight." *Encounter* 61 (Dec. 1983): 68–73.

> Comment by editors, ibid. 62 (April 1984): 77.
>
> Response by Straight's lawyer, ibid., pp. 77–78.
>
> Reply by Hook, ibid., p. 78.

1984

"Pluralistic Societies at Stake." In *Challenges to the Western Alliance*, ed. Joseph Godson, pp. 177–81. London: Times Books, 1984.

"The Philosopher as a Young Man." Review of Kenneth Blackwell et al., eds., *The Collected Papers of Bertrand Russell*, vol. 1. *New York Times Book Review*, 29 Jan. 1984, pp. 7–8.

"Judging Brecht." *Times Literary Supplement*, 3 Feb. 1984, p. 111. Reply to John Willett, ibid., 13 Jan. 1984, p. 37.

> Response by Willett, ibid., 17 Feb. 1984, p. 165.
>
> Reply by Hook, ibid., 9 Mar. 1984, p. 247.

"Breaking with the Communists—a Memoir." *Commentary* 77 (Feb. 1984): 47–53.

"New York Intelligentsia." Letter to the editor. With Arnold Beichman. *New York Times Book Review*, 25 Mar. 1984, p. 26.

> Reply to Nathan Glazer, "New York Intellectuals—Up from Revolution." Ibid., 26 Feb. 1984, pp. 1, 34–35.

"Mill on Nonintervention." Letter to the editor. *New York Times*, 25 Apr. 1984, p. A22.

> Comment on "Moynihan to Quit Senate Panel Post in Dispute on C.I.A." Ibid., 16 Apr. 1984, pp. A1, A8.

"Bertrand Russell: A Portrait from Memory." *Encounter* 62 (Mar. 1984): 9–20. Reprinted in *Out of Step: An Unquiet Life in the 20th Century*, 1987.

Comment by Peter Campbell, *Encounter* 62 (May 1984): 80.
Comment by Robert E. L. Fans, ibid. 64 (Feb. 1985): 78.
"Memories of the Moscow Trials." *Commentary* 77 (Mar. 1984): 57–63.
Correction by Hook, ibid. 77 (May 1984): 13.
Reply by Tom Milstein, ibid. 78 (Aug. 1984): 8.
Reply by Jeremy Murray-Brown, ibid.
Response by Hook, ibid., pp. 8–9.
"The Myth of Necessity." Review of Alexander Zinoviev, *The Reality of Communism. Times Literary Supplement*, 6 Apr. 1984, pp. 365–66.
Reply by Robert Gorham Davis, ibid., 11 May 1984, p. 523.
Response by Hook, ibid., 27 July 1984, p. 841.
"Basics We Must Not Forget." *Times* (London), 23 Apr. 1984, p. 10.
"Humanities, Liberal Democracy Need Not Conflict, Hook Says." Text of Jefferson lecture on "The Humanities and Defense of the Free Society." *Campus Report* (Stanford), 30 May 1984, pp. 17–18.
Comment by Bob Beyers, "Hook Advocates Required Study of Free Democratic Principles." Ibid., p. 17.
"'Geniemoral.'" *Midstream* 30 (May 1984): 33–36.
"Looking for America." Letter to the editor. *Harper's*, May 1984, p. 79.
Response to Philip Berrigan's contribution to "Does America Still Exist?" *Harper's*, Mar. 1984, pp. 45–46.
"Education in Defense of a Free Society." *Commentary* 78 (July): 17–22.
Comment by George Field, ibid. 78 (Oct. 1984): 7–8.
Comments by Joseph R. Aziz, Raymond Garmel, and David Broyles, ibid. 78 (Nov. 1984): 9–10.
Reply by Hook, ibid., pp. 10–11.
"Sweet Are the Uses of Diversity." Letter to the editor. *Wall Street Journal*, 3 July 1984, p. 25.
"God and the Professors." *Free Inquiry* 4 (Summer 1984): 18–27.
Reprinted in *Out of Step: An Unquiet Life in the 20th Century*, 1987.
"Comment on a Comment." *International Journal of World Peace* 1 (Autumn 1984): 41–n.
Reply to Lloyd Motz, "Comment." Ibid., pp. 20–33. Reply to Alexander Shtromas, "To Fight Communism: Why and How?" Ibid., pp. 33–36.

Rejoinder by Shtromas, ibid., pp. 36–41.

"The Principles and Problems of Academic Freedom: Accountability." *Vital Speeches of the Day* 50 (1 Sept. 1984): 701–704.

"'Evil Empire' Label Didn't Hurt the Kremlin's Feelings." *New York Times*, 4 Nov. 1984, p. 24E.

Reply to editorial, "Mondale for President." *New York Times*, 28 Oct. 1984, p. 22E.

"The Use and Abuse of Academic Freedom." *Measure*, no. 63 (Nov. 1984): 1–2.

"The Academic Ethic in Abeyance: Recollections of *Walpurgisnacht* at New York University." *Minerva* 22 (Autumn–Winter 1984): 297–315.

"Questions about a Strange Conversion." *Encounter* 63 (Dec. 1984): 65.

Reply to George Urban, "Portrait of a Dissenter as a Soviet Man: A Conversation with Alexander Zinoviev." Parts 1 and 2. Ibid. 62 (Apr. 1984): 8–24; (May 1984): 30–38.

"The Communist Peace Offensive." *Partisan Review* 51 (1984–85): 692–711. Reprinted in *Out of Step: An Unquiet Life in the 20th Century*, 1987.

1985

"Three Intellectual Troubadours." *American Spectator*, Jan. 1985, pp. 18, 20–22.

"All Is Not Fair in News Reporting." *Wall Street Journal*, 21 Feb. 1985, p. 33.

"Rationalizations for Reverse Discrimination." *New Perspectives* 17 (Winter 1985): 9–11.

Reply by James Kilpatrick, "Do Not Benignly Neglect Injustice." *San Francisco Chronicle*, 16 Apr. 1985, p. 40.

Reply by Jeffrey Hart, "The Evil of Reverse Discrimination." *St. Louis Post-Dispatch*, 14 May 1985, p. 3B.

"English Influence Enlightened India." *Detroit News*, 31 Mar. 1985, p. 17A.

"Will Capitalists Destroy Capitalism?" *Detroit News*, 19 May 1985, p. 15A.

"Encounter with Espionage." *Midstream* 31 (May 1985): 52–55.

"Would It Destroy the World?" Review of Timothy J. Cooney, *Telling Right from Wrong. New York Times Book Review*, 30 June 1985, p. 13.

"Hook on the Stockdales." *American Spectator*, June 1985, p. 7.

> Comment on Harry G. Summers Jr., review of Jim and Sybil Stockdale, *In Love and War*. Ibid., Apr. 1985, pp. 41–44.
>
> Reply by Summers, ibid., June 1985, p. 7.

"Unacademic Campus Tactics." *New York Times*, 3 Oct. 1985, p. A27.

"What's Fair about News Reporting?" *Palo Verde Valley Times*, 18 Oct. 1985, p. 4.

"The Wrong Way to Remedy Abuses of the Academic Ethic." *Measure*, no. 64 (Oct. 1985): 1–2, 5.

"Throw Them in the Melting Pot: Experience Shows Immigrant Children Learn English by Being Taught in English." *St. Louis Post-Dispatch*, 24 Nov. 1985, p. 3G.

"How Has the United States Met Its Major Challenges Since 1945? A Symposium." *Commentary* 80 (Nov. 1985): 47–50.

"Class Consciousness in the Free World." *New America* 22 (Nov.–Dec. 1985): 3.

"Bilingual Ed: Aid or Obstacle?" *Detroit News*, 10 Dec. 1985, p. 19A.

"Academy of Humanism News. Ernest Nagel (1901–1985): A Naturalistic Humanist." *Free Inquiry* 6 (Winter 1985–86): 27.

"On the Existence of God: Duncan and Hook." Correspondence between Homer Duncan and Hook. *Free Inquiry* 6 (Winter 1985–86): 39–41.

"Pluralistic Humanism." *Free Inquiry* 6 (Winter 1985–86): 19–20.

1986

"A Dictionary? Marxism from A to B." *Encounter* 66 (Jan. 1986): 71–74.

> Comment by Tibor R. Machan, "Hook's Marx." Ibid. 66 (May 1986): 76.

Reply by Hook, "Sidney Hook's Reply." Ibid.
Comment by Machan, "Hook's Marx." Ibid. 67 (Dec. 1986): 80.
Reply by Hook, "Sidney Hook Replies." Ibid.
"Between Democracy and Despotism." *Imprimis* 15 (Feb. 1986): 1–4.
"Burden of Proof Is Put on the Defamed." *New York Times*, 6 May 1986, p. A30.

Reply to Stuart Taylor Jr., "High Court Adds Protection for News Media in Libel Suits." Ibid., 22 Apr. 1986, pp. A1, A14.

"Rediscovering Sin." *New York Times Magazine*, 11 May 1986, p. 86. Response to William F. Buckley Jr., "Thou Shalt Not." Ibid., 6 Apr. 1986, pp. 34–36.
"Punishing the Innocent Is Unjust Redress." *New York Times*, 7 June 1986, p. 26.

Response to editorial, "Affirmative (to Most People) Action." Ibid., 24 May 1986, p. 24.

"Who Lives Where, and When?" *Measure*, no. 65 (July 1986): 1, 5–6.
"Anti-Communism on Campus: Misreading of John Dewey, C. G. Jung, and Santayana." *Chronicle of Higher Education*, 6 Aug. 1986, p. 36.

Comment on Michael D. Yates, "South Africa, Anti-Communism, and Value-Free Science." Ibid., 14 May 1986, p. 84.
Comment on Robert S. Corrington, letter to the editor. Ibid., 18 June 1986, p. 37.
Response by Corrington, "John Dewey's Social Theory and University Policy." Ibid., 1 Oct. 1986, p. 46.
Reply by Hook, "Dewey's Opposition to Communism." Ibid., 22 Oct. 1986, pp. 47–48.

"Communists in the Classroom." *American Spectator*, Aug. 1986, pp. 21–24.
"The New School Germanized?" *New York Times Book Review*, 28 Sept. 1986, p. 45.

Reply to Nathan Glazer's review of Peter M. Rutkoff and William B. Scott, *New School: A History of the New School for Social Research*. Ibid., 31 Aug. 1986, pp. 6–7.
Reply by Rutkoff and Scott, ibid., 28 Sept. 1986, p. 45.

"Questions Concerning Student PIRGS." *Measure*, no. 66 (Sept. 1986): 1–2, 5–6.

"The Principles and Problems of Academic Freedom." *Contemporary Education* 58 (Fall 1986): 6–12.

"The New Challenges to Our Schools of Journalism." *Measure*, no. 67 (Nov.–Dec. 1986): 1–2, 4, 6.

1987

Out of Step: An Unquiet Life in the 20th Century. New York: Harper and Row, 1987.

Soviet Hypocrisy and Western Gullibility. With Vladimir Bukovsky and Paul Hollander. Washington, D.C.: Ethics and Public Policy Center, 1987.

Paradoxes of Freedom. With a new introduction by Hook. Amherst, N.Y.: Prometheus Books, 1987.

"Pages from the History of the Association." *Proceedings and Addresses of the American Philosophical Association* 60 (Jan. 1987): 5, 11–13.

"In Defense of Voluntary Euthanasia." *New York Times*, 1 Mar. 1987, p. E25.

Comment by Norman Podhoretz, "A Subliminal Endorsement of Suicide." *Washington Post*, 11 Mar. 1987, p. A19.

Reply by John Lofton to Podhoretz, "Euthanasia's Slippery Slope." Ibid., 1 Apr. 1987, p. D1.

Reply by Hook to Podhoretz, "Does Euthanasia Send Us down a 'Slippery Slope'?" Ibid., 23 Apr. 1987, p. A15.

Reply by Hook, "Grant the Terminally Ill a Right to Relief from Suffering." *San Jose Mercury*, 21 Mar. 1987.

Responses by Felicia Ackerman, Lenore Blumenthal, Eric Kocher, and Isaiah Rackovsky, *New York Times*, 20 Mar. 1987, p. A30.

Reply by Hook to Rackovsky, "Life at Any Price Is a Bargain with Infamy." Ibid., 9 Apr. 1987, p. A26.

"The Affirmative Action Ruling—and the Imperial Judiciary." *New York Post*, 6 Apr. 1987, p. 21.

"The Doctrine of Moral Equivalence Fails on the Facts." *Orange County Register* (Santa Ana, Calif.), 16 Apr. 1987, p. B15. Also published in *New York City Tribune*, 28 Apr. 1987, as "'Moral Equivalence'—a Useless, Outworn Doctrine."

"Santayana: Humanist Misanthrope." Review of John McCormick, *George Santayana: A Biography. Washington Times Magazine*, 27 Apr. 1987, pp. M1, M4.

"Off on Hook." *New Republic* 196 (25 May 1987): 2.

> Reply to Arthur M. Schlesinger Jr., ibid. 196 (4 May 1987): 30–31.

"A Curious Phenomenon: A Report." *Measure* no. 69 (June 1987): 1, 6.

"Educational Statesmanship or Educational Demagogy?" *Measure*, no. 69 (June 1987): 4.

"Hook, Russell, and Atomic War." *American Spectator*, June 1987, p. 9. Reply to Tom Bethell, "A Stroll with Sidney Hook." Ibid., May 1987, 11–13.

"The Communist Peace Offensive." *Freedom at Issue*, no. 97 (July–Aug. 1987): 13–18.

"James Burnham: Radical, Teacher, Technician." *National Review* 39 (11 Sept. 1987): 32–33.

"Old Wine in New Bottles." Review of Tony Smith, *Thinking like a Communist: State and Legitimacy in the Soviet Union, China, and Cuba. Asian Wall Street Journal*, 22 Sept. 1987, p. 8.

"Communists, McCarthy, and American Universities." Review of Ellen Schrecker, *No Ivory Tower: McCarthyism and the Universities. Minerva* 25 (Autumn 1987): 331–48.

"Why 'Back to Basics' Isn't Good Enough." *American Educator* 11 (Fall 1987): 24–28, 42. [Interview by Thomas Main.]

"A Common Moral Universe?" *Free Inquiry* 7 (Fall 1987): 29, 31.

> Reply to Yaakov D. Homnick, "Hook Is Mired in Secular Confusion." Ibid., pp. 28–29, 30.

"Philosophy and Faith." *Commentary* 84 (Nov. 1987): 2, 4.

> Reply to Hilton Kramer, "The Importance of Sidney Hook." Ibid. 84 (Aug. 1987): 17–23.
>
> Comment by Lewis S. Feuer, ibid. 84 (Nov. 1987): 4–6.
>
> Response by Kramer, ibid., p. 6.

"How to Blow Your Own Horn Effectively." Review of William Zinsser, *Inventing the Truth: The Art and Craft of Memoir. Wall Street Journal*, 23 Nov. 1987, p. 24.

1988

Introduction to James Burnham, *The Machiavellians: Defenders of Freedom*. Washington, D.C.: Regnery Gateway.

"Making the Case against Socrates." Review of I. F. Stone, *The Trial of Socrates. Wall Street Journal*, 20 Jan. 1988, p. 24.

> Comment by Kate Regan, "Izzy at 80: Wisdom through the Ages." *San Francisco Chronicle*, 6 Feb. 1988, p. C3.
>
> Reply by Hook, "He Was Praised." Ibid., 29 Feb. 1988, p. A16.

"Absence of Core List of Texts 'Fatal' to Worthwhile Course." *Campus Report* (Stanford), 20 Jan. 1988, pp. 12–13, 17.

"Emotion and Invective Dominate Western Culture Debate." *Stanford Review*, Jan. 1988.

"The Event-making Man." *World & I* 3 (Feb. 1988): 583–92.

"The Attack on Western Civilization: An Interim Report." *Measure*, no. 70 (Feb. 1988): 1–5.

Letter to the editor. *New York Times Book Review*, 6 Mar. 1988, p. 2. Reply to Stephen Schwartz, "Intellectuals and Assassins—Annals of Stalin's Killerati." Ibid., 24 Jan. 1988, pp. 3, 30–32.

"The Uses of Death." Review of Daniel Callahan, *Setting Limits: Medical Goals in an Aging Society. New York Review of Books*, 28 Apr. 1988, pp. 22–25.

"Educational Disaster at Stanford University." *Measure*, no. 72 (Apr. 1988): 1, 3–8.

"Cultural Philistine." Letter to the editor. *New York Review of Books*, 12 May 1988, p. 61. Reply to M. F. Burnyeat's review of I. F. Stone, *The Trial of Socrates*. Ibid., 31 Mar. 1988, pp. 12, 14, 16–18.

> Reply by Burnyeat, ibid., 12 May 1988, p. 61. [See "Making the Case against Socrates," 20 Jan. 1988.]

"The Color of Culture." *Chronicles* 12 (May 1988): 16–19. [See "Absence of Core List of Texts 'Fatal' to Worthwhile Course," 20 Jan. 1988.]

"Intellectual Classes and Institutional Values." *Society* 25 (May–June 1988): 66–69.

REVIEWS OF SIDNEY HOOK'S WORKS

1927

The Metaphysics of Pragmatism. Chicago: Open Court Pub. Co., 1927.
Reviewed in *Dial* 85 (Oct. 1928): 360; *Journal of Philosophy* 25 (21 June 1928): 356–59 (Scott Buchanan).

1933

Towards the Understanding of Karl Marx: A Revolutionary Interpretation. New York: John Day Co., 1933.
Reviewed in *American Economic Review* 23 (Dec. 1933): 687–89 (Joseph J. Senturia); *American Political Science Review* 27 (Aug. 1933): 657–58 (Selig Penman); *Boston Transcript,* 12 Apr. 1933, p. 2; *Commonweal* 18 (18 Aug. 1933): 390–91 (Ross J. S. Hoffman); *Current History* 38 (Aug. 1933): VI; *Journal of Philosophy* 30 (9 Nov. 1933): 634–37 (George H. Sabine); *Modern Monthly* 7 (Oct. 1933): 571–73 (Harry Slochower); *Nation* 136 (12 Apr. 1933): 414; *New Republic* 75 (28 June 1933): 186–87 (Harold J. Laski); *New York Herald Tribune Books,* 16 Apr. 1933, p. 6 (Max Eastman); *North American Review* 236 (Dec. 1933): 570; *Saturday Review of Literature* 9 (22 Apr. 1933): 550 (Felix Morrow); *Student Outlook* 3 (Nov.–Dec. 1934): 31–34 (Morris R. Cohen); *World Tomorrow* 16 (Aug. 1933): 476.

1934

The Meaning of Marx, ed. Sidney Hook. Symposium by Bertrand Russell, John Dewey, Morris R. Cohen, Sherwood Eddy, and Sidney Hook. New York: Farrar and Rinehart, 1934.
Reviewed in *Saturday Review of Literature* 11 (2 Mar. 1935): 522 (Fabian Franklin).

1935

American Philosophy Today and Tomorrow, ed. Sidney Hook and Horace M. Kallen. New York: L. Furman, 1935.
Reviewed in *New Scholasticism 10* (July 1936): 292–94 (Henry A. Lucks).

1936

From Hegel to Marx: Studies in the Intellectual Development of Karl Marx. New York: John Day Co., 1936.
Reviewed in *American Sociological Review* 3 (June 1938): 295–97 (Howard Becker); *Boston Transcript,* 1 Aug. 1936, p. 4; *Christian Century* 54 (3 Mar. 1937): 291; *Economist* 124 (29 Aug. 1936): 395; *International Journal of Ethics* 47 (Apr. 1937): 405–6 (Harold D. Lasswell); *Journal of Philosophy* 34 (21 Jan. 1937): 47–49 (V. J. McGill); *Nation* 143 (15 Aug. 1936): 188–89 (Harold J. Laski); *New Republic* 88 (30 Sept. 1936): 232–33 (Herman Simpson); *New Statesman* 65 (4 Jan. 1963): 16 (George Lichtheim); *New Statesman and Nation,* n.s. 11 (6 June 1936): 897; *New York Herald Tribune Books,* 23 Aug. 1936, p. 2 (Max Lerner); *New York Times Book Review,* 6 Dec. 1936, p. 40 (Fabian Franklin); *Saturday Review of Literature* 14 (15 Aug. 1936): 11 (Max Eastman); *Slavic and East European Journal* 7 (Winter 1963): 437–38 (Donald S. Carlisle); *Spec-*

tator 156 (12 June 1936): 1090; *Tablet* 168 (19 Dec. 1936): 878; *Times* (London) *Literary Supplement,* 11 July 1936, p. 574.

1939

John Dewey: An Intellectual Portrait. New York: John Day Co., 1939.
Reviewed in *Booklist* 36 (1 Dec. 1939): 125; *Journal of Higher Education* 11 (Apr. 1940): 226–29 (Boyd H. Bode); *Journal of Philosophy* 36 (7 Dec. 1939): 695 (Herbert Schneider); *Nation* 150 (6 Jan. 1940): 22–23 (Eliseo Vivas); *New Republic* 10 (6 Dec. 1939): 206–7 (Paul Weiss); *New York Herald Tribune Books,* 5 Nov. 1939, p. 2 (Ernest Sutherland Bates); *Philosophical Review* 50 (Jan. 1941): 86–87 (Everett Wesley Hall); *Saturday Review of Literature* 21 (11 Nov. 1939): 12–13 (Robert Bierstedt); *Thought* 15 (June 1940): 365–67 (Ruth Byrns).

1940

Reason, Social Myths and Democracy. New York: John Day Co., 1940.
Reviewed in *Annals of the American Academy of Political and Social Science* 213 (Jan. 1941): 199–200 (Hans Kohn); *Ethics* 52 (Apr. 1942): 386–87 (Glenn Negley); *Journal of Philosophy* 38 (24 Apr. 1941): 243–49 (V. J. McGill); *Library Journal* 65 (15 Oct. 1940): 873 (Felix E. Hirsch); *Living Age* 359 (Feb. 1941): 593–95 (Albert Lippman); *Nation* 151 (19 Oct. 1940): 370 (Reinhold Niebuhr); *New Republic* 103 (2 Dec. 1940): 762–64 (Irwin Edman); *New Yorker* 16 (7 Dec. 1940): 105; *New York Herald Tribune Books,* 22 Dec. 1940, p. 6 (A. N. Holcombe); *Saturday Review of Literature* 23 (11 Jan. 1941): 15 (Jacques Barzun).

1943

The Hero in History: A Study in Limitation and Possibility. New York: John Day Co., 1943.

Reviewed in *Annals of the American Academy of Political and Social Science* 229 (Sept. 1943): 197–98 (Glenn R. Morrow); *Atlantic Monthly* 172 (July 1943): 129; *Booklist* 39 (1 June 1943): 385; *Catholic Historical Review* 30 (Apr. 1944): 59 (Geoffrey Bruun); *Ethics* 54 (Jan. 1944): 152–53 (Albert W. Levi); *Foreign Affairs* 22 (Oct. 1943): 155 (Robert Gale Woolbert); *Historical Bulletin* 34 (May 1956): 246; *Journal of Philosophy* 40 (14 Oct. 1943): 575–80 (John Herman Randall, Jr.); *Nation* 157 (18 Sept. 1943): 326–28 (Jacques Barzun); *New Republic* 108 (21 June 1943): 834–35 (C. Wright Mills); *New Yorker* 19 (1 May 1943): 67; *New York Times Book Review,* 27 June 1943, p. 23 (Joseph Freeman); *Saturday Review of Literature* 26 (1 May 1943): 6 (Robert Pick); *School and Society* 57 (24 Apr. 1943): 484; *Social Studies* 34 (Dec. 1943): 376 (Walter H. Mohr); *Tablet* 185 (26 May 1945): 250; *Time* 41 (17 May 1943): 90, 92; *Weekly Book Review,* 6 June 1943, p. 16 (Adrienne Koch).

1945

The Authoritarian Attempt to Capture Education. By John Dewey, Sidney Hook, Arthur Murphy, Irwin Edman, and others. New York: King's Crown Press, 1945.

Reviewed in *Journal of Philosophy* 42 (27 Sept. 1945): 548–50 (H. A. L.); *Saturday Review of Literature* 28 (23 June 1945): 37 (Ordway Tead).

1946

Education for Modern Man. New York: Dial Press, 1946.

Reviewed in *Best Sellers* 6 (15 May 1946): 27–28; *Booklist* 42 (15 May 1946): 293; *Catholic Educational Review* 44 (Sept. 1946): 442–45 (George F. Burnell); *Chicago Sun Book Week,* 21 Apr. 1946, p. 5 (Wendell Johnson); *Commentary* 2 (Oct. 1946): 397–98 (Sidney Morgenbesser); *Current History,* n.s. 11 (July 1946): 49; *Ethics* 58 (Jan. 1948): 133–37 (Donald Meiklejohn); *Journal of Philosophy* 43 (7 Nov. 1946): 629–36 (Mason W. Gross); *Kirkus* 14 (1 Apr. 1946): 171; *Library Journal* 71 (15 Apr. 1946): 584 (Thelma Brackett); *Nation* 162 (20 Apr. 1946): 476, 478 (Irwin Edman); *New Republic* 114 (10 June 1946): 840–41 (Jerome Nathanson); *New Yorker* 22 (18 May 1946): 110; *New York Times Book Review,* 26 May 1946, p. 6 (Howard Mumford Jones); *Partisan Review* 13 (Nov.–Dec. 1946): 595–96 (Delmore Schwartz); *Review of Politics* 9 (Oct. 1947): 502–4 (Leo R. Ward); *Saturday Review of Literature* 29 (20 Apr. 1946): 22 (Eric Bentley); *School and Society* 65 (22 Mar. 1947): 209–10 (William Sener Rusk); *Time,* 6 May 1946, p. 88; U.S. *Quarterly Book List* 2 (Sept. 1946): 210; *Weekly Book Review,* 11 Aug. 1946, p. 10 (Albert Guerard).

1947

Freedom and Experience: Essays Presented to Horace M. Kallen, ed. Sidney Hook and Milton R. Konvitz. Ithaca: Cornell University Press, 1947.

Reviewed in *Annals of the American Academy of Political and Social Science* 257 (May 1948): 207–8 (W. H. Sheldon); *Journal of Higher Education* 19 (Nov. 1948): 436 (Ordway Tead); *Modern Schoolman* 26 (Mar. 1949): 257–61 (James Collins).

1950

John Dewey: Philosopher of Science and Freedom, ed. Sidney Hook. New York: Dial Press, 1950.

Reviewed in *Booklist* 46 (15 June 1950): 310; *Ethics* 61 (Oct. 1950): 89 (Alan Gewirth); *Humanist* 10 (Oct. 1950): 223 (Rubin Gotesky); *Journal of Philosophy* 48 (15 Mar. 1951): 192–95 (Harold A. Larrabee); *Journal of Symbolic Logic* 16 (Sept. 1951): 209 (Carl G. Hempel); *Modern Schoolman* 47 (Nov. 1969): 132–33 (Kenneth L. Becker); *New Leader* 33 (29 July 1950): 22 (Ordway Tead); *New York Times Book Review,* 23 Apr. 1950, p. 6 (Thomas Vernor Smith); *San Francisco Chronicle,* 6 Aug. 1950, p. 18; *Saturday Review of Literature* 33 (19 Aug. 1950): 35 (Robert Bierstedt); *Thought* 26 (Summer 1951): 288–91 (James Collins).

1952

Heresy, Yes—Conspiracy, No. New York: American Committee for Cultural Freedom, 1952; New York: John Day Co., 1953.

Reviewed in *America* 89 (6 June 1953): 282 (M. D. Reagan); *American Mercury* 77 (Aug. 1953): 143 (Frank Meyer); *Booklist* 49 (15 June 1953): 334; *Books* 11 (June 1953): 343 (F. Steggert); *Chicago Sunday Tribune Magazine of Books,* 31 May 1953, p. 2 (Alfred C. Ames); *Christian Science Monitor,* 11 Sept. 1953, p. 9 (Saville R. Davis); *Commentary* 16 (July 1953): 86–88 (Robert E. Fitch); *Commonweal* 58 (15 May 1953): 155–56 (John Cogley); *Foreign Affairs* 31 (July 1953): 677–78 (Henry L. Roberts); *Freeman* 3 (18 May 1953): 600–601 (Max Eastman); *Journal of Higher Education* 25 (Mar. 1954): 166–67 (A. Cornelius Benjamin); *Library Journal* 78 (1 June 1953): 992 (James Heslin); *Nation* 176 (6 June 1953): 484–85 (John W. Ward); *New Leader* 36 (8 June 1953): 21–22 (Ordway Tead); *New Republic* 128 (15 June 1953): 20 (Henry Bamford Parkes); *New York Herald Tribune Book Review,* 10 May 1953, p. 7 (August Heckscher);

New York Times Book Review, 10 May 1953, p. 3 (Everett N. Case); *Saturday Review* 36 (13 June 1953): 13–14 (Arthur M. Schlesinger, Jr.); ibid. 36 (20 June 1953): 13, 38 (John K. Sherman); *School and Society* 77 (2 May 1953): 286; *Thought* 28 (Winter 1953–54): 528–46 (Charles Donahue); *United Nations World* 7 (June 1953): 61–62 (George W. Shuster); *U.S. Quarterly Book Review* 9 (Sept. 1953): 328–29.

1955

Marx and the Marxists: The Ambiguous Legacy. Princeton, N.J.: Van Nostrand, 1955.
Reviewed in *American Sociological Review* 21 (June 1956): 397–98 (Paul W. Massing); *Library Journal* 80 (15 Sept. 1955): 1904 (H. H. Bernt); *Review of Politics* 18 (Apr. 1956): 254–56 (Gerhart Niemeyer).

1956

American Philosophers at Work, ed. Sidney Hook. New York: Criterion Books, 1956.
Reviewed in *Booklist* 53 (15 Jan. 1957): 236–37; *Commentary* 24 (Nov. 1957): 454–60 (Kathleen Nott); *New Leader* 40 (1 Apr. 1957): 23–24 (R. G. Ross); *New Republic* 136 (17 June 1957): 16–18 (Robert E. Fitch); *New York Herald Tribune Book Review,* 27 Jan. 1957, p. 12; *New York Times Book Review,* 23 Dec. 1956, pp. 3, 14 (Reinhold Niebuhr); *Thought* 32 (Winter 1957–58): 620–21 (W. Norris Clarke).

1957

Common Sense and the Fifth Amendment. New York: Criterion Books, 1957. Reviewed in *Bookmark* 16 (June 1957): 210; *Chicago Sunday Tribune Magazine of Books,* 19 May 1957, p. 3 (Willard Edwards); *Cleveland Open Shelf,* Nov. 1957, p. 20; *Critic* 16 (Aug.–Sept. 1957): 16 (Albert H. Miller); *Kirkus* 25 (1 Mar. 1957): 203; *Library Journal* 82 (15 Apr. 1957): 1053 (Louis Barron); *New Leader* 40 (10 June 1957): 22–23 (Carl A. Auerbach); *New Yorker* 33 (11 May 1957): 163–64; *New York Herald Tribune Book Review,* 9 June 1957, p. 6 (William H. Edwards); *New York Times Book Review,* 26 May 1957, pp. 3, 12 (John B. Oakes); *Saturday Review* 40 (10 Aug. 1957): 32–33 (Harry Kalven, Jr.); *Time* 69 (27 May 1957): 111–12; *Yale Review,* n.s. 47 (Autumn 1957): 117–25 (Charles L. Black, Jr.).

1958

Determinism and Freedom in the Age of Modern Science, ed. Sidney Hook. First Symposium, New York University Institute of Philosophy, 9–10 Feb. 1957. New York: New York University Press, 1958. Reviewed in *Heythrop Journal* 5 (Jan. 1964): 116–17; *International Philosophical Quarterly* 1 (Sept. 1961): 516–32 (Joseph F. Donceel); *Journal of Philosophy* 56 (9 Apr. 1959): 369–73 (Arthur C. Danto); *Library Journal* 83 (1 Apr. 1958): 1081 (Robert W. Henderson); *Modern Schoolman* 37 (Mar. 1960): 246–47 (Joseph F. Collins); *New York Times Book Review,* 16 Nov. 1958, p. 47 (Charles Frankel); *Philosophical Quarterly* 10 (July 1960): 282 (H. J. N. Horsburgh); *Ratio* 5 (Dec. 1963): 213–23 (D. F. Pears); *Review of Politics* 23 (Jan. 1961): 9697 (Karl Kreilkamp); *Revue philosophique de louvain* 60 (Nov. 1962): 622–37 (Gérard Deledalle).

1959

John Dewey: His Philosophy of Education and Its Critics. New York: Tamiment Institute, 1959. University Institute of Philosophy, 21–22 Oct. 1960. New York: New York University Press, 1961.

Reviewed in *Church Quarterly Review* 164 (Jan.–Mar. 1963): 106–7 (W. R. Matthews); *Commonweal* 75 (2 Mar. 1962): 599–601 (Daniel Callahan); *Journal for the Scientific Study of Religion* 2 (Oct. 1962): 130–31 (Kirtley F. Mather); *Jubilee* 9 (Mar. 1962): 52; *Library Journal* 87 (15 Feb. 1962): 775 (LaVern Kohl); *Life of the Spirit* 17 (Jan. 1963): 293; *New York Times Book Review,* 28 Jan. 1962, p. 42 (Reinhold Niebuhr); ibid., 28 Jan. 1963, p. 14 (H. Smith); *Philosophical Quarterly* 14 (Apr, 1964): 186–87 (Basil Mitchell); *Saturday Review* 45 (3 Feb. 1962): 23, 35 (Huston Smith); *Tablet* 216 (31 Mar. 1962): 307; *Theology Today* 20 (Jan. 1964): 583–85 (P. L. Holmer).

1962

Paradoxes of Freedom. Berkeley: University of California Press, 1962.

Reviewed in *Annals of the American Academy of Political and Social Science* 350 (Nov. 1963): 211–12 (John D. Lewis); *Commentary* 35 (Mar. 1963): 260–62 (Lewis A. Coser); *Forum Service*, no. 585 (16 Mar. 1963): 1–4 (Daniel Bell); *Humanist* 24 (Jan.–Feb. 1964): 19–20 (Van Meter Ames and William Van Alstyne); *Jewish Social Studies* 27 (Oct. 1965): 262 (J. L. Blau); *Journal of Church and State* 6 (Winter 1964): 90–94 (Willam G. Toland); *Journal of Philosophy* 62 (29 Apr. 1965): 241–46 (Arnold S. Kaufman); *Library Journal* 87 (15 Sept. 1962): 3053 (Thomas M. Bogie); *New Statesman* 65 (4 Jan. 1963): 16 (George Lichtheim); *New York Times Book Review,* 7 Oct. 1962, pp. 6, 34 (John Cogley); *Progressive* 27 (Mar. 1963): 43–44 (David Fellman); *Saturday Review* 46 (13 Apr. 1963): 80 (Charles A. Madison).

1963

The Fail-Safe Fallacy. New York: Stein and Day, 1963.
    Reviewed in *Book Week* 1 (27 Oct. 1963): 4 (Gerald Wendt); *Library Journal* 88 (15 Oct. 1963): 3856 (Bernard Poll); *National Review* 15 (19 Nov. 1963): 444–45 (Jameson G. Campaigne, Jr.); *New York Times,* 14 Oct. 1963, p. 27 (Harrison E. Salisbury); *New York Times Book Review,* 6 Oct. 1963, p. 3 (Mark S. Watson); *Virginia Quarterly Review* 40 (Winter 1964): xlii.

Philosophy and History, ed. Sidney Hook. Fifth Symposium, New York University Institute of Philosophy, 11–12 May 1962. New York: New York University Press, 1963.
    Reviewed in *American Historical Review* 69 (Oct. 1963): 83–84 (William Gerber); *Bibliographie de la Philosophie* 11 (1964): 199–200 (Paul Kurtz); *Christian Century* 80 (20 Nov. 1963): 1436 (William A. Sadler, Jr.); *Ethics* 74 (July 1964): 302–4 (Frank H. Knight); *History and Theory* 4 (1965): 328–49 (Marvin Levich); *International Philosophical Quarterly* 4 (Feb. 1964): 320–22 (Eugene Fontinell); *Journal of the History of Ideas* 25 (Oct.–Dec. 1964): 587–98 (Frank H. Knight); *Mind* 74 (July 1965): 434–38 (W. H. Walsh); *Mississippi Valley Historical Review* 50 (June 1963): 155; *Personalist* 44 (Autumn 1963): 549–50 (William H. Werkmeister); *Wisconsin Magazine of History* 48 (Summer 1965): 327–28 (William Fletcher Thompson, Jr.).

1964

Law and Philosophy, ed. Sidney Hook. Sixth Symposium, New York University Institute of Philosophy, 10–11 May 1963. New York: New York University Press, 1964.
    Reviewed in *Catholic Lawyer* 11 (Summer 1965): 263–64 (Patrick J. Rohan); *Choice* 2 (May 1965): 192; *Christian Century* 81 (4 Nov. 1964): 1372; *International Philosophical Quarterly* 5 (May 1965):

377

311–16 (Thomas F. McGann); *Nation* 200 (12 Apr. 1965): 398–401 (Hugo Adam Bedau); *New York Times Book Review,* 22 Nov. 1964, p. 10 (Fred Rodell; letters with Rodell's reply, ibid., 20 Dec. 1964, p. 12).

1966

Art and Philosophy, ed. Sidney Hook. Seventh Symposium, New York University Institute of Philosophy, 23–24 Oct. 1964. New York: New York University Press, 1966.

Reviewed in *British Journal of Aesthetics* 6 (July 1966): 303; *Dalhousie Review* 46 (Autumn 1966): 390–91 (Geoffrey Payzant); *Foundations of Language* 5 (Nov. 1969): 567–68 (J. J. A. Mooij); *Journal of Aesthetics and Art Criticism* 35 (Summer 1967): 478 (David Thoreau Wieck); *Journal of the History of Philosophy* 6 (Oct. 1968): 416–17 (John M. Walker); Music *and Letters* 47 (July 1966): 269 (F. H.); *New Statesman* 72 (1966): 367–68 (Richard Wollheim); *Philosophy and Phenomenological Research* 28 (Sept. 1967): 137–38 (Jerome Stolnitz); *Review of Metaphysics* 20 (Sept. 1966): 163 (R. J. Woods); *Saturday Review* 49 (11 June 1966): 60, 62 (George W. Linden); *Southern Review* 4 (Summer 1968): 766 (R. Hollander).

1967

Religion in a Free Society. Lincoln: University of Nebraska Press, 1967; Don Mills, Ontario: Burns and MacEachern, 1967.

Reviewed in *Ave Maria* 105 (13 May 1967): 11 (D. McDonald); *Booklist* 63 (15 July 1967): 1168–69; *Choice* 5 (Mar. 1968): 70; *Christian Century* 84 (30 Aug. 1967): 1104 (John M. Swomley, Jr.); *Journal of Church and State* 12 (Autumn 1970): 497–500 (William G. Toland); *Journal of Value Inquiry* 2 (Winter 1968): 308–14 (Marvin Fox); *Religion and the Public Order*, no. 5 (1969): 183–84

(Thomas J. O'Toole); *Review of Religious Research* 11 (Fall 1969): 92–93 (Eugene A. Mainelli); *Saturday Review* 50 (21 Oct. 1967): 82 (John Calam); *Stanford Law Review* 20 (Nov. 1967): 146–47 (Walter F. Berns).

Human Values and Economic Policy, ed. Sidney Hook. Eighth Symposium, New York University Institute of Philosophy, 13–14 May 1966. New York: New York University Press, 1967.

Reviewed in *American Economic Review* 58 (Dec. 1968): 1384–85 (Kurt Klappholz); *Choice* 6 (June 1969): 550; *Critique* 35 (Apr. 1969): 359–76 (B. Cazes); *Economic Journal* (London) 80 (Mar. 1970): 122–23 (C. W. Guillebaud); *Library Journal* 92 (1 Oct. 1967): 3413 (Richard A. Gray).

1969

Language and Philosophy: A Symposium, ed. Sidney Hook. Ninth Symposium, New York University Institute of Philosophy, 1968. New York: New York University Press, 1969.

Reviewed in *Canadian Journal of Linguistics* 14 (Spring 1969): 142–43 (Zeno Vendler); *Dialogue* 8 (Dec. 1969): 523–26 (Douglas Odegard); *Forum for Modern Language Studies* 7 (Oct. 1971): 413; *Journal of Linguistics* 6 (Feb. 1970): 134–36 (L. Jonathan Cohen); *Journal of Value Inquiry* 4 (Fall 1970): 235–37 (G. Benjamin Oliver); *Linguistics* 111 (1 Sept. 1973): 99–115 (Venera Mihailescu-Urechia); *Philosophischer Literaturanzeiger* 25 (1972): 115–17 (Gharati Agehananda); *Queen's Quarterly* 77 (Winter 1970): 653–54 (P. W. Rogers); *Times* (London) *Literary Supplement* 616 (18 June 1971): 717.

1970

Academic Freedom and Academic Anarchy. New York: Cowles Book Co., 1970.

Reviewed in *Choice* 7 (Sept. 1970): 906; *Christian Century* 87 (7 Jan. 1970): 22; *Christian Science Monitor*, 22 Oct. 1970, p. 9 (C. Michael Curtis); *Humanist* 30 (May–June 1970): 42–43 (Edward Chalfant and Gordon W. Keller); *Library Journal* 95 (1 Jan. 1970): 57 (Henry J. Steck); *Minnesota Law Review* 55 (1971): 1275–85 (Nelson W. Polsby); *Modern Age* 15 (Winter 1971): 96–99 (C. P. Ives); *National Review* 22 (27 Jan. 1970): 91–92 (Russell Kirk); *New York Review of Books* 14 (12 Feb. 1970): 5–11 (Henry David Aiken); *New York Times Book Review*, 8 Mar. 1970, pp. 25–29 (Edgar Z. Friedenberg); *Philosophical Forum* (De Kalb) 11 (Summer 1972): S77–S87 (Paul Kurtz and Gail Kennedy); *Review for Religious* 29 (May 1970): 483 (V. Bourke); *Saturday Review* 53 (24 Jan. 1970): 67–68 (Lewis B. Mayhew).

1971

In Defense of Academic Freedom, ed. Sidney Hook. New York: Pegasus, 1971.
Reviewed in *Choice* 8 (Sept. 1971): 880; *Library Journal* 96 (1 Nov. 1971): 3604 (James Ranz).

1973

Education and the Taming of Power. La Salle, Ill.: Open Court Pub. Co., 1973.
Reviewed in *AAUP Bulletin* 61 (Oct. 1975): 248–51 (Ronald M. Johnson); *Change* 6 (Apr. 1974): 58–60 (John K. Jessup); *Educational Studies* 5 (Winter 1974–75): 246–47 (Richard Gambino); *Library Journal* 98 (15 Nov. 1973): 3373 (Adeline Konsh); *Modern Age* 19 (Fall 1975): 423–25 (Hugh Mercer Curtler); *National Review* 26 (30 Aug. 1974): 992 (Aram Bakshian, Jr.); *New Republic* 170 (9 Feb. 1974): 30 (Joseph Featherstone); *News From Open Court,* 25

Nov. 1973, pp. 29–30; *Review of Education* 1 (May 1975): 298–302 (Terry Nichols Clark and Priscilla P. Clark); *Saturday Review/World* 1 (27 July 1974): 52 (John Calam).

1974

The Idea of a Modern University, ed. Sidney Hook, Paul Kurtz, and Miro Todorovich. Buffalo, N.Y.: Prometheus Books, 1974.

Reviewed in *Bibliographie de la Philosophie* 22 (1975): 243–44 (Loy Littlefield); *Change* 6 (Sept. 1974): 56–57 (Sol Cohen); *Choice* 11 (Nov. 1974): 1362; *Commonweal* 101 (4 Oct. 1974): 18–22 (Dennis O'Brien); *Educational Studies* 6 (Fall–Winter 1975): 217–18 (Milton K. Reimer); *Humanist* 35 (Mar.–Apr. 1975): 33–35 (David Sidorsky); *International Philosophical Quarterly* 16 (June 1976): 248–51 (John Donnelly); *Library Journal* 99 (Aug. 1974): 1944 (Adeline Konsh); *Review of Education* 1 (May 1975): 298–302 (Terry Nichols Clark and Priscilla P. Clark).

Pragmatism and the Tragic Sense of Life. New York: Basic Books, 1974.

Reviewed in *Commentary* 59 (June 1975): 86, 88 (Michael Novak); *Encounter* 45 (Oct. 1975): 37–45 (Lewis S. Feuer); *Humanist* 35 (July–Aug. 1975): 39 (Steven M. Cahn); *Journal of the History of Ideas* 36 (Oct.–Dec. 1975): 739–46 (Philip P. Wiener); *Journal of Philosophy* 74 (Mar. 1977): 172–76 (Frederick A. Olafson); *Library Journal* 100 (15 Feb. 1975): 396 (Robert Hoffman); *Midstream* 21 (Dec. 1975): 70 (Reuben Abel); *National Review* 28 (23 Jan. 1976): 44–46 (Frederick L. Will); *New Republic* 175 (18 Sept. 1976): 35–37 (William K. Frankena); *Philosophy and Phenomenological Research* 36 (Dec. 1975): 275 (Henry W. Johnstone, Jr.); *Review for Religious* 34 (May 1975): 491 (P. Reardon); *St. Croix Review* 8 (June 1975): 48.

1975

Revolution, Reform, and Social Justice—Studies in the Theory and Practice of Marxism. New York: New York University Press, 1975.

Reviewed in *Choice* 13 (Mar. 1976): 104; *Economist* 262 (8 Jan. 1977): 101–2; *Humanist* 36 (May–June 1976): 36–37 (Marvin Kohl); *Journal of Economic Issues* 11 (Dec. 1977): 904–6 (Howard Sherman); *New Republic* 174 (14 Feb. 1976): 24–25 (Irving Howe); *Political Studies* 25 (Dec. 1977): 629 (David Miller); *Review of Metaphysics* 29 (June 1976): 737–38 (Michael P. Malloy); *Sociology* 12 (Jan. 1978): 180–81 (Peter Lassman); *Studi internazionali di filosofia* 9 (1977): 193–95 (Donald Weiss); *Times* (London) *Literary Supplement,* 8 Apr. 1977, p. 427 (Ghita Ionescu).

The Philosophy of the Curriculum: The Need for General Education, ed. Sidney Hook, Paul Kurtz, and Miro Todorovich. Buffalo, N.Y.: Prometheus Books, 1975.

Reviewed in *Change* 7 (Sept. 1975): 58–59 (Maurice Hungiville); *Choice* 12 (Nov. 1975): 1215; *Chronicle of Higher Education* 14 (11 Oct. 1976): 17 (Leon Botstein); *College and University* 52 (Winter 1977): 240 (Robert A. Scott); *Encounter* 45 (Oct. 1975): 37; *Higher Education* (Netherlands) 5 (1976): 349–50 (Samuel E. Kellams); *Humanist* 35 (Nov.–Dec. 1975): 38–39 (Robert Simon).

1977

The Ethics of Teaching and Scientific Research, ed. Sidney Hook, Paul Kurtz, and Miro Todorovich. Buffalo, N.Y.: Prometheus Books, 1977.

Reviewed in *Contemporary Psychology* 23 (May 1978): 371 (Dennis Regan); *National Association of Secondary School Principals Bulletin* 62 (Mar. 1978): 114 (Weldon Beckner); *New Scientist* 75 (7 July 1977): 30 (Tim Robinson); *Religious Studies Review* 7 (Jan. 1981): 53; *Review of Metaphysics* 31 (Dec. 1977): 320 (Milton Goldinger); *Science Books and Films* 13 (Mar. 1978): 197 (Rachelle D. Hollander).

1978

The University and the State, ed. Sidney Hook, Paul Kurtz, and Miro Todorovich. Buffalo, N.Y.: Prometheus Books, 1978.

Reviewed in *Booklist* 75 (1 Sept. 1978): 6; *Change* 10 (Oct. 1978): 60 (Joseph Barbato); *Choice* 15 (Dec. 1978): 1419; *Educational Studies* 11 (Spring 1980): 77–80 (M. M. Chambers); *Journal of Church and State* 22 (Autumn 1980): 540–41 (Timothy J. Hansen); *Journal of Higher Education* 51 (Sept.–Oct. 1980): 569–72 (Jerry A. May); *Library Journal* 103 (Aug. 1978): 1505–6 (Carol Eckberg Wadsworth); *New England Law Review* 14 (Summer 1978): 144–45; *Publishers Weekly* 214 (3 July 1978): 56.

1980

Philosophy and Public Policy. Carbondale and Edwardsville: Southern Illinois University Press, 1980.

Reviewed in *America* 142 (31 May 1980): 464–65 (Robert F. Drinan); *American Spectator* 13 (Aug. 1980): 40–41 (Arnold Beichman); *Canadian Public Administration* 25 (Fall 1982): 421–22 (Willard A. Mullins); *Choice* 18 (Sept. 1980): 161–62; *Christian Century* 97 (23 Apr. 1980): 476; *Commentary* 70 (Oct. 1980): 74, 76–77 (Werner J. Dannhauser); *Educational Studies* 11 (Fall 1980): 315 (Walter P. Krolikowski); *Encounter* 55 (Nov. 1980): 71–73 (Constantine FitzGibbon); *Ethics* 93 (July 1983): 834 (Peter G. Brown); *Horizons* 8 (Spring 1981): 191–92 (Joseph W. Devlin); *Library Journal* 105 (15 May 1980): 1169 (Peter Vari); *Modern Age* 25 (Summer 1981): 308–10 (J. Brooks Colburn); *Modem Schoolman* 60 (Jan. 1983): 130–31 (Vernon I. Bourke); *Nation* 231 (20 Dec. 1980): 680–81 (Philip Green); *National Review* 32 (31 Oct. 1980): 1335–36 (Jeanne Wacker Sobran); *New Oxford Review* 48 (Jan.–Feb. 1981): 26–28 (Erazim Kohák); *New York Times Book Review,* 30 Nov. 1980, p. 9 (Nathan Glazer); ibid., 8 Feb. 1981, pp. 7, 24–25 (Hilton Kramer); *Perspectives in Religious*

Studies 8 (Summer 1981): 175–79 (R. M. Helm); *Philosophical Books* 22 (Oct. 1981): 232–34 (Antony Flew); *St. Louis Post-Dispatch*, 30 Mar. 1980, 4C (Joseph Losos); *Time* 115 (28 Apr. 1980): 92 (Stefan Kanfer); *Wall Street Journal*, 3 Sept. 1980, p. 26 (Carl Gershman).

1983

Marxism and Beyond. Totowa, N.J.: Rowman and Littlefield, 1983.

Reviewed in *American Scholar* 52 (Autumn 1983): 558–63 (Lewis S. Feuer); *Best Sellers* 43 (1 Apr. 1983): 30 (James O'Malley); *History Teacher* 20 (Nov. 1986): 126–27 (John W. Long); *Library Journal* 108 (1 Mar. 1983): 502 (Robert C. O'Brien); *Midstream* 29 (Nov. 1983): 51–54 (Lewis S. Feuer); *National Review* 35 (11 Nov. 1983): 1422–23 (Joseph Sobran); *New Leader* 66 (16 May 1983): 7–9 (Irving Louis Horowitz); *New York Times Book Review*, 10 Apr. 1983, p. 16 (Judith K. Davison); *Publishers Weekly* 223 (21 Jan. 1983): 76; *Studies in Soviet Thought* 28 (Oct. 1984): 245–49 (Maurice A. Finocchiaro); *This World* 5 (Spring–Summer 1983): 149–53 (Mark Lila); *Village Voice Literary Supplement*, no. 24, Mar. 1984, pp. 1, 10–14 (Paul Berman).

1987

Out of Step: An Unquiet Life in the 20th Century. New York: Harper and Row, 1987.

Reviewed in *American Scholar* 56 (Autumn 1987): 577–86 (Edward Shils); *American Spectator* 20 (June 1987): 36–38 (William McGurn); *Booklist* 83 (1 Jan. 1987): 668 (Bryce J. Christensen); *Book World* (*Washington Post*) 17 (3 May 1987): 5–6 (Nathan Glick); *Boston Sunday Globe*, 29 Mar. 1987, A11, A13 (Robert Gorhain Davis); *Choice* 24 (July–Aug. 1987): 1706 (R. H. Evans); *Christian Science Monitor* 79 (23 Apr. 1987): 21 (Merle Rubin); *Chronicles* 12

(Jan. 1988): 34–35 (Paul Gottfried); *Commentary* 84 (Aug. 1987): 17–23 (Hilton Kramer); *Congress Monthly* 54 (Sept.–Oct. 1987): 16–18 (Irving Louis Horowitz); *Foreign Affairs* 66 (Fall 1987): 195 (Gaddis Smith); *Fortune* 115 (13 Apr. 1987): 122 (Daniel Seligman); *Forward*, 21 Aug. 1987, pp. 26–27 (Albert Glotzer); *Freeman* 37 (June 1987): 236–38 (John Chamberlain); *Grand Street* 7 (Autumn 1987): 185–94 (John Patrick Diggins); *Humanist* 47 (Sept.–Oct. 1987): 45–46 (John P. Runden); *Insight* (*Washington Times*) 3 (27 Apr. 1987): 62–63 (Paul Johnson); *International Herald Tribune*, 10 Apr. 1987, p. 16 (John Gross); *Kirkus* 55 (1 Feb. 1987): 197–98; *Library Journal* 112 (15 Feb. 1987): 142 (Raymond Frey); *Nation* 244 (30 May 1987): 726–30 (Robert Westbrook); *National Review* 39 (14 Aug. 1987): 43–44 (M. E. Bradford); ibid. 39 (11 Sept. 1987): 61–62 (Jeffrey Hart); *New Leader* 70 (23 Mar. 1987): 14–15 (John P. Roche); *New Republic* 196 (4 May 1987): 30–31 (Arthur M. Schlesinger, Jr.); *New York Times*, 31 Mar. 1987, p. C17 (John Gross); *New York Times Book Review*, 12 Apr. 1987, pp. 14–15 (Dennis H. Wrong); *Policy Review*, no. 42 (Fall 1987): 82–84 (Richard Grenier); *Publishers Weekly* 231 (13 Feb. 1987): 85–86; *Reason* 19 (Dec. 1987): 49–51 (Robert Nisbet); *Reference and Research Book News* 2 (Summer 1987): 1; *St. Louis Post-Dispatch*, 24 May 1987, p. 8C (Joseph Losos); *San Francisco Chronicle Review*, 11 Oct. 1987, p. 6 (Marion Fay); *Society* 25 (Nov.–Dec. 1987): 94–97 (Paul Hollander); *Time* 120 (30 Mar. 1987): 72 (Stefan Kanfer); *Wall Street Journal*, 15 Apr. 1987, p. 32 (Nathan Glazer); *Washington Times*, 6 Apr. 1987 (Paul Johnson).

Contributors

GARY BULLERT obtained a BA in philosophy at Stanford University and an MA and PhD in government at Claremont Graduate School. He is a professor at Washington State University (Tri-cities) and the author of *The Politics of John Dewey* and *The Hunthausen File.* His articles have appeared in several journals, including *The South Atlantic Quarterly, Journal of Politics, Modern Age, Educational Theory, Journal of Social, Political and Economic Studies, The World & I, Journal of East and West Studies,* and *Journal of Church and State.* Recent publications are "Reinhold Niebuhr and *The Christian Century*: World War II and the Eclipse of the Social Gospel" (*Journal of Church and State*) and "John Dewey and the Neo-conservatives" (*Political Science Reviewer*).

STEVEN M. CAHN is professor of philosophy and former provost and vice president for academic affairs at the Graduate Center of the City University of New York. He has edited or authored numerous books, including *Classics in Western Philosophy* (ed.), *Saints and Scamps: Ethics in Academia*, and *Morality, Responsibility, and the University*.

MATTHEW COTTER is currently in the PhD program at the Graduate Center of the City University of New York. He obtained his BA from William Paterson University, where he majored in philosophy and history. His dissertation explores Sidney Hook's long career as a teacher at New York University.

MICHAEL ELDRIDGE teaches philosophy at the University of North Carolina at Charlotte. He is the author of *Transforming Experience: John Dewey's Cultural Instrumentalism* (Vanderbilt University Press, 1998) and contributed the introduction for the second volume (1919–39) of the CD-ROM *Correspondence of John Dewey* (InteLex, 2001). He was the 1999 Center for Dewey Studies' Democracy and Education Fellow, and he is currently editing a reprint series on pragmatism and religion for Thoemmes Press.

BARBARA FORREST is professor of philosophy in the Department of History and Political Science at Southeastern Louisiana University. Her doctoral dissertation examined the influence of Sidney Hook's philosophical naturalism on his philosophy of education. She is the author of "Methodological Naturalism and Philosophical Naturalism: Clarifying the Connection," *Philo*, Fall–Winter 2000; "The Possibility of Meaning in Human Evolution," *Zygon: Journal of Religion and Science*, December 2000; "The Wedge at Work: How Intelligent Design Creationism Is Wedging Its Way into Cultural and Academic Mainstream," in *Intelligent Design Creationism and Its Critics: Philosophical, Theological, and Scientific Perspectives*, ed. Robert T. Pennock (MIT Press, 2001); and *Creationism's Trojan Horse: The Wedge of Intelligent Design*, with Paul R. Gross (Oxford University Press, October 2003).

NATHAN GLAZER was born in New York City in 1923. He became an editor of the new magazine *Commentary* on its founding in 1945, where he had occasion to work with Sidney Hook as a contributor. He was a member of the American Congress for Cultural Freedom. He left *Commentary* to work as an editor of the new Anchor Books in 1953. In the late 1950s, he joined a project designed to document the role of Communism in US life and wrote the book *The Social Basis of American Communism*. He became a professor of sociology at the University of California, Berkeley, in 1963, became a critic of the student movement of the 1960s as it became more radical, and wrote *Remembering the Answers*. He moved to Harvard in 1969. In 1973, he joined Irving Kristol as coeditor of the journal of public policy *The Public Interest*, replacing Daniel Bell, and remained as editor until 2003. His major scholarly work as a sociologist has dealt with US ethnicity, race relations, and social policy, and his books include *Beyond the Melting Pot* (with Daniel P. Moynihan), *Affirmative Discrimination: The Limits of Social Policy*, and most recently *We Are All Multiculturalists Now.*

NEIL JUMONVILLE is the William Warren Rogers Professor of History at Florida State University, where he teaches US intellectual and cultural history. He is the author of *Critical Crossings: The New York Intellectuals in Postwar America* (1991), *Henry Steele Commager: Midcentury Liberalism and the History of the Present* (1999), and "The Cultural Politics of the Sociobiology Debate" in the Fall 2002 issue of the *Journal of the History of Biology.*

389

MARVIN KOHL is adjunct professor of the New School University and emeritus professor of philosophy at the State University of New York at Fredonia. He is the author of *The Morality Killing* and editor of *Beneficent Euthanasia and Infanticide* and *The Value of Life*. His recent *Encyclopedia of Ethics* articles include "Beneficence" and "Life and Death."

PAUL KURTZ is professor emeritus of philosophy at the State University of New York at Buffalo. He is chairman of the Committee for the Scientific Investigation of Claims of the Paranormal and the Council for Secular Humanism, as well as president of the International Academy of Humanism. He earned his BA at New York University and his MA and PhD at Columbia University. He has authored forty or more books, including *The Courage to Become*, *Embracing the Power of Humanism*, and *Skepticism and Humanism: The New Paradigm*.

TIBOR R. MACHAN is professor emeritus in the Philosophy Department at Auburn University, Alabama, and Freedom Communications Professor of Business Ethics and Free Enterprise and Distinguished Fellow at the Leatherby Center, Argyros School of Business and Economics, Chapman University. He is a research fellow at the Hoover Institution, Stanford University. A cofounder of *Reason* magazine, Machan is the author of numerous articles in scholarly journals, as well as a frequent contributor to some of the United States' most notable newspapers. Among other titles, he is the author of *Marxism: A Bourgeois Critique*, *Liberty and Culture: Essays on the Idea of a Free Society*, and *Classical Individualism*. His most recent books include *The Liberty Option* and *Putting Humans First, Why People Are More Important than the Wilds*. *Neither Left nor Right: Selections of Machan's Columns*, and his *Objectivity: Recovering Determinate Reality in Philosophy, Science and Everyday Life* will be published in 2004.

CHRISTOPHER PHELPS teaches history at The Ohio State University. He is author of *Young Sidney Hook* (Cornell University Press, 1997) and wrote the introductions to two of Hook's books: *From Hegel to Marx* (1936; Columbia University Press, 1994) and *Towards the Understanding of Karl Marx* (1933; Prometheus Books, 2002).

EDWARD S. SHAPIRO received his BA degree from Georgetown University and his PhD from Harvard University in history. He taught at Seton Hall University for three decades. His books include *Letters of Sidney Hook: Democracy, Communism and the Cold War* and *A Time for Healing: American Jews since World War II*. He is currently writing on the Crown Heights riot of August 1991.

DAVID SIDORSKY is professor of philosophy at Columbia University, where he has taught since 1959. His fields of philosophical interest have been moral philosophy, political philosophy, and literary theory. Related to the current essay on Sidney Hook, he has published several reviews and essays on the history of twentieth-century philosophy, including an interpretive introductory essay in *The Essential Writings of John Dewey* and "Pragmatism: Method, Metaphysics, and Morals" for *The German Encyclopedia of Pragmatism*. His recent articles include "The Historical Novel as the Denial of History: The Unreality of Joyce's Waking Nightmare" (*New Literary History*, 2002); "Incomplete Routes to Moral Objectivity: Four Variants of Naturalism" (*Social Philosophy and Policy*, 2001); and "The Third Concept of Liberty and the Politics of Identity" (*Partisan Review*, 2001), which is projected as part of a forthcoming book, *Liberty, Equality, Fraternity: Skeptical Perspectives*.

391

ROBERT B. TALISSE is assistant professor of philosophy at Vanderbilt University. He is the author of several articles and books in the areas of political philosophy and US pragmatism. He is the editor (with Robert Tempio) of *Sidney Hook on Pragmatism, Democracy, and Freedom: The Essential Essays* (Prometheus Books, 2002) and the author of the forthcoming book *Democracy after Liberalism.*

BRUCE WILSHIRE is Senior Professor of Philosophy at Rutgers University. His recent books include *Wild Hunger: The Primal Roots of Modern Addiction*; *The Primal Roots of American Philosophy: Pragmatism, Phenomenology, Native American Thought*; *Fashionable Nihilism: A Critique of Analytic Philosophy*; and the just completed *Genocide, Terrorism, and Righteous Communities.*